JET MAN

DUNCAN CAMPBELL-SMITH is a former *Financial Times* and *Economist* journalist whose career has also included working in the City, consulting with McKinsey & Co., and jobs in publishing and corporate communications. His other books include *Crossing Continents: A History of Standard Chartered Bank* and *Masters of the Post: The Authorized History of the Royal Mail*, which won the Wadsworth Prize for business history.

JET MAN

The Making and Breaking
of Frank Whittle,
Genius of the Jet Revolution

DUNCAN CAMPBELL-SMITH

An Apollo Book

This is an Apollo book, first published in the UK in 2020 by Head of Zeus Ltd

This paperback edition published in 2021 by Head of Zeus Ltd

9 7 5 3 1 2 4 6 8

A catalogue record for this book is available from
the British Library.

ISBN (PB): 9781788544702
ISBN (E): 9781788544689

Typeset by Adrian McLaughlin

Printed and bound in Great Britain by
CPI Group (UK) Ltd, Croydon CRO 4YY

Head of Zeus Ltd
5–8 Hardwick Street
London EC1R 4RG

WWW.HEADOFZEUS.COM

COVER IMAGE: Frank Whittle in April 1946, with the cigarette lighter presented
to him by his wartime engineering team – made out of the detachable core of
a miniature steel component (the double-sided impeller in the foreground)
engraved with all the team-members' names.

ENDPAPERS: These show (*inside front cover*) an 'Installation' drawing for the front of
Whittle's W.2/700 jet engine and (*inside back cover*) complementary lateral drawings
of the entire W.2/700, traced for assembly work in 1945 and based on drawings dated
July 1944.

To Morwenna

Contents

Acknowledgements

I owe particular thanks to three individuals. My first debt is to the late Alec Collins. One of the most distinguished aero-engineers of his day, Alec joined Rolls-Royce in 1952 and rose to the top of its engineering hierarchy in a career that spanned forty-three years. In his retirement he devoted endless hours to the Rolls-Royce Heritage Trust (RRHT), while pursuing his own research into the technical evolution of the early jet engines. We met at the RRHT's museum on Derby's Osmaston Road shortly after I began my research for this book in 2017. I think Alec took it as a challenge to find a non-engineer asking innocent questions about the nature of Frank Whittle's achievements. With consummate patience and generosity, he thereafter set aside the time for many long discussions – complemented from time to time with explanatory forays out of our meeting room into the surrounding hangars of the museum, home to a unique collection of historic aero-engines. Shortly before his sudden untimely death in December 2019, we made a joint visit to the Churchill Archives Centre in Cambridge so that Alec could delve for the first time into Whittle's own private papers and marvel over some of his personal artefacts (including one faintly nicotine-stained slide rule). It was a memorable day. No doubt this book makes judgements that Alec might have questioned, and I must absolve him from any posthumous responsibility for its telling of Whittle's story. Without Alec, though, I doubt I could have written it.

And it was entirely due to Alec that I was also able to draw on a substantial archive deposited at the RRHT, amassed by a former aviation journalist who worked for many years on a planned biography of Whittle. With an unrivalled knowledge of aero-engine history, Ken Fulton (1928–2011) came to know Whittle personally and built up an enormous private collection of papers, including hundreds of documents copied from The National Archives. With too many other interests competing for his time, and dogged by ill health in his later years, Ken never got around to writing his intended book. After his death, his collection might have been lost but for Alec Collins' intervention: Alec shipped it home and spent three months cataloguing it before arranging for it to be given permanent shelf space at the RRHT. Access to 'the KF archive' fired my initial research and I owe much to Ken Fulton's years of trawling through the public records. I hope his surviving family will see *Jet Man* as at least a partial fulfilment of his long-held determination to see a life of Whittle into print.

My third special debt is to Ian Whittle. To be approached by a total stranger declaring that he would like to write a biography of your father would surely put most sons on their guard. Ian, a retired commercial pilot, had reason to feel especially wary, having himself written and lectured authoritatively on his father's work for many years without the satisfaction of seeing any independent account of it that, in his view, came close to telling the full story. Concealing the scepticism he must certainly have felt, Ian responded kindly to my initial enquiries early in 2017, putting his own private papers at my disposal and granting me permission to quote from his father's voluminous papers. Later he scrutinised the finished text with an eagle eye that I hope he won't mind my comparing with his father's attention to detail. Ian offered many helpful amendments and I am extremely grateful to him for his support in the final stages of the book's preparation.

Many others helped along the way. I must thank first the staff of the Churchill Archives Centre at Churchill College, Cambridge, under its Director Allen Packwood and Senior Archivist Andrew Riley, for their assistance over the course of several visits – made all the more enjoyable by accommodation in the college's splendid Cowen Court building that had just opened when I arrived for my first stay. In Derby, my research at the RRHT was made much easier by the kindness of its staff under Peter Collins, and latterly Neil Chattle who also assisted with securing Rolls-Royce's permission to use some of the many photographs archived with the RRHT. At Cranfield University, Anne Knight and Karyn Meaden-Pratt assisted my work on the Kings Norton Papers. At London's Science Museum, Hannah Nagle, Natasha Logan and Alex Smith helped me find my way to the papers I needed to see at the Dana Research Centre and Blythe House. At the tiny Lutterworth Museum, close by Power Jets' former site, volunteers look after a charmingly miscellaneous collection of Whittle memorabilia and Geoff Smith generously lent me several precious papers to take away and prepare as illustrations. Brian Riddle, Chief Librarian at the National Aerospace Library in Farnborough, guided me to the most useful articles on Whittle from its many shelves of bound periodicals and to additional online material – including the many historic BBC radio broadcasts by famous names from aviation history, accessible via the National Aerospace Sound Archive. Frank Armstrong, another distinguished career engineer turned historian, found time to read a section of the book at short notice and suggested several wise amendments. Jonathan Glancy pointed me towards some useful clues to Whittle's character. Nicholas Jones of Quanta Films provided me with the script of a long interview with Whittle that he and his father Glyn Jones filmed in 1986 (and that Nicholas subsequently used in a BBC Horizon documentary about Whittle's achievements). Chris Weir, whom I met by chance at the Churchill Archives Centre, sent me useful background material about the work of those who developed the fuel atomiser adopted by Whittle and manufactured for him by the Joseph Lucas company. Louise Essex, Ann Brine, Ruth Long and Joe Moseley on the staff of Warwickshire County Council's Resources Directorate enabled me to make use of some of the many photographs of Whittle kept at Rugby Library. I would also like to thank Mark Copley, Tom Gillmor, Robert Cutts and Wayne Davis for their help with picture research, as too Gary Haines at the Royal Air Force Museum in Hendon. My research involved many interviews, and I am once again indebted to Nicki Brown and her colleagues at Transcribe It for their expertise at turning long tape-recordings into immaculate scripts for me. I am grateful to David Thomas and Peter Simpson for reading early drafts of the text and providing excellent suggestions on how to improve it.

Special thanks to all those who saw the book through from concept to publication, starting with Bill Hamilton at the A. M. Heath agency. Bill seemed to have a total grasp of the book's final shape from the outset and offered shrewd advice at every turn. I am hugely grateful to Anthony Cheetham at Head of Zeus for his belief in the book and to all the staff at HoZ who kept their 2020 publishing plans going despite the great difficulties posed by the pandemic, especially Anna Nightingale, Clémence Jacquinet and Richard Collins. Holding everything together, my editor Richard Milbank performed virtual miracles from his virtual desks out of the office and deserves a real medal.

And finally, thanks to my wife Morwenna for her constant support (not least of the IT variety), critical views and good humour in sharing our first three years of married life with the subject of this book.

List of Plates

List of Text Illustrations

Author's Note

This is not a traditional biography. Frank Whittle's life covered most of the twentieth century (1907–96) and a conventional account of it would dictate a rather different book. No other period of his life, though, remotely compared with the intensity of his two decades from 1928 to 1948 that revolved around his pursuit of the jet engine. So *Jet Man* deals only sparingly with what came before and after. It is almost entirely concerned with the intervening years of his twenties and thirties – through most of which Whittle displayed a phenomenal single-mindedness. His drive to launch a successful jet plane, at first to fulfil a youthful vision and then to help vanquish Hitler's Germany, quickly became – no other word will do – all-consuming. He had virtually no social life after 1934, few if any friends beyond his immediate circle of colleagues at work, no significant other interests except flying and almost nothing to distract him from his pursuit of the jet save the demands (and these all too constrained) of his immediate family. All work and no play, warns the proverb, makes Jack a dull boy. There was never any danger of Frank becoming dull. He was on a mission, after all, to change the world. And even while absorbed in problems that challenged all his prodigious abilities as a mathematician and an engineer, he had the imagination to see jet propulsion in a broader context that was lost on most of his contemporaries. For he was by nature a man of rare intellectual energy, constantly questioning what others took for granted. As close colleagues observed from time to time, he often seemed to have more on his mind than they could fathom.

None of them ever felt they had taken his full measure. Indeed, his slightly elusive character was part of what so intrigued many colleagues and forged friendships that lasted a lifetime. This dimension of his life needs emphasizing. Few men can ever have documented their own lives as comprehensively as he did, while at work on the jet; but his myriad file notes and memoranda, diaries and private letters provide only indirect clues to what made him such a source of inspiration to those around him. He used his papers mostly to chronicle his progress, or lack of it, and increasingly to vent feelings of frustration, anger and resentment. To judge solely from the written record, he might have been a forbidding and unfriendly personality – a martinet, humourless and inclined to be overly critical of others even at the best of times. He was never one to suffer fools gladly and some of his wartime peers, less than sympathetic to his situation, certainly thought him unduly difficult. Yet he was unquestionably a hugely charismatic figure, in public and private alike. Audiences large and small were captivated by him as a witty and engaging speaker. Caught on film in his later years, he exuded an easy charm. As for his colleagues in the workplace, it is plain that many of them loved the man. Several youthful companions devoted their careers to backing his engine project. Many of the young graduates who rallied to his cause during the war cherished their memories of working with him for the rest of their lives. The women in his life are harder to discern at this distance in time, but all gave him constant support. Though his first wife Dorothy was kept at arm's length from his work and so now seems a shadowy figure, her selfless devotion (until well after the war) was vital to him, not least through some long periods of illness. Those few women who found a place in his engineering world – most of them, inevitably, secretaries – clearly found him immensely endearing.

All who knew him well could agree, above all, that he was blessed (and sometimes burdened) with a brain quite out of the ordinary. Several of his contemporaries in the world of aeronautics, generally acknowledged as masters of their trade, ceased to regard themselves in quite the same way after meeting Frank

Whittle. They doffed their caps to him. Only by heeding this can we make sense of the jet engine's emergence in England by 1939. Some revisionist histories of the jet revolution would have us believe that it arrived on the back of a broad development process, pushed forward inch by inch in various industrial locations under the guidance of several inspired engineers. In this light, however brilliant, Whittle was merely one of the leading contributors. No doubt it is important to remember that the evolution of the modern jet engine was a complex business, and drew on the work of many firms from an early date. To see modern jet travel as his legacy alone would be absurd. To try telling the tale of the jet's origins without assigning Whittle a central role, though, is to rehearse *Hamlet* without the Prince. This perspective also leaves out of account the story of a personal drama, not to say tragedy, which ought never to be forgotten. It lies at the heart of *Jet Man*.

'His career witnessed every stage in the development of any revolutionary new invention. Viz (1) it's ridiculous – don't waste my time; (2) it's possible – so what? (3) I always said it was a good idea; (4) I thought of it first'

Arthur C. Clarke, science writer and futurist, in a letter of condolence to Frank Whittle's widow, 22 August 1996

'There is, of course, a great deal to say about Whittle's career and frustrations, but at least he ended with the Order of Merit and a magnificent tribute in Westminster Abbey'

Lord Kings Norton (formerly Harold Roxbee Cox) to the son of one of Frank Whittle's closest colleagues, R. D. Williams, 24 March 1997

Prologue

Stories about things that happened in the Second World War are numberless. Central to Frank Whittle's life is the story of something that did not happen, though it might well have done. It could have resulted in a different narrative for some of the most familiar events of Britain's war. We must imagine that a secret dimension of the Royal Air Force's rearmament from 1936 had produced a fully operational jet-propelled aircraft by the end of the Phoney War in May 1940. This plane could have taken full advantage of the country's new coastal radar defences. The Battle of Britain might have ended within days of the first Luftwaffe incursions over the white cliffs of Dover. Few if any German bombers might ever have reached London to unleash Adolf Hitler's intended Blitz. The RAF's bombardment of the Third Reich, from heights of 40,000 feet, might have wrought havoc with only minimal losses to the aircrews of Bomber Command. Extravagantly counter-factual fantasies? Over the page are the opening and closing paragraphs of a remarkable document submitted to the Air Ministry almost a year before the outbreak of the war:

Memorandum on the Jet Propelled
Interceptor Fighter

By Squadron Leader F. Whittle, 25 October 1938

Introduction

The primary function of the interceptor fighter is
to carry a pilot and his machine guns to within the
vicinity of a raiding bomber for a sufficient length
of time to enable him to achieve its destruction,
preferably before it has reached its target.

For this purpose, sheer performance in climb and
speed is the major requisite, and matters such as
fuel consumption are of secondary importance.

It is commonly accepted that ten minutes is the
sort of interval to be expected between the first
report of a raid, and the falling of the bombs on
London. Allowing two minutes for the 'quick getaway'
of the intercepting fighters, the latter have eight
minutes in which to reach the flying height of the
raiders (which may be 15,000–20,000 feet) before the
bombs are dropped, and about twenty-five minutes
before the raiders have re-crossed the coast on the
return flight.

It can be seen that even with the latest interceptors,
it is very doubtful whether successful attack on the
raiders can be made before they drop their bombs, as
the margin of speed between the modern interceptor
and modern bomber is not so great that minutes would
not be lost in 'closing' after the interceptor had
reached the height of the raiders.

It is the purpose of this memorandum to show that the
'jet propulsion engine' now undergoing development by
Power Jets Ltd makes possible the production of an
interceptor fighter of much higher performance than
is possible with the internal combustion engine.

It will, in fact, be shown that it is reasonable to expect to be able to produce an interceptor capable of climbing to 10,000 ft in 1 min 43 secs, and to 20,000 ft in 3 mins 48 secs, and to be capable of a top speed of from 465 m.p.h. at sea level to over 500 m.p.h. at 20,000 ft.

The main reason why these figures are possible is that the jet propulsion engine is so very light in proportion to its power, that notwithstanding its extravagant fuel consumption, the all up weight of an interceptor propelled by this means would be little more than half that of a machine propelled by the normal engine and airscrew for the same thrust horsepower.

[In the body of the memorandum are sections describing key features of the existing engine and of a fighter plane designed around it, backed with a wide range of predicted performance data for the plane including speed/thrust and rate of climb statistics.]

Conclusion

It may be seen from the above that the jet propulsion engine now in course of development is likely to provide a propelling plant which, when installed in a suitable interceptor fighter, would provide so substantial an advance in performance as compared with what appears to be possible with normal power plant, as to at least double the chances of successful interception before the raider dropped his bombs.

The interceptor would be a smaller aeroplane, with a very simple engine burning paraffin and hence it should be both cheap and capable of rapid production.

Attached to the memorandum was a preliminary sketch of the jet aeroplane envisaged by the author (Fig.1). In July 1939 he gave the Air Ministry formal design proposals for this plane, and

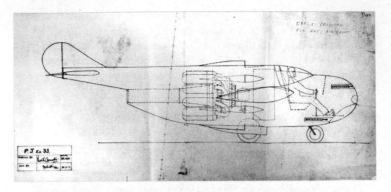

Fig. 1. Drawing of a jet plane (complete with guns)
sent to the Air Ministry in October 1938

for a flight engine based on a proven power plant that had been
fully tested on the ground. As the war broke out, plans were being
laid for an aircraft capable of flying at speeds of up to 700 mph.
Yet the RAF only took delivery of jet planes in the early summer
of 1944. It was immediately obvious that they marked the start of a
new era: jet versions of the Avro Lancaster bomber and the Spitfire
went into their planning stages during preparations for the final
onslaught against Japan. So, might a dramatic break with the past
have happened years earlier – and if so, what forestalled it?

1

False Starts

Pre-1930

Among the boffins of the aircraft world in the autumn of 1929, none was more respected than Alan Arnold Griffith. His formal title was Superintendent of the Air Ministry Laboratory, a modest research facility tucked away behind the Royal College of Science in London's South Kensington. Here, though still only thirty-six years old, he ran a small team of British government scientists employed to help ensure that the Royal Air Force was kept abreast of the latest thinking in the aeronautical sciences. All were in awe of the gaunt-faced and slightly imperious Dr A. A. Griffith. He was famous for the brilliant work he had done during and after the Great War in the esoteric field of 'crack-propagation' theory: he had shown that incessantly repeated strains on a brittle material like glass could cause it, one day, to fracture at less than its theoretical breaking point. (This discovery was critical to a later generation's work on what came to be called 'metal fatigue' in aircraft structures.) In the jargon of the engineering profession, he had been 'a stress man'. In more recent years, though, he had turned his attention to another subject: aircraft engines and in particular the 'gas' turbine. This would run – one day, all being well – on the same basic principle as a steam turbine, with blades on a wheel being blown round and so turning a shaft bearing a propeller. Instead of steam, though, the gas turbine would be driven round by compressed air with a hydrocarbon fuel burning inside it.

A memorandum arrived on his desk one morning in the middle of November 1929 from the Air Ministry's Adastral House on Kingsway, central London. It came from Lawrence Tweedie, a young Technical Officer in the Ministry's Scientific and Industrial Research arm whom Griffith knew quite well. With a degree in chemistry, not to mention a growing reputation as rather an artful Whitehall fixer, Tweedie was already marked out for a bright future at the Ministry. Now in his late twenties, though, Tweedie was still charged with various junior tasks. One of them involved sifting through any new ideas submitted to the Ministry as future research topics. Might Dr Griffith be prepared, asked Tweedie in his memo, to spare a few moments to talk about his current interest in gas-turbine technology with a young RAF man, one Pilot Officer Whittle? We can suppose that a short background briefing accompanied this request, and it must have caused Griffith considerable surprise. This fellow Whittle was only twenty-two and had just passed out of Cranwell cadet college the previous year. He had no professional engineering qualifications at all. Nor had he any public school or family connections: he had had to join the RAF as a humble sixteen-year-old apprentice fitter. Yet an appointment for him had been urged on the Air Ministry by his Commanding Officer at the Central Flying School at RAF Wittering, where he had begun training a few weeks earlier to become a flying instructor. It seemed that Wittering's Group Captain 'Jack' Baldwin, no engineer but a shrewd judge of his young pilots, rated this Whittle chap highly. At the behest of one of his lecturers, Baldwin had agreed to a private meeting at which he had been hugely impressed, albeit slightly nonplussed, by a spirited presentation on the future of the gas turbine as an aircraft engine. Baldwin thought others should listen to it. In short, the Ministry's research department felt under some obligation to the RAF to give P/O Whittle a hearing. What Tweedie's memo to Griffith proposed was that he should review whatever drawings and calculations the novice pilot brought with him and then – if they were genuinely worth a further discussion – the two of them would call on the Superintendent to ask for his views. Griffith trusted Tweedie not to waste his time with some maverick young inventor and agreed to a provisional arrangement for a few days later.

Whittle was duly invited to call at Adastral House in the last week of November. We have no contemporary record of what followed that day, and Whittle's autobiographical account of it many years later runs to barely a dozen lines. He alluded to it many times in later life, however, so we know enough to infer what happened with some confidence – and to picture how a most unlikely encounter unfolded.

He turned up in full uniform – he was, and would always remain, intensely proud of his status as a serving RAF officer – but he cut a diminutive figure (at 5 foot 7 inches) and was still some way short of being able to grow a service moustache. Notwithstanding his boyish appearance, he positively radiated self-confidence. Once seated at the table in Tweedie's office, he proceeded immediately to lay out the set of diagrams and calculations that had rather bamboozled his Commanding Officer at Wittering and began his presentation again. Tweedie listened quietly for a few moments. Then, with a bluntness that Whittle would never forget, he interrupted to offer some advice. He had done some homework of his own on the gas turbine. He had dug out a report written nine years earlier by a Dr W. J. Stern, one of Griffith's predecessors at the Kensington Laboratory. It was only fair, said Tweedie, to make clear straightaway that the Ministry stood by the findings of this 1920 document. The author of Engine Sub-Committee Report No. 54 had looked carefully into the futuristic idea of driving a plane's propeller with a gas-turbine engine. Even the smallest feasible turbine by Sterne's calculations would have to weigh about 10,000 lb, which was roughly ten times heavier than the most popular aero-engines of the day. Nothing had happened since then to make the prospect of a turbine engine any less impractical. So it seemed most unlikely that turbines would ever compete with existing power plants –

especially given the rapid advances currently being made with piston engines by all the leading manufacturers.

If Tweedie imagined a few condescending remarks were going to deflate his visitor, he had mistaken his man. He was well aware of the 1920 report, said Whittle – which to Tweedie must have been surprising enough in itself – and he would not have presumed to take up the Air Ministry's time with a proposal that had anything in common at all with the turbine described there. Dr Stern had supposed a turbine wheel made of brass, and a main engine casement of cast iron. He might just as well have envisaged an engine built of stone. His calculations were of no practical value at all, in Whittle's estimation. In their place, he would like the Ministry to take stock of a radically alternative approach. And he was encouraged to believe his own ideas might be of serious interest, given the recent publication of seminal books on the theory of a gas-turbine engine. What Whittle cannot have known – for it was classified as secret and had probably been shown to very few outside Ministry circles – was that a radical paper on the potential for an engine with a turbine-driven propeller had been produced by the distinguished Dr A. A. Griffith himself in 1926. Tweedie, well aware of this paper, was perhaps now feeling a little uncomfortable. It was soon clear to him that Group Captain Baldwin's protégé ought to meet Griffith in person. Confirmation of their appointment was quickly made, and the two of them set off for South Kensington.

That 1926 paper by Griffith had greatly embellished his reputation among his peers by confirming a theoretical case for the gas turbine as an aero-engine. Contrary to what Tweedie had said about current thinking, some engineers had been aware of its potential for many years past. With very few moving parts, it offered the prospect of one day providing an equally powerful but far lighter and more reliable alternative to the piston engine that had been universally adopted for planes since the Wright brothers' first manned flight in 1903. (As it happened, the first primitive gas turbine had been run successfully that same year, 1903, by a Norwegian inventor called Ægidius Elling.) Certainly the gas turbine was an exciting idea – but it faced a serious snag. A steam turbine – of the kind employed in factories for decades and adapted around the turn of the century to power ships, transforming the maritime world – could easily derive highly pressurised steam by simply heating water in a closed container. A gas turbine, however, demanded a much cleverer way of sourcing pressurised air. It needed a 'compressor', a device that could suck in air and squeeze it tight. As of 1926, no such device had existed, or at least none capable of producing the necessary levels of compression, while also weighing little enough to be practical for an aircraft. Griffith's seminal paper had proposed an 'axial compressor' in which a series of discs – each containing carefully designed vanes, using the latest aerodynamic technology and mounted on a single shaft – would raise the pressure of an airflow along the axis of the shaft. Revolving at high speed, this compressor would feed pressurised air into a combustion chamber to be mixed with burning fuel. The resulting hot gas would hit the turbine, producing enough power to drive both the compressor and a propeller on the same shaft.[1]

To examine the practical viability of Griffith's proposal, a 'single-stage' prototype of just one disc with vanes had been tested in 1928, at the government's Royal Aircraft Establishment (RAE) in Farnborough. The results had been encouraging. The compressor had done its job, delivering the modest pressure ratio for which it was designed and so confirming that Griffith had produced a good basic design. The next step, however, was to progress to a 'multi-stage' prototype involving a shaft with a row of discs capable of producing the much greater air pressure required for a working gas turbine. At this point, things had become more complicated. At full speed, according to Griffith's sums, his multi-stage axial compressor would be the perfect answer. Unfortunately, the same mathematical calculations showed that running it at lower speeds might be difficult or even impossible. He responded to this conundrum by devising a much more elaborate version of his original concept, based around an ingenious but fiendishly complex scheme that he described as a 'contra-flow' arrangement. A long series of experimental tests would be needed to establish the feasibility of such a compressor. None could doubt these would prove difficult and extremely expensive.

This was awkward for Griffith. His work in government service since acquiring his engineering doctorate in 1915 had all been heavily theoretical. In truth, he was much more of a scientist than an engineer. He had sufficient practical skills to supervise research experiments; but he had never until now embarked on a project calling for a prolonged series of rig tests in the workshop with constant minor adjustments. He was nonetheless confident that his contra-flow axial design would live up to its theoretical billing in the end, if only he could raise enough money to keep going. Early in November 1929 – that is to say, days before receiving the Adastral House memorandum from Tweedie about a possible meeting with Pilot Officer Whittle – he had sent a formal report on his progress to his masters at the Ministry's Aeronautical Research Committee (ARC), in which he had taken an uncompromising line:

> The turbine is superior [i.e. in theory] to existing Service engines and to projected compression-ignition engines in every respect examined. The efficiency is higher and the weight and bulk less... A form of experimental unit is proposed, with which the definite predictions of the theory could be checked [i.e. in practice] and data collected for the construction of a complete installation.[2]

With these words, Griffith was signalling his determination to press on with the development of a gas turbine. So Tweedie's unprompted memo must at least have intrigued him. A conversation with a former RAF apprentice was hardly going to be enlightening but it was timely enough and could do no harm.

What followed was a sharing of minds – or more accurately, perhaps, a non-sharing – that must rank as one of the most luckless missed chances in the history of twentieth-century technology, not to say in the history of the Second World War. The illustrious head of the Ministry Laboratory paid his guest the courtesy of a proper hearing, and Whittle this time talked through his presentation without interruption. Perhaps Griffith was merely being polite – but, just as plausibly, he was rather taken aback. For this trainee flying instructor wanted to propose a gas-turbine engine that was in many ways entirely familiar, while suggesting it be harnessed to a new concept of flight that was so fanciful as to be scarcely worth discussing.

The engine itself, sketched out in a set of diagrams that soon lay across the table between them, presented the same combination of compressor, combustion chamber and turbine as the gas turbine that Griffith himself had mooted in 1926. True, there was a significant difference insofar as his troublesome axial compressor was replaced by, to Griffith's mind, a much cruder variant, a 'centrifugal' compressor which would whirl the incoming air away from the axis instead of along it. But the essential structure of the engine was unsurprising – except in one rather crucial respect. The shaft driven round by the turbine only extended forwards as far as the compressor. There it ended, which was entirely logical since it had no further role beyond the compressor. Whittle's design had no propeller. He was proposing instead that the hot gas expanding through his turbine should be vented through a nozzle at the back of his engine, providing all the propulsion it would need in order to thrust an aircraft forwards in the opposite direction, as per Newton's Third Law of Motion. And we can be sure that Whittle, warming to his presentation, strayed far beyond the basic layout of his engine – enlarging on the promise of jet propulsion and its revolutionary implications. It would enable aeroplanes to fly at great heights, where they could reach speeds almost as fast as sound itself. It would take aviation into a new era.

At this point, probably affronted by such certitude from one so unqualified, Griffith seems to have lost patience with the ardent young pilot. We can imagine him reminding Whittle that there were sound reasons for linking any putative gas turbine to a propeller. In moving a large mass of air (relatively) slowly backwards, to propel an aircraft forwards, a propeller wasted very little residual energy. In expelling a much smaller amount of air backwards at very high velocity, by contrast, a gas turbine would leave a huge amount of energy simply unused. The mathematical foundations of all this were a commonplace, at least to those with a proper engineering background. To Whittle's great surprise, Griffith did not question the feasibility of the gas turbine itself. The demonstrable inadequacy of jet propulsion on theoretical grounds was all that really seemed to concern the Superintendent. Pausing only to point out an error he had spotted in Whittle's sums, he brought their conversation to a close.

It had been friendly enough, but nonetheless extraordinary. Setting aside Griffith's abject failure to offer his youthful visitor any hint of encouragement, let alone a few words of praise, this exchange on a wet November afternoon in South Kensington was especially notable in two respects. Griffith had spent more than three years championing the potential of the gas turbine as a power plant for aircraft. Confronted with a mystifyingly well-informed student of gas-turbine theory, it was egregiously mean-spirited of him that he chose to reveal nothing of his own practical experiments since 1926. Of course, the confidentiality of government work must have limited the scope to share the finer details, even with an RAF officer. His 1926 paper was still a classified document. But Griffith might easily have congratulated Whittle and disclosed to him in broad terms how momentously their thoughts had converged on a radical vision of aviation's future. In the event, he said nothing whatever about the progress report he had only recently submitted ('The turbine is superior… in every respect…') and he made no mention at all of the test rig built for his axial compressor.

Tweedie took his lead from Griffith in drafting a subsequent letter to Whittle that brushed aside his work in devastating fashion.[3] Posted a few days later, it avoided disclosing any details on the axial compressor research to date but hinted tantalisingly at the existence of gas-turbine experiments that meant Whittle was less than up to date with his thinking: '… it must be remembered that a tremendous amount of work is being done and while it is not possible at present to publish any complete details of the results of this work you may rest assured the criticisms [by Dr Griffith] of your scheme were made with the full knowledge of the results achieved by actual experiment.' The letter enclosed copies of Whittle's supposedly erroneous calculations, which he had left behind for them to review at their leisure. But Tweedie merely confirmed there had been no change of heart in South Kensington: 'it can be stated clearly that no reason has been found for any alteration of the preliminary comments [by us]... nor of the criticism advanced against your various assumptions.' True, a turbine engine would 'almost certainly one day be developed' but it would have to wait on huge improvements in the current state of the mechanical arts. The letter, to someone Tweedie probably expected never to meet again, closed with bland words of praise that might almost have been calculated to humiliate: 'it has been a matter of real interest to investigate in detail your scheme and I can assure you that any suggestion, backed by careful and considered theory, that is submitted by people in the Service is always welcomed.'

The second striking aspect of Griffith's handling of this November conversation is that he seems to have completely ignored the essential point of Whittle's proposition. The inefficiency of jet propulsion at sea level, especially compared with the efficiency of a propeller engine, was not in dispute between them. The mathematics set out by Whittle that afternoon showed how he proposed to compensate for that poorer propulsive efficiency. By flying at high speeds and high altitudes – where a propeller, whether driven by a gas turbine or a piston engine, would scarcely function at all – his jet-propelled aircraft would encounter much lower drag. With no propeller or gearbox, its engine would also be much lighter. And by flying faster, the propulsive efficiency of its turbine would rise significantly. The net result would be a plane that could travel incomparably faster, and further, than anyone had yet thought remotely possible. If there was one individual in the world equipped to grasp Whittle's thinking, it was Griffith. The notion that he inexplicably failed to understand the importance of the altitude factor is hardly credible. Yet he chose to pretend as much, so avoiding any intellectual engagement with the gist of Whittle's presentation.

Why he reacted to Whittle in this way can only be a matter of speculation: he himself never offered any explanation. But their encounter had shades of the apocryphal 'when-Salieri-met-Mozart' contretemps. Doubtless the drily reserved Griffith was both irritated and disconcerted by Whittle's cocksure manner. The older man generally thought himself cleverer than any of his peers. Nobody in government circles challenged this assessment and his design of an axial compressor had only confirmed his status as a slightly unworldly figure, dedicated to brave initiatives and independent thinking. (Years later, the novelist Nevil Shute – himself an aeronautical engineer and 'stress man' before becoming a full-time author – would take Griffith as the model for Theodore Honey, a boffin whose courageous stand over metal fatigue on transatlantic airliners saves the day in his book *No Highway*, published in 1948.) Of course, a more generous and less aloof individual might have acknowledged Whittle's proposition as both brave and independent, too – but it touched on the future of the gas turbine, which Griffith regarded as his special field. He had little interest in anything that other engineers had to say on this subject, and even less interest in the thoughts of an uneducated Pilot Officer.

Years later, after Whittle's genius had long since become apparent and he had become Sir Frank, many would ask what might have happened if his ideas had received a 'ready welcome that November. Tweedie was right to say a 'tremendous amount of work' had been done at the RAE on topics closely related to Whittle's proposal. So if the RAE's research engineers, at Griffith's bidding, had felt able to bring Whittle back for more discussions and to examine his workings properly, might a powerful synergy have been achieved? Might their joint efforts have brought about a quantum leap in technology that could have transformed the RAF? One of the key figures on the RAE payroll at Farnborough was Hayne Constant, whose career would culminate in a stint as Chief Scientist (RAF) at the Ministry of Defence in the 1960s. In a letter to one of the leading official historians of the Second World War in 1961, Constant acknowledged the counterfactual possibility:

Most of the mechanical problems that Whittle met in the late thirties and early forties had been encountered and to some extent mastered by the RAE in the twenties. A very considerable engineering feat had, therefore, been accomplished. It is clear why this development was started [as part of the RAE's research into using exhaust gases to power turbo-chargers for piston engines] but not so clear why it was abandoned in the early thirties, when persistence might have given us the jet-propulsion gas turbine in time for the second world war.[4]

Constant called this an 'unfortunate failure to persevere' – no mean understatement, given the arms race in the air that was to follow later in the 1930s. In fact, it was the first occasion on which a historic opportunity to advance the jet engine's cause went for nought – though it was to prove far from the last.

If Griffith had alerted the RAE to his conversation with Whittle, he could easily have persuaded his colleagues to hear more about the jet idea. Instead he drew a veil over the whole business. After his 1929 report met a lukewarm response a few months later, his own turbine research was effectively shelved. Hayne Constant looked back on this as something of a mystery, and it is plain that Griffith was deeply disappointed. For years afterwards, he disparaged all talk of jet propulsion as though Whittle had never called on him at all. Yet this audacious young man had left school at the age of fifteen and never been inside a university engineering laboratory in his life. He had produced a set of mathematical calculations that covered several pages and tackled abstract concepts of formidable complexity. It seems inexplicable that Griffith should not have been curious, at the very least, to know how a fledgling pilot could possibly have pulled all this together. Learning something about Whittle's background might not entirely have resolved this enigma – there can be no accounting for genius – but it would at least have provided a clue to the drive and imagination evident on that November afternoon in South Kensington. It might also have served notice that Whittle's rebuff that day was most unlikely to put an end to his aspirations.

ii

Frank had been turned down before. A first and potentially even more crushing rejection had come almost seven years earlier, when he had tried and failed to join the RAF as a fifteen-year-old apprentice. He had sailed through some written tests at a recruitment office in his Midlands home town of Leamington Spa shortly before Christmas 1922. Then the schoolboy known as 'Grub' to his classmates was turned down after a medical – not on account of some hitherto unsuspected malady but simply for being too small. Grub-like, indeed. Refusing to accept his rejection, he went back to school while adopting a Spartan lifestyle with daily exercises geared to expanding his height. He had six months in which to grow three inches taller.

It was inconceivable to the young Frank that the RAF could turn him down. He had been obsessed with planes since his childhood. Indeed, he and the flying machines had more or less grown up in parallel: he had been born on 1 June 1907, a year before the Wright brothers – having made little impact on the American public since their initial flights in 1903 – caused a sensation in France with the first public flying displays that truly confirmed the start of manned flight. His upbringing alongside three younger siblings had been shaped – not to say regimented – by two topics of conversation within the family home above all others. One featured the purity of their thoughts. His father, Moses Whittle, ran a devout Wesleyan household that meant Bible readings in the home every day and dutiful attendance at chapel every Sunday. (Frank would lose his faith in Christianity, while retaining a strong sense of order and propriety – and a lasting attachment to biblical stories.) The other topic featured the contents of the Whittle family workshop and the progress of its latest invention.

Moses came from a long line of cotton-mill operatives – and a family of eighteen siblings – in Lancashire. He had moved south with his new wife, Sarah (née Garlick), just ahead of baby Frank's arrival, to take up a job as foreman in a machine-tool factory in Coventry, close to the heart of Britain's world-beating engineering industry. He had left school at the age of eleven but seems to have been an unusually gifted mechanic, always making space at home for a workshop that might one day bring a marvel into the world (as in a sense it did, though not quite as Moses expected). After nine years of saving every spare penny, he had amassed enough money by 1916 to buy a tiny business of his own. The Leamington Valve and Piston Ring Company was less august than it sounded – a large shed housed just one single-cylinder piston engine and there were no employees when Moses acquired it – but it was a name known to local engine manufacturers in the Midlands and notched up steadily growing sales in the heated wartime economy of 1917–18. In its factory Frank tinkered with every tool his father owned and was trusted to turn metal for valve stems and piston rings. It was not a bad way to have trained for the role of an RAF mechanic.

The young boy also acquired a passionate interest in all things aeronautical. The war years brought alluring stories of the brave men flying the latest biplanes into combat over the Western Front, and even occasional sightings of them in the air. (He would often recount in later life how he had been out playing as a nine-year-old, on Hearsall Common near his home in the village of Earlsdon, when a plane flew so low over his head that it blew off his hat and almost decapitated him.) Frank was equally fascinated by what he saw of the biplanes in local workshops. The war forced ahead constant improvements in their designs, and in the engines that powered them. About a thousand aircraft were built at the Standard Motor Company's works in Canley, on the outskirts of Coventry. His father took him there on several visits to see work progressing on planes like the B.E.12, the R.E.8 and the Sopwith Pup, all to survive as legendary names in later years. Frank was hooked even before he reached his teens. One day, he would learn to fly.

He then acquired a compelling interest in all things scientific. The shelves in his local Free Library in Leamington Spa were well stocked, by his own account, with books on a wide range of subjects from astronomy and physiology to chemistry and engineering. He spent his evenings alone there, poring over these volumes – and the evidence of later years suggests he must indeed have studied many of them very carefully. Under different circumstances – which is to say, in a different educational environment such as he might have encountered in Germany or the United States, with their far deeper regard for technical subjects – Frank might have had teachers more alert to his unusual fascination with science. In the event, his formal education went awry. He puzzled the masters at his municipal secondary school in Leamington, showing a cavalier disregard for the normal demands of school life and the established classroom curricula. Perhaps he was predisposed to be a loner by nature, but his disengagement from the routines of his schoolmates can only have made this outcome more likely. His teachers urged him in one direction, so Frank went in the other. He often neglected homework, which he loathed, and took it as a challenge to divert as little as possible of his own precious reading time into preparing for any exam – or, as he remembered it, 'to scrape through with the least possible effort'.[5] He had a passion for experiments, on the other hand, and chemistry in particular. The school indulged this by letting him loose in the laboratory while his peers were on the sports field. But he went mostly un-supervised, even after one set of experiments had exploded in his face, which might have cost him his eyesight.[6] At the age of fifteen, he gained a mediocre six passes in his School Certificate examinations with not a single distinction, not even in chemistry.

This scarcely bothered him, since he was by now intent on leaving school to join the RAF. He had one other motive, too, for wanting to leave home in short order: hardship and downright poverty had overwhelmed his family since the end of the war, and he was determined to break free of his background. As a small child, as he recalled in later life, he had been 'a street urchin on six days a week and a carefully dressed little boy on Sunday'.[7] So long as the war had lasted, the family had enjoyed the rewards of his father's enterprise in running his own business. The end of the war had curtailed this brief prosperity abruptly. Demand for component parts had collapsed, and Moses had had the misfortune to fall foul of a contractual misunderstanding that bankrupted his business and saw his family evicted from their home. Frank and his younger siblings briefly found themselves having to sleep in the loft over their father's workshop and some desperate times followed. Seeking a way out, Frank by 1922 had come to see the RAF as his ladder to a better life. He was not going to let himself fall at the first rung.

By the summer of 1923, or so he always claimed later, daily bouts of muscle control had left him three inches taller and three inches broader round the chest.[8] Reapplying for another medical at RAF Halton, the station in Buckinghamshire that he had visited six months earlier, the new and enlarged Frank discovered that failed candidates were ineligible. For the RAF's clerks, it seemed, the medics' first decision was final. Letters appealing against the rulebook got him nowhere. In fact, all seemed lost – until one day it occurred to him to submit a fresh application to the Leamington recruitment office as though he had never stepped foot in the place before. None of the record-keepers rumbled this simple ruse, and it earned him an invitation from the RAF to sit the same written apprenticeship tests that he had passed already. It may then have been fortuitous that RAF Halton (scheduled to be rebuilt) had no room to accommodate the next intake of recruits. He was summoned instead to the 'No. 2 School of Technical Training' at RAF Cranwell, an academy set up in 1920 like Halton but in a much more remote location amidst the turnip fields of Lincolnshire. Whichever medical officers confronted him there, no one recognised him and his new physique saw him through. By September 1923, he was installed at Cranwell for a three-year apprenticeship as Whittle, F., Boy 364365.

iii

Whittle entered the RAF convinced that it would be the making of him. His apprenticeship, though, brought him three years of hardship and tedium that came as an unpleasant surprise. In his 1953 memoir, *Jet: The Story of a Pioneer*, he would be guarded in his verdict on the whole experience ('I cannot pretend that I enjoyed my three years'). In old age he was more forthcoming, recalling at least one occasion when he had 'seriously contemplated desertion'.[9] The teenager hitherto so set on becoming a pilot must at times have been sorely disillusioned by the harsh reality of the RAF in its early years.

It was only just beginning the process of establishing itself as a new dimension of the armed services. Its predecessors had been the Royal Flying Corps, part of the army, and the Royal Naval Air Service, part of the Royal Navy. These two bodies had been amalgamated in 1918 to form the world's first independent air force, free from generals and admirals alike. Inaugurated in November 1919 as one of its corner stones, and the world's first 'air academy', Cranwell College was the brainchild of the RAF's founding father and combative first Commander, Sir Hugh ('Boom') Trenchard. The Aircraft Apprentice Scheme was his creation, too, launched in 1920. Those trained by it were to be known for years as 'Trenchard's Brats'. Both the College and its Apprenticeship Scheme were inspired initiatives. Over the years ahead they were to make significant contributions to the development of a distinctive RAF culture. As of 1923, though, Trenchard was still struggling to ensure his service's very survival: post-war Whitehall resented the cost of adding to the armed forces, and the generals and admirals had not yet given up all hope of clawing back their two air arms. While Trenchard and his supporters fought their political battles, the men running operations at a day-to-day level were left to adopt some familiar routines. In a bid to raise standards, a large cohort of demobbed NCOs and physical instructors from the British army were let loose on Cranwell and all other RAF stations to apply their delicate skills on the parade ground.

The result was a harsh environment, very different from the service life that Whittle had anticipated. Its rigours were noted in a contemporary account, later to become famous:

> The laboured nerve-strain of the constant supervision and
> checking and abuse and punishment of squad-life has ironed

the last eagerness out of us: or rather has covered it, for I suspect that essentially we retain our inbred selves and secretly
remember our dreams.[10]

The author was T. E. Lawrence, who served in the lowest rank
of the RAF in 1922–3 in a strange and clandestine bid to escape
his fame as Lawrence of Arabia, leader of the wartime Arab Revolt
against the Ottoman Turks. Having enlisted under a false name,
as Aircraftman (A/C) Ross, Lawrence kept a day-by-day record
of his (brief) time at RAF Uxbridge, a training depot. His notes
were turned into a book, published posthumously in 1955 as *The
Mint*, offering a powerful recollection of his experience. Even
after the rigours of his desert war, Lawrence was dismayed at the
physical brutality of a regime seemingly designed to eradicate
all traces of independence and self-respect in the ranks. He was
an enlisted man, not an apprentice, and had had the misfortune
to join a station ('a savage place') run by an especially sadistic
cadre of officers and NCOs. His personal chronicle is nonetheless suggestive of the environment that Whittle encountered, too.
The RAF had yet to discover, as Lawrence put it, 'that the soldier
and the mechanic were mutually destructive ideals'.[11] Those in
the RAF's lowest ranks, comprising both the Aircraftmen (A/C 1
and A/C 2) and the apprentices hoping to join them, had to face
many hours a week of drill and physical training as well as the
inevitably robust life of the barracks. None of this appealed in
the slightest to the bookish boy from Leamington Spa with a
Wesleyan background who had found even the gentler disciplines
of secondary school a tiresome business.

After a lengthy reassignment to the army, Lawrence returned to
the RAF in August 1925 as A/C Shaw. He was posted to Cranwell.
He wrote in *The Mint* of how much his fellow aircraftmen there
resented having to teach the apprentices – 'the men don't like the
boys... [and] there is jealousy and carping' – but on one of those
apprentices, now in his third year, he made a deep and lasting
impression. Lawrence's real identity was an open secret around
the college and Whittle was soon drawn to him. Attached to the

same Cranwell squadron, and sharing a fondness for powerful motorbikes, they became friends. Whittle read all the books he could find about the Arab Rising, and by his own account managed to elicit Lawrence's scathing verdict on at least one of them (by the American journalist Lowell Thomas – 'All lies! All lies!'). Before leaving for a posting to India late in 1926, Lawrence completed *The Seven Pillars of Wisdom* – he signed off the Acknowledgements from Cranwell – and approved an abridged edition entitled *Revolt in the Desert*, which appeared in 1927. Whittle, by then a twenty-year-old cadet, was enthralled by it. He wrote an essay about the book as part of his English Literature coursework, and embellished it with his recollections of the author:

> Colonel T. E. Lawrence... is a very modest and unassuming character. It is hard to believe that the small flaxen haired airman who was lately stationed at Cranwell... has been known as the 'Uncrowned King of Arabia'. He is an eccentric, and anyone who has met him is liable to think him mentally unbalanced or nearly so. He has many extraordinary characteristics which many would ascribe to insanity. He is modest to an extreme and loathes publicity of any sort...
>
> As this book is a masterpiece on its literary merit alone, this combined with its historical and geographical value, also its pure interest as a story, ranks it as the greatest book I have ever read.[12]

How strange that the RAF should have brought together in one place these two singular figures of the twentieth century from such different backgrounds. As Whittle was perhaps vaguely aware in penning this brief profile, there were several aspects of Lawrence's character – his cleverness and charismatic leadership, his aversion to authority, his dread of publicity and his innate sense of being always a non-conforming outsider – that would turn out to be defining features of his own character, too. (After the Second World War, Whittle had his portrait painted by the distinguished war artist Eric Kennington, who had been close to Lawrence and a pallbearer at his funeral. Whittle read Kennington's private copy of *The Mint*, as yet still unpublished, and noted in his diary that they had had 'many discussions about T. E. Lawrence' – sadly adding no further comment.[13])

Whittle's simple aim in his apprenticeship years was to survive the course, in the hope of becoming eligible for a cadetship. And in engaging for the first time directly with aeroplanes and their maintenance, he found plenty of consolations to help him weather his early despair – and indeed to 'remember his dreams'. He shared them with a childhood sweetheart he had left behind in Leamington. Her name was Barbara, and many of Whittle's letters home to her in 1925–6 fizz with humour and the sense of a young man enjoying life to the full.[14] He was now a voracious reader and regaled her with book lists (Thackeray, Scott, Wodehouse and Shaw), as well as snippets of the foreign languages he was dipping into and, of course, brave accounts of his latest flying adventures (by the spring of 1925 he had flown five times, courtesy of the cadet-college instructors). Full of playful ardour, they are letters written by a sparkling and inventive mind – not shy of the odd missive penned in cod Elizabethan English ('Havynge now sent ye greetynge meet for one so faire, methinks 'twere well that I gotte me donne unto the purpose of this mine epistle...') and usually signed off with a flourish (on one occasion, 'Yours 'till the moon turns green, and whiskers grow on margarine and pimples sprout on pickled pork'). No wonder Barbara kept them safely, though who she was and how his affectionate letters came to survive in his own papers has gone unrecorded.

His rising spirits owed much to Whittle's confidence that his apprenticeship, for all its unwelcome rigours, had much to offer. It gave him precious scope to develop his skills as a craftsman, and also involved classroom studies that engaged his intellect far more directly than any teachers at Leamington College had done. We know his imagination, first stirred by those sightings of wartime planes, had soared by the end of the 1920s. So how exactly was it fuelled in the three years up to 1926? Three positive aspects of his life as an apprentice made a huge and lasting impact.

First came the opportunity to immerse himself in the basic skills of the workshop. His 1923 cohort was broadly split into three groups, to train either as aero-engine fitters, wireless-operator mechanics or as 'carpenter-riggers'. The latter had to master every aspect of the wing and fuselage assemblies for their planes. Whittle was made a carpenter-rigger and put under the supervision of an RAF instructor, Wing Commander George Lees, an avuncular figure with a huge handlebar moustache. Lees recognised his young charge's unusual talents and offered him constant encouragement. (It would frequently happen to Whittle during his career that others would find themselves so drawn to him that a working relationship developed into lasting personal friendship. So it proved now: George Lees was to be the first of many who would fall under his spell in this way.)

In addition to familiarising him with the building blocks of aircraft design – and with the extraordinary precision that was demanded of all those engaged in the maintenance of aircraft – Whittle's workshop role also put him directly in touch with the wider world of technical controversy over future aircraft designs. The carpenter-riggers, as their title would suggest, were mostly handling struts and spars made of wood. Almost all aircraft in 1923 were still built of predominantly wooden airframes, covered with a linen fabric that had been soaked with liquid cellulose ('dope') and then stretched into place before it dried taut. Since 1919, a debate had been growing steadily louder in design circles over the merits of metal as a permanent alternative to wood. It was not until 1927, the year after Whittle's own apprenticeship ended, that the RAF first advertised vacancies for 'metal-riggers' as well as 'carpenter-riggers'. But we know Whittle spent plenty of his time dealing with blacksmiths and coppersmiths at Cranwell, in servicing the needs of its two squadrons, and he must certainly have taken a lively interest in the progress of the wood/metal debate. Nothing could better have alerted him to the intriguing potential of new technologies in the world of aeronautics. If all-wood planes could be replaced by all-metal ones, what other far-reaching changes in aircraft design might soon follow?

The second crucial element of the teenage Whittle's training was the quality of the teaching at Cranwell, and the way he responded to it. During his year in the Sixth Form at Leamington, he had become more receptive to classroom learning. Now it was doubly appealing, not least as an escape from the ghastly business of drill routines. As Whittle explained in later life: 'the education officers were civilians who treated us quite differently from the NCO instructors of the workshops and parade ground. In school we were accepted as human beings rather than as mere numbers.'[15] Though he was too modest to mention it, the classroom at Cranwell was also where he made a pleasing discovery about 'mere numbers'. He had always found that mathematics came to him easily, but had made little of it. Now, when his teachers began using mathematics to solve practical problems involving atmospheric pressures, wing velocities, air resistance and the like, Whittle felt motivated to apply himself properly – and showed a conceptual grasp of the subject that instantly put him in another league from his teachers, let alone his peers. Other subjects could be fascinating, and his extra year at school now stood him in good stead, but it was mathematics ('clearly relevant to the kind of engineering in which I was interested') that really fired him.[16] He acquired his first slide rule and began to attract attention for the brilliance of his classroom contributions. As his apprenticeship years wore on, he came to a sense of his own gifts. Stories about the tiny teenage boffin meanwhile travelled up the ranks at Cranwell. The college's Commanding Officer, a veteran who had flown on the Western Front called Wing Commander Robert ('Biffy') Barton, took to confiding in friends that he had a genius on his hands.

iv

Excellence on the sports field was always seen as marking out a potential officer. Far from excelling on it, Whittle failed to appear at all if he could possibly absent himself. This must at first have caused him considerable difficulties. It was not too long, though, before the senior officers at Cranwell began making allowances for him because of his evident cleverness – and the fact that he had found an unusual outlet for his talents. This was Cranwell's Model Aircraft Society, to which he began devoting every hour of his time that could be salvaged from the formal timetable. Rather as he had done at secondary school, in fact, Whittle pushed the orthodox agenda of his peers to one side so that he could concentrate on what really interested him. The Model Aircraft Society in this way comprised the third critical aspect of his life as an apprentice. Many pioneering theorists of flight in the nineteenth century had used models to test out their ideas. Whittle did the same. He built a series of exquisite models, all of which challenged his understanding of aircraft design and his grasp of the mathematics of flight. They also needed to be assembled by teams, which required him to hone some leadership skills. The model society at Cranwell was run by officers, but they soon learned that Apprentice Boy Whittle would insist on being his own team leader for each of his projects and was quick to dismiss interference by his less gifted peers. The society came to revolve largely around his activities. Biffy Barton himself took a keen interest in this development, and in due course most VIP visitors to Cranwell found a tour of the Apprentices' Wing included a viewing of Boy Whittle's models.

They were splendid affairs, powered by tiny two-stroke petrol engines. Since there existed no means of controlling them in flight, they had to be flown on an open expanse of ground with plenty of room to take off and land unimpeded. Each had to be built with meticulous care, with its wings and rudder trimmed to allow for a generously circular flight and a gentle glide down when the fuel tank ran dry. Sir Philip Sassoon, the Tory Under-Secretary of Air since 1924 (and cousin of the poet Siegfried), was so impressed on a tour of the collected models early in 1926 that he commissioned a new one for himself. Whittle was delighted and assembled a small team for the project, as he recalled years later. He persuaded one of the laboratory assistants at Cranwell to make an engine for it, but he himself took direct charge over all other aspects of the job – 'the design of the airframe, the drawings, wooden jigs for the construction of the delicate wing ribs and other parts of the structure, and the fabric covering'.[17] He presented the finished article to a beaming Sassoon in person on the day of Cranwell's annual Passing Out ceremony in July 1926 (*Plate 1a*). (Sadly, the model never flew: its two spark plugs both failed at the last minute. Whittle never forgot his disappointment. As he recalled sixty years later, only half in jest, 'I think that gave me a very strong prejudice against piston engines if nothing else did!'[18])

This occasion marked the end of the 1923–6 apprentices' training. The outcome, all knew, would see most of them classified as first- or second-class Aircraftmen. A minority, perhaps one in five of the apprentices, would be awarded Leading Aircraftman ('LAC') status. And for the half a dozen emerging with the best final grades, there would be the biggest prize of all: a formal discharge from the RAF, to be followed immediately afterwards by readmission with the award of a paid cadetship at Cranwell to train as a Pilot Officer. This was another of Trenchard's innovations. He insisted that lifting the ablest of the apprentices into the cadet school would eventually inject an essential element of meritocracy into the RAF's officer class, otherwise still comprised almost exclusively of young men educated at Britain's most expensive fee-paying schools like Eton, Haileybury and Wellington. Whittle had a passion to fly – but had always been well aware that simple merit would not guarantee him a ticket into training as a pilot. As he had confided to Barbara three months earlier, in April 1926:

> I am Wing Commander's Orderly next Thursday afternoon which means that I am in the running for a cadetship or corporal. The object is that the Wing Commander wants to ask a dickens of a number of questions, relating to one's dark past, one's parents, and to find if one speaks and behaves like a gentleman. A good deal depends on next Thursday afternoon.

Indeed it did – and Whittle (having striven long ago to ditch his Midlands accent) thought afterwards that he had done his chances no harm with Biffy Barton.

The apprentices' final grades were decided by a formal selection committee, but every CO customarily had discretion over 'efficiency marks' that allowed him to push forward his personal views. When the selection committee tallied up the ranking of the 1923–6 apprentices for passing out, Whittle came seventh – and cadetships were lined up for just the first six names. (Two additional candidates were nominated from Flowerdown, the RAF's other technical training centre where Trenchard's Brats specialised in wireless telegraphy.) Barton requested that his brilliant model-maker's name be added, under the standing rules governing efficiency marks. His fellow officers on the committee objected. Brains were not the stock-in-trade of their RAF, and Whittle had won not a single trophy on the sports field. Nor had he ever shadowed the Commanding Officer as 'Leading Boy', as all promoted apprentices had done to date. Barton's colleagues thought Whittle a difficult lad, inclined to be surprisingly uncompromising with his views. In short, he did not seem quite the right type to fit in as a cadet.

Barton was enraged. As he would later recall: 'Having known the boy for three years, I was aware that he was no good at games and had a poor personality [sic], but at the same time I realised that we had somebody whose brain was streets above any of the other boys and that if he did nothing else he would develop into a most valuable technical officer.'[19] With no time left for gentle persuasion, he went straight to London and appealed directly to the Personnel Branch in Adastral House for their support. He did not get it. Only former Leading Boys, said Personnel, could be considered as future cadets. Barton found his entreaties falling on deaf ears. (Not for the first time or the last, it seemed Whittle was fated to win the support of those in uniform while falling foul of their civilian peers.) Any other Cranwell commander might have let the matter drop. Luckily for Whittle, Barton had one other card to play: he was a former comrade-in-arms of the RAF's Chief, having served under him as a young subaltern in the Royal Scots Fusiliers in 1910. Passing down the corridor out-side Trenchard's office in Adastral House, he dared to beard the great man at his desk. He was fortunate with his timing. Trenchard laid down his papers and listened. With no preamble, Barton pitched the case for making an exception of Whittle, telling Trenchard the RAF had its very own mathematical genius in the making. The founding father of the service was famously a man of few words, but those used on this occasion would be many times retold. He heard out his unannounced visitor, then challenged him in typical style: 'You've usually been right in the past, Barton, but are you sure you're right this time?' The Cran-well commander was adamant, and Trenchard was ready with a snap judgement: 'All right, Barton, but if you've made a mistake with this young man, I'll never forgive you.'[20]

Returning to Lincolnshire, Barton had all the backing he needed to face down the committee. Whittle's name was duly added to the recommended list, as he learned on 12 July. Thus began an eventful few days, described in a subsequent letter to Barbara.[21] The nine candidates were sent straight off to London for their medical test ('frightfully stiff'). Three of them failed it, but not Whittle. On 15 July, the surviving six were interviewed at the Air Ministry by an Air Vice Marshal, Sir Charles Longcroft, and an Air Commodore, Hugh Dowding. Barton sat in on the process, and afterwards told his protégé privately 'the Air Vice Marshal was absolutely delighted' at his performance. Late that evening, a jubilant Whittle arrived back at Cranwell to a hero's reception. 'They knew I had passed before I got back, and started clapping when I walked in. I wondered what on earth was the matter.'

The Air Council made a formal announcement of the Passing Out results a week later. Out of 529 apprentices in Cranwell's 1923 entry, 81 had been made Leading Aircraftmen and 5 of these had been awarded cadetships. The fifth was Frank Whittle.[22] On 23 August 1926, the names of all six nominees – the sixth was a Boy from Flowerdown – appeared in *The Times*. Two of them had been awarded valuable scholarships. Barton's homespun genius had no such luck, but a place alone was triumph enough for now.

2

From Thesis to Turbo-Jet

July 1926 to November 1931

i

As Whittle was making his way back to RAF Cranwell that July, flushed with confidence after his successful interview, he heard the news that a cadet had had a fatal crash during the afternoon. Accidents at the college were not uncommon – flying any plane was still horribly dangerous – and the apprentices at Cranwell were no strangers to the gallows humour that had been the stock-in-trade of the RAF from its earliest RFC days. Sure enough, next morning on the parade ground, a caustic sergeant major rose to the occasion in predictable style. 'If I was you, Whittle, I wouldn't go up there,' he said, pointing to the cadet wing. 'They kill people there!' His young charge reported the quip a few days later in a letter to Barbara, though he paid it no real heed ('I don't think that will put me off').[1] He had been yearning to join the RAF's officer ranks for years, and nothing was going to stand in his way now.

Assuming, that is, he could manage to surmount the class barriers ahead of him. Cranwell took in a fresh entry every six months, assigning each successive cadre to four half-yearly terms. It surprised Whittle, despite his three years as an apprentice, to discover how many ritualistic indignities were heaped on the trainee pilots in their first term – and how many tiny humiliations the RAF's officer class had in store for the unwary social climber. Trenchard's edict that six apprentices a year be appointed to the College had not gone unopposed. 'Certain Air Ministry colleagues, more conservative in outlook, argued that the innovation would "lower the tone" of the service.'[2] Arriving there at the end of August 1926, Whittle had come some distance from his days as Grub of Leamington Secondary, but he was still a relative stranger to the world seemingly inhabited so easily by the twenty-eight cadets around him. As a promoted Trenchard Brat, Whittle was paid seven shillings a day, which comprised his sole income.[3] Most of his peers (or their parents) were paying stiff fees to be there, having just emerged from an equally expensive public-school education. Cranwell was no less a bastion than Sandhurst (its army counterpart) of Britain's institutionalised class system, as it was to remain throughout the interwar years. 'Of the 929 schoolboy entrants who passed through [Cranwell] between 1920 and 1939, all but ninety-three went to fee-paying schools.'[4] Theirs was a close-knit culture to which Whittle – the product of a rather drab state education, now happily professing to be an avowed socialist and making no effort to conceal his loathing of competitive games – scarcely belonged at all. All he really shared with them was a pride in the service and the sheer love of flying.

Moving into a Spartan wooden hut with four others – not counting their batman, who had his own small room – the working-class boy with no middle name discovered one of his peers had a triple-barrelled surname. When they all prepared nightly for dinner, the former Apprentice Boy had to confront the joys of formal dress for the first time in his life – mess kit was black tie, with a blue waistcoat – and the many little niceties of etiquette in the mess. One of his fellow hut mates helped him through some early embarrassments. Rolf Dudley ('Willie') Williams was a jovial and easy-going West Country man, the son of a Plymouth tradesman and a year younger than Whittle. He was struck from the outset by how different his new friend seemed from all the other cadets. Only nineteen, Whittle had a sense of purpose about him and a driving intellectual curiosity that Williams had never encountered before. He found him instantly engaging. As he would recall much later in life:

> I was attracted by the intensity of his eyes and the keen, crisp way he spoke. He was a great man for challenging accepted beliefs, religious, economic, whatever. He was a socialist, whereas I rather accepted matters as they stood. I found myself very attracted to this critical being. He forced me to think.[5]

Whittle repaid his kindness in the mess by helping Williams to cope with the demands of their cadetship in the classroom. A friendship was formed that would change both their lives.

Over the next couple of years, Whittle found many conventional views worth challenging. Two early preoccupations, though, were more personal. He confronted some mounting doubts about his strict Wesleyan upbringing and came to the conclusion that science and his Christian faith were not compatible. He went on attending chapel on Sundays for much of his cadetship, but he abandoned all his former religious beliefs long before the end of the course. And he reappraised his love life. At the start of 1926 he had met Dorothy Mary Lee, the daughter of a well-to-do chartered surveyor, three years older than him and living with her family in Coventry. By the close of the year he was writing her almost daily letters. This brought the curtain down on his relationship with Barbara, to whom he penned a revealingly brusque final missive in November: 'I found your [latest] letter in the drawer in which I place all letters to be answered. I have to do that as I get so many.'[6]

However heartless, this was probably the truth. In pocket diaries that have survived, Whittle kept a daily record of his correspondence.[7] He was evidently busy from his earliest months as a cadet, writing audacious letters to anyone in the aeronautical world whose views he thought might be of interest. They included authors and journalists as well as academics and engineers in the aircraft industry. Their names are scattered amidst the jotted diary notes of a determined young autodidact. Shaping his schedule from one week to the next, meanwhile, were his classroom courses and his flying lessons. The latter were at first less frequent than he had expected – and he did not go solo until halfway through his second term – but the coursework was demanding from the start. The Cranwell syllabus embraced an impressive range of subjects.* Whittle worked hard and was running ahead of all his peers by the start of 1927. He would come easily top of his cadre over their first year, doubtless to the relief and satisfaction of Biffy Barton. And whatever the multiple demands on his time, he managed to go on puzzling over the basics of aeronautical science. He had had to leave behind his model-making days – but he went on, in Dudley Williams' phrase, forcing himself to think.

It fascinated Whittle that aeroplanes had come so far, so fast, within his short lifetime. Just a decade or so had sufficed to see powered planes go from the Wright brothers' jaw-dropping exhibition flights in France in 1908 to the sixteen-hour non-stop crossing of the Atlantic by Alcock and Brown in 1919. And recent years had seen further progress made in a host of ways that the teenage Whittle had been following avidly in books and magazines. Trained as a carpenter-rigger, he knew all about the latest views on wing and fuselage construction. Above all, though, it was the evolution of the aero-engine that to his mind was the crux of the matter. Chemists researching the properties of the various hydro-carbon ingredients of petrol had produced a much-improved range of fuels which in turn had opened up many ways of boosting engine performance. Metallurgists had begun to identify new alloys, picking and mixing from a smorgasbord of exotic minerals to find additives for either steel or aluminium that could make them immeasurably stronger yet

---

* It comprised no fewer than sixteen graded subjects: General History, Aeronautical Science, Armament, Naval Organisation, Law & Administration, Sanitation & Hygiene, Morse, Engines, Rigging, Wireless Telegraphy, Airmanship, Air Pilotage, Practical Flying, Meteorology, Observation Training & Reconnaissance, Drill & General Efficiency. In addition to practical tests, cadets had to write regular essays and one science thesis each term.

at the same time much lighter. This was producing ideal new materials for engine components, from the tiniest valves to whole cylinder blocks. And the mechanical engineers, taking their cues from the men in the laboratories, were coming up with better designs for almost every facet of the engine itself – from ignition and lubrication to cooling and carburettors.

Whittle revelled in the details. At some point in 1927, though, a small spark of genius goaded him into noting something unsatisfactory about the bigger picture. His peers were confident of the scope for continual improvements to aero-engines. Yet a broad consensus seemed to have emerged, that nothing was likely to supersede the internal combustion engine – or indeed even its basic layout, as exemplified in the best designs available by the early 1920s. Whittle began to ask himself: why not?

For his contemporaries, the question simply did not arise. The latest engines were regarded as the culmination of an extra-ordinary era of experimentation, driven ahead by the cataclysmic events of 1914–18. Britain's military had started the war with fewer than three hundred aircraft, with manufacturers turning out perhaps fifty a month. The RAF had ended the war with 22,000 aircraft, and manufacturing output up to almost 2,700 a month. This breakneck expansion had been accompanied by rapid advances in aircraft design, and especially by constantly improved versions of the internal combustion engine to provide more power for less weight – always the Holy Grail of aero-engineering. The outcome looked dramatic by any measure. The pre-war aero-engine industry had been dominated by French companies, and the first squadrons of the Royal Flying Corps had mostly relied on a single French design, an air-cooled 'rotary' engine that was the first standardised power plant to be turned out specifically for planes rather than automobiles. Unlikely as it may now sound, the 'Gnome' of 1914 comprised seven cylinders that whirled round with the propeller as a single unit, revolving on a stationary crankshaft fixed into the fuselage. Pilots needed to be wary of changing direction, unleashing powerful gyroscopic forces, and had to contend with exhaust pipes belching castor oil that was added to the fuel in copious quantities as a cylinder lubricant. A mere five years later, the rotary design had been left behind and a range of infinitely more sophisticated and reliable engines were producing several times as much horsepower as the Gnome (and no castor oil from their exhausts). The leading names included several British firms, including Derby-based Rolls-Royce – famous around the world for the excellence of its state-of-the-art automobiles – whose V-12 'Eagle' engine had carried Alcock and Brown over the Atlantic and powered another Vickers Vimy on the first multi-leg flight from England to Australia the same year.

Within a few years of the war's end, engine designers had settled on two classic designs. One was firmly identified with the Rolls-Royce Eagle and comprised twin banks of water-cooled cylinders in a V-shaped pattern. (A variant of this set the cylinders vertically 'in-line'.) It looked hard to beat, and it was: every subsequent Rolls-Royce piston engine of any consequence, and indeed almost all military engines in every air force of the world, would essentially conform to the Eagle's layout. The other design, only really established as a classic at the start of the 1920s, featured a 'radial' pattern that had several air-cooled cylinders fixed in a circle round the crankshaft. It was epitomised by an engine called the 'Jupiter', launched by the Bristol Aeroplane Company in 1922 and almost exclusively used in civil aircraft. By the time Whittle began writing essays as a Cranwell cadet, several other engines had already become famous in the wake of the Eagle and the Jupiter – but all served to confirm the dominance of these two designs. As a UK government memorandum would put it, looking back twenty years later:

> The [post-war] problem was no longer one of ascertaining the form of optimum engine, it was one of extracting the maximum power from basic layouts which had already been discovered to give the best performance… [The story from 1919] is one of meticulous and painstaking development of the V and radial types.[8]

What defined a 'best performance' engine was its power-to-weight ratio, with the power traditionally measured in horsepower (hp). The V-shaped and radial engines available by 1922 were not significantly heavier than their predecessors but were capable of delivering 400 hp or more, roughly twice as much as the engines that had powered the final versions of the best wartime fighters produced in Britain, France or Germany. (Britain's celebrated Sopwith Camel relied on a French rotary engine capable of just 130 hp.) Without any further boost to their underlying power output, engines like the Jupiter and a new engine from Rolls-Royce, the 'Kestrel', were being continuously enhanced in successive versions to fly aeroplanes faster and more reliably. Over the course of the 1920s, accordingly, the record books had been regularly rewritten. Hugely popular speed trials and competitions were not necessarily an accurate guide to the average performance of aircraft in the RAF, but they did affirm the onward march of aero-engineering at its best. In the most famous race of all, the annual Schneider Trophy, the winning speeds had climbed steadily up from 145 mph in 1922 and by 1927 seemed certain, soon, to approach 300 mph.

To Whittle's fellow cadets, these events added immeasurably to the glamour and excitement of becoming a pilot – all the more so after it was agreed, early in 1927, that Britain would be represented in that year's Schneider Trophy by an RAF team. (A dedicated unit known as the 'High Speed Flight' was assembled for the job at RAF Felixstowe, a station on the Suffolk coast where experimental seaplanes were put through their paces. One of its pilots flew the Trophy winner that September.) Whittle, though, saw things differently, even as a mere cadet. The glamour of high-speed racing seemed to him, if not exactly frivolous, at best a distraction from more serious thinking about the potential of the aeroplane. Racing pandered to the popular appetite for competitive sports, but offered no real clues to the future. Far more significant, to his enquiring mind, were the feats of the long-distance aviators who were breaking records of another kind, with their brave inaugural flights over the oceans. The South Atlantic from Cape Verde to Buenos Aires had been crossed early in 1926, and in May 1927

Charles Lindbergh made his celebrated solo flight from New York to Paris. Flying such huge distances non-stop required engines with unprecedented levels of reliability. Intercontinental routes also challenged current thinking about speed in ways that made the Schneider hardly relevant. Facing a flight across thousands of miles, what difference did it make to go an extra twenty, forty or even sixty miles in each airborne hour? Whittle's imagination was fired by the idea of planes linking the continents on a regular basis. That would require them to fly at speeds perhaps twice as fast as any foreseeable Schneider Trophy winner – fast enough to cross, say, the North Atlantic in less than half a day. Lindbergh had taken more than thirty-three hours to reach Paris from New York.

Searching for a way to turn this high-speed vision into a practical proposition, Whittle turned instinctively to mathematics. The resulting train of thought led him to a logical conclusion from which there could be no retreat, though it would be hard to square with a world dominated by piston aero-engines, trophy-winning or otherwise. He began from first principles. An aircraft in flight encounters two kinds of resistance. 'Profile drag' is a function of the aircraft's shape and of the air's reluctance to give way to it. 'Induced drag' is incurred by the aircraft as a result of its redirecting the airflow downwards over its wings in order to overcome its weight as it moves forward. (Both could be calculated for a given aircraft, using already established equations.) Crucially, as an aircraft picks up speed, the induced drag declines as the profile drag rises. Pictured as two lines on a simple graph, there must plainly be a point (that is, a speed) at which the two lines cross. This represents 'the optimal speed', at which the aircraft will encounter 'minimum total drag'.

There is one other factor, however, that also governs an aircraft's optimal speed – namely, its altitude. This is true because of a constant relationship between air density and velocity. Given the two drag calculations, it is straightforward to calculate an aircraft's optimal speed at sea level; but the calculation is subject to any change of height. The variance can be stated as an equation, which is perhaps the only truly inescapable equation for any proper understanding of Whittle's thinking:

$$\text{'optimal speed'} = \text{the density of the ambient air} \times \text{the aircraft's velocity, squared}$$

As the aircraft climbs in height, the air density decreases. Therefore the velocity can be increased without changing the product of the equation. The implications of this are rather startling. Take an aircraft with an optimal speed at sea level of 300 mph. If it were able to fly at 40,000 feet, where the density of the air falls to a quarter of its sea-level value, then the equation dictates that its velocity could be doubled and it would still be flying at 'optimal speed' – but this would now be a velocity of 600 mph. Or to put it another way, an aircraft designed to encounter minimum total drag at 300 mph at sea level could (in theory) go 600 mph if it flew at 40,000 feet *without encountering an ounce of additional drag.* And the higher it went, the faster it could go.

Here, as the teenaged Whittle grasped in the course of 1927, was the key to his vision of intercontinental flights at high speed. Long distances could be covered in (relatively) short trips by aeroplanes enabled to fly extremely fast by flying at very great heights. He fully appreciated that the thinness of the air would leave piston engines gasping for breath anywhere near 40,000 feet and render propellers next to useless. Necessity would have to be the mother of some other kind of engine.

ii

By the start of 1928 Whittle was ready to explore in detail the idea of flying higher in order to fly much faster. In addition to weekly tests and regular written essays, Cranwell's cadets were required to write a thesis in each of their four terms. They could choose their own topics. Whittle had devoted his first three efforts mostly to his youthful passion for chemistry, though not without including a passing reference ('the speed of an aeroplane must increase with altitude'[9]) to the idea that was increasingly preoccupying him. He decided to make it the subject of his final thesis.

Over the next six months, he pulled together all his thoughts to date. Early in June 1928, the first aeroplane to fly across the Pacific Ocean from the United States to Australia – a monoplane called *Southern Cross* with a four-man Australian crew – landed in Brisbane, to great excitement. This gave Whittle a nicely topical 'Introductory' paragraph for a thesis that stretched to forty-seven handwritten pages by the time he submitted it in July. He called it 'Future Developments in Aircraft Design', a paper intended to survey 'the "middle" future, with a certain amount of speculation which will probably overlap [with] the immediate future'. Preserved today by the Science Museum in London, it is a breathtaking document.[10] Under individual headings such as 'Methods of Obtaining Lift', 'Increase of Speed', 'Range Allowing for Fuel Consumption' and 'Decrease of Structural Weight', Whittle worked out from first principles why aeroplanes could logically be expected, one day, to meet performance goals way beyond those of the 1920s. The resulting stream of equations, with a four-page appendix, evidently floored the professor who marked it and appended an evasive but not ungenerous note at the end. ('It would be difficult to comment on this without re-writing the thesis. The thesis shows much careful and original thought and also a good deal of private reading.')

Leaving aside the baffling fact that all this flowed from the pen of a twenty-one-year-old less than two years out of an apprentice-ship, the paper was touched with genius in two main respects. In the first place, Whittle drew on his imagination to convey an inspired vision of the future. In this respect, the mathematics comprised the small print. He was depicting, in effect, the modern era of jet travel. He invited his reader to imagine planes flying at spectacular speeds and altitudes: 'if practical difficulties could be overcome, an aeroplane which could fly at 60 mph at ground level would be able to fly at 600 mph at 120,000 feet if the power were available.' At this height its passengers and crew could be safely cocooned in 'a totally enclosed cockpit into which warmed air is pressure-fed' and would be untroubled by the weather and atmospheric disturbances far below them. He saw aircraft carrying people and goods on long-haul routes between the continents in ways, familiar enough today, that had simply not occurred to any of his contemporaries.

And second, Whittle firmly and eloquently identified the single most important prerequisite for this whole phenomenon: the invention of an 'air-turbine' engine. He devoted almost half of his 1928 thesis to an analysis of 'Power Units'. Here he did the sums and embraced the air-turbine as an inevitable innovation:

> It seems that, as the turbine is the most efficient prime mover known, it is possible that it will be developed for aircraft, especially if some means of driving a turbine by petrol could be devised. A steam turbine is quite impracticable owing [to] the weight of boilers, condensers etc. A petrol driven turbine would be more efficient... [and would operate with] a constant pressure cycle... My aim is to show that the air turbine will be more efficient than the petrol internal combustion engine and would be more suitable for high altitude work.

With several pages of detailed workings, graphs and diagrams he then accomplished this aim to his own satisfaction, and rounded off his thesis with a straight prediction: 'The most important developments which will take place [in aircraft designs of the future] will follow as a result of the development of a more suitable prime mover, i.e. an air turbine.'

His conviction that the 'air turbine' – that is, the gas turbine – would triumph in the end was born of all those long hours he had spent as a teenager in Leamington Spa library. His immersion in the subject had been further aided by the timely English-language publication in 1927 of a seminal textbook on turbines that had hitherto been available only in German. Aurel Stodola was a Slovak physicist, born in 1859 when his hometown was still part of Hungary. A professor at the Zurich Institute of Technology, Stodola had been teaching there since 1892 and was widely regarded as the most authoritative figure in the whole turbine field. (One of his students at the Zurich Institute was Albert Einstein.) In 1903 he had published *Die Dampfturbine* – The Steam Turbine – and by the 1920s the book had already gone through several editions and done much to establish the esoteric discipline of thermodynamics. Its principal subject was the behaviour of steam within a revolving turbine; but an appendix, added in 1906, also examined the theoretical workings of a gas turbine. We can be sure that Whittle by 1928 was entirely conversant with the translation in every respect. He also knew that all attempts to build a gas turbine had so far proved futile. A dispiriting chronicle of mechanical failures – linked, above all, to the want of a powerful compressor – stretched back almost a quarter of a century. But Whittle swept this history aside in his thesis. He provided a detailed analysis of how a gas turbine might work, based very largely on his own calculations. And for good measure, he even included a diagram of a turbine with a combustion chamber fed by three reciprocating air pumps (*Fig. 2*).

He still had one conundrum to which there seemed no satisfactory answer. His thesis measured the rotary power of a turbine

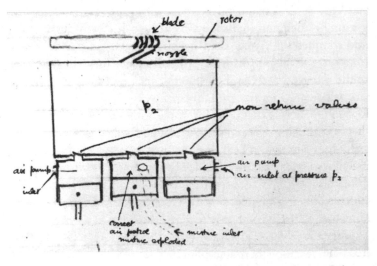

Fig. 2. FW's sketch of a gas-turbine concept for his 1928 Cranwell thesis

connected to a shaft – but this implied the use of a propeller. He noted the unanswerable objection to this – 'an airscrew designed to work efficiently at low altitudes becomes hopelessly unsuitable at great altitudes' – but remained as yet stumped for an alternative. As for the notion of jet propulsion, he referred to it only in the context of rocket power and gave it short shrift. He must have been well aware of a string of patents that had been filed since the turn of the century – mostly by French inventors such as Marconnet (1908), Lorin (1913) and Melot (1920) – to cover engines designed for 'thermal air jet propulsion'. All were linked in some way to reciprocating engines, though, and seemed to him hopelessly impractical. The case for the turbine, by contrast, was compelling. So Whittle opted to stand by the logic of all his equations and to leave the propeller quandary for another day. The 1928 thesis was in this sense unfinished business. It was nonetheless the seed of a revolution in aeronautics.

None of his tutors at Cranwell spotted this, or felt prompted to ask the Air Ministry whether this air-turbine idea was worth serious consideration. National security would no doubt have precluded a fulsome answer – but it was precisely this idea that had been A. A. Griffith's driving obsession at the Air Ministry Laboratory in South Kensington over the past few years. His 1926 paper on the theory of the axial compressor had explored the theory of turbine design on the clear premise that any successful turbine would drive a propeller, hence his talk of a 'turbine airscrew'.[11] Griffith had submitted it to his masters at the Aeronautical Research Committee (ARC). They had passed it along the line to their Engine Sub-Committee, which in turn had invited various experts to run their slide rules over it, much to Griffith's private irritation. By the summer of 1928, as Cadet Whittle was finalising his thesis, the experts' verdicts were being collated and a formal conclusion was only months away. (The prospects were looking none too encouraging for Griffith.)

This lofty debate, of course, belonged to a world far removed from the class work of trainee pilots at Cranwell, let alone Whittle's precocious effort. As for Whittle himself, he had plenty of other matters to keep him busy. July brought graduation. He came second in his year – having perhaps spent more time on his thesis than was intended – but he picked up Cranwell's top prize for academic achievement, the Abdy Gerrard Fellowes Memorial Prize for Aeronautical Sciences. It was not unknown for the same individual to win both this and the 'Best Pilot' accolade and Whittle had proved himself a superb pilot. He nonetheless had to content himself with half the honours: he had disqualified himself from the pilots' prize – which most of his peers fully expected him to win – by getting himself cited for dangerous flying in the final display of the year. His superior officers had finally lost patience with his refusal to heed some basic rules of the college.

Whittle's acrobatic stunts in the cockpit had caused him trouble on several occasions but had also won him a reputation as an unusually fearless flier. His courage was never in doubt. One of his fellow cadets, John Grierson, would much later recall a colourful illustration of it on the ground. The day before his twenty-first birthday in June 1928, Grierson had given him a lift to the local railway station in the sidecar of his Brough Superior motorcycle. They had raced from Cranwell to Newark at breakneck speed and avoided crashing by inches on more than one corner. 'On arrival at Newark station, Frank emerged from the sidecar in a somewhat shaken condition. "Tomorrow", he said, "will be my 21st birthday. I was told by a fortune-teller that I should not live to be twenty-one; I thought this was it".'[12] (Grierson went on to become a brave test pilot, flying some of the first jet engines to go into the air.)

Whittle turned his age into a matter of some consequence at the cadets' Passing Out ceremony. He had become engaged in April to his Coventry sweetheart, Dorothy Lee, and invited her to be there as his guest. She arrived at Cranwell sporting her new ring. No date was yet fixed for the wedding – he and Dorothy were eventually to marry in May 1930 – but Whittle's betrothal flagged again, like his antics in the air, his predilection for cocking a snook at authority. No married man's allowance was available to officers under the age of thirty: the RAF preferred to see its young pilots devoting themselves to the camaraderie of the mess. Whittle's defiance of this convention did not pass unnoticed.

Four weeks after graduation, he was posted as a fresh Pilot Officer to a fighter squadron, No. 111, based at Hornchurch, an Essex town then still just beyond London's north-eastern suburbs. He and a dozen or so other pilots spent most of their time buzzing up and down the Thames estuary and the North Sea coast, practising formation flying in readiness for their participation in the annual audit of the RAF's fighting capacity known as the 'Air Defence of Great Britain' exercises. The aircraft he flew was an Armstrong Whitworth Siskin III, one of several new fighters introduced in the years just after the war. The RAF was delighted with its innovative features: it was the first all-metal plane to go into service. It was nonetheless a biplane, with an open cockpit and a fixed undercarriage, which handled best at speeds of less than 140 mph. Whittle hugely enjoyed flying it. When his service duties each day ended at 4 p.m., he could then look forward to carefree evenings in which to sit alone contemplating how an air turbine might be adapted to power a plane at 600 mph or more, at heights undreamt of by the RAF or anyone else.

The gentlemen on the Engine Sub-Committee of the ARC, meanwhile, were struggling with their own quest. At their regular meeting in October 1928 they reviewed the responses to the paper in which A. A. Griffith had made the case for trying to build a prototype of his gas turbine. Various professors and distinguished engine designers had travelled to Farnborough on the ARC's behalf to see the experimental apparatus set up there by Griffith, and to discuss its prospects with David Pye. Formerly a lecturer in engineering at Trinity College, Cambridge, where he had graduated with first-class honours in 1907, Pye was deputy head of the Air Ministry's Directorate of Scientific Research. The marvel of the piston engine was one of his two great passions – the other was mountaineering: he was a member of the Alpine Club – and he was just starting work on a huge study of the subject that would appear in two volumes a few years later. Less cerebral than the renowned Dr Griffith, Pye was a greatly respected engineer.

Perhaps unsurprisingly, he was deeply sceptical of the whole idea of driving a propeller from a turbine. He had watched efforts to build an axial compressor with interest but little expectation of any useful outcome. The lack of an efficient compressor was just one of the obstacles along the path to a turbine airscrew that he thought might never be surmounted – as he readily opined whenever asked for his views. It could only ensure years of endless frustration. Better by far, in his view, to devote every effort in the laboratory to incremental improvements of the wondrous piston engine.

At its October 1928 meeting, the Engine Sub-Committee felt it had heard enough from Pye and its other experts to reach a verdict on Griffith's prospects. His turbine airscrew, they decided, was 'so problematical that they cannot recommend a continuance of experiments which would demand so great an expenditure of time and energy'. Conceivably one day it 'might satisfy the demand for a cheap power-unit for a wireless-controlled aeroplane' but they reserved judgement on that score.[13] To learn that his proposed engine had failed to make the cut even as a disposable motor for an unmanned plane must have been deeply galling for Griffith. It seemed to him plainly a wrong-headed verdict. Making light as best he could of the Sub-Committee's findings, he pressed ahead into 1929 with a programme of work that he doggedly supposed would oblige his peers, eventually, to change their minds.

No such machinations troubled Whittle, but separately he did shelve for a while his own thoughts on a turbine unit. Instead, he toyed with the idea of a huge fan, to create a jet of air that might propel an aircraft along. This had the great attraction of dispensing with the use of a propeller; but he envisaged powering the fan with a piston engine – and this ran into his growing certainty that the future did not lie with any version of the piston engine. His conviction on this score was in no way shaken by attending the Schneider Trophy event that took place over the Solent off Britain's Isle of Wight in September 1929. (It was the first since 1927, when it had been decided to convert the race into a biannual event.) The RAF's High Speed Flight won the honours again, with a seaplane that flew at almost 329 mph. Reaching a speed roughly twice as fast as the best fighters on active service was no mean achievement – but as Whittle was well aware, it had required intense preparations. A team of engineers at Rolls-Royce had devoted four months to building two versions of a state-of-the-art piston engine called the 'R' – named after Henry Royce, the maestro who presided over the firm's fortunes. The R had been specifically designed for the race – and, even then, it had needed a group of fitters from Derby, given time off work to visit Southampton and watch the racing, to be rounded up from their hotels and pressed into some critical repair work through the night on the engine that next day went on to snatch the Trophy.[14]

The winning plane, a Supermarine S.6, was acclaimed on all sides. Whittle shared in the immediate excitement over its victory, but returned to Hornchurch thinking of the event's significance in a longer perspective. The race had helped, in effect, to make even clearer to him the limitations of the piston engine. It had come a very long way since the Schneider Trophy of 1913 had gone to a plane with a winning speed of 45 mph. It was evidently true that highly skilled engineers could raise the piston engine's performance to ever higher levels. But the attainment of record speeds was now calling for engines of immense size and complexity, which posed daunting problems of maintenance. It was not hard to imagine in 1929 that the R might provide a superb platform for the development in due course of other versions by Rolls-Royce, adapted to general service – and the Supermarine S.6 and the R were indeed to emerge years later as the Spitfire and the Rolls-Royce Merlin. What Whittle could not imagine, though, was another basic design of internal combustion engine that would eclipse the R: it marked, to his mind, the end of the line.

In October 1929, the RAF acknowledged Whittle's rare prowess as a pilot by reassigning him from 111 Squadron to train as an instructor at the Central Flying School at Wittering, near

Peterborough. And it was here, within days of settling in, that Whittle had his eureka moment. It seems to have struck him at the time as anything but life-changing. (Even many years later, he summed up the moment in just ten lines of *Jet*.) It was more a case, sixteen months after the completion of his Cranwell thesis, of the penny finally dropping. The idea that came to him was nonetheless momentous. He would use a turbine rather than a piston engine to drive round the shaft of the engine; and the jet propulsion would come not from a fan, but from the turbine itself. And in place of the fan, he would connect the turbine's shaft to a greatly enhanced centrifugal compressor, to deliver air at several times atmospheric pressure. 'In short, I was back to the gas turbine,' as he would put it in retrospect, 'but this time of a type which produced a propelling jet instead of driving a propeller. Once this idea had taken shape, it seemed rather odd that I had taken so long to arrive at a concept which had become very obvious and of extraordinary simplicity.'[15] Griffith and the other turbine-airscrew theorists were intent on channelling as much power as possible from their turbine to a propeller and minimising the energy to be lost through the exhaust. Whittle would take the opposite tack. After months of thinking about jet propulsion, he now grasped in an instant the true potential of the gas turbine. He would channel only as much power into the shaft as was needed to drive the compressor, maximising the energy to be forced backwards as a jet. 'My calculations satisfied me that it was far superior to my earlier proposals.' To his RAF peers, the notion of flying without a propeller would have seemed as fanciful as flying without wings. To Whittle it was the only way forward.

A few weeks later, he sat down to explain why at the South Kensington Laboratory. There Dr Griffith had just completed his impassioned memo to the Engine Sub-Committee, pleading for the chance to continue his work on the turbine airscrew despite its members' reservations. Perhaps it even came as a relief to the Superintendent to discover that arithmetical error in his visitor's calculations.

iii

The error in his sums did not detain Whittle for long. Reworking all his equations, he discovered a second mistake that had the serendipitous effect of cancelling out the first, identified by Griffith. He made no effort to apprise Griffith and Tweedie of this – one rebuff was enough, for the twenty-two-year-old Whittle had his pride – but it did reconfirm to his own satisfaction that the theoretical basis for his jet-turbine concept was unassailable. The next question was how to turn it into a practical engine. On this score, Tweedie's letter of rejection early in December 1929 at least identified the challenge usefully enough. Whittle's jet would have to rely on three essential components. Only one of them, the turbine, was at all well understood. The other two did not exist in the configurations that he envisaged and seemed to Tweedie most unlikely to be achievable in the foreseeable future, if ever. The combustion chamber would have to deal with temperatures far higher than had yet been envisaged for any other engine. And the air compressor, in order to deliver the necessary pressure, would have to work with an 'efficiency' rating that most engineers thought simply unobtainable. High-performing piston engines of the day were equipped with compressors known as 'superchargers', which forced more air into the cylinder and so increased the power output. It was just such a unit that had helped the Rolls-Royce R engine to power the Supermarine S.6 to a winning speed in the Schneider Trophy. It had been designed by the doyen of the supercharger world, Jimmy Ellor, but even his best offering to date fell well short of Whittle's needs. Ellor's supercharger managed a pressure ratio of 2:1 and worked with 63 per cent efficiency. Whittle's gas turbine needed at least 3:1, with 70 per cent efficiency. In his rejection letter, Lawrence Tweedie suggested to Whittle that he was aiming to combine three highly problematic concepts. Linking them into one system would produce an even more useless engine than the bare mathematics suggested.

Whittle's response to this was almost as audacious as his conception of the jet turbine in the first place. Had his genius extended only as far as mathematics, he might easily have acquiesced in Tweedie's glum appraisal of the practicalities. But his sound understanding of the underlying science, and his self-assurance with all things mechanical, gave Whittle the confidence to believe that existing barriers were no more than temporary impediments. Unencumbered, it must be said, by any formal training as a professional engineer, he saw no reason at all to doubt that he would one day be able to assemble the three components he needed. And if current combustion chambers and compressors were not up to the job, then he would build better versions of his own – designed to match the aerodynamics and thermodynamics of his jet.

From his first days at Wittering, he talked constantly of the 'jet engine' and its potential. Most of his new companions thought it the harmless eccentricity of an otherwise first-class pilot – but, fortunately for Whittle, one of them had a more positive response. Flying Officer W. E. P. (Pat) Johnson was an instructor, four years older than Whittle, and an exceptionally skilled pilot with a strong interest in technical matters. (He would later pioneer the art of 'blind' flying by instruments only: he would take off and land a plane with the cockpit entirely enclosed by a windowless hood to prove his point.) Johnson had been teaching at Wittering for two years, spending most of his time with middle-ranking RAF men who were survivors of the 1914–18 war. The Pilot Officer newly arrived from 111 Squadron made an immediate impression on him as someone quite out of the ordinary. Johnson was fascinated by Whittle's description of jet propulsion. Within a few weeks, he introduced him to the station's Commanding Officer and so triggered Whittle's November 1929 trip up to London. Johnson was on a short service commission in the RAF born out of his love of flying and was planning to return in due course to his professional career – as a chartered patent agent in the City. While admiring his new friend's steely confidence in the importance of his jet-turbine theories, Johnson also took a keen professional interest in their legal status. Over the Christmas period at Wittering, he persuaded Whittle that he ought to prepare for

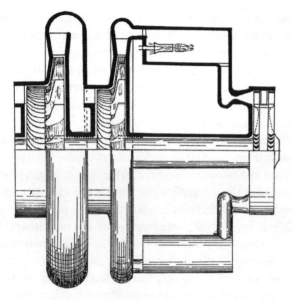

Fig. 3. Illustrative diagram attached to Patent Application
No. 347,206 in January 1930

a future application of his ideas, by taking out a formal patent. Whittle readily agreed, and so began a long and close friendship between the two men.

Johnson helped Whittle draft the necessary papers for a patent. They were filed with the Patent Office as Provisional Specification No. 347,206 ('Improvements relating to the propulsion of aircraft and other vehicles') on 16 January 1930, along with an elegant illustrative diagram (*Fig. 3*). The patent set down Whittle's objective in the most general terms – a power plant capable of flying higher and faster, and with 'simplicity and convenient external form' – but also showed how far he had already grasped the notion of jet propulsion. Indeed, in noting two possible variants on his basic design Whittle referred almost casually to further innovations that would one day serve to reshape the jet industry. He suggested (lines 62–6) that 'a portion of the air only' entering the front of the engine might actually flow through 'the expansion apparatus' while the rest could be channelled down the sides of the engine and out of the back end, where a rush of cold air could serve to reinforce the propulsive power of the hot air from the turbine. (This concept of inhaled air bypassing the core of the engine would be almost universally adopted in the 1960s: all modern jet engines are partly defined by how much air they channel around the core of the engine in proportion to the volume passing through it, known as their 'bypass ratio'.) Perhaps most astonishingly of all, he seems also to have contemplated jet engines on the wing of an aircraft that might be tilted in some way to change the aircraft's direction: 'The final emission of gas may perhaps be directionally controlled for manoeuvring purposes' (lines 107–9). The twenty-two-year-old pilot instructor was musing here over an idea that would lead eventually to aircraft with vertical take-off capabilities.

Whittle was alerted by Johnson to the fact that all the armed services would be notified of the application under Patent Office rules, in case anyone wished to throw a blanket over it on security grounds. Whittle hoped this would prompt renewed interest from the Air Ministry and so allow him to keep his patent secret. He was to be disappointed: none of the services showed the slightest interest. The governing body of the RAF, the Air Council, informed the Patent Office that there was no requirement for the content of Whittle's application to remain confidential (though he had to sign a formal contract acknowledging that the government would be free to exploit his patent if ever it wished to do so). This ruling rendered the UK patent itself an oddly mixed blessing, as Whittle himself appreciated, since the technical information included in it would be freely available for public inspection – not just in Britain but also abroad, where the UK patent would offer him little or no legal protection. By his own recollection much later, he did what he could to allow for this: 'what I drew in the patent drawing was partly intended to look fairly improbable as long as it could get through the Patent Office.'[16] This it duly succeeded in doing: the Complete Specification was accepted on 16 April 1931. And just as Whittle had feared, it soon found its way overseas. The German embassy in London had long maintained a Trade Commission tasked, inter alia, with purchasing copies of all UK technical patents of any interest, for translation and despatch back to Berlin. Whittle's Patent 347,206 was registered in the Berlin Patent Office on 14 August 1931, 'and distributed amongst German aeronautical research establishments as well as aero-engine and airframe manufacturers'.[17] The distribution list would certainly have included the University of Göttingen, one of Europe's pre-eminent centres of experimental physics across a wide range of fields, where it seems that a careful note was made of Whittle's ideas.

Just as Whittle and Johnson were filing their Provisional Specification in January 1930, the vexed debate in Whitehall over the viability of the turbine airscrew was finally coming to a head. Its rejection by the ARC's Engine Sub-Committee in October 1928 had not, after all, finished it off. The chairman of the Sub-Committee was Henry Tizard, the top official at the Department of Scientific and Industrial Research (DSIR), and a distinguished engineer in his own right. When Tizard reported back to his colleagues on the full ARC about the October meeting, it prompted a notable exchange with another member of the ARC, Tizard's long-standing friend (and already a close confidant of Winston Churchill) Frederick Lindemann. Further experiments with a turbine airscrew, explained Tizard, were looking hard to justify. This prompted an unexpected objection:

> Professor Lindemann said a power unit of this type might have the greatest possible value for military purposes and in his opinion it was most undesirable that the work should be stopped by the Aeronautical Research Committee merely because it did not seem to have a commercial application.[18]

Perhaps others on the ARC shared Lindemann's reluctance to abandon the turbine airscrew entirely. Griffith had persevered with it all through 1929 and now, in January 1930, he had produced yet another memorandum pressing his case for more money to build a bigger and better rig. To reach a decision, the

ARC set up a 'Turbine Panel' chaired by Tizard and manned by half a dozen other luminaries including David Pye – but not including Griffith himself, who would be asked to pitch his case one more time in person.

The Panel convened at the Air Ministry on London's Kingsway just four times, in February and March 1930.[19] Its deliberations and the outcome of its work captured the scientific and engineering establishment's agreed stance on the potential of air turbines at this point. They are a fair guide to what might have happened on this front over the next several years if Frank Whittle had never existed. The Panel concluded that none of Griffith's attempts to build a working machine had so far come anywhere near to success – in light of which, the prospect of tying an axial compressor into a successful aero-engine struck the Panel as hardly worth further discussion. 'As to the practical realisation of the claims put forward by Dr Griffith with regard to his turbine power plant, the Panel consider that this must in any case be very remote…'[20] The Panel agreed, though, to finance the construction of another test rig that could be used to pursue some of the wider issues raised by Griffith's work, such as the behaviour of gases in a combustion chamber. This might have proved a fruitful line of research – but it never materialised. Until 1936, when war loomed and word of Whittle's progress began to circulate, the whole topic was simply abandoned. No replacement rig was built; no further work was done at the RAE on the axial compressor; no studies followed on turbine-blade properties; and no further efforts were made to enlist the views of industrialists.

There is no indication that any of the individuals involved in the ARC's proceedings were ever told of Whittle, or had any inkling of his patent application. Probably there was only one man who could have alerted them all to the young RAF officer's relevance to their deliberations and a potentially remarkable turn of events – and that man chose to say not a word about it. In all the surviving documentation of the 1929–30 debate over the gas turbine's future, there was not a single mention by Griffith of Frank Whittle's existence – let alone any reference by him to their November 1929 encounter. He simply took all his own files on the compressor and turbine research and locked them away. Whether he was angry and embittered or just utterly dispirited, there is no way of knowing. But after accepting promotion a few months later to take charge of engine research at the RAE's base in Farnborough from the start of 1931 – a consolation prize, perhaps, to reassure him that his theoretical brilliance was still greatly valued – he left all his work on thermodynamics behind. It was a subject that he had made his own. Now he virtually disowned it, and no one in the government's employ stepped up to sustain it. As a government minister explained in a widely publicised letter of 1934 to a new society launched to promote astronautical research: 'We follow with interest any work which is being done in other countries on jet propulsion, but... do not consider that we should be justified in spending any time and money on it ourselves.'[21]

iv

By February 1930, Whittle had qualified as an instructor, been promoted to Flying Officer and been posted to a Flying Training School. This took him back to Lincolnshire – the school at RAF Digby was only a few miles from Cranwell – but in all other respects his career was moving ahead nicely. Already enjoying a reputation for both his stellar marks as a student and his skill as a pilot, he now discovered another talent: public speaking. His role as an instructor involved giving regular lectures and Whittle found his direct, self-assured intensity could cast a spell in the classroom. Audiences also came to appreciate his predilection for making mischievous and irreverent asides: the twenty-two-year-old's debunking of the pompous or self-important was popular with his peers, if not always with his senior officers. Most important of all was his sheer command of his subject. Whittle could stand before a group of trainees and enthuse them with his brilliance on the very driest of topics. His main agenda, drier than most, was the theory of flight – but of course he had another, much more colourful subject to share with his pupils when time allowed. His readiness to expound on the virtues of his future jet engine quickly became a feature of the instruction available at RAF Digby, and drew Whittle into some lively exchanges. Among those training at the school were university graduates taking up permanent commissions with the RAF. Those with engineering degrees were soon reporting back to him that their professors, told of the jet idea, had scoffed at its impracticality. Every relayed rebuke strengthened Whittle's instinctive belief that there could only be one effective response: he would have to prove the viability of his concept by designing and building a first prototype. Britain's top aero-engineers (unknown to him, of course) had pondered and walked away from it; but he resolved to take on the challenge. He had his patent, and a conviction born of his faith in the mathematics that filled his notebooks. All he needed was a bold manufacturer in the engineering industry ready to back him as a working partner.

First, though, he had a different kind of partnership to settle. He married Dorothy in May 1930. It was outwardly quite a glamorous affair. He flew from Digby to an aerodrome near Coventry, escorted by a squadron of ten Avro trainers flown by his fellow instructors. If Whittle was flouting RAF conventions with his marriage, he was doing so in some style. But there was no concealing other awkward aspects of the day. Dorothy's parents were a little disconcerted by the bridegroom's candid disavowal of any Christian beliefs the day before the service. A Sub-Dean of Coventry Cathedral had to be enlisted to plead with him for a compromise over the precise wording of the vows. And his own parents declined to attend the wedding at all. This marked an unhappy breach with his father Moses that would take some years to heal. Whittle's rejection of his devout Wesleyan background was probably most to blame, though he himself suspected that Moses and Sarah also resented his marrying away from his working-class roots. Not that marrying into a middle-class family made much difference to Whittle's finances. He and Dorothy began their lives together in Spartan married quarters at Digby and had to eke out a frugal existence on his Flying Officer's salary. Fortunately Dorothy seems to have been scarcely interested in such material matters ('I would have married him if he'd been a dustman's son', as she confided to an interviewer half a century later[22]) – and she undoubtedly took pride in being the wife of a handsome RAF officer. Her biggest immediate worry was that Whittle might kill himself with his antics as a daredevil pilot. He crashed twice in the two months before his wedding day, practising dangerous 'Crazy Flying' stunts for air shows.

For all Whittle's rising celebrity as a pilot, the potential of the jet engine was now becoming an obsession. He had already decided, with his usual self-assurance, that he would look for a large engineering firm willing to invest in his idea. Quite what kind of a deal he thought might be achievable, given his status as a serving officer in the forces, is unclear. Perhaps he hoped his patent-agent friend Pat Johnson, still stationed as an instructor at Wittering, might come up with an appropriate scheme as and when they needed it. Certainly he was in constant touch with Johnson – and it was to him that Whittle turned for help in identifying some candidates for a partnership. Their initial list appears not to have included any aero-engine manufacturers. If Whittle supposed for a moment that his vision of high-speed, high-altitude flying might appeal to them, we can be sure that Johnson counselled a more sober approach. They had just filed a patent, after all, describing a new kind of power plant that would have to compete for sales against all existing aero-engines. They needed a potential partner with no vested interest in the piston engine. By the autumn of 1930, Johnson had come up with several promising names. He had also arranged to borrow one of the RAF planes at Wittering for the pair of them to fly round the country for their meetings.

Their timing was unfortunate. The British economy was reeling in the wake of the Wall Street crash. Collapsing revenues and shrinking order books for manufacturers all over the Midlands were fast undermining the appeal of almost any project requiring risk capital. They also had to contend with the aftermath of a calamity that cast a pall over any serious discussion about new modes of flight: the airship R101 crashed on the night of 4 October 1930, shortly after embarking on a flight from England to India. (Airships were abandoned in Britain overnight – despite the fact that the R101's predecessor, the R100, had made a successful transatlantic flight to Canada just two months earlier.) It would not have been a propitious background for a new-business pitch by the slickest and most experienced of entrepreneurs. For a twenty-three-year-old Flying Officer with no knowledge of the business world at all, it probably ought to have dictated a sensible retreat to await happier times. Whittle insisted to Johnson that they nonetheless press on, regardless of the odds. The result was a series of fruitless encounters. Johnson's list of candidates grew steadily shorter.

One of the few remaining names by late October belonged to a large engineering company called British Thomson-Houston (BTH). As late as 1923, it had been the sole supplier of electricity to the Midlands town of Rugby, where it had built up a huge plant since 1900. Its buildings covered several dozen acres on the northern periphery of the town. Originally a subsidiary of General Electric of the US (as the Thomson-Houston Electric Company), the firm had been turning out enormous steam turbines, as well as heavy electrical motors and generators, for more than a quarter of a century. Just as pertinent, Johnson had a brother living in Rugby who was a good friend of BTH's Chief Turbine Engineer, a man called Fred Samuelson. This helped to secure at least an introductory meeting with Samuelson and his deputy, Robert (Bob) Collingham. BTH was later to play an important part in the development of Whittle's first jet engine. This lends an edge to Whittle's subsequent account of a disappointing first discussion. The engine being proposed would in their view demand a budget of around £60,000 – about £2¾ million in today's money – which was far beyond their stricken resources. While generous in his recollection of their response – and the two sides parted on friendly terms, agreeing to stay in touch – Whittle did not forget a notable disclaimer by the two turbine engineers: '[they] argued that as the engine I was proposing was applicable only to aircraft, it was not really appropriate to their field of activity.'[23] Indeed not. Here, after all, were mechanical engineers who had been immersed all their working lives in the practical task of assembling large, heavy industrial hardware built to last a long time. Aero-engines had to meet an entirely different set of criteria, less concerned with robust durability than with matters of weight, precision and compactness.

In fact, the work entailed in Whittle's vision of aero-engineering was doubly detached from the engineering of the steam turbine hall. Piston-engine disciplines represented one jump beyond the traditional power-generation culture. Whittle's thinking involved another leap again, beyond the prevailing aero-engineering disciplines of the day. He wanted to build an engine with hardly more than a single moving part – the turbine, revolving on a shaft that it would share with a centrifugal compressor placed at its opposite end. Success or failure would be determined by the application of mathematics and scientific theories, especially those illuminating the behaviour of gases. This would require, above all else, a knowledge of aerodynamics and thermodynamics that extended way beyond any concept of engineering as it was understood by men like Samuelson and Collingham. As Whittle sat before them speaking of high-powered compressors, constant-burn combustion and jet streams, it must quickly have dawned on them that he was talking of a very different line of business from theirs. They probably felt secretly half-relieved that their lack of cash offered an easy alibi for steering clear of any direct investment. They were nonetheless intrigued by this most unusual young man – and did agree a few months later to provide him with useful data on the performance of their latest steam turbines.

Taking stock of a frustrating few months, Whittle had to wonder by the end of 1930 what tactics might prove more effective in the New Year. Meanwhile, the RAF had a fresh assignment for him. Just after Christmas he was given a new posting to which he seemed ideally suited. It took him to Felixstowe on the Suffolk coast and the RAF's Marine Aircraft Experimental Establishment, to serve as a test pilot.

v

Whittle was delighted. His appointment in January 1931 was a further acknowledgement by the RAF of his superior flying skills, and the Marine Aircraft Experimental Establishment outside Felixstowe promised to make the most of them. Its principal mission was to explore the potential of seaplanes as a future extension of naval power. This suited Whittle perfectly. He had long been intrigued by the possibilities for deploying aircraft at sea. (One of the essays he had written as a Cranwell cadet had been entitled 'Sea Power in the Pacific'. He had raised in it the possibility that the American naval base at Pearl Harbor might one day be susceptible to a surprise attack from the air – by Japanese aeroplanes.[24]) Felixstowe itself was a pleasant Victorian seaside town, with a pretty Edwardian pier and plenty of handsome terraced houses along the seafront. It also had a surprisingly large railway station with excellent rail links to Ipswich and London, luckily for Whittle. He and Dorothy had scarcely moved into rooms in a boarding house – where they would stay until the birth of their first child, due in May – before he was back on his travels. He fully intended from the start of 1931 to continue his quest for a partner that could help him build his engine. He was ready to visit any serious contenders for the role – and, despite Johnson's evident misgivings, he decided in light of his autumn meetings that it would now make sense to sound out some of the aero-engine companies for their reactions.

To bridge the gap between their mechanical world and his jet turbine (or 'turbo-jet' as some began to call it), Whittle decided to draw attention to the kind of compressor that he was proposing to use. (He had filed a separate patent to cover his design, a few months earlier.[25]) It seemed a promising tactic, since the compressor was the one component of his jet that would be most readily familiar to the aircraft-engine makers of the day. As a way of deriving extra power, as noted already designers could fit their piston engines with superchargers. These forced compressed air into the cylinders, so boosting the intake of oxygen. They were less than a foot in diameter and were powered mechanically from the crankshaft of the engine. Whittle's compressor would be almost twice as wide, at about twenty inches. It would be double-sided – that is to say, with vanes on both sides of its rotor – and it would be driven round by the turbine. Nonetheless, the essential functions of the supercharger and of his compressor were similar enough. Superchargers were only a boost to underlying performance, but were nonetheless a defining feature of the most successful engines – so Whittle had a hunch his ambitious plans might engage the interest of those at the cutting edge of supercharger technology. Johnson secured him an introduction to Armstrong Siddeley, a Coventry-based firm that specialised (like Rolls-Royce) in both luxury cars and aero-engines, and enjoyed a glowing reputation for its superchargers. A first trip to see them confirmed Whittle's hopes. Armstrong Siddeley's engineers were indeed intrigued by his confidence in his envisaged compressor, and keen to learn how it might work. Briefly it seemed possible that, in exchange for his insights, the firm might put its weight behind the development of a jet engine. Several visits to Coventry followed over the next two months.

By way of complementing this approach, Whittle decided it was time for him to put the merits of the turbo-jet into writing and to lay out the mathematics that would explain its superiority to the piston engine. It was three years since he had begun work on his 1928 thesis. Now he sat down to compile what was in effect a mature sequel to that earlier effort. The resulting 1931 paper ran to more than thirty pages and he called it 'The Case for the Gas Turbine'.[26] It was never published, but much of its text would be privately circulated in later years. (One copy was acquired by Rolls-Royce and has survived in that company's archives in Derby.[27]) Whittle himself wrote of it with some awe in his autobiography nearly twenty years later: 'Its contents foreshadowed my later work to a remarkable degree in view of the fact that I had not then received any advanced engineering training.'[28] To give just one example of its scope and mathematical rigour: Whittle calculated the exact theoretical performance of his jet as it rose to higher altitudes where the air is intensely cold. This was a considerable feat. Inside his engine the temperatures would be very high. Predicting them with precision was important to his performance analysis but posed a problem, because the coldness of the surrounding air would affect what thermodynamicists call 'the specific heat coefficients' (which define the amount of air-temperature rise attributable to a given heat input). He needed to allow for variations in these coefficients at different temperatures. The necessary calculations were so complex and time-consuming that later aero-engineers, faced with a similar challenge, would generally be content to settle for approximations until well into the 1950s. Whittle invented a method entirely of his own in 1931 to yield the numbers he was seeking with pin-point accuracy.

More broadly, Whittle laid out all the fundamental equations explaining the physics of jet propulsion. He showed why the laws of thermodynamics meant the jet engine would become dramatically more efficient as it flew higher and faster. (This was in direct contrast, it hardly needed saying, to the decline in the efficiency of both the piston engine and the propeller, which fell away even more dramatically. The thinning of the air meant a lower power output from the cylinders; but the friction between all their many moving parts was unaffected by altitude, so the energy spent on overcoming it absorbed a steadily greater proportion of the power.) At the heart of his 1931 paper, in a section headed 'The Gas Turbine as a Jet Propulsion Engine', Whittle set down the detailed performance statistics for a putative jet flying at precisely 341 mph. His workings produced a bottom line that he must surely have supposed would catch the eye of any attentive reader. At ground level, the jet would travel 'about 1.573' [sic] miles per gallon of fuel. At 40,000 feet the same jet would go 6.9 miles per gallon.

He sent a copy of the paper to Roy Fedden, Chief Engineer at Bristol Aeroplane Co. and the famed designer of the Jupiter radial engine (which had been by far the dominant engine of the 1920s and by now had clocked up sales of well over 7,500 units). He despatched it in two instalments in February 1931, the first of which bore a slightly plaintive covering note, reproduced in a modern biography of Fedden:

> I enclose the first instalment of a brief summary of my work and opinions, I'm sorry that it is not yet complete but the field covered is rather large. I will send on the remainder as soon as it is complete.... I may have some difficulty, after all, in getting over [to Bristol] on Friday, but I shall know definitely tomorrow when the C.O. returns. I will wire if I cannot come. I hope I am not inconveniencing you, but I hope you will understand.[29]

In the event, his Commanding Officer required F/O Whittle to fly an aircraft down to Farnborough on the Friday and he never did make that journey to Bristol. Fedden, undoubtedly one of the world's most distinguished designers of piston engines, passed the package with a scribbled note ('Have you any comments?') to the head of his design team, Lenny Butler. Neither he nor another of Fedden's close colleagues, Frank Owner, thought the matter worth pursuing. Owner suggested Whittle's engine 'driven by a turbine, running at a temperature we consider it could withstand, wouldn't pull the skin off a rice pudding'. (There would be other scathing references to rice-pudding skins over the years to come.) If Fedden troubled to send Whittle a reply, his letter has disappeared and certainly Whittle never alluded to it. The largest aero-engine manufacturer in Britain had shown no interest in his ideas whatever.

And the news from Coventry, alas, proved no less disappointing. The supercharger specialists at Armstrong Siddeley grew tired of their discussions. Early in March 1931, the firm's Chief Engineer brought them to a halt, decreeing that there was no real mileage in the underlying jet concept – or, at least, none without an expensive research effort which could hardly be contemplated in the stricken circumstances of the Depression. He sent a peremptory letter off to Whittle:

> It seems to me that the whole scheme depends upon obtaining material which will work satisfactorily at a very high temperature.

Personally I doubt very much whether such material is available and this I think prevents the development of the internal
combustion turbine. I fear therefore that I cannot hold out
any hopes that this firm will take any serious interest in your
proposal.[30]

This stubborn belief in the unavailability of suitable metals for
his engine was the second of the two most common objections
levelled against Whittle at this time (the other being the simple
assertion that his engine's components would never achieve the
efficiency he projected for them). He knew it to be a canard,
because he had studied carefully the innovative aspects of the
Rolls-Royce R engine built for the 1929 Schneider Trophy race.
As his new colleagues in the High Speed Flight Unit at Felixstowe
were happy to confirm, its valves were made of new steel alloys
specially produced for it in Sheffield. Whittle was sure those same
alloys – including one, KE965, that was an alloy of nickel and
chrome – would work for his jet engine, too. He was also confident that the finest steelmakers in Sheffield would be capable
of producing even better alloys, once he explained to them his
exact requirements. (His confidence was well-founded. Ten years
later, in 1941, one of his most valued suppliers in Sheffield, a Dr
Hatfield of Atlas Steels, would look back at their long association
in a revealing letter to Whittle: 'Some twenty years ago I realised
that the properties of steel at high temperatures were likely to
become one of the dominating matters of interest, and it is a
matter of good fortune that we just happened [by the mid-1930s]
to have experimental materials going through the properties of
which you were able to take advantage.'[31] Fortune had favoured
Whittle's brave confidence.)

Metal temperatures were not the Coventry engineers' only
concern. They had followed the gist of Whittle's thinking – how
the rotating vanes at the entrance to the compressor needed to be
curved with the utmost precision, and how complex secondary
currents of air had then to be controlled as the main airstream
flowed through the channels between the vanes – but they had
simply refused to accept Whittle's prediction of the dramatic

impact that these adjustments would have on the compressor's performance. They insisted that curved vanes were just a fancy variant of the crudely bent vanes in existing superchargers, and not worth the additional labour involved. A well-known Cambridge academic acting as a technical consultant to the firm, W. S. (Bill) Farren, concurred with this: he thought Whittle's proposal was 'sound in principle' but no real advance on the superchargers already designed by Armstrong Siddeley.[32] A serious misjudgement, as time would prove.

Whittle still refused to abandon the cause. Instead he saw the Coventry rebuff as an instructive episode. The lesson he drew was that he 'would need to convince people of the value of my compressor proposals before I could hope to get them to accept the much more comprehensive scheme for a complete engine…'.[33] Proceeding via experimentation would require spending huge amounts of money, which he simply did not have, so he had no choice but to resort to yet another theoretical paper. Somehow he found the time to write it over the next eight weeks. This one was entitled 'The Turbo-Compressor and the Supercharging of Aero Engines'. Its twenty-six pages went into enormous detail, drawing on some of the Coventry discussions and delineating the shape and internal architecture of a compressor that, by the author's extensive calculations, would deliver the greatly enhanced performance required for a gas turbine. An appendix incorporated the test results that he had gratefully received from the BTH turbine hall in Rugby. Whittle's mathematics, based on his understanding of the way the air would flow through his own proposed design, yielded a pressure ratio of no less than 4:1 and predicated a 'two-stage' compressor with two impellers that would work with almost 80 per cent efficiency. This appears to have impressed even the author. (Jimmy Ellor's best work for the R engine, as noted, had produced a 2:1 ratio with 63 per cent efficiency.) With some encouragement from a sympathetic academic at Liverpool University, William Kearton, Whittle sent his paper straight off to the journal of the august Royal Aeronautical Society. They published it in November 1931.[34]

Engineers many years later would look back in wonder at the brilliance of the compressor proposed in this second paper, and the way that Whittle further refined it in his first practical drawings a few years later. (He switched in due course from proposing two single-sided impellers to a single, double-sided version which allowed the engine's shaft to be shorter and much lighter.) The revised design led to production units in the Second World War that were to prove superior to any other compressor, axial or centrifugal, used in the British, German or American air forces. The commanding figure at Rolls-Royce charged in 1943 with building upon Whittle's work, Stanley Hooker, always spoke of his compressor design with awe. Hooker was the man whose work on superchargers was largely responsible for keeping the RAF's Spitfires and Hurricanes one step ahead (most of the time) of their German counterparts through the war, so his verdict on Whittle's 1931 achievement was praise indeed: 'I was never able to improve his compressor – I made it worse on one occasion, but never better.'[35] In the immediate aftermath of its publication, however, this second paper of 1931 nevertheless sank without trace. Despite its availability in the *Journal of the R.Ae.S.*, it attracted no more interest from the RAE or the aircraft industry in general than Whittle's earlier and unpublished paper sent to Fedden. And so passed another of the opportunities that might plausibly have triggered a national interest in the idea of the jet engine, with far-reaching consequences.

By July 1931 Whittle had spent more than twelve months expounding his ideas and trying to elicit support. All to no avail. He had devoted a huge amount of time to the two theoretical papers he had completed in 1931. He had scarcely found anyone in the business world to offer him a modicum of encouragement, never mind the prospect of a real partnership. Ironically, there was far more popular interest now in the idea of intercontinental flight, which had long dominated his own thinking about aviation's future: record-breaking flights across the oceans by brave aviators – none more celebrated since 1930 than Amy Johnson – were constantly in the headlines. This did nothing, though, for a prophet of the piston engine's demise. At the end of November 1931 – when yet another corporate rejection landed on the mat ('... unless there is the prospect of business within a reasonable time, we cannot afford the time to design and develop special machines on paper'[36]) – his zeal finally gave way to a stoic resignation. His belief in the jet was not a whit diminished, but it seemed the world was not yet ready to listen. He had had enough of pitching his vision to the incredulous and uncomprehending.

3

The Cooperation Squadron

November 1931 to March 1936

i

If the RAF had set out in 1931 to devise a five-year career plan tailored to the personal needs of a uniquely gifted individual charged with reinventing the aeroplane, they could hardly have made a better job of it. Whittle had already been extraordinarily fortunate to have been helped up the ladder from apprentice to test pilot by some shrewd senior officers. The service was now to serve him superbly well with a series of postings that helped him make the most of his abilities – and in the process prepared him for the day when the seed of his jet concept would fall on less stony ground.

The first, as a test pilot at Felixstowe since January 1931, was already affording him many opportunities to test his skill at mechanical innovation. Over the course of 1931–2 he produced a string of ideas for new equipment, acquiring a reputation as the Marine Establishment's in-house inventor. Some led to inspired gadgets, simplifying maintenance chores and the handling of seaplanes with fixed floats. Others were more radical, including a proposal to fit seaplanes with fully enclosed gun turrets and a scheme to improve bomb-loading routines. Like almost all his peers, Whittle probably assumed that any future war would put a high premium on the RAF's bombing expertise – though he gave no explicit indication of his thoughts on this at the time, or indeed in retrospect. Perhaps he even shared the common belief of the day that no war could really be expected in the foreseeable future. (The government, after all, was still standing by the so-called 'Ten-Year Rule' adhered to since 1919, whereby the nation's defence spending had to proceed from the premise that the British Empire would 'not be engaged in any great war during the next ten years'.) Certainly, anyway, none of his armament proposals found any favour with the Admiralty.

For a few months he was assigned to HMS *Ark Royal* to participate in experimental work with the Navy. It principally involved the firing of sea-planes off the carrier with a catapult. Every launch was a hazardous business, and Whittle completed forty-six of them successfully. In another mark of his physical courage, he even agreed to 'pancake' land an ordinary plane into the sea as part of a trial to test out some new emergency-flotation bags – despite the fact that he could not swim. The *Ark Royal*'s Commanding Officer commended his services to the Admiralty, noting, 'his airmanship inspired confidence in all concerned in the trials'.[1] Other officers on the ship hinted to Whittle that a medal was coming his way. This pleased him enormously – nick-named Grub at school, he was to be a stickler for honours, titles and insignia for the rest of his life – but when the medal failed to materialise he felt badly let down. Not for the first time, he thought he had been short-changed by those in authority.

By a happy chance, the work at Felixstowe reunited Whittle with his Cranwell friend Dudley Williams, whose flying-boat squadron was temporarily stationed there. Williams was much less enamoured of life in the RAF – he was to abandon his short commission within a couple of years, on health grounds – and he made no pretence of understanding the science behind the jet. But he adored his clever friend and was quite in awe of him. Where other pilots at Felixstowe were inclined to tease Whittle about his jet obsession, Williams never doubted that something of great moment would come of it. He even made a serious effort to raise money from other members of his well-to-do family, with which to help pay for US, French and German versions of the 1931 patent. (A US patent, in particular, might have improved Whittle's prospects dramatically. It could have drawn American investors to his support, which in turn might have stirred British investors and aero-engine makers to take a much more lively interest in his idea.) Alas, the money was not forthcoming – and foreign readers of the British patent would very soon be able to contemplate building their own engine to Whittle's design or something very like it.

The summer of 1932 marked the end of the fourth year of Whittle's commission. In line with standard practice, he now had to specialise in one of four directions and the RAF made the decision on his behalf. He was posted to the Officers' School of Engineering at 'Home Aircraft Depot', the RAF's principal aircraft maintenance station at RAF Henlow in Bedfordshire. The entry formalities for the 1932–4 course showed how far his independent studies had carried him beyond the world of trainee engineering schemes. He answered every question in the entrance exam to perfection and was awarded 98 per cent (presumably decorum required a couple of missing marks). It was obvious to his superior officers that he was hugely knowledgeable on a wide range of engineering subjects. Sensibly, they curtailed his schedule of lectures and he completed the supposedly two-year 'E' course before the end of 1933, gaining a distinction in all but one of the examination papers.

It had been arranged at the outset that he would spend some months training in the workshops at Henlow, after completing the formal course. Whittle yearned for a more challenging role – especially now that he had decided, in effect, to shelve his jet-engine proposal. When an official letter reached him in November 1933 demanding a fee of £5 (about £250 in today's money) for the renewal of his 1931 patent, thoughtfully pointing out that no public funds were available to cover the charge, Whittle ignored it.[2] Money was short: childbirth had proved traumatic for Dorothy, and he was struggling to cope with the consequent medical expenses. (The patent duly lapsed two months later.) Before the end of 1933, he resolved to find some way of immersing himself in the aeronautical sciences.

Two institutions dominated the field in Britain – Imperial College London and Cambridge University – and Whittle was aware that the RAF had regularly seconded officers to Cambridge in the past to study Mechanical Sciences. (In status-conscious Britain the course title was revealing: scientists, even mechanical ones, were gentlemen; but 'engineering' was still broadly regarded as a trade, and hardly a suitable tag for a Cambridge Tripos.) Exploring this option late in 1933, he learned that the Air Ministry had in fact discontinued the Cambridge scheme. Like so many other aspects of the RAF in recent years, it had fallen prey to budget cuts. The RAF's straitened circumstances had hitherto only intruded marginally on Whittle's personal career, but being denied a ticket to Cambridge would have been a very different matter. Determined as ever to get his way, he compiled a formal application to study for the Mechanical Sciences Tripos at Cambridge as though the old RAF scheme was still intact. (It was all eerily reminiscent of his experience of gaining an RAF apprenticeship.) He also persuaded Henlow's Commanding Officer to support his application, much as Group Captain Baldwin at Wittering and Biffy Barton at Cranwell had backed him in the past. Several weeks passed with no response from the Air Ministry. Then, late in February 1934, a letter reached Henlow to say that 'in view of this Officer's excellent work on the Specialist 'E' Course', his application had been supported. It had been forwarded to Peterhouse, Cambridge, requesting an undergraduate place for him in October 1934. If admitted, he would be given two years to complete the normally three-year Tripos course.

In the meantime, his superiors at Henlow had recognised that workshop training was scarcely appropriate in Whittle's case. Promoted to Flight Lieutenant, he had been placed in charge of the Home Depot section where reconditioned engines were bench-tested before being released for service. This was to give him invaluable experience, over the next several months, of running a team of engineers – though it was also an assignment rich in irony. Having devoted so much thought and energy to the pursuit of his gas-turbine jet, Whittle was back to the world of valves and tappets, crankshafts and carburettors as a certification officer – a daily reminder of the infinite mechanical complications that could plague every piston engine. More pertinently still, his new role gave him an overview of the aircraft in service with the modern RAF – though as he quickly discovered, 'modern' was scarcely the apposite term.

The RAF's fighters and bombers alike all conformed to basic designs that had changed only slightly since the days of the Royal Flying Corps. Whittle's workshop team busied itself on the best piston engines of the day, from Rolls-Royce Kestrels and Napier Lions to Armstrong Siddeley Jaguars and Bristol Jupiters. All were destined for planes that might not have stood out too conspicuously in a museum of First World War aviation. The fighters were without exception single-seater biplanes with fabric-covered wings, fixed undercarriages and open cockpits. Some, like the Bristol Bulldog and the Siskin III that Whittle himself had flown at Hornchurch, had been around for years; others, like the Hawker Fury and the not yet fully operational Gloster Gauntlet, were supposedly to see the RAF well into the 1930s. None could fly much faster than 220 mph. And this was twice the maximum speed of the bombers flying into Henlow for a refit. It had long been the official policy of the RAF (the 'Trenchard Doctrine') that bombing would be its essential strategic role in any future war. Yet engines were still being serviced for bombers like the Vickers Virginia, a lumbering biplane (maximum speed 108 mph) introduced in 1924. Its putative successor made a first appearance at Henlow early in 1934. The Handley-Page Heyford biplane was a monster with two Kestrel engines but was otherwise no less a relic of the past with its massive fixed wheels, open seats for its four-man crew and largely fabric-covered fuselage – unmistakeably a close relative of the Vickers Vimy that had carried Alcock and Brown over the Atlantic in 1919 (and had itself only been retired from the RAF a year earlier).

Whittle must have been desperate for news of his Cambridge application. It was handled at Peterhouse by Roy Lubbock, a Fellow of that ancient college since 1919 and the University Lecturer in Engineering. The letter survives that Lubbock wrote to the Master of Peterhouse on 15 March 1934 – the college now keeps it on public display – recommending a place be found for an apparently exceptional candidate ('I am told that he has received the thanks both of the Air Council and of the Admiralty for technical suggestions which he has forwarded'). The place was duly awarded. The RAF maintained a University Air Squadron at Cambridge and Whittle was attached to it from July 1934. This allowed him and Dorothy to settle in the village of Trumpington, a mile south of Cambridge, in time for the birth in November of a second son, Ian. The new family home, 'Blackamoors', was a small cottage on the main road that had been occupied by a succession of RAF officers. After two years as lodgers with the local vicar and his wife in Henlow, the Whittles were happy with their novel independence and Frank was thrilled at the prospect of two years in academia.

He plunged into the Tripos course, determined from the start to win a First and so repay the RAF for its belief in him. He had little time for the usual distractions of undergraduate life – nor, much more importantly, for thinking much further about jet propulsion. This caused him no grief. Predictably, perhaps, the rigours of the Cambridge course quickly gave him a shrewder understanding of the problems he would have to confront if he ever turned back to his youthful obsession. Indeed, by his own account he had begun to think this unlikely by the end of his first term ('By then I had virtually given up hope of ever seeing the engine take practical shape'[3]). His working routine as an undergraduate rarely took him far beyond the boundaries of a small triangle with Peterhouse at its apex. From its porter's lodge, the Engineering Department was a brisk five-minute walk down Trumpington Street past the Fitzwilliam Museum. If he left the back of the department through a gate onto Fen Causeway and headed over the Cam, it took him scarcely much longer to reach the mess buildings of the University Air Squadron (CUAS). Most weekdays were divided between mornings in the Peterhouse library and afternoons in the department's main laboratory. The latter had a state-of-the-art wind tunnel, which was being used for some pioneering research into aerodynamics – a subject on which it became apparent at some point before Christmas 1934 that the RAF man from Peterhouse was conspicuously knowledgeable. And perhaps it was this discovery that led Whittle to his first proper conversation with a wise guru who was to become an influential figure in his life.

Cambridge at this time was full of scientists of great distinction, working on the most rarefied topics known to man. At the Cavendish Laboratory a team under Ernest Rutherford had split the atom and in 1932 James Chadwick had discovered the neutron. A recently appointed Professor of Mathematics, Paul Dirac, had just been awarded the 1933 Nobel Prize in Physics for his work on the theory of quantum mechanics. Aeronautical Engineering had its own renowned professor, too, though his was a faculty linked much more directly to the outside world – and in particular the fast mounting concerns of the Air Staff. Bennett Melvill Jones, known to his family and old friends as Melvill (his mother's maiden name) and to almost everyone else as 'Bones', had first been elected to his chair in 1919 at the age of thirty-two. He had since then put his department at the heart of Britain's aeronautical sciences, straddling the two worlds of academia and Whitehall. Cooperation between them in the interests of the RAF's future had never been more critical, and few individuals were as central as Jones to the whole dynamic. He led a small research team that liaised closely with the RAF's University Air Squadron, and was a keen advocate of 'scientist-pilots' who could help engineers in the laboratory to test out their theories.

From their very first meeting the professor was hugely intrigued by Whittle. Few undergraduates can ever have arrived before him with a *Journal of the R.Ae.S.* article under their belt. Yet for all his evident brilliance, Whittle seemed rather touchingly aware of the gaps in his formal engineering education and anxious to fill them. He seemed modest and as much in awe of his new surroundings as his younger peers. Jones was charmed and they became good friends. Before long Whittle was explaining to him the merits of the jet engine – and explaining also why, since the end of 1931, he had set aside his hopes of building one. The prevailing view, that aircraft would continue to rely on piston engines for the foreseeable future, had come to seem insurmountable. To his great surprise, though, Whittle now found the tables oddly turned since his encounter with A. A. Griffith in 1929. The professor applauded his bold vision and insisted that he simply could not give up on it. Others were at work on the gas-turbine concept: a trickle of fresh patents had been awarded in Germany, France and the United States since 1930. But nothing had been heard of any progress towards a working engine, and there was only silence from the RAE in Farnborough. Jones thought a way forward might eventually be found, if they could only keep faith with the idea. This optimism must have buoyed Whittle, but he had little time to dust off his jet notebooks – nor indeed any direct incentive to do so.

ii

Whittle also had less time for flying than the Air Ministry had envisaged in approving his secondment – he generally managed only a few hours each month, taking up a plane from nearby RAF Duxford – but he called regularly at CUAS by way of keeping in touch with the service. And it was on one of his visits to the mess, a week or so into his third term starting late in April 1935, that the Commanding Officer's secretary handed him a letter. Whittle was surprised to find it came from his jolly friend Dudley Williams, whom he had not seen since their Felixstowe days together in 1931–2. Whittle little knew it at the time, but the handwritten note was to change his life. The key lines read:

This is just a hurried note to tell you that I have just met a man who is a bit of a big noise in an engineering concern and to whom

I mentioned your invention of an aeroplane, *sans* propeller as it were, and who is very interested. You told me some time ago that Armstrong's had [it] or were taking it up and if they have broken down or you don't like them, he would, I think, like to handle it. I wonder if you would write and let me know.[4]

As Whittle would later recall, he almost wrote back with his regrets that there was nothing to discuss. He was just preparing for his 'Mays', the examinations that would mark the end of his first year and the halfway point for his truncated Tripos studies. He was anxious to avoid distractions – even, for the moment, any further talk of the jet's prospects. On further reflection, or so he would later recall, it occurred to him that Williams might be in touch with people who could one day be helpful 'in connection with other inventions I then had in mind'.[5] He must surely also have felt a twinge of obligation to Professor Jones to give Williams at least a fair hearing. So he replied a few days later with a mildly encouraging (and none too sincere) nod to the jet's potential – 'if anybody were keen on taking it up, I should think it would pay them' – and he invited Williams to visit him at home the following Sunday, 12 May 1935.

Williams turned up on the Sunday afternoon with a friend in tow whose temperament contrasted almost comically with his own. James Collingwood ('Coll') Tinling was well over six feet tall and thin as a beanpole. Like Williams, he, too, was a former RAF pilot, though in his case a short commission had been ended by a serious flying accident a few years earlier. It had left him with a pronounced limp that somehow accentuated a naturally lugubrious manner. As a later colleague would remember the two of them:

[Williams] was a light-hearted, somewhat flippant character, extremely good with people and a sound thinker... Tinling, his partner, was much more serious and a man of unfailing integrity. They seemed an odd pair and yet they worked well together...[6]

They had recently gone into business together, aspiring to be venture capitalists with a string of part-owned enterprises. These had proved hard to find: the less than sparkling jewel in their portfolio crown to date was a small manufacturer of cigarette-vending machines. Since the start, though, Williams had nurtured the idea of one day investing in the unknown genius he had first met at Cranwell. He had always remembered Whittle's jet obsession fondly. Now he was keen to talk to him about it again, or indeed to hear of any other schemes his brainy friend might have dreamed up since leaving Felixstowe.

Within a few hours of arriving at the cottage in Trumpington, the two ex-RAF men pulled off quite a coup. It must have been quickly apparent to them that, despite all his protestations, Whittle still harboured a firm belief in the future of his jet. Making light of all his doubts and reservations, they pressed him hard to take it up again. They themselves had no money and only the vaguest notion of what building a jet might entail. Yet they managed, surely far more easily than they could have expected, to revive Whittle's confidence that his vision might after all be achievable. (Whittle's own version of this episode gilded the romance of it by suggesting he had scarcely thought of the jet for years.) He had to confess to them, of course, that he had surrendered his master patent of 1931. This evidently gave his visitors a brief pause for thought – but Whittle, rapidly warming to their discussion, was quick to insist they could effectively restore all the protection they needed by patenting various detailed improvements that had occurred to him since the filing of the original concept. Despite his looming Tripos examinations, he promised to provide them with the necessary paperwork within a few days. In exchange, Williams and Tinling went away promising to pay the Patent Office's fees and to act as Whittle's agents in the search for investors – to back a construction project that could scarcely have been bolder. They would aim not just to build a revolutionary new engine but to launch a jet-propelled aeroplane. It was agreed that a budget of £50,000 – about £2½ million in today's money – ought to suffice. Indeed, as Williams explained in a perky letter to Whittle a few days later, this implied having a sensible surplus in reserve 'in case of any serious difficulties such as the Machine being broken on its first flight etc'.[7] Williams closed on a characteristically ebullient note: 'I have perfect confidence in you myself, and in the Invention, and I think anyone else will do also if they are approached in the right manner...'

Over the next six months, with the help of his two new promoters, Whittle would indeed win over several key individuals to the cause. First, though, he had to burn the midnight oil preparing his patent applications. Two of them were submitted within a week of the Trumpington kitchen conference.[8] He would claim in his autobiography to have been sceptical of the whole business at this stage ('I did not really believe that the time was ripe...') but he suggested otherwise to Williams at the time: 'Well, I think you are on a good thing, and it seems quite possible that you may make your pile and mine as well.' At the end of May 1935 he had to sit for Part I of his Tripos. To no one's great surprise he was given a First. Peterhouse awarded him two college prizes – one was a copy of Stodola's tome in English – and made him a Senior Scholar. With his academic career smoothly on track, Whittle then turned back to his jet engine and the design – with more than a little help from his professor – of a single-seater monoplane to be powered by it.

Melvill Jones was eager to assist him. He was keen to encourage any venture that could add momentum to a wave of technical innovation just poised to break over the RAF – and we can assume that talking to Jones, with all his Whitehall connections, gave Whittle in return a far better understanding of the political background to the incipient changes. The advent in Germany of Hitler's National Socialist government in January 1933 had changed the international landscape overnight. It had also led within months to a renewed production in Germany of aircraft with evident military potential. The restoration of the Luftwaffe had only recently been officially acknowledged, in March 1935, but by this date the government in London had been growing increasingly perturbed for a year or so over Germany's obvious air rearmament. Nor was it just the breaking of 1919 Treaty obligations on aircraft numbers that had given ministers a severe jolt. The newest designs emerging from Germany's lead-ing manufacturers looked alarmingly innovative. Planes like Dornier's Do 11 'freight transport' and Heinkel's He 70 'mail plane' marked a break with the past in the starkest terms: monoplanes with all-metal fuselages, enclosed cabins and retractable landing gear, they were forcing Britain's Air Staff to acknowledge the RAF's latest planes as the flying fossils they truly were. An energetic new Secretary of State for Air had just been appointed in June. This was Lord Swinton (formerly Sir Philip Cunliffe-Lister), whom Melvill Jones had known for many years – Swinton had served in several ministerial posts since 1920 – and who was fiercely committed to a radical overhaul of the RAF, starting immediately. None of this guaranteed an audience for Whittle's radical idea. Nonetheless, if he was going to team up with Williams and Tinling in search of investors ready to back it, the background was perhaps as propitious in mid-1935 as it had been unhelpful in 1930–31. Or so it seemed.

As it happened, Williams and Tinling came up with a first promising introduction almost immediately. The man whom Williams had described in his note as 'a bit of a big noise' had gone very quiet. In his place, though, they had come across a consultant engineer with a high profile in the international aircraft industry. Danish-born, his name was Morgens Louis ('Bram') Bramson. If he could be stirred to take an interest in their venture, doors might open in the City of London. An appointment was made for a day in July and Whittle, taking a set of his working papers with him, called on him at his London office in the Aldwych, just a stone's throw from the Air Ministry's head offices on Kingsway. The meet-ing went well. By Bramson's subsequent account, Whittle's papers 'consisted solely of thermodynamic and aerodynamic calculations and diagrams; there were no engineering designs'. But both men were pilots as well as engineers, and their conversation soon ranged far beyond strictly theoretical matters. When they parted, Whittle even agreed to leave his papers behind for Bramson to read them all again. It was more than a little reminiscent, in fact, of that ill-fated trip that Whittle had made to Kensington in 1929

– but the outcome this time was very different. Bramson studied the papers for two weeks, and found them more than persuasive. As he recalled over thirty years later, he 'got quite excited' over the papers. He saw 'the dramatic advance in aviation technology implicit in Whittle's theories' and quickly decided nothing could be allowed to stand in the way of it: 'I suddenly felt "This must be done!"'[9] Whittle was delighted. This was the kind of response he had been seeking for years. Close colleagues in the RAF and at Cambridge, subjected to endless explanations over time, had offered precious moral support; but here at last was an authoritative outsider who had looked hard at the science behind the jet and come away convinced by it. He was hugely gratified.

It was almost certainly at Bramson's behest that Whittle sat down early in August 1935 to write out – for the first time – exactly how he envisaged seeing his concept turned, step by step, into a working prototype. The result was a simple four-page memorandum, 'A Brief Outline of Development Procedure – High Altitude Engine', that he completed later that month.[10] Bramson forwarded it to one of his many useful contacts in the investment world, a banker called Oswald Falk. This was a fortuitous introduction for Whittle, drawing him to the attention of a rather special City firm.

Falk was a well-known figure in Whitehall as well as the City – he had been a close friend and confidant of John Maynard Keynes for many years – and had formerly been senior partner at one of the City's leading stockbrokers. He and three others had gone their own way in 1932 and had set up a small firm, O. T. Falk & Partners, devoted to making high-risk investments. The other founding partners included Sir Maurice ('Bongie') Bonham Carter, a Liberal Party politician who had been Prime Minister Asquith's Principal Private Secretary in the First World War. One of Bonham Carter's countless friends in high places was Montagu Norman, the Governor of the Bank of England; and it was Norman who one day sent along to the firm someone he had recently met and recognised immediately as the kind of adventurous intellectual with eclectic interests who would interest them.

Lancelot (Lance) Law Whyte was an idiosyncratic thirty-nine-year-old former Cambridge physicist. The son of a Calvinist minister in Edinburgh who had married into the Scottish aristocracy, he had been educated at a famously unconventional late-Victorian public school, Bedales, which in many ways represented the antithesis of his upbringing. It had left him with a lifelong interest in radical ideas. His education was interrupted by the Great War, in which he served with distinction: he served on the Western Front as a second lieutenant in the Royal Field Artillery, winning the Military Cross for his bravery and surviving the Somme in 1916, the Battle of Arras in 1917 and the German Offensive in the spring of 1918. After the war he went up to Cambridge, studied Natural Sciences at Trinity College and briefly worked on experimental physics under Rutherford.[11] Turning to the philosophy of science, he spent a year in Berlin (1928–9) where he met and befriended Einstein. (They had conversations together about the possibility of a unified theory to reconcile relativity with quantum theory, and Einstein recommended him as the translator for a long article he had penned for the *New York Times*.[12]) By 1932, Whyte had written a short book on the philosophy of science, *Archimedes, or the Future of Physics*, and was set on a writing career. So he needed an income, and turned to the City for a job.

Montagu Norman's hunch paid off. Falk and his partners hired Whyte and gave him the task of searching out innovative technical processes that might offer investment opportunities. He revelled in the work, spending a lot of time theorising about systemic ways of spreading risk by pooling many ventures into one fund. But in his heart, Whyte was always prospecting for gold: 'my secret hope was that something would turn up for which I would throw over everything else.' And in September 1935, it did. Falk took a call from Bramson that sounded intriguing. After discussing it with Bonham Carter, the two partners asked Whyte if he would like to meet a young RAF pilot who claimed to have invented a totally new kind of aero-engine. Whyte needed little persuading to accept the invitation – though he did worry about the scale of investment that he supposed might be needed for a genuinely new engine – and he went off to meet Whittle at Bramson's Bush House office in the Aldwych.

As on so many past occasions, Whittle's exposition of his thinking simply bowled his man over. Whyte recorded the episode, many years later, with more eloquence than any other convert ever managed:

> It was like love at first sight: the impression he made was overwhelming. I have never been so quickly convinced, nor so happy to find one's highest standards met. Whittle held all the winning cards: imagination, ability, enthusiasm, determination, respect for science, and practical experience – all at the service of a stunningly simple idea: 2,000 hp with one moving part. This was genius, not talent. Though I have known a number of the greatest living scientists and thinkers, this meeting with Frank Whittle gave me a thrill I have never experienced otherwise...
>
> That night I told my wife that I had met one of the great inventive engineers of our time. To explain my excitement I said that it was like what I imagined was the experience of meeting a saint in an earlier religious epoch: one surrendered to the enchantment of a single-minded personality born to a great task.[13]

Whittle's own memory of their first conversation was a little more prosaic ('I warned him that anyone putting up money should do so on the basis that the chances of success were 30:1 against') but his enthusiasm had cast its spell again. Lance Whyte left Bush House with his mind already made up. He would do everything in his power to help Whittle fulfil his vision of 'great jet planes that in ten or twenty years would be speeding round the globe at incredible heights'.

First he had to set about persuading Bonham Carter and Falk to part with some money. This was settled in principle within days, though it had to be the blindest leap of faith. The magic of Whittle's vision was apparently enough for Whyte's colleagues, as it had been for him, and they were all keen to back it with some seed capital – subject only to a positive report from a suitably qualified aero-engineer, just in case they had fallen for a dazzling white elephant. Whittle was happy to cooperate, but insisted that the author of the report had to be Bramson himself. Fortunately Bramson accepted the brief, with some enthusiasm, and he began work immediately. His final report, dated 8 October 1935, was a little masterpiece of its kind.[14] It offered 'an independent step by step check of the theories, calculations and design proposals... [for] the achievement of practical stratospheric transport'. The investment objective was taken to be a transatlantic mail plane that would cruise at a speed of 500 mph at a height of 69,000 feet, with a range of approximately 5,000 miles. At the end of an extensive analysis, Bramson gave this outlandish idea his unequivocal backing: 'The proposed development though necessarily speculative as regards time and money required, is so important that it should, if possible, be undertaken.'

The O. T. Falk partners were delighted and needed no further endorsement. Within days Whittle found himself sitting through a series of meetings at the firm's City offices in Old Jewry, a stone's throw from the Bank of England, to discuss the financial arrangements. They agreed to set up a company, to be called Power Jets, which they were confident would attract funding from the City. Whittle would, of course, be key to the company's future, though there was no question of his abandoning his RAF career. The equity in Power Jets would be structured to allow him to share effective control of the company with Williams and Tinling, while allowing stock to be acquired by investors for cash. O. T. Falk would provide the company with initial capital of £2,000, and the firm had an option until July 1937 to invest another £18,000 ahead of any third parties.

So after years of delay, Whittle had at last found a way forward – just as predicted by Melvill Jones, to whom a copy of Bramson's report was swiftly despatched – and his excitement was palpable. 'Things are going fine', as he wrote a few weeks later to Williams and Tinling, 'and I'm as braced as hell.'[15] His Tripos studies were plainly going to have to allow for some extracurricular activities after all.

iii

As he began his second year at Cambridge, 1935–6, Whittle turned to planning the actual construction of his jet engine. His first goal would be a relatively inexpensive unit that would run on a bench. He could leave until later the whole business of financing a more ambitious flight engine. Everything hinged for the moment on creating that very first, self-sustaining creature – a practical machine, the begetter of a totally new kind of power that he was certain would change the world. And actually *making* it was the critical objective, more important by far than just arriving at a plausible design. Gas-turbine sketches had now adorned the pages of learned periodicals for some years. They had failed to shake the general consensus among engineers and industrialists that nothing practical would come of them, at least in the foreseeable future. Greatly encouraged by Bramson's support in London and the faith in his ideas shown by Jones and the Cambridge Engineering Faculty, Whittle was determined to prove the consensus wrong. No engine made of iron and steel was going to be wrought in the laboratory on Trumpington Street, though. His first task was to find an industrial contractor for the job. They would have to work under his close direction to pull together a compressor, a combustion chamber and a turbine – and all three components were going to pose as yet imponderable difficulties. All would require novel materials and designs which would allow them to function with a record-breaking efficiency that most of his contemporaries regarded as, if not impossible, at best extremely improbable. So where was he going to find an engine manufacturer willing and able to rise to this challenge?

The obvious choice might have been one of Britain's five world-beating aero-engine makers – industrial companies with the skilled workmen and machine tools to speed his project ahead. From Cambridge, he could conveniently have reached out to, say, Armstrong Siddeley in Coventry or de Havilland Aircraft, based at Hatfield in Hertfordshire. Whittle had made clear to Williams and Tinling over the summer, however, that this was not his intention. He wanted nothing to do with any of the established aero-engine makers – and the notion of turning to one of them as a principal contractor was out of the question.

Much was to hinge on this decision. Whittle had some rational motives. Every history of technical innovation was littered with examples of inventors thwarted for a while by entrenched business interests – the telephone's pioneers, for instance, encountering a hostile telegraph industry – and he was acutely aware of this possibility. As Pat Johnson had pointed out in 1930, the jet engine – if successful – was eventually going to rival the piston engine. The leading names in the traditional aero-engine business had invested heavily in piston-engine technology for a quarter of a century. Whittle feared they would take up the jet only to stymie its development. His animus against them was undoubtedly also fuelled by an understandable sense of grievance that his overtures in 1930–31 had been so blithely ignored by companies like Bristol Aeroplane and Armstrong Siddeley. His socialist ideals, too, played a part in his thinking. Surely underlying all these considerations, though, was a deeper psychological factor. The big companies were part of an acknowledged oligopoly – along with a dozen specialist airframe manufacturers, they comprised what was known as 'the Air Ministry Ring' – and its clubbiness struck him as a subtle form of coercion, to which he reacted with his usual aversion to being told what to do. By temperament an outsider, he preferred to remain his own man. The truth, awkwardly for any sympathetic account of his later travails, is that Whittle's prejudice in this matter must answer for many of his subsequent difficulties. Insofar as making a success of his jet engine was almost certainly going to dictate partnering with an existing aero-engine company sooner or later, he was going to have to amend his views one day – or else see them overruled. It might have been infinitely better if he had made this calculation for himself at the outset in 1935–6. There was never any suggestion that he was ready to do so.

The only feasible alternative had to be a large and resourceful engineering firm with no significant niche in aero-engineering.

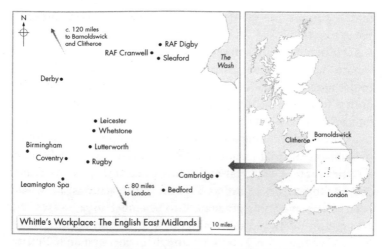

Fig. 4. Map of the key places in FW's RAF life,
most of them located in the East Midlands

His patent-agent friend Pat Johnson had led him to British
Thomson-Houston (BTH) in October 1930 on the back of a family
connection. Now Whittle had a personal reason of his own to think
of BTH again. Its sprawling plant – one of the largest industrial
sites in Britain – lay just to the north of Rugby and therefore only
a short drive from the Coventry home of Dorothy's parents (*see
Fig. 4*). Visiting them for the weekend was one of poor Dorothy's
few effective ways of separating her husband from his work. On
one of these weekends, early in October 1935, he arranged to leave
Dorothy and the boys with her parents while he drove back to
Rugby to pay another call on BTH.

He had been in touch with them intermittently since 1930 –
notably to enlist their help with his paper on superchargers – but
this weekend meeting must nonetheless have been a piquant
occasion. The two men who met him were the engineers who had
turned his jet proposal down five years earlier: Fred Samuelson,
Chief Engineer of the Turbine Department, and his deputy Robert
(Bob) Collingham. They were obviously more than intrigued by
his return. There was no denying his persistence, after all, and

that 1931 paper on superchargers had certainly been impressive. What exactly passed between them at their initial 1935 meeting is unclear, but within a matter of days Samuelson had authorised work to begin on some preliminary drawings to show that BTH could meet Whittle's requirements. The company sent him a first draft – 'Proposed Blading for Experimental Gas Turbine for Flying Officer Whittle' – and it was dated 28 October 1935.[16]

As he began making other enquiries of firms that he identified as potential material suppliers, Whittle realised he was embarking on a project that would far outlast his secondment for the Tripos course. To pursue it beyond his final examinations, he would need to become a postgraduate. In December 1935, he took the plunge and submitted a formal request to stay on at Cambridge. His college tutor, Roy Lubbock, strongly endorsed it and wrote to the Air Ministry just after Christmas affirming the warm support of the whole Engineering Faculty ('... the advice and experience of members of the staff will always be available [to him]'[17]). A postgraduate year was not in the gift of his superior officers in the uniformed RAF, so Whittle was effectively passing his career at this point into the hands of the Ministry. And his application – probably unprecedented in the history of the service – posed a slightly uncomfortable dilemma for Ministry officials.

Having deemed his work of no interest in 1930, the Ministry had already reassessed it once and had come to an unflattering conclusion. Back in June, the Ministry had received the reworked patent submissions and initial sketches of his proposed engine that Whittle had prepared in the wake of that first meeting with Williams and Tinling in his cottage at Trumpington. Given his growing reputation as one of the cleverest (and bravest) men in the uniformed service, the Contracts Department had reviewed the papers and approached several colleagues anew about his jet-engine idea. Did it look, after all, like an invention of any consequence? And, if so, should ownership of it be deemed a security issue? The Engines directorate within the Ministry passed the query on to its Engine Development arm, which left the business of penning a reply to the head of its Engine Research Contracts section. Unfortunately for Whittle, this turned out to be none other than Lawrence Tweedie, who had written to him so dismissively after his ill-fated meeting with A. A. Griffith in 1929.

Notwithstanding Whittle's distinguished service record in the meantime – which he must surely have known about, given Whittle's intermittent exchanges with the Ministry over all those ingenious gadgets he had devised at RAF Felixstowe – Tweedie's response in October 1935 was unambiguous. He made light of the whole business, not least by drawing an unfavourable comparison between Whittle's submission and the work of his nemesis several years earlier:

> In many ways the invention described... is similar to an invention of Dr A. A. Griffith which was experimented with at the Royal Aircraft Establishment some years ago. Although Dr Griffith's scheme was in many ways more promising than the one now submitted, the experiments proved disappointing and the scheme was eventually dropped. This invention is considered unlikely to prove of any practical value to the Royal Air Force in the light of present knowledge. It is considered, in the circumstances, to be a minor matter.[18]

This was a shamefully casual thumbs-down from Tweedie. It is hard to avoid the suspicion that, mindful of the way that he and Griffith had brushed Whittle aside in 1929, Tweedie felt disinclined to face the embarrassing possibility that Whittle's proposal was not so fanciful after all. So he simply hastened to bury the 'minor matter' – an invention that would one day reconfigure the geography of the world – back in the 'For Record Only' files of the Contracts Department. Whatever his motive, anyway, his verdict was probably reassuring for some of his colleagues. Any more positive appraisal might have raised eyebrows, given that nothing more had been heard from the RAE men at Farnborough about gas turbines since 1930. In the event, the Ministry decided there was no cause to worry about secrecy and Whittle was informed – eventually, and after five weeks of intermittent correspondence – that he was free to enjoy all the rights secured under his patents ('subject to the usual agreement reserving to the

Crown the right of user of the invention free of royalty or other payment...').

At the start of January 1936, the Ministry was in receipt of yet more papers from Whittle relating to a further round of patent applications. The man's persistence was probably becoming rather an irritant to Tweedie, but he sensed now that a more senior and authoritative response was needed. Accordingly, he conferred with his boss, the head of Engine Development. This was Major George Bulman, formerly of the Royal Flying Corps and a formidable figure within the corridors of the Air Ministry. Bulman scanned Whittle's latest patent applications and effectively concurred with the view taken by Tweedie of the jet engine three months earlier. The Ministry could safely ignore the idea and leave it to Whittle as his pet project. Bulman did take the trouble, though, to set down some specific criticisms. He wrote to David Pye, the great piston-engine authority who was now Deputy Director of Scientific Research at Farnborough, casting doubt on some technical features of the drawings that were included in Whittle's applications. With a certitude that he had come to display in such matters after many years in charge, Bulman added his own highly influential imprimatur to Tweedie's black mark:

1. Before these files are returned to the Contracts Department you should, I think, see them, representing as they do, further patent activity by Flight Lieutenant Whittle.

2. The high speed coupling, so far as one can judge from the description, is not likely to have practical success.

3. The scheme of attachment of the turbine blades is not easy to follow, and I am not sure how near it gets to the American form of exhaust turbo construction.

4. The third mention seems to me quite impractical, representing, in effect, the provision of a species of 'mud guard'.

5. There would seem to be no point in regarding any of the schemes as secret, or meriting a trial at departmental expense.[19]

To judge from the tone of his note, Bulman appears at this stage to have known much less than Tweedie about Flight Lieutenant Whittle. His easy dismissal of the design ideas to be patented – including that species of 'mud guard' – suggests he also knew little or nothing of Whittle's growing reputation at Cambridge.

Nor were he and Tweedie yet aware, presumably, of Whittle's request to press ahead with his engine project through a post-graduate year. This revelation – and the news that the Cambridge boffins were fully behind him – must have come as quite a surprise to them both when they heard of it in the second week of the New Year. They and their colleagues elsewhere in the Ministry were given further surprises within days. The partners from O. T. Falk chose this moment to bring officials up to date with their by now elaborate plans for a jet-engine venture. Discussions between Whittle and BTH had gone well in December. The Rugby firm was open in principle to going ahead with the work. As for the funding of the project, Whittle and his two associates Williams and Tinling had been helped by the Falk partnership to draft the articles for their newly registered company, Power Jets. So the Ministry faced not only a decision over Whittle's personal career; it also had to reach a broader view on the future of his putative jet engine and the highly irregular notion of a serving RAF officer throwing in his lot with a commercial enterprise.

Ministry officials set aside the decision over Whittle's career for the moment, to focus on Power Jets. While making no attempt to disguise their astonishment that anyone should want to invest in the company, they insisted on several changes to its legal structure. To acknowledge its unique provenance, the articles would have to include the Secretary of State for Air as a party to it. There could be no possibility, though, of taxpayers' money going into the equity, since the jet engine evidently had no military application (though any agreement between the bankers and the Ministry would have to take aboard the 'Free Crown User' condition governing the jet project's patents, just in case this view proved mistaken). By way of a concession to the Power Jets company, it was agreed that only 25 per cent of any future commercial profits would belong to the Air Minister, rather than the 40 per cent that the Ministry's standing rules might have required. All this looked rather academic, though, given that everyone in the Ministry – and those at the RAE who were asked for their view, almost certainly including A. A. Griffith – regarded the jet engine as a long-term research project at best. The chances of it ever making any money were deemed extremely remote, though the Ministry warned that it might revisit the 25 per cent quota if this outlook should ever change.

By the end of January, all were ready to sign what was christened 'The Four-Party Agreement'. The equity in Power Jets would be divided into 'A' shares, to be held only by the founders and effectively ensuring them of control, and 'B' shares, available for purchase by outside investors. Whittle was assigned 56 of the 98 'A' shares but undertook to hold 14 of them in trust on behalf of the Air Minister as the fourth party. This left him with 42 shares while his two ex-RAF friends Williams and Tinling took 21 shares each. (Whittle of his own volition subsequently increased from 14 to 24 his holding on the Minister's behalf.) Lance Whyte, fulfilling his hope of finding a venture worth all his time, became the company's chairman. Bramson agreed to be its Technical Consultant. No attempt was made to define executive responsibilities – unsurprisingly, since most of these would devolve to the one individual who could not be formally assigned any executive position. Whittle was told he could serve the company, which would be incorporated in March 1936, as 'Honorary Chief Engineer' for a period of five years. As for the extent of his commitment, the letter of the Agreement stipulated that he should work 'in any one week… a total of six hours'.[20] Since the spirit of the Agreement plainly acknowledged that Whittle would effectively be seconded to Power Jets, this six-hour condition was odd. It has been suggested, plausibly enough, that it was merely a face-saving clause to avoid having to acknowledge in writing 'that Whittle was assigned full-time to a privately financed company for the purposes of developing an engine that many regarded as fanciful…'.[21]

The mere fact that Whittle was being allowed to remain at Cambridge for another year was certainly a substantial concession by the Ministry. Whether it amounted to a gesture of confidence in his engine may be doubted. As Lance Whyte would recall: 'the Air Ministry said to us, "It is for you City people to gamble on Whittle. We cannot give you money but we will help you by lending Whittle's services free as chief engineer to your company, because we expect to get valuable scientific information from your failure".'[22] Whittle had been ignored by the scientists in 1929 and spurned by the engineers in 1931. Now his jet idea had been pigeon-holed by the civil servants as a matter of very little consequence. The gap between the Ministry's perception of this young officer and the RAF's high regard for him by 1936 does seem puzzling. This was the first occasion on which Whitehall's officialdom might have taken stock of Whittle properly, consulting Professor Jones and his colleagues at Cambridge to reach a far more considered – and more positive – view of his radical proposal. Instead, with a slightly disdainful air tinged with a snobbish suspicion of a man risen from the ranks, he was treated as little more than a well-meaning eccentric. This view of him, once filed, was going to prove hard to dislodge. It was to prevail inside the Ministry until the summer of 1939.

iv

Before the Four-Party Agreement had even been signed, and leaving Williams and Tinling to finalise the details, Whittle had meanwhile pushed ahead with his plans. The Air Ministry's lack of interest in his scheme seems not to have bothered him one jot. After another session with Samuelson and Collingham early in January 1936, he addressed a full technical conference with all the relevant engineers in Rugby a week later.[23] A meeting with the BTH Board followed, at which he and Whyte tried to persuade the directors to take a share of the financial risk by buying some 'B' shares in Power Jets. They pleaded in vain: the directors would only sign a 'cost-plus' contract, and BTH invoices would need to be settled monthly. The Rugby firm also extracted a promise that it would be awarded the contract to make the first hundred units, if the engine ever went into full production. In the meantime, work on an experimental engine would have to proceed without any kind of BTH subsidy.

The first stage of the project involved reaching full agreement with BTH on drawings. As Whittle had long known, priority would have to be given to drawings that could show exactly how, and at what speeds, the air would flow into, and through, the engine. In particular, they would have to capture precisely the aerodynamics of the compressor. Whittle had been sketching drafts for months. One of his fellow undergraduates, Arnold Hall, would later recall seeing the latest revisions regularly scattered by Whittle across the floor of his own rooms at Clare College, while his friend – 'a small figure bubbling with enthusiasm and exuding vitality' – pored over them on his hands and knees, pointing out where he needed help with some calculations.[24] These 'flow path' drawings, as they later came to be called, had to be completed ahead of work on the 'General Arrangement' ('GA') drawings that would present an outline of the whole engine and its mechanical construction. This sequence, though, ran counter to the approach generally used for piston engines, where the GA drawing came first. The turbine engineers at BTH assumed the same would apply to the jet. After receiving Whittle's preliminary sketches in January 1936, they went away and tackled a draft GA drawing to see the project off to a speedy start. Unfortunately, this well-intended initiative only served to show how far the jet concept was still beyond their grasp. Shown their work several weeks later, Whittle had to set it aside and substitute new drawings of his own. Some difficult discussions followed – his diary noted 'much argument as to the nature of the layout'[25] – as Whittle insisted that his own requirements needed following to the letter. Early in April he handed the BTH team his own preliminary drawing, 'Proposed General Arrangement of Shafts' – which he proudly headed 'Power Jets Ltd' and signed off as 'Technical Adviser'

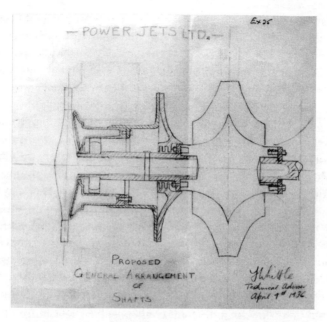

Fig. 5. FW's first 'General Arrangement' sketch,
handed to BTH in April 1936

(*Fig. 5*). The whole episode left him with a keener understanding
of the task ahead. He would have to monitor every stage of the
paperwork in detail, signing off every drawing personally and
meticulously delineating all mechanical parts so that BTH and its
suppliers could proceed to shape them exactly as he specified, for
the first 'Whittle Unit' – or the 'WU' as it was christened from the
outset. (It will be referred to here as the WU1, to avoid confusion
with subsequent reconstructions.)

Whittle also turned in the early months of 1936 to the sourcing
of suitable metals for his engine. It puzzled the BTH men that the
steel plate and ingots stored on site in Rugby were not seen as good
enough. Whittle drew on their inventory for parts of his design, but
insisted on buying fresh stock for his critical components. For the
rotating wheel of the compressor – the 'impeller', with its precisely
angled vanes – he needed a combination of low weight and high

resistance to stress that went far beyond anything available with standard steels. He found it in Slough, where a business called High Duty Alloys had been set up in 1927 by Wallace C. Deveraux, an engineer-businessman who had been thinking hard about the design of aero-engines for many years. Deveraux had since then been pioneering the improvement of aluminium-based metals. Other companies generally relied on castings of aluminium, pouring the molten metal into shaped containers and extracting the solidified metal as their final, *cast* product. High Duty Alloys worked hard on the metal as soon as it began to cool, beating it to form a *forged* solid that was considerably more expensive but much tougher. The aluminium Whittle acquired from them was called Hiduminium RR56, and it had been developed with Rolls-Royce's metallurgists for the R engine. Its properties were not widely appreciated beyond Derby, but Whittle had learned of them at Felixstowe from his RAF friends in the High Speed Unit.

The rotating turbine and the blades inserted into its hub presented Whittle with a different challenge: heat-resistance rather than lightness was the top priority here, to cope with metal-melting temperatures in the jet's gas stream. He went to Sheffield to consult Firth Vickers, a producer of the stainless steel that had been famously invented in its pre-war research laboratory by Harry Brierley. (Some insisted Brierley had *discovered* it, citing a popular story that he mixed several steel alloys and threw them all into a bin. Only weeks later did he notice that all had begun to rust except the steel mixed with chromium which remained wholly untarnished – the world's first scrap of stainless steel.) Brierley had moved on to another firm, but Firth Vickers remained at the forefront of the steel business, and Whittle signed them up for his turbine wheel. Once again the R engine figured in the story: Firth Vickers provided Whittle with 'Stayblade', a material developed for the R's exhaust valves.

Slough and Sheffield were but two of the stops on Whittle's frenetic round of visits early in 1936. Other destinations included Coventry, to talk to the machine tools specialist Alfred Herbert, and Chelmsford in Essex where Hoffman Manufacturing turned out the highest quality of precision ball bearings available in Britain. For one of his requirements, though, he had no well-known name to approach and was slightly at a loss where to turn. To crack the engine's combustion process he needed a supplier who could provide not just components but also advice and rare expertise. By any measure it was the aspect of his gas-turbine design that posed the single most daunting challenge – or, actually, three challenges. First, a system had to be devised that would allow controllable amounts of liquid fuel to be injected with great precision and at any altitude. Second, a combustion chamber had to be designed such that the injected fuel could be burned away completely, within a tiny space. And third, metals had to be sourced that would be capable of withstanding some warm work. Stainless steel would melt at temperatures around 1,400°C and the flame that Whittle was contemplating might burn a few hundred degrees hotter even than that. It would mean a 'heat release', as the engineers put it, about twenty times as great as any delivered to date for a ship's boiler. As he would later confess, he 'felt rather out of my depth with the combustion problem...'[26] So he was looking for someone with a deep knowledge of the mysteries of combustion.

He found him in February 1936 at a trade fair in Birmingham. Whittle went round its stalls for a morning, outlining his radical requirements in a tortuously cryptic fashion which met with a shake of the head from a succession of puzzled sales reps. Then he approached the stand of Laidlaw, Drew and Company, a family firm based just outside Edinburgh. On show were photographs of its standard product range, including the basic combustion kit used in glass manufacturers' furnaces and in boilers destined for ships built on the Clyde. Whittle asked again about the possibility of acquiring a burner rather out of the ordinary – and found himself being cross-examined by Mr A. B. S. Laidlaw. The ensuing conversation intrigued Laidlaw, who guessed at the outset that a gas turbine was at the heart of the matter (or so at least he always claimed later). Whatever his suspicions, he agreed to work on the mystery project. Whittle thereafter arranged a series of visits to Edinburgh, borrowing one of the planes from the Cambridge

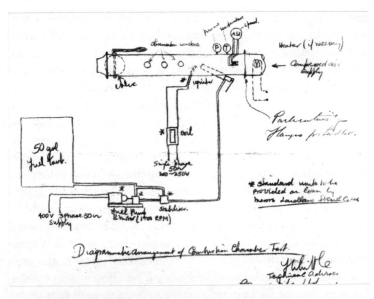

Fig. 6. FW's first sketch for a combustion-chamber test assembly

University Air Squadron to fly up there from Cambridge. He was soon working on the design of a primitive combustion chamber that could be built with Laidlaw, Drew components for some initial test work (*Fig. 6*).

His membership of CUAS also proved invaluable when the time came to look for someone who might champion the jet project as consistently in Whitehall as Professor Jones had backed it at the university. Whittle was never an accomplished networker. Identifying potentially important contacts in high places – never mind hanging onto them – was not his forte. He was deeply averse to anything that smacked of mere self-promotion, as opposed to explaining his work to those worthy of his attention. (In this respect, intriguingly, he had much in common with Wilbur and Orville Wright, famously uncompromising pioneers with the same aversion.) Even he could appreciate, though, that the annual CUAS black-tie dinner on the last Friday of the Lent term represented a rare opportunity to make some useful friends. It was always a grand affair, held at the University Arms Hotel. The 1936 event promised to be no exception, though black waistcoats were to be worn out of respect for the late King George V who had died on 20 January. Each of CUAS's hundred or so members could nominate personal guests, and Whittle invited all the directors of Power Jets – Lance Whyte and Sir Maurice Bonham Carter as well as Williams and Tinling – to join his table. When they met there on the evening of 6 March, they duly found themselves in promising company. In addition to the Air Minister himself, Lord Swinton, and the Chief of the Air Staff, the turnout boasted one Field Marshal, several Air Marshals 'and lesser fry without number' (as reported in the following week's edition of *Flight* magazine[27]). And among all the non-uniformed dignitaries were more than a few panjandrums of the aeronautical research world, of particular interest to Whittle and his friends. One of them, tall and stern, was Harry Wimperis, Director of Science and Research at the Air Ministry for the past ten years and the current President of the Royal Aeronautical Society.

As an exercise in building bridges, the Power Jets team's manoeuvring got off to a poor start. Dudley Williams recognised Wimperis and had the temerity to introduce Whittle to him, explaining that Power Jets had just been established to create a gas-turbine plant that would one day power a plane with jet propulsion. A man who had seen more aeronautical inventions come and go than most of his peers, Wimperis waspishly observed that it might be entertaining to see the rise and fall of their scheme. Whittle could still recall his words half a century later: 'One can only marvel at how many people have burnt their fingers on gas-turbine projects. And I don't suppose that you, Mr Williams, will be the last.'[28] Perhaps Wimperis had in mind A. A. Griffith, whose fingers had at least been recovering since 1930 thanks to his decision that year to drop all work on gas-turbine engines.

As it happened, the man who had had to preside over that decision was also at the dinner – Henry Tizard. Both now in their fifties, Tizard and Wimperis had been friends and colleagues for years. Their joint efforts had only recently given rise to a committee that was currently working, under Tizard's chairmanship, on the technology that would later come to be known as radar. But Tizard, later the same evening, gave Whittle and his friends a far more sympathetic hearing. He was surprised to learn of their plans for a gas-turbine engine, and intrigued to hear that some initial funding had been raised in the City. He had known nothing until now about either Whittle or his jet. At some point towards the end of the evening, Tizard sought out Whittle for a proper conversation.

The two men struck up an instant rapport. Their careers to date had much in common. Like Whittle, Tizard had been an outstanding mathematician in his youth with a keen interest in chemistry. During the war, he had learned to fly with the RFC, becoming a test pilot by 1917, and his subsequent research on petroleum chemistry in the 1920s had combined pure science with applied technology in ways that Whittle much admired. (He had virtually invented the use of 'octane numbers' to classify different grades of petroleum.) In more recent years, he had moved into various administrative roles in science and education, hence his chairmanship of the Engine Sub-Committee for the ARC in 1929–30. He was now chairman of the ARC itself and of a sister body, the Committee for the Scientific Survey of Air Defence. He had also been Rector of Imperial College since 1929 (the year it became part of London University). Tizard, in short, was exactly the kind of potential patron that Whittle had hoped he might encounter at the CUAS dinner – and the younger man seized the moment to talk again of the vision with which he had dazzled so many listeners already.

Without question, Tizard was impressed. Like many well-placed contemporaries in Whitehall, he was already persuaded that a war was coming. The notion of a new kind of aero-engine outperforming all piston engines had his full attention. More than that, Whittle's vision had an obvious relevance to the discussions that had begun some months earlier, under Tizard's own chairmanship, about the possibilities of a radar network for air defence. Tizard saw at once the potential for linking high-speed interceptor fighters to the radar detection of enemy planes. In the conversation that ensued, it seems safe to assume that he spelled out for Whittle the wider ramifications of his jet idea. Given their company at the dinner, Tizard can hardly have avoided alerting Whittle also to the broader political background. The guest of honour, Lord Swinton, had hurled himself into rebuilding the RAF. As his chief enforcer, Swinton had two months earlier brought Air Vice Marshal Wilfrid Freeman into his Ministry, as 'Air Member for Research and Development' (AMRD). These two men were together intent on creating, in effect, an air force that would be at least as large, powerful and attuned to the needs of an imminent war as Nazi Germany's Luftwaffe. Their plan – known in Whitehall as 'Scheme F' – marked the real start of a massive rearmament drive for the RAF. The number of its squadrons would be doubled, and they would be equipped with several thousand of the very latest aircraft. (As Tizard must have known, the prototype of an exciting new fighter, the Supermarine Spitfire, was scheduled to make its first flight later in the month, powered by a new engine from Rolls-Royce's Derby factory, the R-descended Merlin.) The necessary expansion of production capacity for the enlarged service was going to come from government-financed 'shadow factories', to be set up and run by existing car manufacturers under guidance from the top aircraft firms. If Whittle had still been thinking of his jet as a mail plane at the start of the evening, he knew by the end of it that more vital applications beckoned.

Indeed, the whole occasion can only have left Whittle and his colleagues struck by how ominously the context for their jet project had changed since May 1935. In his after-dinner speech, Swinton reminded his audience of the huge expansion that he and Freeman were presiding over: he had just agreed the 'Air Estimates' for government spending on the RAF in 1936–7 – they would appear in *The Times* the next morning – and the headline number was going to be £39 million, up from £21 million in 1935–6. Then he extolled CUAS as the 'Aeronautics Co-operation Squadron' and proposed a toast hymning the value to the RAF of the research being done in

Cambridge. The alliance between its scientists, British industry and the Air Staff 'was one of the greatest things in the world'. The Power Jets directors presumably raised their glasses cheerily enough to this encomium from the Air Minister who was now their fellow shareholder. And Tizard must have retired to his college rooms that night thinking he had stumbled most unexpectedly on an exciting instance of Swinton's Co-operation Squadron in action. Next day, Tizard telephoned Lance Whyte asking to be sent a copy immediately of the Bramson Report on the jet-engine proposal. It is far from clear with whom he discussed the report, or whether he tackled anyone in the Ministry directly about Whittle's personal situation. His enquiries, though, may have made their mark. Just a week after the dinner, Whittle heard from the Chief Instructor at CUAS that a letter had been received from the Air Ministry. It brought news that the Air Council had decided to accede to the Flight Lieutenant's request to remain at Cambridge for a further academic year.[29]

4

'Making the Thing Work'

March 1936 to September 1939

i

During the day following that CUAS dinner in Cambridge, 7 March 1936, the threat of another war in Europe suddenly assumed a greater and more frightening plausibility. German troops goose-stepped across the Hohenzollern Bridge in Cologne to begin the remilitarisation of the Rhineland, in yet more defiance by Hitler of the Treaty of Versailles. Reactions to the crisis in Britain generally exacerbated the growing schism in political circles between those intent on confronting Hitler and those anxious to appease him. For many of the individuals whom Whittle had met the night before, concerned above all with Britain's progress in the aeronautical sciences and the parlous state of the RAF, this latest challenge from Berlin was another reminder that the country faced a remorseless arms race in the air. Whittle could hardly have had a more graphic confirmation of Tizard's views within twenty-four hours of their first encounter.

Taking aboard the implications over the next few months, Whittle would rapidly come to view the progress of his project in a new light. The question hitherto had been: could he construct a working jet engine? The amended question would be more demanding by far: could he construct one in time for it to make a difference to the arms race and any war to come with Germany?

Before starting to grapple with the idea of such a chilling time-table, though, he had another more pressing deadline to contend with: his final Tripos exams. Despite all his distractions, he was still quite determined to gain a First Class – a distinction claimed in most years by fewer than one in ten of the Engineering Faculty's students after following a three-year course. Whittle immersed himself in his revision work so intensely that by the time his examination days arrived early in June 1936, he had made himself physically ill – an omen of ailments to come. He struggled through most of his papers, but missed one exam entirely. Someone must have spoken up for him when the marks were assembled. Perhaps it was Melvill Jones, convinced that giving this man less than a First would later reflect badly on his faculty. Whittle, anyway, was duly awarded his coveted First Class. His achievement was all the more striking, given how much time he had spent on the jet project since the turn of the year. His friend Arnold Hall, who later became another luminary of British aero-engineering, would look back in awe: 'I think it is a very important thing in understanding this man to realise that he did the almost impossible in getting a First...'.[1] Whittle's senior officers in the RAF were well aware of this at the time. As one of them put it in a subsequent note to the Air Ministry's new head of Research and Development, Wilfrid Freeman, Whittle deserved great credit for gaining a First while managing also 'to devote his spare time to the development of his inventions, which if practically developed will prove of great utility for the Royal Air Force'.[2] The uniformed service by now had a fair sense of their ex-apprentice's potential.

Once his exams were over, Whittle picked up on the development of his principal invention with barely a moment's pause. By the time he took Dorothy to London on 14 June 1936 to celebrate the publication of his degree, he had already been to Rugby for a confirmation of the final working drawings at BTH. Days later, the first steps into the manufacturing process were taken and Whittle, having lined up his suppliers, was ready to embark on a Herculean feat of supervision and coordination. Somehow, in addition to all his constant travelling and long days at Rugby spent on directing the incremental business of building an engine, he also found the time to maintain a daily diary with details of all his activities.

The diary began as a matter of itemising significant data so that he would have his own summary record of how the work was evolving, but soon grew into something much more comprehensive. Steadily more voluminous entries turned into running commentaries on the whole project. They included very few references to his domestic life: Dorothy and the two boys, David and Ian, were rarely mentioned. But his personal and professional lives were otherwise so intertwined – he had by now virtually no interests outside his work – that any aspect of a typical day might prompt a careful note (aided by his use of Pitman's shorthand, which he had taught himself while a cadet at Cranwell). So statistics, sketches and diagrams had increasingly to jostle for space with detailed accounts of every discussion. Here Whittle's obvious need to be brief had to contend every day with his unusual ability to recall conversations verbatim. As yet, he had no secretary and could indulge in extensive for-the-record memoranda only sparingly. Nonetheless, the infinite care with which he recorded every aspect of his theoretical work and experimental results would be extended to cover all his dealings with the various groups in a position to influence the growth of Power Jets. The pages of his diary would register his progress on both counts.[3]

He set about engaging the support of the RAE engineering establishment with a characteristic fearlessness. Any neutral observer might have expected this to be a protracted business, on several counts. Not yet out of his twenties, Whittle's youth was conspicuous for a start. Those at Cambridge and at the RAE soon to emerge as the dramatis personae of his diaries were mostly of the same generation as his professor, Melvill Jones. Several of them had come together as colleagues in the early expansion of the RAE's precursor, the Royal Aircraft Factory, and had built on that wartime experience to assume leading roles in Whitehall and Oxbridge colleges through the 1920s. They were the leading lights of the aeronautical world before Apprentice Boy 364365 had even begun working his way up the ranks. And here was a second dimension to the challenge facing Whittle. His peers in the establishment were almost all scions of upper-middle-class families, privileged alumni of the great public schools of England. In the profoundly class-conscious society of Britain in the 1930s, Whittle's humble background was hardly disguised by a brief albeit glittering flying career. Rumours of his courage as a test pilot and reports of his distinction as an undergraduate only added to his reputation as a curious phenomenon – a former Cranwell Boy, obsessed with an intriguing but most unlikely ambition. Many were still intensely sceptical of the jet idea but no longer quite as dismissive as they had been in the past. David Pye, the Deputy Director of Scientific Research at the Air Ministry, captured their slight bemusement perfectly in a cagey note of December 1935: 'I wish you every success in your bold venture outside the limits of designs which have hitherto been built, and shall be very interested to hear how matters progress.'[4]

Yet Whittle now made his mark within months. As he embarked on his postgraduate year with his Tripos behind him, the jet engine fast became an all-consuming passion. The young pilot with a vision had matured into the engineer with a mission. Armed with a fierce self-belief and a brave confidence that his fellow engineers would have to acknowledge the merit of his ideas, he approached the leading men of his day as equals just as he had once written to magazine editors while a young schoolboy. This led inevitably to another encounter between Whittle and the man whose chilly rejection of his youthful exposition on jet propulsion had been so mortifying to him – Dr Alan Arnold Griffith.

The two men had not met since the end of 1929. Arnold Griffith had left his post at the South Kensington laboratory in 1931 to become head of engine research at the RAE's airfield base in Hampshire. We have only a scanty record of his research activities over the intervening years – he published no papers at all after 1928 – but it is clear that nothing had been done at Farnborough by 1936 to build on his earlier axial-compressor work. Exactly when

Griffith first heard again of Frank Whittle, and what then passed through his mind, no one knows. Always an aloof character, he never let slip any indication of remembering their earlier encounter. It is certainly intriguing, though, that early in 1935 he put forward the idea of an unmanned missile powered by a simple turbojet engine.[5] The proposal was rejected and soon forgotten – but perhaps Griffith had taken more note of Whittle's jet-propulsion concept than is generally supposed. Whatever the truth, he was ready by the summer of 1936 to accept the appointment of a deputy at the RAE with a special interest in axial-compressor technology. This was Hayne Constant, a formidably talented engineer who had enjoyed a high reputation at Farnborough in the early 1930s but had left in 1934 to become a lecturer at Tizard's Imperial College. He had quickly become disillusioned with the academic life, and Tizard – who had been prompted by his meeting with Whittle at the CUAS dinner in Cambridge to think it was high time the RAE resumed the quest for a gas-turbine engine – had persuaded him to return to Farnborough. This was duly agreed with Griffith, on the explicit understanding that Constant would devote most of his time to advancing the RAE's knowledge of compressors. He was to report directly to Griffith, though in reality he would be the force behind their joint work.

The new RAE colleagues were soon contacted by Melvill Jones from Cambridge, who told them of Whittle's plans and suggested the three of them should meet. They welcomed the idea and Whittle wasted no time following up:

> I flew to Farnborough on the 10th August [1936] and talked to Constant and Griffith. They were fairly optimistic about the possibility of obtaining my estimated compressor performance (they had read my thesis on compressor losses). They expressed willingness to help.[6]

This terse entry suggests Whittle saw no point in referring to the past. He was far more interested, anyway, in the future cooperation that Griffith and his deputy seemed ready to contemplate. For his part, Griffith seems to have borne Whittle no grudge.

Three weeks later Whittle was back at Farnborough for a further meeting ('Talk with Griffith on the combustion problem and other matters'). More conversations followed over the next several weeks. It was confirmation at last that Whittle's thinking was now of genuine interest to the leading aeronautical minds of the day. He found himself embraced by the engineers as one of their own, which more than consoled him for any frustrations encountered elsewhere.

And other aspects of his jet project were indeed proving less welcome. Whittle was deeply indebted to Dudley Williams and Coll Tinling for their success in establishing Power Jets Ltd as a vehicle for his work. This corporate approach, though, had drawbacks that soon became apparent. Whittle was drawn into some vexing correspondence with the Air Ministry, for example, over the financial ramifications of his role. (Having initially sought a 25 per cent share of Power Jets' equity for the state, the Ministry subsequently demanded 35 per cent and then began angling for rather more.) He was also dragged into many hours of negotiation with Lance Whyte and the O. T. Falk partners over the commercial prospects for the jet engine. Neither activity much appealed to him. He was far happier nourishing his ties with other engineers, especially those with some influence in public life.

The most eminent of these, with whom he had yet to engage properly by the autumn of 1936, was Tizard. Their discussion at the CUAS dinner in March had augured well, and Whittle could have had no doubt about the potential importance of Tizard's interest. His busy schedule over the summer of 1936, though, had scarcely left Tizard a single moment to think of Whittle. A body set up a year earlier to explore ways of defending Britain against air attack had evolved, under his leadership, into a taskforce – the 'Tizard Committee' – promoting the development of radar. Through most of August and September 1936, Tizard had personally supervised a crucial series of trials at RAF Biggin Hill to establish how the radar detection of enemy bombers might be used to orchestrate a successful counter-attack by the RAF's newly formed Fighter Command. It was a momentous advance, for which Tizard was to be knighted the following year. No longer could anyone in government, challenged over defence strategy, glibly cite Stanley Baldwin's notorious assertion of 1932 that 'the bomber will always get through'.

Tizard had also had to contend, over the summer, with a distressing clash of wills over the best way to pursue radar's potential. His erstwhile friend and fellow scientist Frederick Lindemann, one of the key advisers to Winston Churchill in the latter's vigorous campaign to promote rearmament, had challenged the Tizard Committee's approach as woefully lacking in urgency. (This was a portent of another similar intervention over Whittle's work four years later.) Determined to accelerate radar's development at almost any cost, Lindemann had arranged a private meeting for Churchill with the pioneering scientist behind it, Robert Watson-Watt. A celebrated row had ensued, Tizard accusing Lindemann of interference, prompting several acrimonious letters and many resignations. Lindemann had retreated in the end, allowing the radar project to proceed under a reconstituted Tizard Committee but leaving his relationship with Tizard in shreds.

By the start of October 1936, with the unfortunate Lindemann affair resolved and the Biggin Hill trials completed, Tizard found the time at last for other matters. Having looked again at the report on the jet concept that he had been sent in March, he soon uncovered the exciting news that a jet engine was actually under construction. He wrote immediately to Lance Whyte to offer some personal encouragement:

> I am very glad to hear of the progress of F/L Whittle's unit. It is time that someone made a bold experiment of this kind. I feel sure that there is no <u>fundamental</u> objection to it although I think that you may have to be prepared for a long series of costly experiments before you can get the overall efficiency which will be tolerable.[7]

Nothing ever pleased Tizard more than the discovery of a new engineering idea in search of a patron. He was soon chasing

Whittle for a summary of his test results to date, and invited him to a private lunch in London at the Athenaeum Club on 15 October 1936.

Tizard's renewed interest offered Whittle a cue to reach out for some government assistance, which until now had been largely unforthcoming. Indeed, where specific requests for help had been submitted to the Air Ministry on Whittle's behalf, they had all met with a stony indifference. Whittle knew Tizard was probably the one individual brave enough to champion his cause, if persuaded of its merits. So much was going to hang on their lunch. Armed with a copy of his compressor thesis, several blueprint drawings of the engine, photographs of a wooden model of it and a mass of calculations, Whittle turned up in ebullient mood. He took Tizard through the whole case for the gas-turbine jet, from the elegant simplicity of the concept to the vision of a radically new kind of aviation. Tizard was captivated. As he recalled some years later: 'Whittle's suggestion was undoubtedly streets ahead of any other suggestion for the development of aircraft engines at the time. I knew it would cost a great deal of money; I knew that success was not certain; and yet I felt that it was of great national importance to spend the money.'[8] This was not an instance of being wise long after the event: Whittle noted in his diary that same evening that Tizard had 'agreed that the importance of the work was such as to justify action by the Aeronautical Research Committee'.

Naturally the ARC would need first to review all of the working papers, including the detailed drawings of the proposed engine's mechanical design. Whyte raised no objection on commercial grounds. Whittle, ever conscious of his status as a serving officer of the Crown, agreed unreservedly to hand them over. The sequel was richly ironic. On 2 November 1936, almost exactly seven years after their first meeting, Whittle travelled up to the Air Ministry for another appointment with Lawrence Tweedie, to deliver by hand his report and working papers. This time he was received with rather more deference. There were to be other echoes of that earlier 1929 visit, too. Tweedie's brief was to bundle up the material and pass it to the one scientist in Britain whom the ARC felt it could trust for a reliable appraisal: Dr A. A. Griffith. The committee asked Griffith to present an official paper on Whittle's project by the end of February 1937. It would be reviewed at the March meeting of the ARC.

Griffith, to his credit, gave Whittle's project a great deal of thought over the next three months: he was genuinely intent on making a study of the relative merits of the gas turbine and the high-performance piston engine. He made only a single visit to Rugby where the engine's parts were gradually being honed, but he had several long conversations with Whittle and pored over the mathematical calculations behind 'the jet propulsion system' for weeks. He even advised a significant alteration to the WU1's design, giving the centrifugal compressor not one but two impeller wheels because he still refused to believe that a single wheel could possibly deliver more than a 2:1 pressure ratio. (Whittle stuck to his single, double-sided wheel.) Then, penning his conclusions, Griffith contrived to miss the whole point of Whittle's vision almost as oddly as in 1929. He was prepared in his February 1937 report to acknowledge the potential value of jet propulsion 'for special purposes, such as the attainment of high speed or high altitude for a short time, in cases where take-off requirements are not stringent'.[9] But the overwhelming theoretical superiority of the jet over the piston engine at high altitudes – the primary rationale for Whittle's whole endeavour – was otherwise largely ignored. The bulk of the report propounded the disadvantages of the jet, especially its high fuel consumption on take-off and at low altitudes, as compared 'with a conventional power plant in any case where economical flight is demanded'. In his defence, Griffith almost certainly knew nothing at this stage about the breakthrough with radar, which might yet have created the 'special purpose' for the jet engine that Tizard had already identified. Even so, his final verdict on Whittle's engine was an almost comical misjudgement: '[to] become a competitor in the field of economical flight, a large improvement, of the order of say at least 50–100%, must be made in the ratio of take-off thrust to power plant weight.' To do something for which it was not designed, in other words, it would have to be radically redesigned. Griffith had no grasp at all of the different future for flight that Whittle had in mind. Had Britain's jet project hung on his report, it must now have been shelved altogether.

Immersed in final preparations for the inaugural run of his engine, Whittle paid Griffith's report surprisingly little attention. Perhaps he already sensed in March 1937 that Griffith's appraisal had been overtaken by events. And indeed, Tizard had been working behind the scenes for several weeks to stimulate interest in the gas turbine's potential. When his Engine Sub-Committee of the ARC convened on 15 March 1937 and reviewed Griffith's work, Tizard soon made his own views clear. One of the country's best-known engineers was sitting at the table and volunteered that 'he would stake his whole reputation on his opinion that the [Whittle] scheme would not work, and that it would be a waste of money to encourage it'. Tizard, who could be notoriously prickly when crossed, replied that he 'would guard against the loss of the gentleman's reputation by omitting his opinion from the Minutes'. (It was so omitted – but Tizard recalled it twenty years later.[10]) Those minutes closed with a formal recommendation 'that the Air Ministry should take up the question of the development of the internal combustion turbine as a matter of urgency and make all possible arrangements for its production at the earliest possible moment'. Yet still no one knew: with (as some still thought preferable) or without an added airscrew, was the gas turbine a concept that could really be made to work in practice? Now that Henry Tizard had led the RAE engineers to espouse its cause so openly, much was riding on Whittle's efforts at the BTH plant in Rugby.

ii

Work on the WU1 engine went forward in a small yard just outside BTH's main turbine hall. The company's managers issued no formal notice about it, nor were many people privy to the background: 'surprisingly little information (had) leaked out, and only a few of those actually working on the project knew what it was all about'.[11] As it took shape, some in the BTH workforce supposed it a secret weapon – or, rather, said the wags, an open-secret weapon. It was surely big enough to contain at least one turbine; but it also sported an enormous pipe that appeared to have been tied round the body of the unit in a knot. (Whittle never concerned himself much with the aesthetic appeal of his designs.) If its dimensions were puzzling, early indications of its purpose were downright baffling and by early 1937 were prompting occasional concern. The business of assembling and testing the combustion process – overseen by Mr Laidlaw from Leith, as Whittle's closest external assistant – caused particular alarm. 'Large pools of fuel would collect underneath [the apparatus],' as Whittle later recalled. 'Sooner or later flaming drops set them alight and we, conducting the tests, would be stepping between the pools of flame like demons in an inferno.'[12] The noise, smoke and vibrations led to several protests from female staff working in a first-floor office just above the yard, which they certainly thought too close for comfort.

Months were spent shaping, refining and patiently assembling the different parts of the engine. Whittle set out with a coherent design but inevitably ran into unexpected difficulties that several times forced him back to the drawing board. To take just one example, he had to resolve a tricky practical dilemma posed by the compressor, the unit at the front of the engine to which he had devoted so much thought in the past. It comprised both a rotor (the 'impeller'), to accelerate the air passing into it, and an elaborate exit passageway (the 'diffuser') which would slow the air down. It had to operate on an unprecedented scale, gulping in 1,500 lbs of air per minute, compared with the 120 lbs or so sucked in by the high-performing supercharger on a Merlin piston engine. Whirling the air up to a high speed, about 700 mph, would invest it with a lot of kinetic energy. Leaving the impeller, the air had then to be slowed down to about 200 mph in order to convert the kinetic energy into just the right amount of potential energy, which is to say pressure.

This could be done, in the diffuser, by directing the air into the narrow end of a megaphone-shaped channel. Expanding through it, the air would slow automatically. An identical process might be imagined for a river: a fast-flowing current must slow where the banks on either side of the river diverge from each other. The angle of divergence is of critical importance: if the two banks head away from each other too suddenly, the current will slow too abruptly and break up into uncontrollable eddies. As for the water in the river, so for the air through the gas turbine's diffuser. The deceleration process had to be gradual, with the walls of the diffuser opening out at a maximum angle of 11°. (The angle was established by a Swiss mathematician in the eighteenth century called Daniel Bernoulli, a key figure in Whittle's private pantheon of kindred spirits.)

As so often, though, the gas turbine threw up a complication. Whittle decided there was virtually no scope to vary the total length of the whole engine: this was determined by the length of the shaft linking the turbine to the compressor, which for good mechanical reasons could not feasibly be made any longer. Needing plenty of space for the combustion process, he had to run it through a long pipe bent around the engine. The same constraint meant he had virtually no scope to lay the diffuser horizontally as he had initially envisaged: it would have needed a channel a few feet long if it was to slow the air as gradually as required, respecting that maximum angle of 11°. Whittle devised a typically inspired solution. In place of one long horizontal channel, he substituted eight much shorter channels arranged vertically in a honeycomb pattern. The air entering the first channel would pass up through walls diverging at exactly the appropriate angle, before streaming into a second channel – and so on to the eighth. Thus would his 'honeycomb diffuser' deliver the requisite deceleration of the air, within the limited space available.

Comparable challenges, some rather more intractable, slowed work on both the combustion chamber and the turbine. Whittle resolved them one by one, drawing on all his knowledge of thermodynamics and aerodynamics to complement his basic mechanical

Fig. 7. The Whittle Unit (WU1) engine ready for its
first ignition, April 1937

and engineering skills. He toiled over endless drawings at home
in Trumpington, driving over to BTH at frequent intervals and
sometimes staying overnight at Rugby's Grand Hotel. Step by step
the engine took shape: the turbine hall produced the steel plates
he needed, manufactured the various components of the engine
out of the alloys he sourced, tested each part separately insofar as
this was possible and then pieced them all together. The result,
eventually, was a rather clumsy-looking contraption that bore no
resemblance to any product of the turbine hall and left most of
his BTH assistants flummoxed. Finally, in April 1937, Whittle
judged it ready to be run as a complete unit. A 'test assembly' was
finalised, with the engine attached to a control panel sporting a
dozen vital dials (*Fig. 7*). Over the second weekend of the month,
mounted on a heavy wooden platform, it was relocated to a
gallery inside the turbine hall where the end of the engine had to
protrude rather comically out of a small window.

Whittle arrived on the Monday morning of 12 April for an
event that had been almost two years in the making. After a series
of last-minute checks, he put the date at the top of page 75 in his
1936–7 Note Book for Workshop & Laboratory Records, set down
a few details on the power required of the starter motor to rotate
the whole unit at 1995 rpm and 990 rpm, and then wrote 'Starting

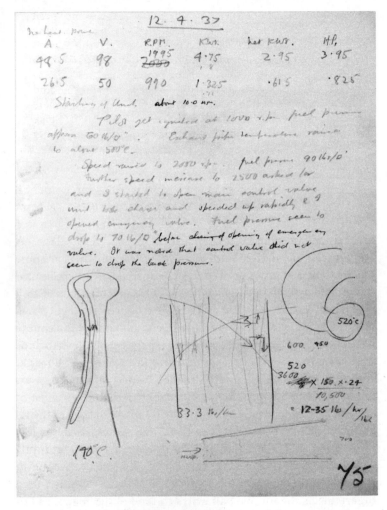

Fig. 8. The entry in FW's Workshop Note Book for 12 April 1937:
'Starting of unit'

of Unit' (*Fig. 8*). The pencil jottings and diagrams that followed
were the basis of a more polished description that he wrote out
much later in the day – but even the refined version betrayed no
sign of elation at the first ever running of a jet engine:

Starting of Unit. Pilot jet successfully ignited at 1000 rpm. Speed raised to 2000 rpm by motor. I requested the further raising of speed to 2500 rpm and during this process I opened valve B and the unit suddenly ran away. Probably started at about 2300 and using only about 5 HP starting power. Fuel pressure was much below expectations being 90 lb/sq in. at 2000 rpm and dropping to 70 lb/sq in. when control B was used, though there was no apparent drop in back pressure. Noted that return pipe from jet was overheating badly. Flame tube red hot at inner radius. Combustion very bad…[13]

There was nothing here to suggest what a pivotal moment it was for him, though he did close the entry with a note of a 'Congratulatory wire from Sir Maurice, Whyte & Bramson' that had arrived that afternoon. With an almost impossibly tight budget and scarcely any margin at all for miscalculation in the plethora of equations and mechanical minutiae that had underpinned the design and assembly of his jet, he had built an entirely new concept of a power plant. It had run for less than a minute, but it had nonetheless worked *at its very first ignition* – the real hallmark of his genius, for many engineers.[14] (The giant Swiss turbine business Brown Boveri had been trying in vain to fire up a gas turbine since 1918. It would take that company another two years to pull it off.)

The principal reaction of most of those present at that first firing appears to have been blind panic. Jet propulsion was like some mythical beast – a Wagnerian dragon, perhaps – abruptly woken and pulled from its lair. The sound of the engine, never heard before, began as a deep whine but turned rapidly into a high-pitched scream that was neither a piston engine's growl nor the whirr of a steam turbine. Whittle himself later described it as 'a rising shriek like an air-raid siren' and admitted he had 'rarely been so frightened'.[15] As soon as it began, the BTH team fled to safety. Even those listening from the turbine hall ran for cover. Whittle was left standing alone with his clipboard beside the engine, surely allowing himself at least a brief moment of triumph that ignition had in fact been achieved. He was quickly aware, though, that the engine had run out of control. Red-hot patches were creeping across the steel casing. It might perhaps have been about to explode, which would probably have been the end of him. Fortunately, closing the fuel pipe choked the engine abruptly. Its noise died away as quickly as it had begun.

Clearly the test had not gone quite as anticipated. Still, Whittle had set out to show that a self-sustaining gas-turbine engine could work, and it had (albeit briefly). Now work could begin on mastering its performance, so that one day it might power an aeroplane through the sky. An extraordinary period followed of initial testing. The terrifying early bursts of acceleration were quickly diagnosed – faulty fuel controls and a leaky pump had allowed tiny pools of kerosene to gather in unexpected places, where they had flared up at random – and the problem was fixed. But the turbine still remained prone to frightening bursts of unexpected acceleration almost on a daily basis. Whittle always affected a steely calmness, but was often under terrible strain. (On more than one occasion, returning to his hotel for an evening meal, he was suddenly overwhelmed by fits of hysterical laughter in reaction to the tensions of the day, 'much to the astonishment of the other occupants'.[16]) Whittle's assistants were always alert to the need for evasive action and it was taken all too regularly. On one morning, the impeller spinning round at 12,000 rpm unaccountably touched the inside of the compressor's casing and the engine screeched to a halt in less than two seconds.

At another test, Samuelson and Collingham joined the team in the gallery to see Whittle's engine for themselves. They were duly dismayed by what followed: 'the engine accelerated smoothly enough at first and for a moment or two appeared to be under perfect control, then once more it ran away with the usual terrifying crescendo of noise, and a great jet of flame from the propelling nozzle.'[17] The two men bolted, Collingham to the fore – he had been edging his way out of the hall even before the engine was fired – and this prompted some hilarity round the plant at their expense. But it made no difference to the heightened respect that both now felt for Whittle. To their credit, they went out of their way to reassure the BTH workforce that Whittle's unnerving project would be allowed to go on without a break. During one works conference around this time, Whittle overheard Samuelson speaking on the telephone in an adjacent office. He heard him confiding in hushed tones 'it looks like being something very big', and had no doubt Samuelson was talking of his jet engine.[18]

iii

For almost nine years, Whittle had peddled a theoretical proposition that industry and Whitehall had treated as little more than a clever young man's fantasy. Now, in the summer of 1937, he had a proven concept and was surely entitled to hope that the world would take a more generous view of his extraordinary scheme. His jet engine had actually worked. At least the RAF acknowledged this progress by placing him on its 'Special Duty List' when his postgraduate year ended, so that he could continue working on his project rather than be posted back to active service. Other parties mostly held back, baffled by the implications of his achievement. What lay ahead was a development process that was indeed impossible to define in advance, but sure to prove expensive. Success within a timeframe comparable to that of 1935–7 would depend on sufficient funds being made available, either from the private sector or from the government. In the event, for reasons that no doubt seemed compelling to many at the time but appear less impressive in light of the wartime crises to come, neither was to deliver the support that Whittle expected – and surely deserved.

He had handed his patents over to Power Jets on the basis of O. T. Falk & Partners' assurance late in 1935 that a growing band of shareholders would subscribe all the capital needed to pay for the development of his engine. The company would then prosper from the commercial returns on high-altitude aviation, and the shares would fly high, too. By mid-1937, however, mounting fears of another war with Germany had made it most unlikely that additional investors would be found for any venture linked to civil aviation. (The timing by Williams and Tinling of their initiative in 1935 no longer looked quite so propitious after all.) To pay off in the foreseeable future, the jet engine would have to be linked to the rearmament of the RAF. For prospective investors, this was obviously problematic. If the day ever came for jet engines to be ordered under a defence contract, an industrial manufacturer would be entitled by virtue of Whittle's status as a serving officer of the Crown to exploit his patents and commercial secrets without paying Power Jets a penny in royalties. O. T. Falk had sunk £2,000 into Power Jets, with an option to subscribe a further £18,000 ahead of any other investors. Within weeks of the successful first ignition in the turbine hall at BTH, Whyte and his colleagues were searching for a more promising 'Plan B'.

Conceivably they might have sought a suitable champion in the existing aircraft industry who would agree to adopt Whittle and his project. Plausible patrons might in theory have included men like John Siddeley or Geoffrey de Havilland, individuals with famous names and industrial resources at their disposal. Lance Whyte and his colleagues appear never to have explored this avenue. They were too well aware of Whittle's antipathy to the industry's big corporate players. They would also have known that arranging any partnership of this kind would have required them to lure Whittle out of the RAF. This might fairly have struck them as a hopeless proposition. Indeed, this was the moment at which Whittle's RAF background, which hitherto had been so central to all his achievements, began to appear in a contrary light. It had hitherto promoted his career in a spectacular fashion. From this point onwards, his status as a serving officer in Her Majesty's forces – and thus an engineer subject to the dictates of the Air Ministry and its officials – would begin to prove in many ways a hindrance.

(The notion of finding a commercial patron fared better in Germany. Covert plans to build a jet plane had been instigated there just over a year earlier, in April 1936, at the behest of another aspiring young jet-engine enthusiast called Hans Joachim Pabst von Ohain, a twenty-four-year-old PhD student at the University of Göttingen. Von Ohain's doctoral research into thermodynamic reactions had fired in him an ambition to make a gas-turbine engine – in all essentials identical to the jet as set down in Whittle's patent of 1931 – if only he could find a sponsor with the necessary engineering resources. His professor had given him an introduction to Ernst Heinkel, head of one of Germany's largest aircraft companies, who found the outrageous idea of an aeroplane with no propeller immensely appealing. Heinkel, a maverick figure in his industry who prided himself on being open to radical new ideas, had his own political reasons for backing von Ohain's proposal. He was far from certain of its feasibility. 'He was a brilliant scientist,' recalled Heinkel of von Ohain in his post-war memoirs, '... [but] a pure theoretician, knowing nothing of technical drawing...'[19] Nonetheless he almost immediately set his engineers to work on building a plane for him in a secret workshop on the edge of Heinkel's main factory airfield.)

Shortly after the war, a Harvard historian of the jet engine's origins – having corresponded with at least one of the O. T. Falk men – observed that the firm had 'realised... from the beginning that the entire undertaking would ultimately have to be a partnership with the state...'.[20] Whatever the true timing of this decision, they were certainly ready to broach the partnership idea with Whittle by the end of May 1937. Various ploys were explored, but they settled in the end for the simplest. 'We discuss our attitude to the Air Ministry,' noted Whittle later, 'and eventually agree that absolute frankness is best, and draw up proposals for selling them the unit and carrying out a research contract.'[21] It looked a compelling proposition, until it was put to the Ministry on 2 June 1937 – or, more precisely, until Whyte in the course of a meeting that day quoted £16,000 (about £800,000 today) as the purchase price of the engine. This was 'not well received'.[22] The officials knew the cost of the project to date was rather less than £5,000. Given the RAF's largesse in making Whittle freely available to work on the project, it seemed to the Ministry men that Lance Whyte had rather overstepped the mark. This probably only confirmed their first impression of him. Snappily dressed in an expensive suit, with gold-rimmed spectacles and a silk handkerchief in his breast pocket, no one could have mistaken Whyte for a civil servant. His grand and cerebral manner – as Whittle himself was only too well aware – ruffled Whitehall feathers from the start. Ministry officials probably knew little or nothing of his academic past and suspected that, stripped of all his fine words, Whyte was just a sharp City gent chasing a quick windfall. They rejected his approach out of hand. Indeed, in turning down the idea of any purchase by the Ministry, they questioned whether in fact the engine had any lasting value at all. ('They still require to be satisfied that we have a piece of apparatus capable of continuous running,' noted Whittle.) They left open the possibility of paying for a detailed report on the jet's progress, and of making occasional payments to cover repairs and modifications. But such matters would have to be negotiated at a later date.

Whittle was extremely disappointed. He confessed as much at a private meeting with Henry Tizard later the same day. Power Jets faced a serious financial predicament. The Air Ministry had agreed to let Whittle remain with the project, as envisaged in the Four-Party Agreement, but whether the tiny company could find the money needed to develop the engine now looked doubtful. Tizard promised to investigate further, and two weeks later met Lance Whyte for a conversation that almost led the O. T. Falk partners to think again about expanding their investment. The ARC chairman said he was in no doubt that the Power Jets project was well ahead of any other in the field – by which he plainly meant the RAE's long-neglected programme – and had the 'vision and energy' to sustain its lead. If private investors in the City were holding back, other funding sources would have to be found. In his opinion it was 'undesirable to have any foreign money in the company... [but] the company's work was worth financing and [he] suggested that the Air Ministry might be persuaded to subscribe for shares'.[23]

Whyte took this to mean Tizard would support a sizeable government stake in Power Jets, possibly even a majority holding.

He asked Tizard to send him a written confirmation of his views, which might be shown to third parties, and Tizard wrote back to him a few days later. This letter has often been quoted as evidence of Tizard's historic support for Whittle. Its message for Whyte at the time was quite different. Yes, Tizard was happy to acknowledge what made Whittle such a rare bird. But in the space of those few days – and perhaps after encountering a firm rebuff from the Ministry – Tizard backed away from his earlier suggestion. (The episode was in this respect another ominous portent of things to come.) He was still full of praise for Whittle personally, but he could only wish O. T. Falk the best of luck with its plan to finance the engine privately 'because I think you will have to make up your mind that a large expenditure will be necessary before final success is reached'.[24] This confirmed Whyte's worst fears. Investors would have to dig deep in support of a clandestine venture, with a long gestation and no obvious way of turning 'final success' into any reward at all. Within days of receiving his letter, O. T. Falk drew back. Whyte informed Dudley Williams on 8 July that the financing model devised in January 1936 was now defunct and the option granted to O. T. Falk would be allowed to expire.

Whittle briefly feared the collapse of the whole project. Meetings were held at Falk's Old Jewry office in the City to talk about liquidation arrangements for Power Jets and the subsequent ownership of its patents. The Director of Education at the Air Ministry received a slightly forlorn note from Whittle explaining that he might very soon be 'without official employment'.[25] In the event, collapse was averted and matters were settled reasonably amicably. Control over Power Jets reverted to Whittle, Williams and Tinling, shorn of many complications that had been linked to the O. T. Falk option – and Whyte was even asked to remain as chairman of the company. But the crisis left Whittle henceforth dependent on the proceeds of a hand-to-mouth struggle for money. The O. T. Falk partners were reluctant to be seen abandoning the cause – Oswald Falk himself and Sir Maurice Bonham Carter both retained hefty personal stakes in Power Jets – and they soon agreed to a series of tiny short-term loans to help pay Power Jets' bills. They were not prepared to commit any more of their firm's capital, though, and would no longer be actively marketing the company to institutional investors. Any additional private funds would have to come from selling new 'B' shares to random wealthy individuals, for whom a blind faith in Whittle's vision might amply justify parting with a few hundred pounds. Lance Whyte actually confided in Whittle, at the time of an especially acute cash crisis, his own conviction 'that anybody who becomes a "B" shareholder is a Bloody Fool...'[26]

A possible purchase of Whittle's engine by the state was briefly mooted one more time, in August 1937, with an offer of £10,000 that would be conditional on the engine running successfully up to full speed. The offer was quickly withdrawn two months later, however, following lively objections from the Treasury. So the Air Ministry, almost certainly at Tizard's urgent prompting, instead offered Power Jets a development contract in the autumn worth £5,000 – more or less the sum spent on the engine to date. It would be paid in instalments, but only in exchange for results from pre-defined tests in the course of Whittle's research. (Reaching final signatures on even this modest contract would take several months of tortuous negotiation, lasting into 1938.) Only after agreement had been reached in principle was it fully appreciated by the Power Jets team that even the skimpiest of contracts with the Air Ministry brought with it a lethal side effect. The project would have to be registered on the Official Secrets List, effectively putting paid to any lingering hope of further significant investment from the private sector.

From the summer of 1937 onwards, the survival of Whittle's jet engine therefore depended above all else on government funding. Thus began a financial arrangement that in theory might have lifted him well clear of his hand-to-mouth existence but sig-nally failed to do so over the next three years. As his personal diaries were constantly to attest, the state would take a wretchedly miserly approach. It provided Power Jets with just enough cash to avert insolvency – but not a penny more. Since this outcome was indeed avoided, it might be said that Whittle had good reason to be grateful to the state. Some authors have averred as much in recent times, celebrating a glass half-full for which the Air Ministry in their view deserves some praise. ('It is to the credit of officials that they took the risk of proceeding with Power Jets at all...'[27]) The empty half, though, caused Whittle endless trouble and severely impeded his progress in a hundred ways. He set himself a daunting objective in 1937, more so than he appreciated at the outset. If minor miracles were needed to achieve it – as they certainly were – this was attributable not just to the ground-breaking nature of the work but also to the lamentably meagre resources at his disposal.

The £5,000 released under the first development contract in 1937–8 lasted little longer than the contract's negotiation. At one point in the summer of 1938 Power Jets had only £1,200 (about £60,000 today) left in its bank account, and no idea where to turn for more funds.[28] Technical setbacks to the programme then meant the Ministry had to let it collapse altogether or else provide another, more generous contract. This second one was finally agreed in October 1938, but not without much further rancour and only after months of pressure from Tizard, the RAE engineers and the directors of BTH who by this stage could hardly contemplate seeing all their company's efforts consigned to the bin (along with its equity in the job – BTH had agreed to take 2,400 'B' shares in lieu of payment for its work on a second reconstruction of the engine). The terms dictated by the Ministry presented Whittle with a classic dilemma: he could only receive cash disbursements by agreeing to test results that were not remotely achievable, given the constraints imposed by his shoestring budget. On this unsatisfactory basis he struggled on, with the Ministry breaching its own terms just frequently enough to ensure the funds never quite dried up.

The Ministry's antipathy towards Whittle – for under the circumstances, and given his glittering career to date, this is what its half-hearted support amounted to – reflected more than just a bureaucracy's customary dislike of mavericks. From the outset, officials were acutely uncomfortable with the notion of subsidising a privately capitalised venture that was so completely identified with a serving RAF officer. At no point does the Ministry appear to have considered simply obliging Power Jets to accept a merger with one of the big engine companies. Yet as the company's paymaster it must have enjoyed far more leverage than O. T. Falk to secure this outcome. Whittle was desperate to press ahead. Might not the Ministry have promoted his project as a vital aspect of the RAF's rearmament and marched him into a suitable niche with one of the country's leading firms? We are left to wonder what might have happened, to pick the most obvious counterfactual, had he been obliged to accept a generously resourced facility at Rolls-Royce. There are many reasons to suspect such an arrangement might never have worked. That the Air Ministry failed to explore the possibility in even the most general way, however, is a measure of how egregiously Whitehall neglected the jet engine's potential after the April 1937 triumph in Rugby. (Again, more effective steps were meanwhile being taken in Nazi Germany. Unseen from London, engineers working within the Reichsluftfahrtministerium (RLM) in Berlin were busily fostering interest in a jet-engine programme among the leading German aero-engine companies. Rivalries between them – and disputes over Heinkel's right as an airframe manufacturer to persevere with von Ohain's project – ensured plenty of complications: a tangled web of negotiations, according to the best account of the process, 'resembled the synopsis of an extravagant television soap opera'.[29] It was nonetheless true that leading names like Junkers and BMW were soon being generously provided with all the government funds they needed for jet-engine work.)

Part of the Air Ministry's diffidence can be attributed to a continuing suspicion among officials that, despite its successful ignition, turning the engine into an aircraft's power plant still looked at best a most doubtful prospect. Their concerns were only compounded after the summer of 1937 by the fact that Farnborough was pursuing its own gas-turbine programme under the guidance of the world's best-known authority on such matters, Dr A. A. Griffith – and it was heading off in a subtly different direction from that taken by Whittle. In response to a recommendation by Tizard's ARC Sub-Committee and with the full support of David Pye, the RAE was now pressing ahead with work on a turbine/propeller combination. Griffith and his recently recruited deputy Hayne Constant were also intent on using an axial compressor, designed to ambitious specifications, which the RAE believed would in due course eclipse the centrifugal compressor being employed at Rugby. To help make their engine, the RAE engineers would soon have their own heavyweight industrial partner, Metropolitan-Vickers ('Metrovick'). Whittle noted a briefing on this topic from Lawrence Tweedie in March 1938. A close relationship was envisaged with Metrovick, and 'there is one [RAE] man permanently there in a position similar to my own [at BTH]'.[30] The curious fact that Metrovick and BTH were sister companies, both of them subsidiaries since 1929 of the giant Associated Electrical Industries (AEI), only underscored for many of Tweedie's colleagues what a thoroughly anomalous situation had been allowed to develop.

Above all else, though, officials had little time for Whittle's project because so little time was available to them for *any* business not directly connected with the headlong rearmament of the RAF with the best aircraft already (or very soon to be) available. Any fair-minded criticism of the Air Ministry for neglecting Whittle's cause in the years immediately prior to the outbreak of war has to contend with this: there were, of course, mitigating circumstances of no slight importance. For the second time in two generations, Britain was in an arms race with Germany. Bigger and heavier battleships had once been the measure of it. Now faster and more powerful aeroplanes, powered by bigger and more efficient piston engines, looked set to define the pace of Anglo-German rivalry. Those who believed it would end in war had to be wary of distractions. No one felt this more fervently than the Ministry's head of Engine Development. This was the man who had spotted the species of mudguard on the jet-engine's design at the start of 1936, George Bulman. Now in his mid-forties,

Bulman had been running his eye over aero-engines on behalf of the Air Ministry since the middle of the First World War. He came from a comfortable, middle-class background but was no university man. He had gone straight from public school (Bedford) into a marine-engineering apprenticeship in Sunderland before taking up work in the pre-1914 aero-engine world. He had served as a major in the Royal Flying Corps, 'a smallish, clean-shaven and tough character with a military air'.[31] Appointed Chief Inspector of Engines to the RAF in 1919, he had been in charge of the Air Ministry's development work with engine manufacturers since 1928. (Production work fell under a second arm of the Engines directorate.) He still cut a lean figure in 1937, with a martial bearing and aquiline features well suited to his predatory role hunting out all potential flaws and failings in new designs destined for service with the RAF. His practical knowledge and experience were greatly respected both within Whitehall and among the engine-makers alike. Those serving under him like Tweedie and A. A. (Andrew) Ross, the latter his deputy since 1915, flourished in a disciplined culture shaped by the lessons of the late war. Bulman nurtured it day and night, to promote the strict procedures and exacting standards on which, as he always insisted, everything else depended. He went 'by the book' and regarded imagination as a much overrated faculty. The development of practical piston engines was his trade, not conjuring visions of the future. And on the wall behind his desk hung a photograph of the man he regarded as the patron saint of that trade, the late Henry Royce. Extraordinarily hard-working, Bulman was nominally just a middle-ranking Ministry official. In reality he wielded huge authority over all engine-development matters, in 1937 as for many years past. As he himself put it in his post-war memoirs, 'I never regarded myself as a civil servant, but as an engineer dedicated to the RAF.'[32]

What this had entailed since January 1937 was a total dedica-tion to the campaign being driven forward by Swinton and Air Marshal Wilfrid Freeman to expand and modernise the RAF as quickly as possible. This ensured a massive workload for all officials in the Air Ministry – and it was George Bulman and his Engine Development team to whom Swinton and Freeman were delegating ever more of the infinitely complicated day-to-day tasks. Immediately after the Munich Conference of October 1938, in an unprecedented move, Freeman promoted Bulman and put him in charge of Engine Production as well as Engine Development – so he now ran the whole of the Engines directorate (also known as ED&P) as one. As Bulman would proudly recall later, he was 'the only man other than Freeman to carry both burdens'.[33] Understandably under the circumstances, Bulman was disinclined to spend time on non-urgent matters. 'The ultimate criterion,' as he explained in his memoirs, 'became "Is it fit for war and vast production?" rather than a merely technically interesting experimental aircraft as had been sought too often.'[34] Over the course of his career he had developed an intense suspicion of clever university men trying to sell him world-beating new designs of aero-engines and their component parts. They were among the most frequent visitors to his office, and the most dispensable. He called them his 'Wild Inventors'.[35] The looming war with Germany gave him a perfect pretext to ignore them all.

Fortunately for Whittle, his jet engine captured the imagination of the two individuals in the Ministry probably best placed to ensure that his project was not terminally ignored. One of them was none other than Wilfrid Freeman himself. The Air Marshal, later to prove one of the most distinguished of Britain's war leaders, had many fine qualities. Among them was a brave willingness to back the unorthodox. (After an acrimonious divorce in 1935, he had married a young woman half his age which upset many of his peers and for a while had threatened an end to his RAF career. Freeman, who had become secretly engaged to his future second wife in 1932, was undeterred. By a curious chance, his first wife's closest friend was married to George Bulman.[36]) As the Air Member for Research and Development since 1936, Freeman had already made his mark as a risk-taker in at least two significant ways. He had been one of the most effective champions of radar: a network of twenty radar stations down Britain's east coast might have been fatally delayed in 1937 but for his personal intervention (it emerged complete as the 'Chain Home' system in 1940, making a critical contribution to the air war). And he had begun talking to Geoffrey de Havilland about the possibility of building a super-fast but completely unarmed bomber made entirely of wood – which would later emerge as the de Havilland Mosquito, an aircraft known to all as 'Freeman's Folly' until it turned out to be one of the RAF's most successful planes of the war. At some point in 1937–8, Freeman also took a keen interest in another development project that he heard was under way in the East Midlands. In the autumn of 1938 he decided the aircraft industry was encumbered by an excessive number of designs and took steps to curtail the portfolio. At a Progress Meeting in the Ministry, though, he insisted that one putative engine in particular should go on being developed – and displayed a shrewd grasp of what it might offer:

> This engine is based on jet propulsion and the results of tests already carried out had exceeded expectations... [If successful] it would be cheap to produce, as it contained comparatively few mechanical parts. It... required no airscrew.[37]

Freeman had no time to involve himself at this stage in the minutiae of the Ministry's dealings with Whittle, but his genuine interest in the jet engine was now on the record. It probably helped ensure the conclusion of the second funding contract for Power Jets.

The other hugely influential figure keeping a sympathetic eye on Whittle's progress took a more direct approach to its finances. Lord (William) Weir was a rich Scottish industrialist who had been an unpaid adviser to Swinton since 1935, giving the Air Minister – and later Freeman, too – the benefit of his own un-paralleled experience of coping with the practical problems of aircraft production. (Having been 'Controller of Aeronautical Supplies' in the First World War and Air Minister in 1918, he had remained closely involved with the politics of the RAF and its aircraft-industry suppliers for twenty years.) Weir was chairman of his family firm, a Glasgow engineering group, and G. & J. Weir began acquiring 'B' shares in Power Jets in 1937. Over the next two years it would build up a significant stake in the company – too little to make much difference to Whittle's financial situation, but a more eloquent gesture of moral support than anything on offer from the Ministry's officials.

iv

After the war, with the jet engine poised to conquer the world of aero-engineering, BTH was proud to recall its association with Frank Whittle. A lavish company booklet explained the relevance of its skills 'acquired in the building of other turbines and compressors of high rotational speeds'. It set out a detailed textual account of its work on the project, with almost a hundred illustrations, all prefaced with a portrait gallery of those who had worked with Whittle (*Plate 4*). It included nineteen engineers, draughtsmen and fitters 'who comprised the team which designed and manufactured for Power Jets Ltd the first experimental jet-propulsion gas turbine...'[38] Posterity was invited to celebrate a glorious partnership between the Rugby firm and the Air Commodore who inspired them all. The truth was very different.

Setting out to develop an improved version of the WU1, Whittle expected to encounter many technical difficulties. What he did not anticipate was a lack of interest from BTH's most senior men, which turned in some cases to outright hostility when the exacting nature of the project became clear. None caused Whittle more distress than the Chief Engineer, an American called Henry (Harry) Nathan Sporborg. Originally an employee of General Electric of the US, he had been sent across the Atlantic in his mid-twenties to help set up BTH in 1902 as an autonomous subsidiary of GE. With an expertise in electrical engineering and power systems for trams and railways, he had been the chief architect of the Rugby plant's successful expansion and had been a Board director of the business since 1910. His had been an impressive career to date – but when an intense young RAF officer began conducting noisy experiments directly outside his Turbine Hall, Sporborg made it clear that he regarded the whole business as a tiresome distraction.

He took no interest in the extraordinary events of April 1937, but finally found the time late in August to attend a test run of the jet. Whittle organised it partly as a first demonstration for Hayne Constant, who travelled up from Farnborough for the day to see it. He planned to run the engine up to 14,000 rpm, which was 80 per cent of its theoretical maximum speed. After the jet started accelerating, however, Sporborg grew visibly alarmed. After fifteen minutes, the engine had reached 13,600 rpm and Sporborg's nerves could stand it no longer. He demanded it be shut down immediately. At a hastily convened meeting in his office, he announced that no further tests would be allowed to take it beyond 11,000 rpm. They were a danger, he said, to all concerned. Bombastic and opinionated, Sporborg was not interested in discussing the finer points of the jet's workings. Within weeks, he was indicating his intention to cancel BTH's involvement altogether.

Sporborg relented, insofar as he was prepared to let BTH go on manufacturing and assembling parts for Power Jets, but he had made up his mind that test runs of the engine posed a physical threat to his workforce. An alternative test site would have to be found. This was awkward for Whittle, not least because Power Jets had just bought a house for him in Rugby. As an RAF officer on the Special Duty List, it no longer made any sense for him to be based at the cottage in Trumpington, especially since he was now entitled for the first time to a marriage allowance on top of his basic salary. As their first real family home, he and Dorothy had lighted upon a suburban villa ('Broomfield') located in a cul-de-sac off one of the main roads out of Rugby. Whittle had no idea whereabouts he might have to continue with his project. Some anxious days ensued. Then he received a telephone call from Sporborg to say that BTH had after all found some space that could be made available. It was located seven miles north-east of Rugby, outside a

Fig. 9. BTH's disused foundry at Ladywood Works,
early in Power Jets' tenure

tiny market town called Lutterworth. Whittle made his way there
with Dudley Williams and Coll Tinling early in October to see
what was on offer.

It turned out to be a disused BTH site called the Ladywood
Works, surrounded by arable farmsteads and connected to the
main road by a private lane. The main premises comprised an old
foundry with two large brickwork bays, attached to a building
with ground and first floors that had obviously once provided
several small offices. There was also a workshop, about forty feet
square, where BTH had maintained several machine tools in
years past. Gas and electricity links had been cut off long ago, and
the only running water was a solitary domestic tap. Whittle was
unimpressed, perhaps even a little dismayed. But when he, Williams
and Tinling huddled round a table in Lutterworth's Denbigh Arms
public house for lunch, his two friends found ample reasons to
press ahead. BTH wanted only a peppercorn rent for a site that at
least offered plenty of floor space for future development, and the
distance from the plant in Rugby was just about manageable. An old

water well existed on the site, fed from a local spring, and BTH had promised to install a telephone. The company had also undertaken to pay for some modest restoration work. Since Power Jets had no money to pay anyone a commercial rent, Williams and Tinling soon talked Whittle round. Power Jets agreed to the relocation. A hand-painted sign, 'Power Jets Offices', went up on the wall (*Fig. 9*) and by December 1937 Williams was busy supervising the site's conversion into an engine-testing station.

So it was here, in a thoroughly incongruous rural setting, that Whittle embarked on a development programme to turn his unruly WU1 unit into a reliable engine, capable of running at high speed for long enough to persuade all parties that it could be a power plant for a 'jet plane'. Williams and Tinling attended to a modest rebuilding of the premises; Lance Whyte came up from London for regular business discussions; and they hired their first employee: Victor Crompton, another ex-RAF man who had been working as a laboratory technician in the Engineering Department at Cambridge and now joined Power Jets as Whittle's assistant, later to become the Works Manager. Meanwhile Whittle applied himself to his work. On most days, he either pored over drawings and test results at the foundry with only Vic Crompton for company, or drove back to Rugby to confer with the members of his small BTH team. For the next two years he devoted himself to a relentless process of testing, redesigning, rebuilding and testing again that stretched his abilities to the limit.

It stretched his relations with BTH to the limit, too. Many of its managers took their cue from Sporborg's attitude and had to be constantly chivvied by Whittle to provide the assistance he needed. Frequent misunderstandings, though, stemmed from two more fundamental difficulties which constantly plagued his relations with the Rugby factory. The first concerned the nature of the work itself: BTH manufactured massive turbine machinery and had no real concept of the delicate machine that Whittle was seeking to develop. As he himself ruefully confessed in retrospect, relying on BTH to turn out the component parts he needed had been 'a bit like expecting the makers of Big Ben to make a good job of a lady's wrist-watch'.[39] The second problem came down to Whittle's own personality. He could be extremely demanding. In the workplace, he was a perfectionist and applied meticulous standards to whatever tasks were at hand. In discussions over theoretical matters, his mind would fly ahead and leave others often struggling to keep up with him. And in both contexts he was for ever taking notes, which many found disquieting. These fed into diary entries that often caught a flavour of Whittle's own exasperation – especially with any individual engineers who seemed to him insufficiently on top of their own trade as turbine-makers. One extraordinary row centred on a fundamental aspect of aerodynamics known as 'vortex theory'. Whittle was startled to discover, late in 1937, that none of the engineers at BTH had any inkling of it. (It mattered hugely to the jet engine because it explained the behaviour of the air propelled from the turbine, which in turn dictated the need for the turbine's individual blades to be subtly twisted.) One of the BTH team, Forslind by name, tried to make light of the issue and incurred Whittle's wrath for weeks. The diary noted as much: '24 March. Talk with Forslind. He says he's always believed in the vortex, but thinks the presence of blades with small clearance nullifies it. <u>The chump</u>!'[40]

Whittle's often volatile dealings with BTH over the next few years confirmed what might easily have been predicted on the basis of his track record to date. He was a supremely gifted individual, but his relentless drive needed careful handling. Ideally, others would help him to work in the kind of environment he really needed – carefully structured where necessary, yet at the same time entirely open to his own way of doing things differently whenever this seemed to him likely to yield better results. Until he outgrew it, active service with the RAF had suited him perfectly in this respect (once he had survived that harsh apprenticeship), as, too, had his academic days at Cambridge. It was much less clear that he was suited to working in partnership with any business enterprise, even one drawn from the engineering world. BTH's unsympathetic managers, often obstructive and incompetent, caused him terrible anguish. (Lance Whyte, travelling up from London for the day, was more than once shocked to find how distressed he had become over some maddening oversight in the workshop.) If he was to flourish as the driving force behind his engine project, Whittle would need in due course to be linked up with a more enlightened workforce or perhaps assisted to build his own. In this sense, the managerial dimension to his project was going to be a key determinant of its success, almost as crucial as his progress with the engine itself. Whittle himself understood this from an early stage. Of those in Whitehall to whom he would later turn as guardian 'minders', some had a much better grasp of it than others.

When Whittle began to give lectures after the war about the origins of the jet, he gave himself permission to pass quickly over the interminable engineering problems encountered in the two years from mid-1937: 'I cannot possibly give an adequate picture of that heart-breaking period... Even if the whole lecture were confined to this period of testing, it would still be no more than an outline.'[41] A brief genealogy of the engine's successive designs, though, has to note three main stages. The WU1 that marked the jet's debut in April 1937 lasted until the autumn, at which point Whittle decided further modifications were ineffective and a wholesale reconstruction was needed (albeit recycling most of the first engine's constituent parts, since there was no budget for replacements). The resulting WU2 unit, assembled like its predecessor at the BTH plant, was shipped by lorry to the Ladywood Works over the Easter weekend of 1938. It looked nothing like the first engine: a much more compact combustion cylinder replaced the huge sausage-shaped pipe that had steered gas to the turbine in the WU1, and the new design was essentially symmetrical round its central axis (*Fig. 10*). With ten jet pipes leading from the back of the turbine, it also looked more obviously like an engine. From its very first run, though, it posed problems. One BTH engineer whom Whittle had come to respect greatly, Leslie Cheshire, had the temerity to suggest the WU2's component parts were not up to the job – cheekily asking, as Whittle noted in his diary, 'why we

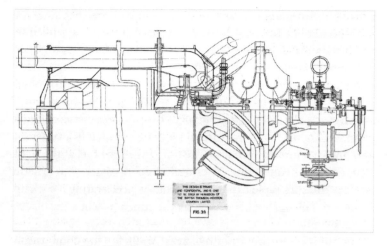

Fig. 10. The BTH design drawing for the WU2, autumn 1937

got our combustion equipment from Woolworths'. Three weeks later the WU2 self-destructed and had to be towed back to Rugby as salvage. Even Whittle was briefly disheartened by the severity of this setback. Hayne Constant came up to the BTH plant to see the shattered unit and to offer his sympathies. The two of them afterwards went to the restaurant at Rugby's railway station for lunch. Constant asked Whittle outright how he would feel about abandoning his solo effort at Lutterworth and being posted by the RAF to work as an engineer at Farnborough. 'It wouldn't break my heart' was Whittle's reply.[42] Within days, though, his spirits had revived. Work began on a second reconstruction. The revised design for this third engine, the WU3, was finally going to produce the properly working jet he had been seeking from the start.

Critical to this fresh design was a fundamental reappraisal of how to provide for the combustion process. Whittle's thermodynamic calculations required the compressed air from his honeycomb diffuser to be mixed with fuel (he soon settled on kerosene) and then burned at temperatures – or more accurately, with an intensity of heat – far beyond anything demanded of, say, the boiler fuelling a ship's steam turbine. And whereas the space for the flame under a ship's boiler might run to several square yards, the chamber for the jet had to be tiny – about the size, as Whittle always liked to say, of a standard suitcase. Within it, once ignited, the gas mixture had to burn continuously – in contrast to the cyclical combustion of the piston engine. (Popular descriptions of the jet engine often refer wrongly to its modus operandi as 'suck-squeeze-bang-blow', which is actually a description of what happens in a piston engine's cylinder. There is no bang inside a jet engine, merely a constant and finely controlled furnace.) The burning of the fuel at the right temperature – converting its potential energy back into kinetic energy – meant a rapid expansion of the air, accelerating it back up from 200 mph to about 700 mph by the time it reached the blades of the turbine.

In addition to constructing metal walls for the combustion chamber that would withstand fearsome temperatures, Whittle had to devise an appropriate shape for the chamber so that the airflow through it from diffuser to turbine would satisfy various requirements. One of the more important of these was that all the fuel, inserted into the mix near the air's point of entry, should have sufficient time to burn up completely before reaching the turbine. Ensuring the necessary time interval meant directing the flow through a chamber several feet long, hence the 'sausage' pipe on his WU1 design. For the ill-fated WU2, Whittle had devised a much better alternative – a shorter passageway that doubled up on itself inside a compact combustion chamber. Air was fed into it via ten separate discharge pipes from the compressor, nicknamed 'the elephant trunks'. Fuelled and ignited, the air as hot gas travelled down one passage from front to rear of the engine and was then sent round a hairpin bend to flow back along the second passage in the reverse direction. After the WU2's hasty demise, Whittle took this 'reverse flow' idea one critical stage further. Instead of one combustion chamber, the WU3 would have ten – one chamber for each of the elephant trunks from the compressor – and they would sit round the waist of the engine like a kind of giant buoyancy jacket. Each would be a tenth as big as the single chamber on the WU2, and would similarly house a passage doubled up on itself. Within each of the ten chambers, vaporised fuel would be injected at the point where the compressed air made its first 180° reversal. All ten would be cleverly interconnected so that just two spark plugs would be sufficient to ignite the combustion process, which would thereafter be self-sustaining. The ten burning gas streams would be combined before reaching the turbine – and would be reversed again to flow backwards into the turbine, so passing through it the 'right' way. The gas would then be propelled from the engine via the rear nozzle and a single exhaust pipe rather than the ten pipes used on the WU2.

This new design meant the WU3 took months to build – despite the fact that the rest of the engine, notably the whole compressor assembly, was largely cannibalised from the original engine – and only in September 1938 was it finally brought from Rugby to Lutterworth. It was fired for the first time on 10 October. The 'ten-can' combustion chamber immediately proved a hugely successful innovation. Whittle had arrived at a layout for his jet engine that laid the basis for a whole new industry: the design and

Fig. 11. Simplified diagram of the basic jet engine,
used for post-war training

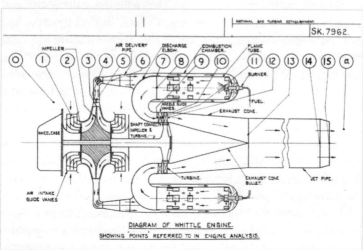

appearance of the WU3 are now broadly familiar to every student of aero-engineering. Indeed, when engineering instructors after the Second World War compiled a diagram to show the workings of 'the Whittle engine', the result fairly represented the structure of the WU3. Innumerable modifications would be made to it over the years ahead – notably in respect of the combustion process – but they were to involve refinements of its critical components while requiring no fundamental changes to the basic arrangement of the engine (*Fig. 11*).

As of the autumn of 1938, Whittle nonetheless faced a daunting range of practical difficulties, especially over the fuel system and combustion arrangement. Work on these led to a steady deterioration in Whittle's relations with the senior men at BTH. By December, the scene was set for a series of ugly confrontations that crystallised many of the reservations that each side had had about the other from the start. Just before Christmas 1938, a blazing row between Samuelson and Whittle seemed to presage a final parting of the ways. Both agreed it would be 'quite impossible to go on'.[43] That very evening happened to be the occasion of the Engineers Christmas Ball, a great event in Rugby's social calendar attended by all self-respecting members of the profession living in the East Midlands. Whittle and his wife went along and had a party of guests at their table. Hardly had they sat down before Fred Samuelson sailed into view, giving them all a cheery wave. He had had a terrible quarrel with Whittle that morning, he announced to the table, but they 'were not the sort of people to let it last as long as twenty-four hours!'. This bravado went down well with the ladies and Samuelson later invited the Whittles over to his table, going out of his way to be charming to Dorothy. It all helped restore a modicum of civility at the factory, and work on the second reconstruction of the engine continued apace. But Whittle's relationship with BTH, riddled with distrust, never properly recovered.

His relations with the Air Ministry's officials, meanwhile, were scarcely more trusting. Nothing revealed the Ministry's dismissive attitude more tellingly than the way in which it deliberately constrained Whittle's dealings with the government's own scientists and engineers at the RAE. The successful ignition of the first engine in April 1937 had made a big impression on the RAE, and most of its staff engineers were well aware that the gas-turbine project in Rugby depended entirely on Whittle's extraordinary determination to keep going. Making regular visits to Farnborough, Whittle drew steadily closer to Griffith's deputy, Hayne Constant, a dry bachelor whose reserved and cerebral manner intimidated many of those around him. Constant's penchant for severe dissection of technical issues held no terrors for Whittle, who soon began to see him as a powerful ally in the struggle to elicit a more positive response from Whitehall – 'He agrees with me that far more energy should be shown on the whole of the gas turbine problem'.[44] Whittle also conferred regularly with William Farren, who had moved from Cambridge to the Air Ministry in 1937 to become Deputy Director of Scientific Research. Farren was yet another brilliant Cambridge mathematician who had originally been drawn to flying as a young man in the First World War. It frequently occurred to Whittle that the logical outcome of his dealings with these kindred spirits would be a close partnership between Power Jets and Farnborough. The Air Ministry gave any notion of a partnership short shrift. Far from encouraging the two parties to work together, the Ministry made clear its disapproval of too close a liaison. Constant had to confess to Whittle more than once that he was withholding information at the Ministry's behest. Others cautioned him to the same effect. The best engineers in the aeronautical establishment, unquestionably fascinated by his jet project and ready to assist it, were discouraged from doing so. It might be conjectured that officials were deliberately cultivating two separate jet-engine initiatives, trusting that in due course each might usefully complement the other. Just such a de facto policy would emerge much later, but there is no evidence of it being consciously adopted in the pre-war years.

Far more plausibly, Whittle's activities were simply being squeezed aside as a distraction from the preparations for war. These were gathering pace, though many still doubted the Chamberlain government's resolve. A political row in May 1938 swept Swinton out of office. He was replaced as Air Minister by a former Post-master General, Sir Kingsley Wood, known in Whitehall as 'Little Sir Echo'. A thorough reorganisation of the Ministry followed and Sir Wilfrid Freeman, previously head of Research and Development (and knighted in 1937), had his fiefdom enlarged to cover all industrial production for the RAF as well as the R&D support for the service. George Bulman's brief, as noted already, was then widened in parallel with Freeman's extended responsibilities. Indeed, Bulman's authority within the Ministry was now on a par with his high reputation over the years. After the Munich Crisis in September 1938, Freeman decided to com-mission a new plant capable of turning out four hundred Merlin engines a month – it was an engine far superior to anything else available to the RAF. He sent Bulman to the Treasury to secure clearance on the costs. 'It now seems incredible,' recalled Bulman in his memoirs, 'but the fact is that I walked out of the Treasury in five minutes armed with verbal financial authority for £5 mil-lion [about £250 million today] to be confirmed in writing in a few days!'[45]

No such largesse came Whittle's way. He nonetheless per-severed – and even began in 1937–9 to contemplate some radical ways of spending money well beyond the budget for his engine. He had taken aboard the notion of an interceptor jet fighter from Tizard, and within months of the first ignition in April 1937 began sounding out makers of light aircraft about building a jet plane. The founding entrepreneurs behind one small firm, Phillips & Powis, met him at the BTH plant in August 1937.[46] An engineer who had already designed some tiny monoplanes for Phillips & Powis was a lively character called Fred Miles, who introduced himself to Whittle early in 1938. Whittle took Lance Whyte with him to the Savoy for a lunch with Miles and the three men talked in earnest about the notion of launching a small jet plane. 'We discuss the possible basis on which the aeroplane could be built,' noted Whittle in his diary that evening. '[Miles] hovers round the figure of £10,000 [about £½ million today]. Argues that the

Air Ministry would pay for it if the engine did its stuff. Would be willing to do the design work free. Does not hold out much hope of RR [Rolls-Royce] cooperation financially. Suggests we send him a rough specification.'[47] Another company keen to win a construction contract from Power Jets was General Aircraft, which had made a name for itself building a fighter biplane called the Hawker Fury and was currently making stretched-skin wings for the Spitfire. Its managers told Whittle, within days of the Savoy lunch with Miles, that they thought they could deliver an aeroplane for his jet within nine months.

The setback encountered with the WU2 engine at Lutterworth in May 1938 appears to have temporarily sidelined these conversations, but Whittle went on devoting plenty of time (and most of a rare family summer holiday on a farm in Devon) to further research into the potential of a jet-powered interceptor fighter. By late in October 1938 he was ready to commit his calculations to paper – and the result was the memorandum 'On the Jet Propelled Interceptor Fighter' quoted in the Prologue.[48] Anticipating war with Germany, he laid out a proposal in plain English, with only the barest of technical details, for the kind of fighter that he could see Britain urgently needed – and that he now believed had been made possible by his WU3 engine. It would offer, as he suggested with a rare flourish, a 'startling performance'. In any indictment of Britain's failure to exploit the jet as one of the great missed opportunities of the Second World War, this paper would rank as a key exhibit. Its eight pages rang with the same brilliance and self-belief as that youthful thesis of 1928 at Cranwell, fortified in 1938 with all that its author had learned across the intervening years. Whittle asserted as a simple truth that 'sheer performance in climb and speed is the major requisite' for any aircraft tasked with protecting London from German bombers. The engine still under wraps at Lutterworth would power a plane to 20,000 feet in less than four minutes and let it fly there at more than 500 mph. Almost as important under the circumstances of the day, it would power a plane that would be 'both cheap and capable of rapid production'. He attached to the memorandum a preliminary drawing of the plane that he had just completed with his assistant, Vic Crompton (*see Fig. 1*).

Britain's aircraft industry had many engine designers of great distinction – men like Roy Fedden, Frank Halford, Harry Ricardo and Arthur Rowledge (the real brain behind the Merlin) whose names were known across the world for their achievements with the piston engine. None of these individuals, though, had ever aspired to design an airframe. The industry could likewise boast several famous aircraft designers, men like Tommy Sopwith and Geoffrey de Havilland whose names had been legendary since the air war over the Western Front – or Sidney Camm, Reginald Mitchell and Roy Chadwick whose work on the Hawker Hurricane, the Supermarine Spitfire and the Avro Lancaster would one day earn them a similar status. But none of these luminaries had ever designed an engine, let alone built one from scratch. Whittle, in other words, brought to bear a unique combination of skills. He alone was comfortable designing both an aeroplane and the engine to power it. He was also, of course, a superb pilot.

The Ministry paid his 'Interceptor Fighter' paper no heed at all. Whittle submitted it scarcely a month after the Munich Crisis, hoping Prime Minister Neville Chamberlain's 'peace in our time' might provide a precious opportunity for the Ministry to explore his proposal. This was extraordinarily optimistic, since he was well aware that his whole project had just come close to being shelved altogether. Word had reached him, at the height of the scare over Hitler's designs on Czechoslovakia, that in the event of war he would be ordered to abandon his work in Rugby, probably to report for technical duties at Farnborough. The defusing of the crisis seemed to make no difference at all in this respect: there was no sign, over the following months, of Whittle's situation being given any further thought. His 'Fighter' memorandum drew no response, and his days in Rugby seemed indeed to be numbered. When he called at the Ministry in February 1939 to seek some clarification of his personal future, Farren explained with some apparent embarrassment that he could offer Whittle little reassurance 'in view of

the fact that we had not produced more results than we had...'.[49]
Apparently the Ministry had had enough of the repeated setbacks
to his programme since 1937. Its officials – men who until a few
years earlier had anticipated presiding for the foreseeable future
over an air force of biplanes with open cockpits – felt that the jet
concept had fallen some way short of the grand claims made for
it. As a result, said Farren, he himself 'was likely to find himself in
difficulties, having made promises based on [Whittle's] promises
which in effect were not being kept'.

At a chance meeting in Rugby with the Minister of Labour
a few weeks later, Whittle suggested the Air Ministry's attitude
towards him was 'rather chilly'. If this was meant to imply that
he was none too concerned, the state of his health suggested
otherwise. Concern over his career and status at the Ministry
were just another source of worry, to be added to the financial
problems of Power Jets, the sticky relationships at BTH and the
relentless struggle to conquer the technical problems of the jet
itself. For several months past, he had begun to suffer from signs
of debilitating anxiety that went far beyond the occasional fits of
hysterical laughter that he had experienced in 1937. In addition to
regular headaches, he was also being plagued by recurrent boils
and intermittent bouts of digestive trouble. In March 1938 he
drove to Leicester for a first session with a chiropractor, hoping
some alternative medicine might help him to recover the robust
health he had enjoyed as a youth. In the meantime, he continued
to rely on a more familiar remedy for stress, smoking fifty or sixty
Capstan Full Strength (unfiltered) cigarettes a day.

Whittle's ailments were an added strain on his marriage,
which by the end of the 1930s had problems of its own. The doctors
had warned Dorothy against having any more children after the
difficult birth of their first son. The arrival of a second son, Ian, in
November 1934 left her determined to avoid the risk of a further
pregnancy at all costs. By 1939 this had undoubtedly robbed the
marital home of the warmth and intimacy of earlier years.[50]
Whittle's workaholism can hardly have helped: he was toiling at
Lutterworth six days a week and spending most of his Sundays at

Broomfield sitting in an armchair, slide rule in hand, pondering the past week's test results.

While seeing too little of Dorothy and too much of his engine, though, Whittle was not entirely starved of female company away from home. Just before Christmas 1938, Williams and Tinling had found him a secretary. She was not the first young woman to try for the job, but Whittle had rejected other hopefuls after the briefest of trials. Mary Phillips was different. She met his exacting standards in taking dictation and typing, which instantly lightened his diary-keeping routines by letting him dictate notes in place of writing them all out. (The diaries nonetheless went on filling up. Whittle's need to set everything down in writing only seemed to grow more compelling over the years. As well as listing his phone calls and visitors, he was soon keeping a daily record of life's minutiae – the day's weather, the money spent on tips, the departure and arrival times of trains – with almost the same care that he lavished on engine-test results.) With strong, refined features that gave her a slightly patrician mien, Mary was twenty-eight and single, living with her elderly father with whom she shared a semi-detached house in Rugby's Bilton Road, a ten-minute walk from the Whittles' home. Within a matter of months, a strong bond had grown up between them and Mary had become indispensable.

For her part, she plainly adored her new boss from the start. In the otherwise all-male world of engineering, she was treated by Whittle with a courtesy and respect she had never encountered before in a series of unhappy office jobs in Rugby. She was always reliably discreet in her dealings with him in public, but they soon came to enjoy a working relationship that was none too formal in private. Mary was a great fan of Charlie Chaplin's films and the physical similarity between Chaplin and her employer was hard to ignore. Like the Hollywood star, Whittle was small with a strong head of dark brown hair and a modest moustache. He was also undeniably a handsome man, like Chaplin, with an impish twinkle in his eye that was part of what made him such a captivating speaker in front of an audience. Within a year or two,

Mary was teasing Whittle about the likeness, as she would go on doing through the war and into a long post-war correspondence. There were not many people in Whittle's life who felt able to take that kind of liberty with him. As the burden of his responsibilities for the jet engine grew ever more onerous, Mary brought a cheerfulness and humour to her secretarial duties that he badly needed.

Her employment prospects clouded within three months of her starting the job, when Hitler's Wehrmacht marched into Prague in March 1939 and it looked as though war with Germany might be imminent. Lawrence Tweedie warned Whittle he should once more prepare to abandon the jet project. Here was Whittle's single biggest worry of all – that despite his feverish efforts to complete testing of the third version of the engine as quickly as possible, he and the BTH team would simply be overtaken by events. The timing looked cruel. The engine was tested successfully on fourteen days of March, running comfortably up to 13,500 rpm, and the prospect of a jet flight was coming closer by the day. When Constant came up to Lutterworth at the end of the month, he confided to Whittle that he was now finally converted to the cause. 'He stated that he had changed his own opinion about the usefulness of the unit and was no longer [merely?] interested but regarded it as worthy of immediate application to aircraft.'[51] Whittle promptly resumed his quest for a plane, visiting the Gloster Aircraft Company in April 1939 to talk to its Chief Designer, George Carter, who was the acknowledged doyen of his profession. (The Spitfire's designer, Reginald Mitchell, had died of cancer the previous summer.) Carter and Gloster Aircraft's two illustrious test pilots, P.E.G. ('Gerry') Sayer and Michael Daunt, now heard of the jet engine for the first time and did not conceal their excitement: 'we agreed that we should try and get the Air Ministry to make official contact with the Gloster Company.'[52] Indeed, Whittle made a note of Carter telling him 'they had got a new machine coming along in which there might be considerable possibility of installing an engine like ours'.[53]

The Ministry, as ever, remained to be persuaded. Farren's boss, David Pye, told Tizard on 2 May that he was still pessimistic about

Whittle's position. Then, with a suddenness that surprised many of those close to the whole business, various conversations in Whitehall began to convey a subtly different message. On 12 May, Lance Whyte arranged a meeting with Pye and Farren, to implore that Whittle not be moved off the jet project at this point. He found himself pushing on an open door. 'Whyte's net impression,' noted Whittle later, 'was that for some reason unknown to him a generally much more favourable view of the engine was taken than ever before...'[54] Whittle's great concern was that a declaration of war might overtake his enterprise. But there was perhaps one other hidden dread lurking within the corridors of Whitehall, which may just have edged rather closer to the daylight – the awful fear that Germany, with its widely admired industrial prowess and rapidly expanding factory capacity, might secretly have forged ahead in the aeronautical arms race by developing a jet engine of its own.

v

Five days after Neville Chamberlain's apparently triumphant return from Munich on 30 September 1938, Whittle joined Lance Whyte for a private lunch at a flat on Grosvenor Square. The host was Air Commodore James Weir, younger brother of Lord Weir and a fellow director with him of the family company in Glasgow, G. & J. Weir. The Air Commodore had some interesting news for Whittle. The business in Glasgow had recently recruited an experienced German engineer called Räder. The man had come straight from working in the German aircraft industry, and had told his new Scottish colleagues that he had personal knowledge of several aeronautical engineers in Germany 'working on jet propulsion'. Whittle noted the news in his diary without comment. Perhaps it came as no surprise: Constant had told him more than a year earlier of reports that a highly efficient single-stage impeller had been successfully tested in Germany.[55]

In fact, the Germans' intense interest in the possibility of jet flight could hardly be doubted. There were more signs of it in the months after that Grosvenor Square lunch. In February 1939 the Institution of Mechanical Engineers in London hosted a lecture on gas turbines by a Dr Adolf Meyer of the huge Swiss company Brown Boveri. Its state-of-the-art turbine products – mostly manufactured, as it happened, in a plant at Mannheim in Germany – were built for industrial use, but Dr Meyer and his colleagues were much respected for their knowledge of the whole field and were just pioneering a switch from steam to gas (that is, compressed air mixed with a burning fuel). His talk drew an unusually large audience of German as well as British engineers and prompted a lively Q&A discussion. Whittle, attending the event with Bramson, could not resist speaking up for the potential of gas turbines as the aero-engines of the future.[56] Providing background reading for the IME lecture, meanwhile, was a timely run of articles published in the leading German aviation magazine *Flugsport*. It devoted many pages of its January and February issues of 1939 to 'A Survey of Patents Dealing with Thermal Air Jet Propulsion'.[57] Courtesy of the German Trade Commission in London, the series included copies of drawings that had been filed with Whittle's patent submissions, much to his dismay. It was read with grave misgivings by officials in the Intelligence Directorate of the Air Ministry. Their data-gathering efforts had been notoriously lacklustre for years past, but any noteworthy events in Germany were now receiving far more intense scrutiny in the wake of the Munich Crisis. The disclosure in *Flugsport* of so much information on jet propulsion stirred immediate suspicions. At this point in the arms race, the survey was surely more than just the quasi-academic exercise it purported to be. Had the magazine's editors perhaps got wind of a radical development in the Reich's research activities for the Luftwaffe, but prudently shrunk from publishing anything too specific? Intelligence sources within Germany were primed to look out for more clues. Rumours of a Nazi-backed jet soon began to circulate in Whitehall.

For those who were privy to the speculation, Frank Whittle's jet-engine project suddenly appeared in a rather different light.

As of March 1939, Whittle was afraid his project might be con-
demned to a lengthy postponement, perhaps even cancelled
altogether. It was, by Whittle's own account, 'perhaps the most
critical moment in the whole history of the development'.[58] Yet
by the close of July, the Air Ministry had authorised a renewal
of Whittle's special status, a fresh set of contract payments, a
new version of the engine and a new plane to make the most of
it. Official attitudes had been transformed in the space of three
months. So what had happened?

No doubt several factors contributed to this decisive swing
in official sentiment. Most obviously, the test results achieved at
Lutterworth from early May had begun to look much more persuasive, creeping ever closer to the performance specifications
that Whittle had predicted. His own personal commitment to
the jet also made a strong impression. He had always talked of his
RAF career as sacrosanct in the past. Now he was making clear
to everyone that he wished to see his project through to fruition,
even if this required his resignation from the service. And the
broader context of the work, meanwhile, looked more propitious,
too. Whittle was promising a new kind of interceptor fighter, and
this chimed perfectly with a drastic shift in British defence policy
that had involved a reappraisal of the role of the RAF. Until 1938,
its bombers had been given precedence in the belief that their
offensive capabilities would be decisive in any war; now fighters
were instead seen as the real key to RAF strategy, defending the
nation against enemy attack. By the middle of 1939, due in large
part to Freeman's leadership within the Air Ministry and to the
resolve of Air Chief Marshal Hugh Dowding at its head, Fighter
Command had been given paramount importance long enough
to have realigned priorities throughout the RAF and the aircraft
industry behind it.

However influential these various considerations, though, the
sheer suddenness with which Whittle's jet was reassessed leaves
room to wonder about the covert influence of Whitehall's intelligence reports. Some word of a rival jet programme in Nazi
Germany would certainly help to explain a dramatic change of

heart by David Pye, the Ministry's Director of Scientific Research
(DSR). He was scheduled to visit Lutterworth on 12 April to watch
a trial of the reconstructed WU3. Pye still took a gloomy view of
Whittle's prospects at this point, and a disappointing outcome to
the trial might have been fatal. Then fate took a hand. Cracks were
discovered in the vanes of the impeller, forcing a postponement
of Pye's visit. By the time the engine was ready for him to see it,
on 30 June, his attitude to the project had changed completely.

Pye was upbeat from the moment he arrived at the Ladywood
Works. Whittle and his team had their WU3 fully prepped in its
test shed for a demonstration run (*Fig. 12*). It did not let them down.
The engine accelerated smoothly up to 16,000 rpm, where it gave a
useful amount of thrust and ran without a blip for twenty minutes.
Visibly excited, Pye launched into a fulsome endorsement of Power
Jets' whole vision. He walked several times round the Works with

Fig. 12. The WU3 on its trolley bed, with 'porthole' doors
to be opened before ignition

Whittle and Lance Whyte, talking of plans for a rapid expansion of the site, the importance of renewing Whittle's personal contract – which, by chance, was due to expire that very day – and the practical advantages of having the Ministry take ownership of the project (much as Whittle and Whyte had proposed in vain almost exactly two years earlier). Then he broached the crucial next step:

> We discussed the possibility of a flight engine and it was agreed that we should aim at a light weight unit… Pye said that *he did not think there was any reason why we should not proceed at once with the unit for flight* [author's italics] and hinted strongly that we should be asked to tender for it so that that engine also would be Air Ministry property.[59]

Whittle had the perfect response to this. Dashing over to his office, he re-emerged with a blueprint that he had already compiled for a plane that could take the flight engine. Even in Whittle's typically deadpan account, it seems plain that Pye was amazed. When Whittle told him of plans for a successor to the WU3, which would be a flight engine, Pye urged him to push ahead without delay. He thought it likely to compare well with any existing RAF engine, even if it fell slightly short of expectations – and he readily agreed with Whittle 'that the aeroplane ought to be going on at the same time as the new engine'. A lively discussion followed about the possible timing. 'Whyte and I said that we could be flying within a year if the aeroplane was built at the same time as the new unit, and Whyte asked Mr Pye if he did not agree that we ought to aim for this…'[60] Yes, replied Pye, he most certainly did agree. And this could mean the RAF would have a prototype jet fighter by the summer of 1940…

By the time he had to leave for his train back to London, Pye – the great authority on the evolution of the piston engine – had buried all his past reservations. Whittle drove him to the station at Rugby and was treated to a memorable sermon:

> I had the curious experience of having him recite to me all the advantages of the engine. His manner of doing so was almost as

though he were trying to convert a sceptic. I was tactful enough
not to point out that he was preaching to the first of all converts.
It was a measure of the degree to which he was carried away by
his enthusiasm.[61]

Whittle had spent more than two years hoping for an excited
reaction of this kind. He was puzzled by Pye's conversion, but
nonetheless delighted. It tallied, in fact, with his own private
opinion that the WU3 finally confirmed the potential suggested
two years earlier by the fiery and frightening performance of the
WU1. When the head of the US aerospace corporation Pratt &
Whitney, Art Wagner, wrote to Whittle in 1987 to congratulate
him on the fiftieth anniversary of the first ignition – 'a remarkable breakthrough that revolutionized every facet of the aerospace
industry' – Whittle replied: 'To me, making the thing work was
more important than the invention...'[62] He had now made it work.

Whatever the full explanation for Pye's abrupt volte-face in
June 1939 – and the possible influence of a rival German programme seems not to have occurred to Whittle – the repercussions
followed at a brisk pace. A letter from the top contracts man at
the Ministry on 4 July assured Whittle there was no question of
his being posted away from Rugby. He could continue with his
project for at least the next twelve months, assuming the Treasury
agreed – 'and in the light of recent developments I feel sure that
they will'.[63] Whittle had waited a long time for this moment and
he seized it with characteristic bravura. He submitted two formal
memoranda within days that laid out detailed design proposals
for both the flight engine and the aircraft that would test it.[64] At
Whyte's suggestion, he christened the flight engine the 'W.1' (not
to be confused with the WU1).

The W.1's specifications, for any Whitehall readers unfamiliar
with the gestation of the jet since 1936, must have come as a shock.
Whittle proposed building an engine of consummate simplicity
that would weigh approximately 850 lbs. It would power its aircraft up to 40,000 feet in less than ten minutes and would fly at
speeds in excess of 500 mph. He provided fuel calculations for

speeds up to 700 mph. The papers made no references to the performance of the best available power plant of the day, but no informed reader in Whitehall would have needed them. The superbly crafted but high-maintenance Merlin engine now being installed in the RAF's Hurricane and Spitfire fighters weighed just over 1,600 lbs and delivered a top speed of around 350 mph. A Merlin-powered Spitfire could reach 34,000 feet in about a quarter of an hour, and that was its ceiling height.

George Bulman and his colleagues in the Ministry's Engines directorate again offered no response. Perhaps they never even saw these latest papers, so immersed were they in supervising a breakneck production of new aircraft that might be needed by the RAF within months or even weeks. So there ensued a curious splintering of responsibilities between the different sections of the Air Ministry that might never have been tolerated under normal circumstances. Plans for the construction of a jet aircraft were overseen by an RAF officer, Group Captain Liptrot, who was based in Adastral House on Kingsway. He and a small team of fellow uniformed officers were now as supportive of Whittle's project as were Pye and the RAE engineers. Initial discussions with the aircraft manufacturers raced ahead through July and August. The uniformed branch welcomed Whittle's active participation in their choice of a manufacturer for the jet plane. General Aircraft and Shorts were sidelined in favour of Gloster Aircraft Company, not least because Whittle had already begun forging a good relationship with Gloster's designer, George Carter, who was one of his warmest supporters. The Ministry confirmed in the last week of August 1939 – less than eight weeks since Pye's Damascene conversion at Lutterworth – that Whittle's design proposals would be taken as the basis for the new plane. Work on it would continue even in the event of war. So Whittle felt now that he had all the backing he needed to start serious work on the actual flight engine.

In the very same week that Britain's Air Ministry agreed to Whittle's design proposals, on 27 August 1939, a tiny jet-powered monoplane took off from a factory airfield close to the Baltic coast of Germany owned by the Heinkel aircraft company. It was the first outing for the jet plane that Ernst Heinkel had commissioned from his young protégé Hans von Ohain, and that had been under construction at the Heinkel plant since April 1936. Despite a small bird disappearing into its 'He S3' engine just as it left the tarmac, the 'He 178' remained airborne for six minutes and landed safely. How soon news of this momentous event reached Whitehall is tantalisingly unclear. A file in The National Archives dated 1939 contains a black-and-white photograph of this first plane ever to have flown with no propeller. The file carries no details of the picture's provenance, but a German caption suggests it was extracted sometime later from a magazine. If the Air Ministry learned more immediately of the He 178's flight, it must have had access to a well-placed source. This seems entirely possible. Eight months later, the Air Ministry was to launch a monthly report of 'Scientific Intelligence Summaries' and early editions of the report would carry explicit references to someone in Germany who had provided secret information on Heinkel's jet programme. (Rather mysteriously, he was reported to have found his way to London 'and it may be worth repeating here that he is available for interrogation'.[65]) Perhaps this same individual could have reported the He 178's first flight soon after it happened. Whatever the truth, no word of the He 178 reached Whittle.

Even had it done so, it could hardly have added to his motivation. As a former fighter pilot, Whittle was immensely proud to think that he was now on the brink of delivering a new kind of plane that might actually alter the balance of any air war decisively in the RAF's favour. His only regret was that events were moving too fast: he still needed more time to get a jet plane into the air. His mixed emotions were evident in a letter that he wrote to Hayne Constant on the first day of September: 'My feeling is that as soon as we settle this combustion business, we are practically home... P.S. It looks as though we are about a year too late.'[66] Two days later, he sat down in his small office at the Ladywood Works with Mary Phillips and his BTH assistants to listen to Prime Minister Chamberlain's Sunday morning wireless broadcast from Downing Street. The war had begun.

5

The Jet and the Dragonfly

September 1939 to May 1940

i

Britain's reluctance to mobilise immediately for all-out hostilities with Germany and the curious drift into a state of 'phoney war' averted a sense of national crisis that might have swept the jet project away. In fact, having taken such a favourable turn at the end of June, Whittle's situation only went on improving. The war brought no immediate inconvenience for him personally, except that he 'could no longer walk about in disguise' as he told a friend, and had to dress in uniform (as he anyway preferred to do). On the other hand, it ensured there would be no respite for the Ministry's technical departments as they went on desperately preparing the RAF for war, leaving all their officials – with the sole exception of Tweedie – little or no time to second-guess papers relating to Power Jets. In keeping with the new groundswell of support for the company, this paperwork included an extraordinary surge of fresh contracts from the Air Staff in Adastral House and the promise of more cash than had been imaginable just nine months earlier.

Up to August 1939 the Air Ministry had paid Power Jets a total of just £10,300 (just over £½ million today). Two weeks into the war, Whittle took a call from Tweedie informing him 'that the Air Ministry have decided to give Power Jets an order for a new engine of new design in addition to the W.1'.[1] This would be worth several times the pre-war disbursement. By the start of November, Power Jets could look forward to government payments for continuing research on the experimental WU3 engine, for the supply of a finished W.1 engine and a successor engine, to be called the W.2, plus the cost of all necessary spare parts. And within weeks it was confirmed that Power Jets would receive a formal order for the first jet plane, a fighter with the official specification E.28/39, on the understanding that the actual building of the plane would be sub-contracted to Gloster. (The plane was later christened 'the Pioneer', but the name never gained much traction and it remained the E.28/39 for most purposes.) The Ministry even agreed, as a way of extracting Treasury approval for an additional payout, to buy the WU3 engine for £7,600. Truly, Christmas came early for Whittle in 1939.

As important for his state of mind, he was also being fêted by his peers for what he had accomplished with his engine. George Carter, the Chief Designer at Gloster, had agreed to work on the E.28/39 almost entirely on the strength of his conversations with Whittle in the summer, without actually seeing the magical beast that could fly with no propeller. Visiting Lutterworth on 5 September for his first encounter with it, the fifty-year-old Carter was almost lost for words. He wrote to Whittle the next day 'to express my sincere admiration for the great work you have done in connection with your engine and for the very remarkable results you have now achieved'.[2] He spent a week going through a file of Whittle's projections for the E.28/39, then wrote a second note to endorse their feasibility: '... I confirm my earlier impressions that the association of this engine with a fighter aircraft presents no special difficulties so far as can be ascertained from a brief general survey of this project.'[3] This was a signal tribute to Whittle personally. The production line at Gloster's had been going flat out on the delivery of Hawker Hurricanes since the start of 1939. Yet Carter and his team saw no obstacle, at this of all moments, to contemplating a tie-up with an engine-design outfit that was virtually a one-man band. Whittle was invited over to the Gloster factory the next day and shown a preliminary General Arrangement drawing for the kind of plane they thought would suit his engine. It had an 'all-up' weight of 4,800 lbs. Whittle insisted the first jet plane should be stripped of all non-essentials 'to go all out for maximum performance' – with a weight of 2,800 lbs. Those of Carter's colleagues who were meeting Whittle for the first time were astounded by his grasp of aircraft design. 'They agreed that there was a good deal of force in these arguments and decided to proceed on this basis.'[4]

Gloster was part of the larger Hawker Siddeley Aircraft Ltd, one of whose directors was Tommy Sopwith, whose colourful career to date had included founding the firm that made the celebrated Sopwith Camel in the First World War. Carter wasted no time getting him to Lutterworth to see the jet engine for himself. Several of the RAE's engineers, including Whittle's close Cambridge friend Arnold Hall, were there the same day. All were deeply impressed by a flawless demonstration of the WU3. The RAE men told Whittle he could rely on their 'utmost assistance' in developing the E.28/39. Not to be outdone, the irrepressible Sopwith confirmed his firm's readiness to start on it immediately. Lance Whyte penned a record of the discussion, pointedly copied to Pye at the Ministry, noting 'all parties were agreed… the urgency of the situation justified the immediate giving of the word "Go" to all people concerned, so that no time may be lost'.[5] Nor was Sopwith only concerned to back Gloster's work on the airframe. He was so astonished by the jet that he insisted the entire top executive cadre of his group's engine division, Armstrong Siddeley, travel the short distance to Lutterworth from Coventry the next day to witness another run. The discovery of such a radical development on their own doorstep within a few weeks of war being declared seemed to them all quite extraordinary. Whittle was soon being given VIP lunches at Armstrong Siddeley's plants at Coventry and Kenilworth as they sought to capture the job of turning out future jet engines on a production line.

But, of course, an option to make the first 100 engines had been awarded to BTH early in 1936, as part of the deal to secure the

Rugby firm's services. So now that the jet project appeared to be passing beyond the experimentation stage, some critical choices would have to be made. Despite the frequent and often acrimonious quarrels over the two reconstructions of the first engine, BTH's executives had no intention of dropping their involvement with the jet. Bob Collingham, having stepped into Samuelson's shoes as Chief Turbine Engineer, was only too well aware that other Midland firms might try to lure away the genius behind it. A blunt Yorkshireman, Collingham repeatedly pressed Whittle in September to talk about their future together, even suggesting to him at one point that BTH had tentative plans to build a shadow factory for large-scale production of the W.1 when it was ready.

Whittle was carefully non-committal. Yet another confrontation would have been ill-timed at this point. He had important work in hand with BTH engineers like Leslie Cheshire whom he had more or less co-opted onto the project team. Whittle had conceived a new way of locking the blades of a turbine into its central hub, by giving the root of each blade a 'fir-tree' shape that could be slotted into a matching aperture. The exact specifications were still being refined with BTH's help – and the eventual outcome would yield an inspired design that is still employed for turbine blades to this day. While still in daily contact with BTH, though, Whittle had by now made up his mind to look elsewhere for a manufacturing partner. He had finally given up any hope of the Rugby firm delivering the high-quality workmanship critical for jet engines. Successive breaches of good faith had left him feeling doubtful about the directors' real intentions, but he was in no doubt at all that lax management of the turbine plant had led to a series of avoidable delays. (A few months into 1940, Whittle would sit down to write a formal appraisal of BTH's performance for the Air Ministry. He gave the firm's employees credit where he thought it due, but in general his verdict was harsh. 'It seemed impossible to fire the imagination of the people concerned with the nature of the scheme and they always treated the job from a purely business point of view.'[6] His meticulous critique ran to five closely typed pages.)

His years of working with BTH had left Whittle with a broad conviction that was far more important than all the piecemeal lessons he had learned in Rugby about the gulf – to use his own metaphor – between building Big Ben and creating a lady's wrist-watch. He had come to believe that the successful production of a working jet engine would require him to supervise the evolution of the manufacturing process, going far beyond making occasional amendments to any prototype. Those responsible for supervising the manufacturing of the engine had to understand the science behind its design. They also needed to have a sound grasp of the particular manufacturing techniques that had been developed during the making of the initial prototypes. Since Power Jets (i.e., he and a small band of BTH men) had effectively hand-built the first engine, the company had, in his view, to remain in charge of developing it through to the point of line production – albeit in close association, at every stage, with the eventual manufacturer. He would seek to build a substantial company at Lutterworth accordingly.

This was a breathtakingly bold aspiration. Building up any fresh enterprise, in a country at war, would be at best problematic. Making the task even harder, Whittle would also be aspiring to a kind of specialised design-and-development role at Power Jets for which the aircraft industry had no obvious template. Engines were almost invariably designed and developed by teams that were closely integrated with the line-production function. Men like Arthur Rowledge at Rolls-Royce and Frank Halford, working with de Havilland and more recently Napier, were superb mechanical engineers coordinating the resources of large, established firms. Power Jets had yet to acquire any substantial resources at all – Lutterworth's permanent staff at the outbreak of the war comprised Victor Crompton and Mary Phillips, plus two nightwatchmen and their dog, a mongrel called Sandy from Battersea Dogs Home. And even assuming Whittle could pull to-gether an operation capable of assembling hand-built engines, he would then need an industrial partner willing and able to respond to meticulous instructions in turning the prototype into an engine fit to be made on a line. As an engineer and mathematician of rare gifts, he had shown that he was capable of predicting the jet's behaviour to the *n*th degree before it even existed. Now the manufacture and assembly of its parts would need to respect his design accordingly. He would need subcontractors prepared to work with him in novel ways, acknowledging his unique grasp of a whole new field of engineering. Whatever the difficulties, the jet engine's potential had to be realised urgently in the interests of the nation. Under his lead, Power Jets would deliver it.

He set off for this goal by insisting that Lance Whyte, Dudley Williams and Coll Tinling join him working in Lutterworth on a full-time basis. Pat Johnson had recently returned to active duty – having left the Air Force in 1932 to pursue his City career as a chartered patent adviser – and Whittle prevailed on the RAF to post him, too, to Power Jets. (Johnson supposed that he was going to be needed as a test pilot for the first jet plane, but soon knew better. 'I rapidly found myself immersed in a lot of miscellaneous duties, each of which was more essential at its time than flying.'[7]) Much of the day-to-day administration of the Works would fall to this loyal quartet. Whittle also turned to a serving Wing Commander ten years older than himself and a rank above him – George Lees, who had been one of his first instructors on the Cranwell apprenticeship course of 1923–6. Lees had followed his protégé's career admiringly for fifteen years. Now he became his de facto deputy, known to all as 'Daddy' Lees. There was indeed a kind of father/son relationship between them. Lees was always at hand to offer the benefit of his experience and Whittle often turned to him for his advice and common sense as well as practical assistance with the needs of the day.

Then the search began for the first engineers and draughtsmen. Collingham, briefly eager to please, agreed to the loan of Leslie Cheshire, just the first of several BTH men who asked to remain working full-time on the jet project. (Whittle told Collingham one morning that 'he would get a shock if he knew how many BTH employees had applied to Power Jets…') They joined a steadily growing payroll: Power Jets had fifteen employees by the end of

December 1939, and twenty-five by the end of January 1940. Whittle gloried in the business of building up a close-knit team, displaying all the enthusiasm and natural authority that he had shown in running Cranwell's Model Aircraft Society as a teenaged apprentice. There was something special about this 'external' recruitment process from the outset. Vacancies had to be advertised with no specific details at all. Dozens of applications were nonetheless received for every job and Whittle suspected that many of the young engineering applicants had a shrewd idea of what was afoot at the Ladywood Works despite its Top Secret status. Perhaps, for many of them, the secrecy surrounding the project only added to its appeal. Choosing among them, he almost exclusively selected young men graduating with the highest honours and awards from the finest university faculties in the country. (Several were Cambridge men, but certainly not all.) He was looking not just for employees but for disciples, the best and brightest of the coming generation of aero-engineers in Britain who would measure up to the demands of a new era that they themselves could do much to shape. It is striking that he found so many of them – gifted young men ready to take up employment in a ramshackle group of buildings in the middle of the Leicestershire countryside. And whatever their motives for joining, it seems plain enough why almost all of them stayed: they soon fell under the spell of Whittle's personal charisma. One of the early recruits, Reg Voysey, later recalled:

> The thing I most remember about Frank Whittle at that time [c.1940–41] was his total absorption in what he was doing – a total concentration which impinged itself on the atmosphere surrounding him. It was very hard for anybody to evaluate him, because he was a many-sided person who had a charming naïveté. He trusted people, and believed that everybody was motivated by a common good. I had the utmost respect for him as a leader and, of course, for his genius.[8]

Later Voysey would become less enamoured of Power Jets as a business, but he remained in awe of Whittle's leadership in the workplace for the rest of his life.

As for the bricks and mortar of that workplace, the Ladywood Works began at last to resemble a serious industrial enterprise. Another of the new recruits later provided a good guide to the site as it was to appear in May 1940, by which time there would be more than forty employees.[9] The two bays of the old foundry were given concrete floors and were equipped with heavy work benches. (The fuselage of an old Hawker Hart bomber was hung from the roof of one bay, and new arrivals would be kidded that Whittle planned to fly it again once a jet engine had been installed in its tail.) The ground-floor accommodated two engineers' offices and a small chemical laboratory. The upper floor housed Accounts and Buying departments plus a drawing office, directors' offices and Whittle's own private room. To help furnish all these, Tinling and Williams brought up the modest contents of their General Enterprises office on Piccadilly. In the large workshop just across the driveway, different areas were segregated from each other as a machine shop, a sheet-metal-working station and a welding department. Along one wall was a row of alcoves, each equipped for the testing of combustion chambers. (Combustion was still the single most troublesome aspect of the evolving engine.) And then there was the most important feature of all: the engine test shed, a modest space enclosed by a brick wall where the one and only jet engine yet in existence slumbered on its trolley between one fiery test and the next.

For mere mortals in the service of the engine, meanwhile, living quarters were found for the new arrivals in and around the local town. These were less than palatial, but all made the best of it. Williams' wife Helen later recalled the gamekeeper's cottage that she and her husband leased: 'It was terribly primitive with two up and two down, one small sink and water from a well which was some distance away.'[10] Lutterworth had several pubs and two larger establishments, the Hind Hotel and the Denbigh Arms, which could help with meals for visitors to the works and provide overnight accommodation when it was needed.

Their facilities were soon in regular demand. The local railway station with its London North Eastern Railway (LNER) line down to London's Marylebone Station delivered a steady trickle of visitors, not least from the RAE in Farnborough. The most frequent caller was Hayne Constant, who had been converted to the jet's cause rather sooner than had David Pye. Visiting in October, Constant told Lance Whyte that Pye had asked him for his advice on 'the whole problem of the wartime development of jet propulsion engines and aircraft'. He had told Pye that it was no time to be ambivalent: 'there were only two proper courses for the Air Ministry to take in relation to the Whittle Engine: either to drop it altogether or to do everything to force its development [ahead] so that it could be of military value in this war.'[11]

But could jet fighters flying 500 mph at 33,000 feet really be delivered to the RAF soon enough to make a difference? Two early discussions between Power Jets, Gloster and RAE representatives, in October and November 1939, took a sanguine view of the answer.[12] Carter, a hard-headed veteran of the aircraft business, thought prototypes of the E.28/39 might be ready by October 1940. Lance Whyte even submitted a formal memorandum to the Air Ministry, proposing that the W.1 engine might in the meantime be flight-tested in an existing aircraft.[13] (The idea attracted some support from the RAE – adding the W.1 to an Avro Anson was thought to be one possibility – but the Ministry took it no further.) Constant, committing himself wholeheartedly to the rapid development option, thought 'small-scale production [of an engine] could be reached in about eighteen months'. The axial-compressor engine always favoured at Farnborough would not be abandoned. (Indeed, no fewer than seven axial-compressor designs were to be tested there – all assigned girls' names from Alice and Anne in 1938–9 to Freda and Doris in 1941–2 – and the progress made with them would prove critical to the development of the jet engine in the long term.) The RAE would continue with its own research programmes and a complementary relationship between it and Power Jets could now – at last – be encouraged. But Constant readily conceded the kind of engine being championed at Farnborough by Arnold Griffith 'was much further from being a practical job' – and there was no longer any ducking the fact that

'Power Jets had already got an engine working'.[14] As for Whittle himself, he never had a shred of doubt that a war plane could be delivered in quite short order. As an experienced test pilot, he was already presenting his peers with designs for the inside of the cockpit on the putative fighter that might make it easier to fly. And through all these discussions, it was tacitly agreed by all that Whittle's direction of the project would go on being the key to success. One of his RAF colleagues, Squadron Leader 'Mac' Reynolds, reported back to him a conversation with Pye's deputy, William Farren, at the Air Ministry in September: 'he asked Mr Farren what the position would be if by chance a bomb eliminated Whittle, and Mr Farren's reply was that we should all be sunk in that case.'[15]

Two important visitors early in the New Year left Whittle more confident than ever that his plan to equip the RAF with jet fighters was realistic. He had heard very little from Sir Henry Tizard since the summer of 1937 and was delighted to receive him at Lutterworth on 24 January 1940. The castings had only just arrived for machining work to begin on the W.1 – with some machines newly installed on the site – but the WU3 engine was ready for inspection and its state of readiness seems to have taken Tizard completely by surprise. He reacted to a faultless run by declaring rather grandly that 'a demonstration which does not break down in my presence is a production job'. He offered Whittle his personal congratulations on 'a really practical engine' and the two men eagerly exchanged thoughts on next steps. Whittle outlined his plans for the W.2 and explained why he thought 'it would be a very great advance upon Engine W.1' – swapping the W.1's water-cooled turbine for an air-cooled design, for example – while Tizard speculated about the desirability of a twin-engined aircraft that he thought might make the most of its potential. (He would push this idea hard over the next few months, prompting the Air Ministry to ask Gloster Aircraft for a design.) Implicit in everything Tizard said was the need to press ahead quickly, though he only alluded in passing to a consideration he may not have felt able – or knowledgeable enough – to say much about:

There are vague rumours of German applications of the gas turbine to flight which [Tizard] thinks may be along considerably more complicated lines to [*sic*] ours, based on Swiss work [;] though he has no evidence that Germany are definitely on this, the possibility is another reason for getting ahead as rapidly as possible.[16]

Both men agreed on the need to begin thinking immediately about ways of manufacturing any successful design. Plainly, the Lilliputian enterprise at Lutterworth with which Whittle proposed to assemble his first prototypes was a far cry from the kind of heavy industrial plant required to turn out battle-ready engines by the score. He told Tizard he was anxious to talk about a future production partnership, but also to have his support for experimental production at the Ladywood Works. The fast-expanding Power Jets wanted to gain experience 'on development manufacture...' – a clumsy phrase to pull together two activities, designating the greyish area that would link the first to the second.

The winter weather over the following days was severe: the BBC pronounced it the coldest winter since 1894. Heavy snow blocked the roads around Lutterworth and forced Whittle to travel to and from the site by train. But the drifts did not deter Arthur Tedder, the resolute Air Vice Marshal who had been brought into the Air Ministry by Freeman in 1938 to run its Research and Development arm. (This left Freeman himself, though formally responsible for these activities, much more time to concentrate on the all-important task of overseeing aircraft production.) A rising star in the top ranks of the service, Tedder was to play an important part in Whittle's life over the course of 1940. He had previously held several prominent posts, including command of all RAF stations in the Far East in 1937–8, and was a man renowned for his shrewdness and practical good sense. (He would rise to the very top eventually: his distinguished wartime career included being appointed Supreme Deputy Commander of the Allied Expeditionary Force under General Eisenhower in 1944.) Tedder had spent the first months of the war adjudicating on the prospects of success for numerous development ventures, insisting that all should be thoroughly investigated – however fanciful they appeared to be. One of them, according to his post-war biographer, was the helicopter. A practical machine had been given a promising demonstration in the United States in the middle of September 1939. Tedder had taken note of it, but decreed that its potential 'had to be sacrificed, for the time being, in the interests of more immediately vital aircraft'.[17] The jet engine might have suffered the same fate, despite Freeman's interest in it, had Tedder not been converted to its cause. He himself was no engineer. When Tizard had first outlined the basic workings of the jet – and explained that the higher it went, the better it worked – Tedder told him he would have dismissed the same explanation from anyone else as a confidence trick. But the more he had learned of the jet from Pye and his colleagues, the more it had intrigued him. He knew that Freeman wanted the jet engine to be given full support. Within days of the outbreak of the war, Tedder had given orders that nothing should be allowed to impede its progress.

Tizard's response to seeing the jet in action prompted Tedder to set off for Lutterworth himself. His official car made it to the site in swirling snow as darkness fell on the late afternoon of 29 January, bringing Tedder up from London in the company of Whyte and Squadron Leader Mac Reynolds.[18] Whittle took them straight to the engine. By his own recollection, Tedder was slightly alarmed by its ramshackle appearance, sitting 'in one corner of what looked like, and I believe was, a derelict motor garage…' He must have wondered if his difficult journey had really been worthwhile. But when the jet burst into life, all his doubts were dispelled. He was transfixed by its performance, 'the glowing combustion chamber and the blazing blue jet flame roaring out into the open…'[19] He told Whittle he had been thrilled by earlier reports of the engine, and was impressed now to find it delivering a thrust even greater than predicted. Before leaving to drive across the Cotswolds to visit Carter and his team at Gloster, Tedder promised Whittle his full support. As he wrote to him a couple of days later: 'It really is a fascinating and impressive job and, having seen it, I shall certainly feel even more than before that it is up to me to do all I can to help it forward.'[20]

ii

Many of the most illustrious names in the British car industry of the interwar years belonged to factories scattered around the Coventry area of the Midlands where Whittle had grown up. One of them was the Hillman Motor Car Company, founded in 1907 by William Hillman. He had six daughters, one of whom married a young solicitor called Spencer Bernau Wilks. Five years later, in 1921, Hillman died and Wilks took over the management of the family company. The following year, he gave his eighteen-year-old brother Maurice a job on the shop floor as a trainee mechanic. Spencer proved to be a shrewd businessman, and Maurice – benefiting from a two-year stint with General Motors in Detroit in the late twenties – became an auto-engineer of some note. Under their combined leadership, Hillman prospered. But in 1929 the business was acquired by another, equally ambitious pair of brothers in the motor trade, Billy and Reggie Rootes. The Wilks brothers fell out with them and moved on together to work for another Coventry car firm, Rover Company. They were still at Rover in 1940, Spencer as Managing Director and Maurice as Chief Engineer, and their partnership was well on its way to becoming one of the legends of the industry. Rover was making solidly respectable saloon models at the upper end of the price range and, having weathered some lean times in the Depression years, enjoyed a reputation as one of the most profitable firms in the British car industry.

It happened that Maurice Wilks' wife had been at school with Nancy Tinling, wife of the Power Jets director, and they were still close friends. At some point in the New Year of 1940, as the result of a conversation between the two wives that Nancy relayed to her husband, it occurred to Coll Tinling that Rover might be a much more satisfactory candidate than BTH as the kind of reliable manufacturing partner he knew Whittle had in mind for Power Jets. Whittle welcomed the suggestion. He had lost all patience with Harry Sporborg and BTH, and his talks with Armstrong Siddeley had petered out. He told Tweedie this was 'chiefly because of the personalities involved' – John Siddeley was a notoriously autocratic figure, not at all the kind of partner that Whittle was seeking for the future – but he had also backed away because of his long-standing fear of being swallowed whole by one of the leviathans of the traditional aircraft industry. Rover had no aero-engine turf to defend. It seemed the firm might nonetheless offer Power Jets a more extensive range of engineering skills and facilities than BTH had ever mustered. Indeed, since 1937 Rover had been one of several car firms enlisted into the shadow-factory scheme organised by Swinton and Freeman. It had built a plant in the Acocks Green area of Birmingham, equipped at the Air Ministry's expense, to turn out Hercules and Pegasus engines under the guidance of their designers at Bristol Aeroplane. The Rover/Bristol relationship had not always worked smoothly: Rover had criticised Roy Fedden's design work and had constantly tried to improve on it, to little avail. Fedden would share his irritation over it with Whittle a year later ('It was evident that Fedden felt very sore about this'[21]) but as of January 1940 the works at Acocks Green looked to Whittle much like the kind of designer/producer arrangement he was envisaging for his jet engine – and so it came about that Maurice Wilks was invited to Lutterworth for lunch.

He braved the snowy conditions to join Whittle, Tinling and Williams at the Denbigh Arms on 27 January. Their discussion went well and within days a second meeting was convened, this time at Rover and including Spencer Wilks. It was mooted that Rover might invest a hefty chunk of capital in Power Jets – perhaps £50,000 (£2½ million today) for a 10 per cent slice of the equity – as part of a close partnership on the jet's development, to be followed by subcontracts to manufacture line models. But before going any further, said Spencer Wilks, he planned to consult the Ministry. He and George Bulman spoke by telephone later the same day.

Plate 1. Up through the ranks: Whittle as an apprentice rigger (*top left*) at RAF Cranwell in July 1926, presenting a beaming Under-Secretary of Air, Sir Philip Sassoon, with a model made especially for him; as a proud cadet that autumn (*above*), starting his 1926–8 course at Cranwell College; and as a newly-promoted Flying Officer (*left*), taken for his wedding in May 1930 – seven years too soon for a married man's allowance.

Plate 2. One naysayer and two enthusiasts: Dr A. A. Griffith (*left*) who as head of the Air Ministry Laboratory listened to Whittle expounding his ideas in 1929 and then buried them; and 'Coll' Tinling (*below left*) with Dudley Williams, ex-RAF pals who sought out Whittle in 1935 and offered to find him some investors.

Plate 3. Another mission accomplished: Whittle and his wife, Dorothy, on the day he collected his First Class degree in the Mechanical Sciences Tripos at Cambridge in the summer of 1936, aged twenty-nine.

Fig. I.

Air Commodore Frank Whittle, C.B.E., R.A.F., M.A., (Hon.) M.I.Mech.E., F.R.Ae.S.,
and the BTH men who comprised the team which designed and manufactured for
Power Jets, Ltd., the first experimental jet-propulsion gas turbine ; and subsequently the flight engine which was installed in the first successful jet-propelled
aeroplane in the world—Flown in England, 15th May, 1941.

Plate 4. Recalled with pride: the opening page of a brochure produced by British
Thomson-Houston immediately after the war, making the most of a relationship
that helped Whittle to get started but later often left him close to despair.

Plate 5. Two of Whittle's early champions: Henry Tizard (*left*) in 1937, a portrait taken to mark his receipt of a knighthood for his work on radar; and Air Marshal Arthur Tedder (*below*) in February 1944, shortly after his appointment as Deputy Supreme Commander for the D-Day landings.

Plate 6. The indefatigable secretary: Mary Phillips, who joined Whittle at the start of 1939 and devoted herself tirelessly to her role for almost ten years. After her health collapsed in 1948, she was to remain virtually bedridden until her death in 1972.

Plate 7. Triumph and tribulation: Whittle's historic handshake (*above*) with Gloster's chief test pilot P. E. G. ('Gerry') Sayer on 15 May 1941 after the successful maiden flight of the E.28/39; and his welcome to the Ladywood Works in July 1941 (*below*) for John Moore-Brabazon, the Minister for Aircraft Production whose constant requests for news left Whittle feeling 'like a hunted man'.

Plate 8. Rest and recreation on the mission to America, June–August 1942: with a secretary beside the ocean at Lynn, Massachusetts (*left*), taking a break from meetings at General Electric; and at Malibu Beach, California (*below*) with new-found friends whose company Whittle enjoyed for ten riotous days as a house guest in Santa Barbara.

Bulman was aghast. Tizard and Tedder had just come away from Lutterworth signalling their joint intention to put the jet engine on a list of 'potential war winners' to be given 'Priority' status. Such a precipitous decision was alarming enough to an official schooled for years in the cautious business of engine procurement. And now here was Whittle, a man with virtually no physical resources of his own, talking about plans for line production with one of the country's vital shadow-factory firms! Spencer Wilks' call prompted a flurry of departmental minutes about what on earth had been going on at Power Jets in recent months. It was no longer possible to ignore Whittle's project as a piece of long-term research for the Pending tray. The Engines directorate would have to take an immediate interest in the future of the jet. The timing was poor: hugely overworked since the outbreak of the war, Bulman was deeply enmeshed in crisis meetings over a new bomber that had looked highly promising but was now in danger of being scrapped because its two recently developed new Rolls-Royce engines had proved so disappointing. (The Avro Manchester would soon be rescued by substituting four Merlin engines for its two underperforming Vultures, emerging in due course in the slightly modified shape of the Avro Lancaster.) Setting this and other urgent matters aside for a morning, Bulman dug out of his files all the Ministry's past correspondence and official minutes on Power Jets, including his own advice in January 1936 that the gas-turbine idea (complete with that 'species of mud guard') did not merit a trial at his directorate's expense. Plainly the concept had come a long way since those days. It seemed just as obvious to Bulman, though, that his superiors were in urgent need of a little sober counselling about the dangers of visionary engines in wartime.

This was a Dragonfly moment for the head of Engines. When confronted by the aircraft industry with any novel idea that had won overly enthusiastic reviews, he had long been fond of reminding colleagues of a seminal episode from his own past. Never had it seemed more relevant. In 1917, when the young George Bulman had been working as an officer in the Weybridge station of the RFC's Aircraft Inspection Unit, he heard about a new engine called the Dragonfly being developed by a small Surrey-based manufacturer, ABC Motors. Like its predecessor from this factory, the Wasp, it promised to be an exciting advance in aero-engineering. The Dragonfly comprised a nine-cylinder radial design and featured a striking simplicity of construction. Largely for this reason, and before a single finished engine had even been bench-tested, the Air Ministry ordered the production of 10,000 units – enough to keep busy almost the entire capacity of Britain's aero-engine industry at the time. The young Bulman opposed the whole business vehemently but in vain. He was proved right in the end, though. By the time a thousand units of the Dragonfly had been built, the engine was still hopelessly overweight and well short of its predicted power. Bulman would recall the implications half a century later:

> Had the War dragged on into 1919, the Dragonfly would have lost it for us in the air. We would have been beaten out of the sky; it was a hideous episode illustrating the effect of a single unwise decision, based on 'cleverness', and should never be forgotten by any future arbiter of high responsibility.[22]

The lesson he had drawn from this experience seemed especially pertinent in January 1940, as all were toiling day and night to save the RAF from possible destruction. (The Ministry was about to oversee a doubling of the monthly production figures for Hurricane and Spitfire fighters.) The Dragonfly had come close to sinking the RFC 'just because the engineers, hard-bitten, maybe cynical, from their accumulation of experience, were not strong enough to counter the arguments of the uninitiated enthusiasts'. Bulman was too wily ever to mention that the Air Ministry man responsible for placing the Dragonfly order had been one William Weir, then the Director of Aeronautical Supplies and now a keen investor in Power Jets. He was quick, though, to suggest to colleagues that the Whittle Unit and the Dragonfly might have other parallels that were worth noting. His problem was that the circle of admirers rallying to Whittle's side with such (to his mind) alarming haste included not just influential engineers and industrialists like Tizard and Weir, but also two of the most senior RAF officers in the Ministry – Tedder and the top man himself, Wilfrid Freeman. If the Engines directorate officials were to rein back this jet business effectively, they would first have to gain proper control of it.

Power Jets' activities were formally the responsibility not of the Engines directorate but of the Director of Scientific Research, David Pye, to whom Tweedie was seconded. Bulman hastily contacted Pye and his deputy, William Farren, and reminded them both that their first loyalties had to lie with Farnborough and its own jet-engine programme under way with Metropolitan-Vickers. And in anticipation of talks with the kind of industrial firms that might be capable of taking on a long-term development of the jet, those already talking to Power Jets were cautioned against jumping the gun. Bulman sent off an advisory letter to Spencer Wilks to this effect on 3 February. Awkwardly, from the Ministry's point of view, Spencer's brother Maurice two days later read it over the telephone to Whittle. Straining to catch every word, Whittle scribbled down the letter in his Pitman's shorthand. Bulman insisted in it that Power Jets needed neither additional equity capital nor further manufacturing resources. As for the idea of anyone at Rover accepting an invitation to Lutterworth, he issued a slightly sinister warning: 'You tell me that Mr Maurice Wilks has been in direct contact with certain persons [sic] and that it is proposed that he should see the apparatus. We do not think that any useful purpose would be served and advise you to tread warily.'[23]

Whittle was startled by the hostile tone of this letter and the advice it contained. Urging the Wilks brothers to stay away from the Ladywood Works seemed to him quite contrary to the spirit of his recent exchanges with Tizard and Tedder, let alone the whole tenor of his dealings with Glosters and the RAE since the outbreak of the war. He immediately sought an urgent meeting with Tedder, and was duly given an appointment at the Ministry's new premises in Harrogate for 3 p.m. the very next day, 6 February 1940.

The Air Vice Marshal, ignoring the advice of his Ministry officials, spared almost a whole afternoon for this encounter. Whittle's record of their conversation suggests he found it entirely reassuring. Tedder responded positively to an extensive shopping list of the plant and equipment needed for Lutterworth, which Whittle had drawn up on his train journey that morning. He listened sympathetically to a blow-by-blow account of the soured partnership with BTH, and a catalogue of complaints about BTH's unsuitability for the jet project. Best of all, he was apologetic about that 'most unfortunately phrased' letter from Bulman. Whittle asked if 'strings were being pulled in the background'. Not at all, insisted Tedder, while stressing 'with considerable emphasis that he wanted the job to go ahead at full speed'. He also remarked pointedly that 'he would not allow any large concern to rob the parents of their child'. This Whittle took as a cue to reaffirm his existing plans: he had a 'very good impression' of the Wilks brothers and believed they had 'excellent facilities to act as sub-contractors'. Obviously he himself was going to remain in control of the whole operation – it was 'both in the interests of the Company and the Air Ministry' that he should do so. Tedder went along with all this, merely observing that 'the proof of the pudding was in the eating'.[24]

Tedder avoided giving any explicit confirmation, though, of the leading role that Whittle had assigned himself. Whittle, often trusting to the point of naïveté in conversations with any political dimension, seems hardly to have noticed. He merely recorded Tedder's gentle warning: 'He said that the Air Ministry intended to take a much greater interest in the affairs of Power Jets than they had up to then, and that they wanted to be sure that any arrangement that was made was the best possible one.' In fact, Bulman and his team had already begun to plot a careful intervention. Nothing was said to Whittle about a series of meetings that had been planned between the Ministry, BTH and the Wilks brothers, scheduled for the next few weeks. Probably Tedder knew nothing about them. Desperately under pressure, it is easy to suppose he had handed the jet file over to George Bulman and left the Engines directorate to take charge of the details.

The officials duly pursued their meetings – and arrived in due course at a policy on the jet project very different from the line taken by all concerned since September 1939. Whittle's meticulous analysis of BTH's shortcomings was set aside, and work on the jet engine was judged to be well within BTH's competence. It was decided, though, that a top motor manufacturer would be better suited than BTH to line production. So a subordinate role was planned for BTH, which would ensure some valuable continuity and a useful back-up facility. Then the Wilks brothers were asked if Rover could be readied to take on the job, not as a partner and subcontractor to Power Jets but as primary contractor to the Ministry. The brothers confirmed their firm would be happy to do so. Bulman was delighted: engaging Rover and BTH as active contractors in this way meant the Air Ministry would have effective control over the project begun at Lutterworth. It was a tidy solution to the problem of coping with a new engine venture at this crucial time for the country, just over four months into the war. Unhappily, though, the whole arrangement was discussed with no place at the table for Whittle or anyone else from Power Jets. None of the participants in the talks mentioned a word of them to the man responsible for the jet engine since launching it three years earlier.

Leaving aside the discourtesy, the assumption that Whittle could be sidelined in this way suggests much about the attitude towards him among those in the Ministry who had been in charge of developing new engines over the past two decades. Despite all the praise recently showered on Whittle, the old guard in Whitehall – by no means restricted to the Engines D&P team – still regarded him as a maverick RAF officer promoting a curious project. Insofar as they had noted his progress after the establishment of Power Jets in 1936, it had seemed to them highly unlikely that anything would come of the jet engine, even after its first ignition in 1937. The successful running of the WU3 in June 1939 had given them quite a surprise, but fell far short of persuading them that any practical use could be made of the engine in the foreseeable future. If it had stirred some excitement among those non-engineers in high places inclined to espouse visionary causes – men like Freeman and Tedder – contractual arrangements could be made by the Air Ministry with trusted manufacturers to explore the (long-term) development possibilities. Under no circumstances, though, was the Ministry going to allow the WU3 to be used as a pretext for turning Power Jets into a half-baked manufacturing enterprise.

Word of the agreements reached with Rover and BTH began circulating within the Ministry as early as mid-February 1940. Indeed, William Farren almost let the cat out of the bag at a Farnborough lunch. Sitting next to Whittle, the Deputy Director of Scientific Research made a series of disobliging observations about Power Jets' future. The Ministry, he said, 'intended to keep it as a small organisation' with no hope of orders for anything other than (at best) a few experimental engines, and therefore no hope of any significant return for its private investors. Whittle was appalled. He knew that Farren, normally reserved and wary of all small talk, was not a man to speak lightly of such matters. If the Ministry really did intend to block the growth of Power Jets, Whittle could see it being left horribly vulnerable to a renewed approach from Armstrong Siddeley or one of the other big aero-engine firms. He fired off a letter to Farren the next day, memorably suggesting 'the wolves are gathering round the door' waiting to gobble up his project.[25]

The incident blew over: Farren withdrew his remarks in a telephone call (he had only sought 'to point out the kind of un-desirable things that might happen' and 'agreed with everybody else that Power Jets had done a marvellous job of work').[26] Still Whittle remained in ignorance of the agreements struck with Rover and BTH. He was undoubtedly growing suspicious – nothing, after all, had been heard from the Wilks brothers since the end of January – but once again he was reassured by Tedder. After Whittle sent him a copy of the letter to Farren, Tedder wrote back on 19 February with just the right nostrum from one RAF officer to another ('I dislike wolves as much as you do'). He was looking forward, said Tedder, to discussing a development programme for the jet within a week or so.[27]

So Whittle pressed ahead. He trusted his RAF superiors on the one hand and most of the RAE engineers on the other to back him. At meetings in London, Farnborough and the Gloster works, he continued to show an unrivalled grip on the technical issues facing the jet. True, Power Jets was still a tiny concern. But with new recruits steadily gathering around him at Lutterworth, and assuming sufficient public funding, he believed it could make a contribution wholly disproportionate to its size – and conceivably as significant to the eventual course of the war against Germany as the feats of even the biggest aero-engine firms in the land.

iii

Out of the blue, Whittle received an invitation on 24 March 1940 summoning him and Lance Whyte to a meeting convened by Tedder in his new office at Harrogate in two days' time. They travelled by train to the Yorkshire spa town the next day and spent the night before the meeting at the Queen's Hotel, where they discovered the Wilks brothers were fellow guests. They met briefly, but curiously neither brother showed any inclination to engage in conversation. The venue next day was the Air Ministry's relocated headquarters in the Hotel Majestic, an enormous turn-of-the-century redbrick edifice that looked like one of the grander Victorian railway stations. Tedder had a cavernous office on the third floor. No agenda had been provided in advance, so Whittle and Whyte made their way up the Majestic's enormous spiral staircase with no idea what to expect. It hardly appeared a crucial event as the participants assembled. Harry Sporborg from BTH was supposed to be there but had cried off, said Tedder from the chair, as too had E. L. Pickles who was head of the Contracts Department but had sent along a junior colleague in his place. Apart from Spencer and Maurice Wilks, the only other attendees were David Pye and Lawrence Tweedie, representing the Engines directorate in Bulman's absence.

Tedder made a few opening remarks about the importance of pushing ahead 'with the greatest possible speed' as there was 'a good chance' the jet could be produced 'in time to be of use in this war', all of which must have cheered Whittle considerably.[28] Then the Air Vice Marshal turned to his briefing papers. He had called the meeting, he said, so that they could reach the key decisions together that would form the basis of future policy on the jet engine. It was a shame, he suggested, that Sporborg could not be present, but arrangements would be made shortly to clarify a continuing role for his firm, since 'it would be a great pity if the experience of the B.T.H. to date were wasted'. This observation astounded Whittle – who protested immediately that it would be no great loss at all – but it was nothing compared to what came next.

It might be wondered whether Tedder had had any time to study the brief he had been handed by his officials. He had twice gone out of his way in February to reassure Whittle that his ambitious plans were well understood and accepted. Yet he now announced a set of policy decisions cutting directly across them. The Engines directorate, he declared, had decided 'to call in a firm with considerable production experience, and having suitable plant to undertake development manufacture...' In short, all development contracts for the jet would henceforth be awarded not to Power Jets but to Rover. Ministry contracts for the line production of engines would similarly flow directly to Rover just as soon as the development programme allowed. (The work currently subcontracted to BTH by Power Jets would be allowed to run its course, but would not be taken any further.) Ministry officials 'hoped for a very intimate basis of cooperation' between Rover and Power Jets, but this could have no legal basis in any contract.

Thus did the Ministry propose to demolish at a stroke Whittle's dream of an engineering business like no other, fit under his leadership to transform the future of the aero-engine. He seems to have been too shocked to respond immediately. If the mood can be fairly construed from his own dry record of the meeting, there was a long and awkward silence. Then Spencer Wilks spoke up. He and his brother, though happy to discuss a contract behind Whittle's back, had apparently not been made aware of the Ministry's intended treatment of Power Jets. So Wilks asked Tedder for a little clarification. He was told 'that if Rover came into the picture now they need have no fear that at some future date they would be left high and dry...' But Wilks to his credit was thinking less about Rover's situation, which after all had been agreed, than about the predicament of Power Jets, for which 'high and dry' seemed all too apt a label. He was candid about his unease. The arrangement being proposed by the Ministry, he thought, 'seemed to him to be morally very unfair'.

Tedder accepted this objection. It was one of several moments seeming to confirm his discomfort with the Ministry's briefing. The apparent purpose of the meeting was only now revealed: they were there to identify a level of compensation for Power Jets that all present could agree would be appropriate. (They never did.) Whittle himself took no part in this. He was sitting with Whyte in a state of disbelief – he later wrote of 'the great dismay' that had swept over them both[29] – as all those around them offered Tedder advice on how best, in effect, to abort the fledgling Lutterworth enterprise. Spencer Wilks suggested a licence payment from Rover to Power Jets might work. Obviously, though, 'the Air Ministry would need to join [in the terms of the licence] since it appeared to him that the Air Ministry held all the cards'. Yes indeed they did, replied Tedder – 'especially the Joker'. And he waved a hand in Whittle's direction, inviting Wilks to call the Squadron Leader 'at any time'.

After Tedder had extended this show of sympathy for Whittle, the Engines directorate's envoy hastened to make clear the constraints that would now be applicable to his fledgling company. Licence fees would not be available to it, said Tweedie, since Rover would be working on behalf of the Crown, and the Crown had long since been given Free User rights to all Power Jets' patents. Indeed, since patent royalties and design fees were inapplicable for the same reason, 'there did not seem to be any basis on which Power Jets could officially claim any payment from Rovers'. Tweedie then proceeded to spell out further implications of the proposed jet policy with some relish, piling up the obstacles to any meaningful role for Power Jets. He freely admitted 'he was against the Air Ministry giving any more contracts to Power Jets and [thought] that all further orders for development engines should go to Rovers'. Power Jets would be in no position, for example, to manufacture engine parts or to manage subcontractors for any future work, since it had no staff of its own with experience of production work. For several minutes, Whittle found himself listening to a valedictory for Power Jets – delivered by Tweedie, of all people, the man whose official letter of rejection in December 1929 might have put paid to the jet engine before it even reached a drawing board.

Towards the end of the meeting, Whittle pleaded with Tedder to see the disruption in existing work programmes that would flow from the proposed arrangement – but he could make no impression. When he pointed out how much Power Jets was already doing in anticipation of receiving further contracts for engines beyond the W.2, Tedder reacted badly. Such work was inappropriate, he said, 'because this meant that Power Jets were proceeding with the designs without having the experience of production people [sic] on the job'. Tedder also expressed concern over the size of Power Jets 'and suggested that it was expanding too fast'. These views were totally at variance with the encouragement he had offered Whittle in the engine shed in January and the provenance of Tedder's brief was obvious, as it had been from the start. When Spencer Wilks asked if there was one man at the Ministry who could be relied upon for 'decisive decisions' on the jet project, it was no surprise to hear from Tedder that 'he would instruct Major Bulman to handle the job'. Flexing all his knowledge and experience of the engine industry, Bulman had moved decisively to snatch control.

As Whittle and Whyte gathered up their papers and headed out of the Majestic to catch their train back to Rugby, they could hardly have imagined a bleaker outcome to their visit. As Whittle recalled for his file memo: 'It was agreed in principle by the Air

Ministry people that some way would have to be found by which Power Jets could carry on, but there was no clear suggestion as to how this was to be done.' Perhaps the drift of the meeting had caused Tedder some misgivings, too. As if to reaffirm the commitments he had made to Whittle since January, he dictated a personal note on 28 March for the Ministry's policy files that once again asserted the importance of the jet engine: '… its potentialities, if it is successful, are so great that although it is "futuristic" and a gamble its development should be pushed on as fast as possible with a view to its use in this war.'

This note bore signs of further devious briefing from his officials. Bulman had stressed in briefing papers for Tedder that the jet engine had to be developed 'by a firm which would be able to go over rapidly to production once a reasonable state of development had been reached'. This disqualified Power Jets, given its obvious inability to switch to full production. To make sure the Air Marshal realised quite how small the operation at Lutterworth really was, officials insisted on referring to it in the days after the meeting as a 'design unit'. Perhaps they felt the gravity of the times excused this convenient deception. Nonetheless, as Bulman must by now have known, it was an egregious misrepresentation of what had been achieved by Whittle and his team. It was true that the Ladywood Works had had hardly more than a dozen employees in the first months of the war (though it was recruiting quickly now). Yet with the assistance of a team of engineers, draughtsmen and works staff at BTH, Whittle had overseen the manufacture of the world's first working gas turbine in 1936–7, involving several new techniques in the workshop that BTH managers had initially insisted were not possible. And over the intervening three years at the Ladywood Works Whittle had been responsible for turning a crude experimental engine into a fully tested prototype virtually ready for flight. Tedder, a career RAF officer with a Cambridge history degree and no knowledge whatever of engineering, failed to see how far he had been misled by his officials. Acquiescing in their advice, he had to agree it hardly seemed realistic to give development orders to Power Jets 'who after all are merely a small design unit'.[30] Tedder was astute enough to assert some common sense in spelling out the policy conundrum they faced: 'As a design unit, they are of course the key of [sic] the whole project and their continued existence is vital.' So long as this misnomer for Power Jets lingered on, though, the Air Vice Marshal was going to struggle to find a coherent policy framework for what was actually afoot at Lutterworth.

An indication of this fell on Ministry desks within days. It was a magisterial two-page paper from Whittle entitled 'Immediate Plan for Manufacture of Development Engines', and it described how a first W.1 could be built by Power Jets 'in not more than two months from the date of receipt of limiting material'.[31] The Immediate Plan had been written by Whittle a day before the Harrogate meeting. Evidently disconcerted by the stasis in his talks with Rover, he had decided a short blast on his own trumpet might be timely. The result was a spirited assessment of Power Jets' achievements to date – and an extraordinary prediction:

> The Company... has produced an engine which makes possible aircraft performances quite outside the range of those which can be attained by normal aero engines, and as the result of experience and innovation during this period very great further improvements are expected during the course of the next few months, so much so that the present day aircraft power plant is likely to be almost wholly superseded within the next five years.

Less prescient, perhaps, was a closing rumination on the financial implications for Power Jets. Whittle thought 5,000 engines a year might be made over a ten-year period, at a 'very modest' estimate, with the company taking about £100 per engine from royalties and design fees. Future revenues of approximately £5 million might therefore flow to the company – not a bad return for an outlay of about £50,000. It was probably the fullest analysis he ever made of a subject that never much interested him.

The soaring claims for the jet in this paper probably made Bulman's blood run cold. His own strategy for dealing with the jet, meanwhile, was proving no simple panacea. Power Jets was the driving force behind the project in every detail. Appending both BTH and Rover to it in any meaningful way – let along summarily discontinuing the work at Lutterworth – was always going to be horribly difficult. The task fell to Lawrence Tweedie, and he struggled from the start. He could provide neither company with useful operational parameters, nor were any legal guidelines made available by the Ministry's contracts department. All the familiar bugbears for Whittle of working with BTH's management resurfaced yet again. At a meeting in Rugby on 15 April 1940, for example, the parties clashed over workshop conditions, which had been a bone of contention for the past three years. ('Sqd Ldr Whittle pointed out that with light alloys, close limits could only be obtained in a temperature-controlled shop. Mr Sporborg and Mr Collingham, however, thought that the limits called for by Power Jets were unnecessarily fine.'[32]) Above all else, the notion that either Rover or BTH could prepare their own drawings for the manufacture of prototypes, based on technical and design data obtained from Power Jets, quickly came to grief. Whittle handed over the data, as he was bound to do, but this only led to a series of tetchy and unproductive discussions. These turned quite acrimonious, once Lance Whyte began a feisty rearguard action to shore up what few legal defences Power Jets still had left, to salvage a long-term future for itself. (His persistence soon became counter-productive from Whittle's point of view. Years later, Bulman recalled Whyte 'continually approaching the Ministry, embodying so to speak the impression of a solicitor's letter threatening and menacing on his client's behalf...'[33])

Whittle himself tried to steer clear of the whole imbroglio. He had no shortage of workshop tasks to keep him busy at Lutterworth – where Power Jets' staff numbers were climbing steadily towards the fifty mark – and the outcome of the Harrogate debacle had effectively killed off the talks aimed at selling some equity to the Wilks brothers. But when obliged to attend a meeting at Rover on 22 April, he lost patience with the discussion and tore into the Ministry for its handling of the whole affair:

> I said that I had not had an opportunity to give an opinion...
> and that the Air Ministry's decisions had been taken without
> full knowledge of the opinions of the engineer who had been
> in charge of the job for four years, namely, myself. I said that if
> the Air Ministry wanted to put this job into production in the
> shortest possible time they were not going the right way about it.[34]

Tweedie and his colleagues were at first incensed by Whittle's
outspokenness. Nonetheless, they were forced within days to the
same conclusion. A project led by Rover and BTH, with Power Jets
offering continued support as a kind of glorified consultancy, was
not going to work. Instead of asking how the three firms might
alternatively be realigned in some kind of triple partnership,
Tweedie recommended that efforts to secure cooperation between
them should be abandoned altogether. They should instead be
required to strike out totally independently of each other.

Years later, Whittle came to the view that this might in fact
have served the country's interests and been a blessing for Power
Jets. But it struck him at the time as an even madder option than
consigning Power Jets to a supporting role. Hearing of the proposed revision in a letter from Tedder on 9 May, he rushed straight
back to Harrogate for yet another meeting early the following
day. Despite their heavy schedules, he was given appointments
to see not only Tedder but Wilfrid Freeman as well. First came a
private chat with Tedder. To Whittle's great relief, Tedder made a
point of repeating that he 'had made up his mind very definitely
some time ago that in no circumstances would he allow a small
company to be swallowed by two large companies, and that this
was still his attitude'.[35] (Time spent with Freeman, it seemed, had
stiffened his resolve.) He chided Whittle for his 'very naughty'
remarks at Rover's premises in April, but seemed far more sympathetic to his criticisms than Whittle had expected. This set the
tone for what followed.

'What shall we do about this bloody man Whyte?' were
Freeman's first words, greeting Whittle in the corridor outside
his Majestic suite. The two Air Marshals then remonstrated
with him, as the three of them drew up chairs round a table in

Freeman's office, about what they regarded as an obstreperous and disruptive approach to the civil service by Lance Whyte. Whittle stoutly defended his fellow director. It suited all three men, though, to lay much of the discord since January at Whyte's door. Then they moved to more important matters – and Whittle now had the chance, at last, properly to explain why he so disagreed with the policy adopted at the end of March. He had a receptive audience. Both senior officers readily conceded that Whittle had been magnanimous in delivering all of Power Jets' drawings and design data to Rover, notwithstanding his principled opposition to the car-maker's putative role. Tedder warned Freeman that he was going to hear a lot of serious objections to the Ministry's latest proposal 'for what... were very good and sound reasons'.[36] On cue, Whittle went through them, explaining all over again why building a gas-turbine jet was such a different proposition from anything in traditional aero-engineering.

If there was one man in the Air Ministry fully receptive to this truth, it was Wilfrid Freeman. The individual who, in his biographer's words, 'had laid the foundations of Britain's wartime aircraft economy', had been intrigued by the potential of the jet since first hearing of it in 1937. It was one of the two genuinely radical design initiatives that he had taken to his heart. The other, noted already, was the unarmed wooden bomber that he had backed consistently. (He had personally pushed through the vital decision in December 1939 to place an order with de Havilland for production of the first fifty aircraft to specification B.1/40, which would become the outstandingly versatile Mosquito.) Shortly after Freeman's death in 1953, another Air Marshal delivered a warm tribute to him in a BBC broadcast. He was willing, recalled Sir John Slessor, 'to accept responsibility – to back his own judgement – and to run risks... qualities with which [he] was supremely endowed. Some of his most important and fruitful decisions such as... the Mosquito... and Whittle's jet were taken against formidable technical advice...'.[37] (More of this background might have been evident to later historians, had not all of Freeman's personal papers been destroyed shortly after his death.) Freeman's courage and resolve were well in evidence at this meeting with Whittle in his Harrogate office on 10 May 1940.

He was genuinely puzzled that the Air Ministry should have tried to marginalise Power Jets. As for the proposed policy revision – asking all parties involved to proceed independently of each other – he entirely concurred with Whittle that asking Rover to pursue a jet engine independently of Power Jets was a nonsense. He had no objection to Rover's involvement per se – 'everything had to be darn well tried, and tried fast... there would be no financial restrictions on the whole development whatsoever' – but he was clear about the role he wanted Whittle to play. 'Sir Wilfrid said that his view of my function was that I should have a much more general position in the situation than I had at present, and implied that I was attending too much to detail, and that he would like to see me walking round and kicking the other parties concerned...' As Whittle was quick to observe, this was effectively to suggest that he would be Chief Engineer to the project. There ensued a candid but not unfriendly exchange between Freeman and Tedder, as recalled by Whittle:

> Sir Wilfrid turned to Tedder and asked him if I was a difficult fellow to get on with, adding: 'he seems to be a reasonable enough being in this office'. Tedder smiled and said I was a little difficult at times (in our earlier talk, Tedder had remarked that I had to be regarded somewhat as a 'prima donna' – very important, but needing to be handled gently). I said to Freeman that I hoped that time would show that I was not as difficult as Tedder implied.[38]

Such was Freeman's charm that he could usually draw others into thinking that he and they shared total confidence in each other. It certainly worked on this occasion: thinking they were all of the same mind, Whittle proposed again that the broader role apparently envisaged by the Air Marshal might be best fulfilled by his acting as Chief Engineer. But the two senior officers demurred: 'both Tedder and Freeman were non-committal on this point.'[39]

Yet Whittle had been Chief Engineer in all but title for the past four years. As some of the country's most distinguished aero-engineers would much later observe – Hawker Siddeley's Arnold Hall and Rolls-Royce's Stanley Hooker among them – formally appointing him to the role must have been the most sensible next step. If taken successfully, it could have struck a good working compromise between the option (so feared by Bulman) of giving Power Jets a free rein and the opposite policy (so opposed by Whittle) of trying to marginalise Power Jets as that 'small design unit'. Surely some such compromise must have been considered in the weeks just ahead – had not events intervened. They did so, however, in the gravest way imaginable. Even as Whittle and the two Air Marshals were deep in conversation around Freeman's table, the first news was racing along every floor of the Majestic that the Luftwaffe had that very morning, 10 May 1940, struck at Dutch and Belgian airfields, catching their two national air forces on the ground to devastating effect. Hitler had launched his invasion of the West.

6

Conference at Farnborough

May 1940 to November 1940

i

Ten days after Whittle's meeting with Freeman and Tedder, a Post Office boy arrived at the Ladywood Works with a telegram. It came from the Ministry of Aircraft Production (MAP), which had just been established by Winston Churchill as one of his first initiatives after being appointed Prime Minister on the evening of 10 May 1940. Churchill was determined to ensure that absolutely nothing would be allowed to impede the maximum possible production of new planes for the RAF, in the shortest possible time. So he had set up MAP on 14 May as an autonomous department, moved all the technical units of the Air Ministry into it, starting with Freeman's Development and Production arm, and picked a human bulldozer to run it – the Canadian businessman and press tycoon Lord Beaverbrook. The news from France had confirmed within days the extreme urgency of the task facing 'the Beaver' and his bewildered officials. Hitler's blitzkrieg in the West had drawn the RAF into a series of disastrous engagements over France and the Low Countries. One sortie after another, confronted by German units flying Messerschmitt Me 109 and Me 110 fighters, had incurred shocking losses. Hopelessly outclassed bombers like the Bristol Blenheim and the Fairey Battle had been shot down in terrible numbers. The RAF's own fighter strength in France relied on the Hawker Hurricane – no Spitfires had been shipped over the Channel – and it was generally living up to its pilots' high expectations. But the speed with which the Hurricane squadrons had nonetheless been depleted was another cause for alarm. When the squadrons operating with the British Expeditionary Force in northern France were hurriedly recalled on 19 May, only 66 aircraft were left of an original 261 total. Beaverbrook was appalled by the implications. Nothing could be allowed to slow the production of fresh aircraft. He told his officials to ensure that all resources were concentrated on existing production lines for just five aircraft types. ('We might have only a few weeks to live, he'd declare,' recalled Bulman. 'No use bothering about other types if we were all dead anyway.'[1]) Any other projects would have to wait. One result was the telegram that Whittle read at his desk the next day, 20 May. Power Jets had lost the Priority status awarded only a few months earlier.

He had no idea what this might entail for the jet project, nor did a flurry of mixed messages from MAP in London and the Air Ministry in Harrogate over the following days offer much of a guide. The formal contract for the E.28/39's airframe had just been placed with Gloster, on 12 May 1940. It nonetheless seemed possible that BTH and Rover might both now be barred from further work on the jet, and Power Jets would not be able to rely on parts from any of its own subcontractors for the W.1. But Tedder sent Whittle a scribbled reassurance – 'I want the job to go on but it will have to take second place at the moment'[2] – and subsequent letters from MAP suggested 'second place' need only apply where the jet project clashed directly with the production of war materials. Since design and development work on the jet was still far removed from any production line, this rather belied the point of suspending its Priority status in the first place – and on 11 June another telegram arrived at Lutterworth, confirming that its former status had been restored.

Whittle wanted desperately to believe that a similar reversal would soon restore the personal control over his project that he had nominally lost since the end of March. The start of the war in

September 1939 had unexpectedly left him more scope to pursue his goals than hitherto. Perhaps the emergency measures being rushed into place now would have the same effect, prompting officials to set aside the ill-considered and time-wasting realignment (as he believed) of the engine contracts tabled at the Harrogate meeting. He summarised the 'Harrogate policy' in a letter to Sir Henry Tizard early in June 1940. The Ministry had given large-scale development contracts to BTH and Rover, depriving him in effect of any power to insist on his engine being developed in line with his own very exact requirements. So much for the broad supervisory role advocated by Freeman in May: 'in other words, my position as chief engineer on the job has been seriously weakened and I do not like it much.'[3] Whittle probably resorted to this strained understatement in deference to the sense of deep crisis that had engulfed the country by this point – the collapse of France looked imminent – but it surely concealed his true feelings. He was desperate to push ahead with the plans for a jet fighter that he thought was at last within their grasp.

The latest arrangement involving BTH and Rover was Tedder's attempt to reach a workable compromise with Power Jets. He envisaged all experimental engines being built to Whittle's design, but thought the two manufacturing companies should be left with discretion to propose design changes that in their view would ease the path to full production. These, naturally, would have to be discussed with Whittle. How the process would evolve in practice, Tedder would leave to them. His only stipulation – as he had sharply reminded Lance Whyte in a feisty telephone conversation in mid-April that he arranged to be recorded 'because I regard it as possibly being of rather great importance' – was that all parties should act together 'in the spirit of collaboration'.[4] After four years of collaboration with BTH, this vague prescription did not appeal to Whittle in the slightest. He was convinced that only a firm demarcation of responsibilities could avert constant arguments over design amendments – which in his view, of course, were most unlikely ever to improve on his own drawings. He thought the Priority-status affair might have set them back at least a few months. They could hardly afford further delays if they were to have jet fighters in the air by, say, the middle of 1941.

Unfortunately Henry Tizard, for all his keen interest in Whittle's endeavour, was poorly placed to help. He had been scientific adviser to the Chief of the Air Staff since November 1939, but his position had just been hopelessly compromised by Churchill's appointment of his own man as scientific adviser to all three service chiefs – none other than Frederick Lindemann, with whom Tizard had fallen out so bitterly in 1936. (Tizard was to resign from the Air Ministry before the end of June 1940.) Lindemann was one newcomer causing waves in Whitehall, and there were many others – not least at MAP, where Beaverbrook was bringing in assorted cronies from the business world with the avowed intention of disrupting the status quo. Freeman and Tedder were hard pressed to ward off the potential chaos threatened by their alarming new boss. Neither had much time available to resume the discussion they had had with Whittle on 10 May, though Freeman had at least intervened to ensure the jet project's survival by making sure that no one alerted Beaverbrook to its existence in his first few weeks as Minister. The barnstorming Canadian had tried hard to cancel the Mosquito aircraft and Airborne Interception radar, both still in development. Guessing that he would have even less time for the jet engine, Freeman had hidden away all the Whittle files.[5]

Among the officials alerted to Freeman's rescue mission was an accomplished RAE engineer arriving at MAP on a transfer from Farnborough. He would soon emerge, in Tizard's absence, as one of the key individuals in the Whitehall establishment to whom Whittle could turn for help in his struggle to claw back control. Harold Roxbee Cox, known to his friends as Roxbee, had spent most of the 1930s in a succession of senior research posts. Now he was appointed Deputy Director of Scientific Research to head up various special projects and above all the jet engine. He had already attended a number of pre-war meetings about it, wearing his RAE hat. Just five years older than Whittle, he, too, had grown up in the Midlands and started out as a humble apprentice. Less preternaturally gifted but with a great deal more *savoir faire* than Whittle, he had made his way via a brilliant academic career into a succession of engineering roles in the public sector. He saw the potential significance of the jet engine almost immediately and showed a ready appreciation of its designer's genius from their first meeting. This was of some moment for Whittle, because Roxbee Cox – a dapper figure, always immaculately dressed – would turn out to be a consummate Whitehall operator. Patient, diplomatic and ever alert to the possibilities of a compromise that might advance his goal, he was in many ways the very antithesis of Whittle and his caution would save Whittle some embarrassment on several occasions. (In later life, he was to chair an extraordinary number of committees. Given a peerage in 1965 as Lord Kings Norton, he took as his motto 'Precision and Tolerance'.)

Usefully abetting Roxbee Cox's approach was a younger official who in effect reported to him. Denis Tobin was on secondment from the Air Ministry. He looked as though he was scarcely out of his teens, but had the daunting job of liaising between the civil service and Power Jets. (Another official had the same role at BTH.) Tobin was officially Whitehall's man at Lutterworth, but acted for much of the time as Whittle's man at MAP. Slightly in awe of the jet's inventor, he was in almost daily contact with him by telephone and was also a regular visitor to the Works. Tobin often stayed at the Hind Hotel, when needing to attend early morning meetings or travelling next day to other appointments in the Midlands.

Whittle himself regularly stayed overnight from about the middle of June 1940, though he always slept on a camp bed at the Ladywood Works. Amidst all his other anxieties, he was now prey to a mounting concern over the physical safety of his engine. It was, after all, still the only working version of his jet in existence. A stray German bomb might blow the whole jet project to smithereens. He even began to think it possible that German paratroopers might be dropped on Lutterworth to seek out and destroy the engine. He was determined, in true Home Guard fashion, that they would have to cope with him first:

At first my colleagues were reluctant to accept that this was necessary, but after a short period, during which I supplemented the night-watchmen on my own – sleeping on a camp-bed in my office – the idea became more generally accepted and a group of us took it in turns... I used to get quite a thrill wandering round the almost deserted works on a still night with searchlights eerily sweeping the sky.[6]

It was on one of these solitary midnight patrols, on the night of 24 June, that he heard the sound of German bombers passing overhead for the first time.[7] For a man who had spent so much time contemplating the tactical challenge posed by bombers, the menacing drone of those aircraft flying unopposed through the darkness must have been deeply galling. It can only have added to his desperate impatience to hear that the Harrogate policy had been abandoned. It would surely take only a word from Tedder.

The days passed, and no word came. Whittle was pleased to receive news of his promotion to Wing Commander; but his only real concern now was that effective control over the jet project should be restored to Power Jets. On this crucial matter, he heard nothing at all. It seemed to him inconceivable that MAP could persist for long with its decision to hand the project over to two companies with no understanding at all of the underlying technology. Probably, though, he would have to wait a while for confirmation of a rethink. France had fallen and Britain was facing the prospect of invasion by the all-conquering Wehrmacht: it was hardly an auspicious moment to be seeking a policy clarification from the Ministry. Then, a week into July 1940, he suddenly received a most unexpected summons. It came from Beaverbrook's personal office. He was asked to present himself for a meeting at Stornoway House, the Minister's magnificent white-painted Georgian home overlooking London's Green Park that was temporarily doubling as MAP's headquarters. Having heard about Beaverbrook's tempestuous personality, Whittle organised his papers with more than usual thoroughness. On the train down from Rugby on 9 July he readied himself for a critical encounter. It seemed quite possible that Beaverbrook might be intent on serving the jet engine's last rites in person. On the other hand, perhaps the Minister might be open to hearing a few home truths about the proposed management of the project?

Within moments of meeting him, Whittle realised that his worst fears had been misplaced:

> The Minister asked me what I'd got tucked away and I replied that I had a very good engine. He wanted to know how we were getting on with it and I said that there were still development troubles to be overcome, but that I thought that it would be fit for service before long.[8]

This response appears to have delighted Beaverbrook. Far from wanting to kill it, in fact, he was genuinely intrigued by the potential of the jet engine. Here was a golden opportunity for Whittle. If only he could have spoken out with all the brilliance and authority of which he had shown himself capable on so many previous occasions, he might have dealt the Harrogate policy a fatal blow. He could have denounced Bulman's initiative and Rover's unsuitability so uncompromisingly that Beaverbrook might at least have ordered a reappraisal and might even have reinstated Power Jets as prime contractor immediately. In the event, Whittle's nerve failed him. He managed only brief answers to a fusillade of questions from the Minister about his dealings with MAP and Farnborough – and ducked the vital issue:

> … When he asked me if Rovers and the BTH were doing a satisfactory job my reply was as non-committal as I could make it, saying that the arrangements made by the Air Ministry were so recent that there was not yet time to judge.

Quite why he fluffed his chance so badly is a mystery. Perhaps he was more than a little overwhelmed by his surroundings and by the Beaver's famously combative style. (Whittle himself suggested, in his autobiography, that he had felt MAP's approach to the jet project was 'too complex a subject for a very short interview' – a plausible explanation, given how deeply he had been immersed in his work for the past four years.) Notwithstanding

Whittle's reticence, the Minister promised his support with characteristic panache. After Whittle suggested that the timetable for a first jet aircraft might hinge upon the production of the new plane, he heard from Beaverbrook 'that when we were ready for the prototype I was to let him know and we should have it'. Then the interview was over. It had lasted all of ten minutes, though Beaverbrook assured his departing guest 'that it had been very useful to him, and that he had found out what he wanted to know'.

It is possible that Beaverbrook's whirlwind cross-examination of Whittle had been prompted by reading alarming reports of a jet-engine programme in Germany. As noted already, the Air Ministry had in April 1940 inaugurated 'Scientific Intelligence Summaries'. These were to be monthly papers edited by Dr R. V. Jones, another RAE scientist who had been brought into the Ministry at the start of the war to run its intelligence section (the first scientist ever to work in this line of Whitehall business). The limited circulation list for these Summaries included David Pye, the Director of Scientific Research, who had been among the Air staff transferred to MAP. In the May 1940 edition was a paragraph referring to intelligence received about work on a twin-engined jet aircraft being developed by Heinkel, christened the He 280:

> ... the He 280 is an experimental aircraft fitted with two thermodynamic turbines which drive small propellers at the front, and whose exhaust is used as the main motive power. The development has been kept most secret, and the state of the experiment is uncertain. The machine is to be used as a destroyer, and it is hoped to attain speeds up to 800 kms.p.h. A few of these aircraft have already been built, and they might be used for scare purposes. Mass production is some way off, even if the experiments have been successful.[9]

(Intelligence reports compiled later in the war would confirm the timing of this discovery. 'The existence of designs and wind-tunnel models for a Heinkel jet-propelled aircraft', noted one report in April 1943, 'was established early in 1940.'[10]) The He 280 was actually a much more sophisticated aircraft than the May

1940 edition of the Intelligence Summaries suggested: the German engineers had no more interest than Frank Whittle in resorting to 'small propellers'.[11] Subsequent Summaries from Dr Jones would provide further intelligence on the He 280 – 'The first model is said to have crashed, and the second attained a speed of 594 mph', according to a report noted in the June/July Summary[12] – and it seemed that, in this phase of the arms race, Germany had stolen a significant lead. Hayne Constant certainly believed so, and was not afraid to relay to Whittle later in the summer of 1940 some of the latest information garnered on the progress at Heinkel ('the Germans were using a gas turbine with a single combustion chamber in the wing, fed by a scroll on the compressor...'[13]).

In fact many more jet programmes were under way in Germany than anyone in London or Farnborough yet realised: in addition to the Heinkel project, engineers at Daimler-Benz, Junkers Motoren and BMW had all been at work since the end of 1938, with varying degrees of commitment, on competing projects of their own.[14] Some key individuals within the Air Ministry in Berlin were eagerly promoting these efforts – and egging on the rivalry between them – and had placed a direct contract with Messerschmitt as early as October 1938 for the development of a suitable airframe to take the best performing engine. Those select few in British government circles who were party in the middle of 1940 to the first glimmers of intelligence on this activity must have been dismayed to learn that jet planes were being tested in Germany while Whittle's Gloster Pioneer had yet to make its maiden flight. Only by an egregious oversight could Ministers have been left ignorant of the topic in normal times. Of course the early summer of 1940 was far from normal. Britain was daily facing the possibility of a German invasion. Perhaps the man in charge of MAP was too busy to bother with intelligence reports. Just as likely, though, Beaverbrook had heard of them one way or another – and had immediately sent for Whittle to get a first-hand account of his progress. Perhaps Dr Jones's Summaries had even helped to restore Lutterworth's Priority status.

Anyway, whatever Beaverbrook's state of knowledge, Whittle returned to Rugby feeling elated over the Minister's enthusiastic support. On further reflection, it was a matter of lasting regret to him that he had squandered a precious opportunity to register his disquiet over the involvement of BTH and Rover. (Denis Tobin only added to his remorse by suggesting 'that if Lord Beaverbrook had taken a fancy to me I should probably be made a director of the whole development'.[15]) Whittle was also struck that Beaverbrook had appeared to know so little about his project. It seemed to be further confirmation of the low priority attached to the jet by the Engines directorate. Now relocated a second time and given offices in Thames House North, the erstwhile headquarters of ICI just along Millbank from the Palace of Westminster, their views indeed appeared not to have changed at all since March. Presumably unaware of the German threat, they simply did not rate development of the jet engine as a matter of any urgency. They even remained sceptical of its long-term feasibility, but that would be a subject for discussion in less fevered times. The immediate task, as they saw it, was to shepherd BTH, Rover and Whittle himself into a workable arrangement that would allow the jet project to make steady progress in the background without distracting MAP from the business of keeping the RAF fully equipped in its battle for survival against the Luftwaffe.

Roxbee Cox saw matters differently. He was far junior to Bulman and probably had little if any access to Tedder through the early weeks of MAP's existence. But Whitehall's ways were familiar to him – he had worked for a year before the war as the technical director of the body charged with the regulation of civil aircraft – and his influence seems to have grown rapidly. By July 1940, Roxbee Cox was clear in his own mind that the Engines directorate's intended relegation of Power Jets to a peripheral role was thoroughly mistaken. As the official now responsible for the jet engine, he decided he would do whatever he could to ensure that Power Jets kept effective control of its design and development. And in the wake of Beaverbrook's meeting with Whittle – perhaps even at Beaverbrook's behest – Roxbee Cox began to plan accordingly.

So now, within a ministry struggling from its start with confused and contradictory agendas on many levels, there were two broadly opposed policies on the jet engine. Both were contending hard for Tedder's ear. Whittle would need to cope with conflicting signals from Whitehall and play a careful game – a challenge, of course, for which he had not the slightest aptitude.

ii

By July 1940, even Lawrence Tweedie was beginning to despair of the policy adopted at Harrogate. The rationale for stripping Power Jets of its leading status was clear to him. Whittle and his academic friends were gifted amateurs by comparison with the practical men running huge factories that, week after week, could turn out finished engines by the score. Better, then, to hand over control of the jet's future to them. Unfortunately, the practical men had agendas of their own. BTH and Rover had begun raising design issues that seemed to be less concerned with perfecting the technical state of the engine than with reducing its production costs and so improving its potential profitability in a post-war marketplace. With the very future of the country apparently hanging in the balance, this struck many within the Ministry as inappropriate, not to say distasteful, tactics. Officials in the contracts department were especially affronted by the attitude of Spencer Wilks, always the robust Midlands businessman, who scarcely bothered to disguise his commercial motivation. Roxbee Cox remarked cryptically to Whittle at the time that the Rover men were 'honest within their lights'.[16]

Perhaps detecting a more sympathetic view of Power Jets within the Ministry, Roxbee Cox hastened within days of Whittle's brief audience with Beaverbrook to submit a capital budget of £24,000 (about £1.2 million today) for the Ladywood Works. Paying for the purchase of additional tools and the immediate construction of a row of wooden huts to adjoin the existing buildings, this alone signalled a fresh start for Power Jets' finances.

Roxbee Cox – surely with Tedder's backing – then pulled off the definitive deal for Power Jets when he persuaded the Treasury to move beyond funding of the company via successive research contracts. It was agreed that all its running expenses would in future be settled with a monthly cheque. The arrangement – acknowledging that Lutterworth was effectively a state entity despite retaining some private shareholders – would be confirmed at the end of September 1940, along with the Treasury's acceptance of the capital budget.[17]

The expansion of the Ladywood Works began to accelerate rapidly, starting with the recruitment of dozens of workmen – and twelve lady clerks – in addition to several RAF servicemen. Under Whittle's guidance, Dudley Williams and Coll Tinling went on to hire sheet-metal workers, fitters, welders, machinists, carpenters, millwrights, electricians and general labourers, draughtsmen, designers and general office staff.[18] Power Jets' payroll would rise from 54 in July to 132 by the end of the year. This pell-mell growth must have raised endless difficulties from day to day, given the still primitive state of the Power Jets premises. Fully three years after Whittle and his friends had first visited the site, its buildings were still extraordinarily basic. The newcomers were often quite shocked at the working conditions. G. B. R. ('Bob') Feilden arrived in June 1940 as the forty-seventh hire. Two decades later, he would write a colourful account of his early months:

> The minimum structural modifications had been made to enable us to test engines and combustion chambers, and to manufacture a few replacement parts to keep our development programme going. Conditions in the building were so bad that in the autumn of 1940 the entire staff were given a weekend off whilst three or four brave volunteers, wearing respirators, worked on ladders blowing the thick layer of foundry sand off the rafters and roof timbers. This step was taken in desperation after the repeated failures which we had experienced...[19]

The fifty-second hire was a twenty-seven-year-old secondee from the RAE, William Hawthorne – later to be Professor of Applied Thermodynamics at Cambridge for almost thirty years

– and he brought with him from Farnborough a small group of engineers who would devote themselves to constant improvements in the jet's combustion process. The way had just been cleared for critical progress to be made on this aspect of the engine's construction, for so long the single biggest obstacle in its development.

The breakthrough came with the adoption of a new design for the fuel system. On the original WU in April 1937, the fuel had been injected with a liquid spray from a single jet with a large aperture. This had not prevented the first ignition, but it had been a (relatively speaking) clumsy device. The spray had failed to atomise kerosene finely enough to generate the high temperatures ideally required. Whittle had insisted against Laidlaw's advice that this 'atomiser' should be dropped in favour of a system that vaporised kerosene before injecting it. His decision set off a long-running debate among the engineers between two camps sounding like tribes from *Gulliver's Travels* – the 'atomisers' and the 'vaporisers'. Supporting Laidlaw and the atomisers was a fuel engineer at Asiatic Petroleum, a Shell subsidiary based in London. His name was Isaac Lubbock (no relation to Whittle's Peterhouse tutor), and Whittle was given an introduction to him in January 1938. At his research laboratory in Fulham, Lubbock showed Whittle an atomiser capable of delivering a much finer spray that would provide a hotter flame.[20] (A droplet of any liquid fuel burns on its surface, not from its centre. The smaller the droplet's size, the greater must be the inflammable surface area for a given volume of fuel. So the finer the mist, the faster and hotter it will burn.) Lubbock and his team were intent on designing an entire combustion system that would incorporate this new atomiser and be suitable for the jet engine. Much further work was needed, though, and in the meantime Whittle pressed on as a vaporiser – only much later to admit that sticking with Laidlaw's approach, suitably amended, might have averted many difficulties.

In January 1940 Whittle received a note from Lubbock suggesting his team was on the brink of success ('I appear to have evolved a type of combustion… which one might have thought at first sight could not possibly work…'[21]) and in the middle of July

1940 he received a jubilant telephone call. Lubbock had a whole combustion chamber ready for use. As it happened, Whittle had just parted ways with Laidlaw, after a terminal argument over the quality of the parts provided by his company. He sent a team of colleagues down to see a demonstration of Lubbock's 'Shell chamber'. They were hugely impressed and drove straight back to Lutterworth with Lubbock's device in the back of their car, to be presented for Whittle's inspection. He saw immediately that Lubbock's 'wide-range pressure jet nozzle' could indeed be the solution to the combustion problem, though many experiments would be needed before the atomisers were finally to vanquish the vaporisers. Whittle delegated the task to William Hawthorne and one of Lubbock's colleagues, J. R. Joyce, who was now effectively seconded from Shell to Power Jets. Work began before the end of July on manufacturing ten chambers with atomiser systems, to arrive at a final design ('Combustion Chamber 75') that would eventually go into the W.1 flight engine. Whittle and his draughtsmen produced two beautiful drawings of the engine for MAP, with sections cut away to reveal the structures of the crucial components (*Fig. 13*).

By now the W.1 was just one of several engine designs under active consideration at Power Jets. It was more than a year since the first full run of the WU3 engine which had so excited David Pye. Whittle was totally confident that, when the time came, the E.28/39 would fly perfectly with the W.1 (in defiance of whispered jibes, that he would never forget, from 'certain high officials in the Ministry [who] believed that the aeroplane might prove to be fundamentally unstable with this novel form of propulsion'.[22]) So there had been no reason, in his view, to hold back on planning other engines. One was a modestly revised version of the W.1, classified as the W.1X and intended for experimental use. Far more important, though, was a fresh design envisaged as the power plant for a successor to the E.28/39. This plane was just coming into view. Whittle had been told by George Carter of a request from the Air Ministry prior to 10 May for design drawings of a twin-engined fighter. Gloster Aircraft submitted a first formal proposal to MAP

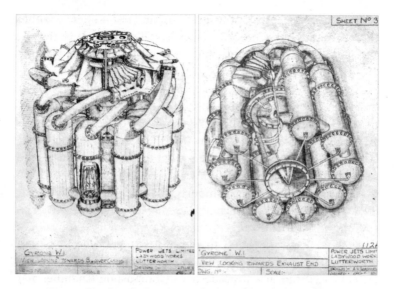

Fig. 13. The first flight engine, the W.1, from front and back,
drawn in July 1940

in August 1940. It would shortly be classified as the F.9/40, later
to be christened the 'Gloster Meteor'.

Whittle's initial design of a significantly enhanced engine for
the F.9/40 Meteor had been derived in most essentials from the
emerging W.1 and was dubbed the W.2. By August, though, it
had thrown up so many problems at the design stage that he had
decided it would have to be superseded by a substantially altered
design. Rover and BTH were both by this point working on W.2
prototypes, but he went ahead anyway with work on its successor,
to be called the W.2B. (No one ever accused Whittle of being fanciful with his choice of engine names. Ironically, his one stab at a
more creative approach fell completely flat. He tried to popularise
'gyrone' as the generic noun for the gas turbine, signifying an
engine that spins round as opposed to the reciprocal action of the
piston engine. The name never caught on.)

In the second week of August 1940, when they met for dinner
at the Grand Hotel in Rugby, Roxbee Cox was intrigued to hear

of the W.2B's inception. He was heartened also to hear of other recent technical advances at Power Jets. These included not just the Shell combustion chamber but the resolution as well of several knotty problems bearing on such fundamental issues as the final choice of alloys for the impeller, the lubrication of the engine's bearings and the fabrication of the sheet metal to be used for the engine's casings. (Whittle had shown BTH's workmen how to roll sheets of stainless steel just 1/64th of an inch thick – to the bemusement of Collingham and his deputy, Randles, who had insisted it could not be done.) It was heady stuff for Roxbee Cox, who had just spent most of his day at BTH and Rover arguing over tedious legalities. This had been dispiriting, but nonetheless useful: 'he had made it clear', he told Whittle, 'that if either of them thought it was possible to dispense with Power Jets, that was out of the question.'[23] Whittle's response was to suggest that, on the contrary, BTH itself was now eminently dispensable. Power Jets had retained its relationship with them only because forced to do so by the Air Ministry. He explained again why any worthwhile cooperation with BTH was in his view no longer possible, and he was scathing about some of the technical points that Sporborg and Collingham had made to Roxbee Cox earlier in the day. ('I told him they were throwing dust in his eyes.') But all was not yet lost, said Whittle: 'there was still time to stop the downhill slide and make quite different arrangements.' Roxbee Cox was not quite sure what Whittle had in mind. He agreed, though, to appeal to Tedder for some formal confirmation that the still-born Harrogate policy had finally been abandoned.

It was not a good moment to be suggesting fresh policy directives. These were days of mounting horror at the scale of the Luftwaffe's bombing raids on south-east England. The middle of August 1940 brought an abrupt change in Luftwaffe tactics and a series of daylight raids on RAF airfields involving massed formations of enemy aircraft. Churchill had warned in June of an imminent 'Battle of Britain' and now it was unmistakeably under way. For those in the top ranks of the RAF and their key officials, it was no time to be agonising over the management of a long-term development project. Understandably, Tedder appears to have given little thought to some new terms of reference for the project, drawn up by Lawrence Tweedie, which were signed and despatched over his name on 21 August. These went some way towards satisfying Whittle and Roxbee Cox, insofar as they addressed Power Jets 'in general terms [about] the co-operative basis on which we want your Company, The Rover Co and The British Thomson-Houston Co to work…'. This was certainly a useful corrective to the dismissive treatment of Power Jets at Harrogate in March. Unfortunately, the rest of Tedder's text was essentially a restatement of the policy adopted there. It closed with a supremely optimistic assessment that the three firms 'did not need more than a general indication of the lines along which to proceed'.[24]

Perhaps the country's dire predicament struck officials as ample justification for any cobbled expedient that could remove the Whittle business from MAP's immediate agenda. Still, Tedder's letter struck Whittle as a poor return on the assurances he had been given by Roxbee Cox at their private dinner in Rugby. It seemed to take no heed at all of what was actually happening at the Ladywood Works. Whittle showed the letter to the Power Jets team and all agreed that some kind of stand had to be taken. Their response to the setback in March had been far too accommodating. This time they would take the first possible opportunity to confront Tedder and insist that he had been badly advised. They did not have to wait long for their chance. Word arrived from MAP that the Air Vice Marshal was on his way to Lutterworth in person to settle any remaining issues.

iii

Why Tedder had failed to back up Roxbee Cox was unclear. Whittle always blamed 'certain officials', which was generally his code phrase for Bulman. Whatever the truth, he felt that Power Jets had again been outmanoeuvred. Roxbee Cox himself wisely concealed his dismay. He was convinced that Tedder's support might be fully restored, if he was properly apprised of the real situation at Lutterworth. Perhaps it was his idea, indeed, that Tedder should pay Whittle an immediate visit. Following behind Tedder's official car on 23 August in a second vehicle were Roxbee Cox himself and Tobin, with Hayne Constant from Farnborough. By the time he arrived at the Ladywood Works in the evening – after a long morning drive and an afternoon meeting at BTH – Tedder seemed largely unaware of the unhappy impact of his letter of 21 August on the Power Jets team. If Roxbee Cox had a good idea of the reception that awaited them at Lutterworth, he had had no chance to warn Tedder. When their cars drew up, Whyte, Williams and Tinling were standing with Whittle to welcome them. The four of them led the Air Vice Marshal and his party up to the drawing office on the first floor, where they sat round a table still strewn with working papers.

Tedder had just spent more than three hours with Sporborg, Collingham and the Wilks brothers, listening to their cavils about the obsessive perfectionist at Lutterworth. He opened the discussion with their complaints still ringing in his ears. He reminded the home team 'that Power Jets' function was purely research, and that this did not include experiments in manufacturing methods'. He was sure that MAP's prescription for the jet project could work smoothly, 'and that the main obstacles to be overcome were psychological ones…' It was an uncharacteristically clumsy way to have opened the conversation, given the sheer intensity of the work schedules at the Ladywood site. Whittle suggested with evident exasperation that the main obstacles were in fact less related to psychology than to the future of aero-engineering, which some people at MAP seemed completely unable to grasp. This led with little preamble to a forthright exchange that visibly disconcerted the Air Vice Marshal. The principal threat to the jet engine, said Whittle, was the risk of allowing BTH and Rover to tamper with its design. It was simply beyond their capabilities. Tedder accused him of being contemptuous of their engineers. Yes indeed he was, replied Whittle, with a vehemence Tedder had not heard before:

I said that that was true and that it was well based. As far as the Rover Co were concerned, though Mr Maurice Wilks might be a good engineer, this engine was so foreign to his previous experience that he was like a child in relation to it. As far as the BTH were concerned, there were no individuals in their organisation, with the exception of Mr Cheshire, who were at all qualified to design the job, and that we had found [this to be true] by bitter experience…[25]

Power Jets alone had the requisite skills, said Whittle. They could take advice from BTH and Rover and could then 'combine with the production facilities of the other two firms to get the most efficient result'.

Tedder was next treated to a brief digression on the engine's technical progress, in which Constant conspicuously endorsed Whittle's views. Then he was taken on a tour of the site. It was so much bigger and more impressive than when he had first visited in January – and than he had been led to expect by Bulman and Tweedie in London. Tedder saw the newly built test houses. He was shown a combustion test in the field behind the Works, always a dramatic affair. He was struck by the sheet-metal working benches and other evidence of Power Jets' incipient manufacturing capabilities. When they all returned to the upstairs office, he spoke quietly and with his usual pipe-smoking deliberation – but his change of heart was unmistakeable. Contrary to his letter two days earlier, said Tedder, Power Jets would be given the opportunity to build at least three more experimental engines beyond the W.1, 'though he made it clear that we could not hope for much in the way of machine tools and would have to sub-contract most of the work'. This proved to be no great constraint. At a finance meeting at MAP attended by Whittle three days later, some long-standing orders were approved for machine-tools ('29th [August] – Mr Tobin rang up and said we could go ahead and purchase… though they thought the price was exorbitant'[26]) and the hiring programme for the rest of the year was confirmed.

Encouraged by these concessions, Whittle decided it was time to tackle the problem of accommodation at the Ladywood Works.

They were running out of room for all their recruits, so extra space was a pressing requirement. A makeshift remedy was found when the LNER company agreed to park a redundant railway carriage in some sidings adjacent to the site. This provided several extra desks for Hawthorne and his combustion team, but a more substantial annex was needed. It was found early in September. A few miles outside Rugby, just off the main road to Lutterworth, a concealed driveway led down beneath a bower of evergreen trees and bushes to a redbrick country mansion called Brownsover Hall.

Designed in the best Victorian Gothic style by Gilbert Scott, architect of the Albert Memorial and a string of nineteenth-century churches and cathedrals, Brownsover Hall actually sported a steeple as well as a corner tower (*Fig. 14*). Tall, arched windows gave it an ecclesiastical appearance, and there were even faux-medieval cloisters inside the Hall enclosing a private chapel. The building was mostly empty in the summer of 1940. Someone in Rugby arranged for its ancestral owners, the Ward-Boughton-Leigh family, to make several of the ground-floor rooms available to Whittle at a peppercorn rent. More or less equidistant between his home in Bilton Road and the Works at Lutterworth, Brownsover Hall offered him the perfect retreat. He set up an office for himself and Mary Phillips to share in a large, high-ceilinged room overlooking the driveway and lawns in front of the house, and more than twenty designers and draughtsmen from Ladywood Works were relocated into what had once been a grand dining room at the back of the building.

Whittle would soon settle into a routine built round mornings at the Works and afternoons at Brownsover. In the study there he could sit at an enormous desk, permanently wreathed in cigarette smoke, reviewing test results and calculations or dictating the latest in an endless stream of meeting notes and memoranda to the indefatigable Mary. These papers, all signed off with 'FW/P', had grown longer and more detailed with every passing month. They had a practical purpose, insofar as Whittle was determined to keep a record of all discussions with which to defend the integrity of his project. He thought its very survival had been thrown

Fig. 14. Brownsover Hall today, looking just as it did
when FW set up there

into doubt by the behaviour of BTH and Rover since March 1940. By taking them on as primary contractors rather leaving them as subcontractors to Power Jets, so depriving Whittle of control over the development and production of the engines he was designing, MAP had in his view opened the door to all sorts of misunderstandings and worse. Leading suppliers, for example, had been puzzled by orders – from BTH in particular – accompanied by pattern drawings that differed in minute but nonetheless critical ways from Whittle's originals. Those who had decided to 'improve' upon his work had usually done so, as he could show, without consulting him. Again, mistrust between the three parties had been fuelled by many disputes over the proprietary nature of this or that design, and its consequent potential as a patentable property. Whittle discovered from a supplier on one occasion that drawings of a compressor casing provided by Rover had actually been 'photostat copies of Power Jets' drawings with all reference to Power Jets removed and no acknowledgement of the origin of the drawing[s]'.[27] By the end of August 1940 Whittle would gladly have parted company with his troublesome partners. When Tobin suggested that the squabbling between them and Power Jets over contracts might yet prompt them to walk away altogether, Whittle confessed 'that would not break my heart'.[28] But while they remained engaged, he would do his best to maintain a paper trail tracking all important decisions.

The meticulous chronicling of his affairs was important to Whittle in other ways, too. He was under appalling strain. Every day brought fresh technical challenges posed by the engine itself – not to mention, since May, the frightful possibility of defeat for the RAF and a German invasion of the country. Radio bulletins on the hour now carried the latest news of the battle in the skies over south-east England and the bravery of the RAF's young fighter pilots. Whittle had been desperate since the earliest days of the war to see his jet engine provide them with planes that would tilt the balance of the air war decisively in the RAF's favour. Yet he was still being forced to deal with officials who plainly had no concept of the new weapon almost within their grasp. The Engines directorate's opposition to his control of the jet project was wearing him down, as were the scarcely concealed manoeuvrings of BTH and Rover. Filing away his own obsessive accounts of every meeting and conversation – even where official minutes were being compiled – was Whittle's way of imposing a sense of order on events that were too often both confusing and dispiriting. Having an extraordinary ability to recall long conversations verbatim, he could also use his own narratives to tease out and correct others' inconsistencies (or worse). And the sheer labour involved in all this work had one other dimension. It kept him and his devoted Mary Phillips busy together for several hours a week.

Their relationship had grown steadily since her arrival at the end of 1938. There was never any doubt that she would follow him to Brownsover. Once installed at the Hall, she would attend most of the meetings to be held there, taking her own notes with which to complement Whittle's later recollection of what had been said. (She is usually there beside him, in the few photographs taken of him at the Hall.) By the late summer of 1940 they enjoyed a close rapport. Any romantic undertones would certainly have been suppressed by Whittle as socially inappropriate and unprofessional. He was always a stickler for appearances. That said, Mary's complicity in the almost daily preparation of memoranda must have added to the comfort that Whittle evidently derived from compiling them. His pursuit of the jet engine left him with few relationships of any kind beyond his working ties with fellow engineers. Nor was there much substance left to his marriage. He was seeing less and less of Dorothy – who seems at this point to have had only the vaguest notion about the importance of her husband's great project. As Whittle confessed much later in his life, he saw its Top Secret classification as a bar to discussing it with her: 'I couldn't put her in the picture, and she wouldn't have been interested if I had tried. She was... very artistic and her mind moved in a world far removed from science and engineering.'[29] Not surprisingly, Dorothy struggled to follow the setbacks he was facing. Mary, by contrast, did everything in her power as a secretary to lighten them.

One of Mary's minor tasks was to keep his desk at the Hall replete with his daily needs, which in addition to copious amounts of tea and cigarettes now included prescription drugs for his various stress-related ailments – and a steady supply of Benzedrine inhalers. Use of Benzedrine, containing an amphetamine-based stimulant, was already rife in the RAF by this early stage of the war. (Bomber Command was later to rely heavily on Benzedrine pills that helped crews stay awake through long missions over Germany. They were especially popular with the rear-turret gunners, the RAF's 'tail-end Charlies' – so much so that the pills themselves acquired the same nick-name.) Whittle became heavily addicted, as he recalled in later life, with doleful consequences. 'When I suffered rapid heartbeat, feelings of tension, anxiety and insomnia I did not make the connection: I assumed these things were due to overwork, frustration and the race with time. So, when I appealed to the doctor to help me with insomnia, it never occurred to me to mention the Benzedrine...'[30] Outward signs of the toll on Whittle's health were also becoming hard to ignore. He was increasingly short-tempered and suspicious of others' motives to the point of incipient paranoia. Colleagues tried in vain to persuade him to take a holiday or perhaps a refresher flying course, and worried that he often seemed overwrought. In particular, his relations with the other Power Jets directors, after months of uncertainty over the company's future, were a growing concern. Simple misunderstandings had drawn him into several bitter arguments – none more acrimonious than a dispute between him and Lance Whyte.

Though often deferring to his advice, Whittle had never liked Whyte on a personal level. He resented his upper-class airs – Whyte's mother was a Scottish aristocrat – and his disdain for his social inferiors, which was a regular source of trouble. (Whyte sparked a row at Brownsover one afternoon, reprimanding Mary Phillips for having the effrontery to take a sip from her tea in front of him.) A dispute between the two men, over who had said what at some Whitehall conference, had escalated through the summer, and at the start of September Whittle used his authority as the principal 'A' shareholder to dismiss Whyte as the company's chairman. He insisted on doing so, despite protests from Williams and Tinling and the fact that Whyte had a contract as Managing Director which all agreed would be allowed to continue. It was a messy and embarrassing saga, and it prompted Tedder to send for

Whittle and ask him for an explanation. Whittle obliged with a typically naïve candour:

> The A.V.M. asked was Mr Whyte an honest man or was he a twister (in words to that effect). I said that he was undoubtedly an honest man... but that he was not fitted for the post that he held.... I said that I thought Mr Whyte had been most unfortunate in having to deal with a man like Mr S. B. Wilks, because he was tarred with very much the same brush, to which the A.V.M. replied that that was very true. I told him that my main charges against Mr Whyte were that he was lacking in tact to an extraordinary extent, and his tactics in negotiating were shocking and did not inspire confidence...[31]

This cannot have done much to boost Tedder's confidence in Power Jets – 'What a racket!' was his instant reaction – and it can scarcely have reassured him to hear Whittle a few moments later offering some frank views on his colleagues Coll Tinling ('too cautious') and Dudley Williams (whom he described rather mysteriously as suffering 'too much from what was usually known as the June temperament').

At least this discussion, though, led to an explicit acknowledgement of the need to appoint a Chief Engineer: someone, as Tedder pointedly remarked, who would be 'free to devote his whole energies to engineering'. And as little energy as possible, it scarcely needed saying, to the politics of the project. The politics, they could both agree, would be better left entirely to 'an able and energetic man, very level-headed, and one who in no circumstances would lose his temper...' As September wore on, Whittle came to see this as the essential next step. Tedder's support had been vital – and it was gratifying that, despite occasional wavering over Ministry policy, the Air Vice Marshal had become increasingly convinced of the jet's historic importance. (Telling Whittle about a visit he had recently made to the BTH turbine hall, for example, he remarked how forcefully 'he had been reminded of the days when wooden ships were still being built and iron ships were just coming in'.) Tedder had also played a crucial part in shoring up Power Jets' financial position.

But given the RAF's current plight, his responsibilities at MAP were almost overwhelming. He simply did not have the time properly to defuse the constant tension at MAP, between those actively backing the jet and those inclined to shelve it. Plainly, the sooner a 'level-headed' man was found for the executive role that they had mooted, the better. As it happened, Whittle thought he knew just the man for the job.

iv

Ironically, he was a senior BTH man. A. P. Young had been the Works Manager of the Rugby plant since 1929. (He generally stuck to using his initials, perhaps because his middle name was Primrose.) Whittle had had little to do with him personally, but knew of his pre-war reputation as one of the country's best-known public speakers on the modern topic of industrial management. Young was also much respected in Whitehall. Indeed, he had been plucked out of BTH at the end of May 1940 and whisked off to the Ministry of Labour at the personal behest of Ernest Bevin, the trade union leader whom Churchill had appointed to head the department at the heart of the Home Front. After a few discreet enquiries, Whittle learned that Young customarily spent his Sundays in Warwickshire, resting at his home in Kenilworth. On 22 September 1940, Young's quiet Sunday afternoon was duly interrupted by the arrival of an unexpected guest.

Young had followed BTH's involvement with the jet project in general terms, without involving himself in any of the details. He was quite happy to hear more about it. As he recalled more than twenty years later, Whittle was soon pacing to and fro across the carpet in his sitting room, pleading the case for his jet and the urgent need to accelerate its development. 'He was bursting to do something to arouse those in authority to quick action, to launch a project which – he rightly felt – might reasonably have a profound influence on the future course of the war.'[32] What was needed was a small 'production committee,' said Whittle, which could be formed inside MAP to give his engine project a critical momentum. So would Young accept an invitation to become its chairman? The BTH man was flattered. He was also completely persuaded of the jet's great importance. But it was not clear to Young how Whittle thought his production committee was going to materialise. Apparently there had been no serious discussion with Tedder on the topic. Nor had Whittle consulted Roxbee Cox, or indeed given any thought to Roxbee Cox's likely reaction to his initiative.

Young suggested to Whittle that any effective committee would have to be championed at the highest levels of the government. So he proposed that he should pen a detailed 'Secret Memorandum' on Ministry of Labour paper the next day, with the full story of the project 'leading up to the present unsatisfactory position', and then hand it personally to Mr Bevin. They could fully expect the Minister to pass it straight to 10 Downing Street. Whittle welcomed this idea and urged Young to go ahead. It was obviously a risky tactic to appeal over the heads of the men at the Ministry: he and Young would be gambling on a positive reaction at the top of government. But Whittle felt drastic times required a drastic measure.

Young did as he had promised. His letter was an impassioned plea for the jet engine to be given the government's full support, comparing the potential value of the jet aeroplane with the impact of the tank on the Western Front in the First World War. He gave the letter to Bevin four days later. As anticipated, Bevin passed it straight to 10 Downing Street. In his later account of the story, Young claimed 'good grounds' for believing this was the first occasion on which Churchill was alerted to the jet project's existence. Perhaps so, and a decision followed almost immediately. On Tuesday 1 October 1940, Whittle received a telephone call from the office of Professor Lindemann. The Prof (as he was known to all) had been asked by the Prime Minister to talk to Whittle in person – so would he please come to Whitehall the next day. As he had done for his July encounter with Beaverbrook, Whittle dropped everything to prepare his case. (He appears to have had no inkling of Lindemann's clash with Tizard in 1936.) He wrote a three-page summary of the projected performance for both the single-engined E.28/39 Pioneer and the twin-engined F.9/40 Meteor.[33] And he added two pages of commentary on the development work, explaining how 'MAP has made a great mistake in the opinion of the writer'. He listed the inadequacies of BTH and Rover, and the spurious reasons given by MAP for its policy since March – based on 'decisions [that] have been taken after making only the most superficial enquiry into the fitness of the firms concerned'.

The interview was fixed for the Wednesday afternoon, 2 October 1940. Arriving in Whitehall at midday, Whittle was appalled to see the latest evidence of German bombing in the very heart of the capital: London had been targeted by the Luftwaffe every night for weeks. He went out to lunch with Denis Tobin and showed him the notes that he had written for Lindemann, including his negative commentary on MAP's track record. Tobin tried to be as supportive as usual, though he was understandably nervous that 'a severe reaction might come back on Tedder' if Whittle's views were fully accepted.[34] Then Whittle set off for Lindemann's office just round the corner from Downing Street. One of the Professor's assistants, a Mr Tuck, received him cordially but warned him to expect plenty of scepticism. In the event, it took Whittle no time at all to win over Lindemann. Having heard little or nothing more about jet propulsion since those committee investigations into Arnold Griffith's work in the late 1920s, Lindemann was enthralled by Whittle's description of the science behind the jet engine. He was astonished – and not a little annoyed – to hear that the first engine had been running for three years, and that flight tests of the E.28/39 could be ready to start by Christmas. He was also quick to deride MAP for doing so little since February to speed the jet engine into production. What followed next caught Whittle by surprise:

> He then took my breath away by asking 'if you were given an absolutely free hand, would it be possible to get the complete

interceptor fighter into production in the spring [of 1941], at the rate of 20 a week'. He commented that as the programme stood it looked like being 1942 before anything materialised... and he then said 'suppose they send 40,000 bombers over next year', or words to that effect.

After some discussion he asked me to give a considered opinion as to whether, given all the necessary resources, facilities, factories, etc, etc and if a tremendous gamble were taken on the success of the job, could it be done. I said that I would consider it... and asked that he should still seriously consider my suggestions, even if we did have to wait till 1942.[35]

Whittle agreed to give him a written answer, though he was 'appalled at the magnitude of the demand' from Lindemann. On his way out, he passed a beaming Mr Tuck who offered his congratulations. He could always tell, he said, when things had gone well with the Prof – so 'I could consider that I had had a very successful meeting and that it was evident that I had convinced Prof. Lindemann and removed his scepticism...'

Returning that evening to Rugby, Whittle plunged into 'a feverish rush to produce the outline for a workable scheme'. Lindemann's request for 'a considered opinion', after all, appeared to suggest that Churchill himself might be taking a direct interest in the jet. Whittle asked Gloster's George Carter and several of the Lutterworth engineers to hurry over to Brownsover Hall the next day for a discussion he promised them would make good use of their time. All agreed to attend a morning meeting. Gathered together in his study, they solemnly endorsed a written plan of action for Lindemann. His goal could be met, they would advise, provided several weighty conditions were met. Whittle drew up eight of them, which amounted to launching a special organisation for the production of the jet aeroplane immediately, and granting it unimpeded access to all the tools, labour and materials it requested. Power Jets and Gloster, both duly expanded for the scope of the job, would be the main contractors. Presiding over their work and all the manufacturing facilities and their suppliers would be a 'Controller Committee' comprising 'men each

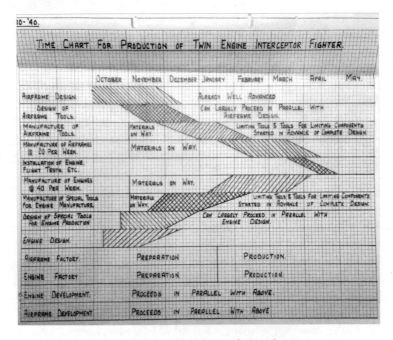

Fig. 15. The time-chart drawn for Lindemann,
proposing jet planes by May 1941

of exceptional ability for his task'. Whittle attached to the report a time-chart showing the critical stages along a path leading to the launch of 'a twin-engine interceptor fighter' by May 1941 (*Fig. 15*). Then he added a cover note for Lindemann. It concluded: 'We estimate that the complete twin engine aircraft [i.e. the Meteor] would be in full production at the rate of 20 per week by May 1st 1941.'[36] That would be almost eighteen months since the running of the WU3 for David Pye, which seemed a reasonable gestation period in the circumstances.

The package went off by hand to Lindemann's office early on 4 October, and Whittle at the same time sent a copy of it to Tobin. Later in the day he began to feel ill at ease for not having done more to keep Tedder abreast of the whole affair. He tried in vain to reach the Air Vice Marshal at MAP by telephone, only to hear from a Squadron Leader Ridley that events had moved on slightly alarmingly. Lindemann had already sent some 'proposals' into the Ministry. They had not gone down well. Even this junior RAF officer felt entitled to opine that they 'seemed calculated to slow up the work rather than speed it up' and he made a peevish remark about Tedder being left out of the loop.[37] Whittle was dismayed. He dashed off a letter to Tedder, expressing some remorse – 'looking back on the affair, it might appear that I intrigued to bring special pressure to bear on the Ministry because of my well-known disagreement with the policy of the Department' – but insisting that his meeting with Lindemann, just like his interview with Beaverbrook in July, had come completely out of the blue.[38] This, of course, was more than a little disingenuous; but his account of Lindemann's interest and the sequel was otherwise truthful enough. (This letter disclosed that Young, off his own bat, had suggested that not only BTH and Rovers but also two or three other firms 'equally capable should be roped in on the job'. Whittle had taken great exception to this, when told of it by Lindemann, and the two of them had concurred 'that this was not the time for new firms to start learning how to do it.') There was no reply from Tedder.

Whittle became steadily more anxious and rang Lindemann's office on 7 October for more news. Tuck told him the jet's future 'was now in the hands of the Prime Minister'. It seemed the prospect of a jet fighter in the air by May 1941 had caught Churchill's attention. But Lindemann's assistant also urged Whittle to be wary of Whitehall's ways:

> Tuck thought I had been rather unwise in mentioning the matter to the Ministry at all, and said that the whole business was now on such a high plane that one had to be very careful. He went on to say that if things happened they would happen fast, but if the decision went against the scheme nothing very much could be done about it.[39]

Tuck was right to warn of quick consequences. He called back later in the day to say Lindemann was sending out invitations to an urgent conference on the jet engine's future. It was to be held at the

RAE offices in Farnborough on 11 October. The Prof would chair it, with two objectives on behalf of the War Cabinet: to establish the technical prospects for the jet engine, and to decide on the feasibility of launching it into production as soon as possible. In addition to Whittle himself, the RAE would be well represented and Tedder would be invited to bring his own team of officials from MAP.

Whittle clearly hoped that six frustrating months of equivocation by MAP might be over at last. Had he heeded Tuck's advice, he would have lain low in preparation for the conference. But he had just put the finishing touches to a masterly summary of the jet's technical history to date ('Memorandum on the Development of the Gyrone Engine') and could not resist sending copies by hand to Tedder and Lindemann on 10 October. He attached two typically unguarded letters, further raising the stakes on the gamble he had taken. He told Tedder the seven weeks since 23 August had exhausted his remaining hopes of achieving 'satisfactory and rapid development... within the present framework'. And in case Tedder was in any doubt about the line he would take at Farnborough the next day, he warned the Air Vice Marshal (not for the first time) that he 'would prefer to be posted right away from the job [rather] than attempt to carry on within the present framework'.[40] In the second letter, to Lindemann, he made a stab at pre-empting any push-back from MAP officials at the conference. Their advice, he suggested, had constantly impeded Tedder ('who has repeatedly expressed his confidence in me'). The Ministry seemed determined to stick by BTH and Rover 'to do things they have never done before, simply on the ground apparently that they are large firms with years of production experience'.[41] And departmental loyalties had been a constant problem. They had served, wrote Whittle, 'to prevent honest expressions of opinion... and I therefore hope that something will be done to prevent this happening at tomorrow's meeting'.[42]

In the event, MAP's officials seem to have expressed few opinions next day, honest or otherwise. Lindemann fired off a long stream of technical questions about the project's progress so far and it was very largely left to Whittle to answer them. His sub-sequent note of the meeting suggests a dry encounter under a characteristically aloof chairman who gave away little of his own thinking. George Bulman was present but he, too, kept his own counsel. Perhaps his workload at MAP since August had simply left him too drained to feel like intervening. (The RAF's intense campaign to defend its fighter airfields against incessant attack by the Luftwaffe appeared to have passed its peak, but it had been a cruel battle of attrition – and MAP's success in replacing lost aircraft faster than the Germans had been critical to the outcome.) It was obviously a fraught occasion – Lindemann was there, after all, to reach a decision that all understood he would pass on directly to Churchill – and Whittle probably added to the tension with some colourful criticism of BTH. Its faulty workmanship, he complained at one point, had led to the scrapping of many parts – including three expensive impeller forgings ('This last caused a mild sensation').[43] Then suddenly Lindemann had heard enough. He stood up and the meeting was over.

Standing around afterwards with Tedder, Constant and several MAP officials including both Bulman and Roxbee Cox, Whittle had no idea whether his appeal to Lindemann had paid off. By his own account written that evening, he extracted several promises from Tedder that a big stick would be waved at both BTH and Rover; but he still could not quite persuade the Air Vice Marshal to give him the level of authority he thought essential in all design matters. Whittle's record of their conversation ended by noting he had 'repeatedly affirmed very emphatically [to Tedder] that the whole development programme lacked clear definition', which probably means the Air Vice Marshal was badgered all the way to the door of his Ministry car, waiting to take him and Bulman back to London.

Just two days later, Whittle heard news from Tobin that left him feeling elated. Evidently Lindemann had intervened to great effect. Tedder had summoned a meeting in his office at MAP and had laid down production goals for the F.9/40 jet fighter 'as the basis for planning'.[44] They would aim for no less than 80 airframes and at least 160 engines a month. It was clear that 'a large proportion' of the engines would have to be manufactured by Rover, but detailed 'terms of reference' would be applied, to supersede the spirit of collaboration that had wilted so badly in recent months. Everything possible would be done to deliver a first production version of the jet fighter by September 1941 – not quite matching Lindemann's challenge to Whittle on 2 October, but not far short of it.

One of the most useful sources for the whole story of the wartime jet is an account written in 1945–7 – and warmly endorsed by Whittle himself – as a first draft of the relevant section in the official history of the war. Its author was Cynthia Keppel (whose former status as a secretary at MI5 rather belied her forensic skills as an investigative reporter).* She interviewed many of those who had been directly involved. To assess the importance of the Farnborough conference of 11 October 1940, she spoke directly to one of the participants. He told her that '[at this] most important meeting... [Lindemann] was convinced by Mr Constant and Wing Commander Whittle of the importance of jet propulsion'.[45] This was the message that Lindemann conveyed to Churchill. In Keppel's view, his doing so contributed directly to 'the remarkable renaissance in jet propulsion during the early and late autumn' of 1940.

A few days later, on 18 October, Wilfrid Freeman and Roxbee Cox drove up to the Ladywood Works to congratulate Whittle in person on the momentous decisions that had been taken about future production. Freeman also had a word of warning, though, about the political reverberations of the bold initiative that Whittle had triggered:

---

* Keppel's 173-page account, 'The Development of Jet Propulsion and Gas Turbine Engines in the United Kingdom', has been retained in The National Archives (AIR 62/2) but its text was heavily redacted before being included in the *Design and Development of Weapons* volume of the Civil Histories of the war eventually published in 1964. Keppel had had plenty of time by then to debate the editing of her contribution – one of the three authors of the book was M. M. Postan whom she had married in December 1944. Her original account is referenced below as Keppel's draft history.

> Sir Wilfrid said that Professor Lindemann had apparently made out to the Prime Minister that he had discovered this engine, and has given the impression that the Ministry were doing nothing about it. Dr Roxbee Cox said that the facts were not like that, to which Sir Wilfrid replied that the important thing was that the Prime Minister thought they were.[46]

Freeman did not elaborate on the dangers lurking here, but he and Roxbee Cox were both well aware of them. Any criticism of MAP was a criticism of their bull-in-a-china-shop Minister, Lord Beaverbrook. It is quite plausible that Beaverbrook had known nothing about the Farnborough conference: his erratic and unpredictable direction of MAP left much of the Ministry's activities to be coordinated by Freeman and his closest colleagues. (In a private letter written before the end of the year, Tedder would deliver his own verdict on this state of affairs: 'the present organisation of the Ministry is chaotic and the methods employed by some of the principal authorities are such as to cause mutual distrust, friction and confusion.'[47]) Lindemann's disparagement of the Ministry, though, was almost certain to have reached Beaverbrook's ear. Some response, however devious, could be guaranteed. Beaverbrook loathed Lindemann: he once famously described Churchill's confidant as an adviser 'whose entry into other Ministers' offices was seldom solicited and whose departure was invariably welcomed'. Freeman and Roxbee Cox cautioned Whittle that some personality clashes might lie ahead, with potentially unfortunate consequences.

Lindemann's other bitter antagonists now included Sir Henry Tizard. As Whittle talked to Freeman and Roxbee Cox that day about ways in which MAP's coordination of the jet project might be made more effective, he was intrigued to hear that Tizard's name had recently been mooted as possible chairman of an 'executive committee'. Tizard had just returned from leading a technical mission to the United States (about which more later). First reports suggested it had gone well, reminding many in Whitehall of Tizard's qualities as an administrator. He was still chairman of the Aeronautical Research Committee and remained the Rector of Imperial College. As a result of his quarrel with Lindemann and resignation in June, though, he had no real perch in Whitehall, no proper job and no office. This seemed anomalous, given his superb connections in the Air Ministry and throughout the RAF. Whittle suggested he would welcome having Tizard's active support. He had, after all, been one of the jet's strongest supporters in its earliest days, and had recently stood up for it on many occasions – not least in May 1939, when Griffith had suggested to the Air Ministry that the experimental engine had reached the end of the road and Tizard had insisted otherwise.[48] Freeman thought a role for Tizard might be helpful, but was unlikely to arise. (He knew that Beaverbrook, irritated that Tizard had not responded instantly to a summons to his office, had refused to see him as he prepared for his trip to the USA. Told of the reason by Freeman, 'Tizard was shocked. "The man must be mad." "Of course he's mad," said Freeman, "didn't you know that?"'[49])

Whittle heard nothing more of the machinations in London over the coming days. And then, quite suddenly, Freeman was gone. At the beginning of November 1940, it was announced that he was leaving MAP with immediate effect. He was to join the Air Ministry as Deputy Chief of the Air Staff under Charles Portal. (It was generally believed that he might have been appointed to the top job a month earlier but for the opposition of the King, who refused to have a divorced man in the role. Portal accepted it, but insisted on having Freeman as his deputy.) Freeman's departure from MAP robbed Whittle of his most influential champion just as the jet project seemed poised to achieve an unstoppable momentum. The news then reached Lutterworth that Freeman's responsibilities for research and development had been reassigned. And Beaverbrook had handed them over to none other than Henry Tizard.

Tizard's elevation offered Whittle at least some comfort: he was a scientist and an engineer, and the two of them enjoyed a good rapport. Two drawbacks, though, came with it. One was quickly apparent: Lindemann turned his back on the project – as no doubt Beaverbrook intended. So as well as losing Freeman,

Whittle also lost his recently acquired line into Downing Street. No word would be heard for the next few months of Churchill's attitude to the jet. The other snag about Tizard's appointment was that nobody could be sure what he had been appointed to do. Beaverbrook failed hopelessly to define a proper role for him with formal powers and responsibilities. It was not even clear how his role was to relate to Tedder's work as erstwhile deputy to Freeman. This source of confusion, at least, was short-lived. Three weeks later, it was Tedder's turn to disappear. At the end of November he followed Freeman out of MAP, suddenly and unexpectedly posted to Cairo as Deputy Commander-in-Chief of RAF operations in the Middle East.

Whittle would have to press ahead without the cover provided for his project by both these senior RAF officers since January 1940. His hopes of delivering a jet fighter for the RAF in 1941 seemed to have been given a huge boost, and he had Tizard to help him cope with the influence of some less sympathetic figures inside MAP. Only in retrospect would it become apparent that these personnel changes late in 1940 had actually been a calamity for Whittle and the progress of his jet.

7

'Say, 1,000 WHITTLES...'

November 1940 to July 1941

i

Late in the day on 14 November 1940, Whittle drove home from Brownsover Hall as usual, dropping Mary off at No. 77 and driving half a mile further down the Bilton Road out of Rugby to reach the little lane up to Broomfield. After supper with Dorothy and the boys he turned back to his papers and was soon poring as usual over the latest test results. Shortly after 7 p.m., he heard the unmistakeable sound of heavy aircraft overhead. Rushing into the blackout darkness of the garden, he saw a rash of explosions from the direction of Coventry. The family house was on a small ridge that set it above the surrounding countryside. He could clearly see fires breaking out, little more than ten miles away to the west, across the city where he had spent his childhood. What followed shocked Whittle to the core. The moonlit night sky filled with the noise of hundreds upon hundreds of enemy bombers, all seemingly heading for Coventry. The distant fires grew into an inferno – 'an awe-inspiring and terrible spectacle' as he later recalled – that stretched along the horizon.[1] There had been several small raids on the city since the start of the year, but nothing remotely like this. Dorothy and the two boys joined him and they all stood transfixed, side by side in the darkness. The bombing continued until well after midnight and Whittle feared for the level of destruction in the city. (In fact, virtually the whole of the city centre was devastated, while thousands of homes and factories all around it were destroyed – including, as it happened, the Hillman motor car factory built at the start of the 1920s by Spencer Wilks' father-in-law.) This was the kind of savage onslaught that he had long been afraid might accompany any new European war. That the bombs were falling on Coventry only compounded his anguish: more than ten years later, he still found it 'impossible to describe my feelings as I helplessly watched my native city go up in flames'. From his vantage point on the edge of Rugby, he could not be sure but strongly suspected that the German bombers were flying over the city with virtual impunity. Dozens of searchlight beams criss-crossed the night sky and anti-aircraft batteries kept up a constant barrage into the early hours. Yet it seemed to him that all the raiders were 'apparently escaping unscathed'. He was not mistaken: the RAF had no nightfighters available and the Luftwaffe that night lost just one aircraft, out of more than five hundred engaged in the raid.

No other event could have impressed on him more vividly the potential importance of his engine and the need to pursue it at almost any cost. A jet fighter, capable of soaring above all other aircraft within ten minutes of take-off, had lain at the heart of his vision for the gas turbine for more than two years. He had set down exactly what he envisaged in that memorandum of October 1938 (see Prologue, p. xxiv). Too much time had been wasted in 1940 arguing about the overlap between development and production. Now he thought there was at last a readiness in Whitehall to back Power Jets with far more resolve – and more funding, too, via the new regular cheques from the Treasury. His W.1 engine would soon be ready for its maiden flight in the Gloster Pioneer, and he was already hard at work on the drawings for the W.2B that Rover was now scheduled to start producing in quantity by September 1941. Every feature of the engine had to be drawn in the minutest detail, to provide for the manufacture of parts – especially the blades and vanes, all with complex angled

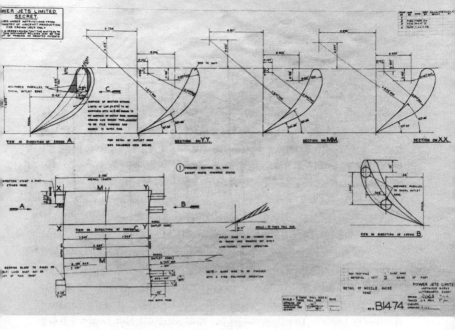

Fig. 16. 'Guide vanes' for the W.2B engine, each to be
made with exquisite precision

shapes – for which there was no precedent in the piston-engine
world (*Fig. 16*).

Though deprived of his supporters in Freeman and Tedder,
Whittle took some satisfaction from Tizard's arrival at MAP. As
a general matter, he applauded the appointment – even as just
an unofficial adviser – of such a distinguished scientist, steeped
for years in aeronautical research. Both the Ministry and the
RAF paid, in Whittle's view, far too little heed to science and
engineering. He had been shocked, as he told Tobin late in
November 1940, to discover that the Chief Technical Officer of
Fighter Command held only the modest rank of Group Captain,
affording little or no access to the top brass. (He asked Tobin
to impress on his colleagues at MAP 'that this was in my view
all wrong and represented a serious weakness, especially as it
was clear many operational problems were engineering matters'.
Tobin agreed to see this opinion 'was spread around a bit'.[2])
Whittle was heartened, more specifically, by the close interest
taken by Tizard in his own progress at Lutterworth. On his first

trip to the Ladywood Works since the beginning of 1940, Tizard expressed open dismay that Whittle still had only the antiquated workhorse of a solitary jet engine to show for all his labours since 1937: 'it was an unsatisfactory state of affairs...'.[3] (When a company like Bristol or Rolls-Royce tackled the creation of a new piston engine, it would have a dozen or so versions under development at the same time. Working on a single unit meant perilous delays.) The working arrangements proposed by MAP in March 1940 had, Tizard agreed, worked out very poorly. He rapidly sized up BTH's inadequacies and gave the Rugby company no real credence as a future partner. 'Mr Sporborg takes the line that BTH know much more about these things than Whittle... and I am inclined to think we shall not get much out of the firm.'[4] Tizard was keen to link Whittle up with leading figures in the world of aero-engine design who could offer advice and perhaps additional ideas in the same way as Shell's Isaac Lubbock had done.

One such individual was Frank Halford (commonly referred to as Major Halford, retaining the wartime rank he had earned in the Royal Flying Corps just like Major Bulman). Halford had been responsible for the 'Gypsy' engines, installed by de Havilland in some of the best-selling light aircraft of the interwar years, most notably the Tiger Moth biplane. Tizard had his own agenda here, too: men like Halford – and several other famous names in the engine business including Harry Ricardo, best-known for his work on sleeve valves for piston engines – could offer him a second opinion on the mechanical progress of Whittle's project. He was also being urged by the RAE to broaden the range of firms engaging with the jet project. Tizard was sensitive to the risk of offending Whittle's pride and sent him a delicately worded letter explaining his rationale for inviting other views. 'We should take all the precautions we can at this stage,' he wrote early in December, 'now that so much depends on experimental units that are going to be made in the near future.' Seeking others' involvement meant 'no implied criticism'.[5] Whittle was not so sure. When Halford arrived at Lutterworth on 30 December 1940, with a couple of de Havilland engineers in tow, their host seemed to them unduly edgy. Their visit passed off well, though, with Halford himself stressing in conversation the importance of requiring sub-contracted manufacturers to work 'absolutely' to designs produced by Whittle, 'whether they liked them or not...'.[6]

Lutterworth was suddenly a magnet for distinguished visitors. It was only eighteen months since the jet project had been on the brink of being discontinued by the authorities. Now some of the highest and most powerful names in the land were pressing for time in Whittle's diary. Their glamorous cars – none flashier than the yellow Rolls-Royce that was Tizard's much treasured ministerial perk – were drawing up quite regularly in front of the drab buildings of the Ladywood Works, so recently all but derelict. And Whittle sent none away disappointed. Influential figures visiting for the first time were invariably bowled over – in one case, literally so. At the beginning of December the Ladywood Works laid on a tour for Air Chief Marshal Hugh Dowding, who was intent on finding out for himself about a project that Tedder had mentioned to him several times. (Dowding had lost his position at the head of Fighter Command just a fortnight earlier, a departure not unconnected with the absence of night fighters so conspicuously evident over Coventry the previous month.) As Whittle showed him around the worksite, Dowding heard the sound of the engine starting up and headed straight for the side of the test cell where its rear nozzle protruded through the wall. Misunderstanding a gesture from Whittle, he strode directly into the jet stream. The invisible blast tore open the heavy trench coat he was wearing, blew his Air Chief Marshal's hat high into the air and hurled the fifty-eight-year-old across the concrete. Famed for his supposed lack of humour, 'Stuffy' Dowding had recovered sufficiently by lunchtime to joke about the incident and it was not referred to again. But it might easily have killed him.

By the end of 1940, Tizard was making obvious headway: the conviction was spreading that Whittle's engine did indeed belong on any list of 'potential war-winners'. The goals recently agreed in October as the 'basis for planning' already looked far too modest. On the second day of the New Year, 1941, Whittle joined a roundtable conference at the executive offices of BTH, convened by Tizard to review the path ahead that would lead to a jet-fighter squadron for the RAF. Its seventeen participants – from Power Jets, BTH, Rover and a few of their main suppliers as well as MAP itself – comprised more or less all those with a significant influence on the project to date. From the chair, Tizard opened their discussion by declaring 'this engine could make a lot of difference to the war if it could be made a production job in time'.[7] (Tizard at this point supposed the war would be over in two years.) Before the conference ended, agreement had been reached on Tizard's own proposal that they aim for production of the W.2B engine at a rate of 2,000 units a year within eighteen months. In the words of Keppel's draft history, 'it was clear [to Tizard]... that if the jet fighter was required at all it would be required in very large numbers and... [so he needed] to arrange for production plans to be undertaken with the greatest enthusiasm and activity'.[8] This was a euphemistic way of describing the most extraordinary gamble that was now to be taken. Gloster and Rover were to be instructed to proceed as quickly as possible with the construction of twelve F.9/40 Meteor prototypes. In parallel with this work, and without any guarantee that the W.2B would live up to its billing, the two companies were also to embark immediately on the planning and assembly of jigs and tools capable of turning out eighty aircraft a month 'to avoid delay when a production order should be approved'.

It was a supremely bold leap of faith on Tizard's part, another brave sally on behalf of a new technology by the man whose leadership had been vital to the breakthrough with radar four years earlier. He was ready to champion the start of line production within a matter of months for an engine that was basically the same as the WU3 that had been designed and developed for less than £20,000 (about £1 million today). Whittle was delighted. The Treasury's mandarins were unimpressed. A letter from MAP conveyed the conference's decision to Great George Street and the reply was a classic of its kind. Requesting some confirmation 'in writing' that Tizard was sure of the gamble's outcome – a contradiction in terms in itself, of course – the Treasury's incredulity was no less menacing for being exquisitely understated:

> There is, as your letter appreciates, a risk involved in going ahead with plans for production of a type [of aircraft] which has not reached the stage at which it can be fully tested... If there is a tendency to suspend judgment for a period on the new engine and airframe, during which period expenditure on the jigging and tooling for the production orders was mounting up, the position would be less attractive.[9]

In other words, any hint of delay in reaching the production stage would bring down the wrath of the Treasury on all concerned.

The day after the conference, 3 January 1941, Whittle and Roxbee Cox went to lunch at the MAP offices in Thames House. Tizard recorded for his own diary: 'Whittle said the spirit of cooperation shown yesterday was better than it had ever been.'[10] It had indeed been a memorable day for him. After all the jockeying for control of the project through 1940, it was a moment to be savoured. BTH's Harry Sporborg had agreed, albeit rather gracelessly, to continue making experimental units of the W.2B on contract to Power Jets, though it was now generally understood that BTH would not be considered as a future line manufacturer under contract to MAP. Spencer Wilks gave an undertaking that Rover would also make test units, and would gear up for quantity production in a No.2 shadow factory. All had agreed to abide by Whittle's design for the W.2B. In the event of any need arising for design amendments, as part of the final preparations for large-scale production, Whittle was to be regarded as the principal arbiter. Very minor changes to the *mechanical* aspects of the design would be acceptable, but other changes would only be permissible at his discretion – most especially those affecting any aspects of the engine touching on 'its general aerodynamic characteristics'. Any serious disagreements would be referred to Tizard for a final decision.

This encouraging state of affairs was mostly Tizard's doing, ably assisted by Roxbee Cox. Whittle had been sufficiently reassured by their involvement to set aside his deep misgivings over Rover's capacity to deliver what he required of them. His only regret at this point was that Tizard's overtures to other aero-engineering firms had not included an approach to the one name that Whittle esteemed above all others: Rolls-Royce. Not for the first time, he had asked Hayne Constant during the conference at BTH 'if there was any chance of getting some of our work done at Rolls-Royce'.[11] No hope at all, replied Constant. The firm's magnificent Merlin engine was probably the single most indispensable item in Britain's wartime armoury. Most of its development engineers were at full stretch, devising improvements for the next Merlin upgrade and its next state-of-the-art supercharger. Besides, as Tizard had reminded Whittle a few times since November, the Derby firm had its own in-house gas-turbine project, in the shape of A. A. Griffith's CR1 contra-flow design. Not for the first time, in fact, Griffith's endeavours with gas-turbine technology were impeding Whittle's progress – though whether either Tizard or Whittle noted the irony of this at the time may be doubted. (Years later, in an autobiography entitled *Not Much of an Engineer*, one of Rolls-Royce's most distinguished alumni suggested he had already instigated discussions between Lutterworth and Derby by this date.[12] Stanley Hooker recounted visiting Power Jets in January 1940 and building a close bond between the two companies over the subsequent eighteen months or so. Had this version of the past only been true, an impending tragedy might have been averted – but Hooker, as will be seen, was not much of a diarist and had muddled his dates.)

ii

Despite his New Year optimism, Whittle was sceptical that Tizard had yet brought all his MAP officials fully round to their proposed way forward. He half-expected some pushback soon from the

Engines directorate. On 15 January 1941, though, he took a phone call from Denis Tobin, who had some unexpected news. George Bulman had decided he was wrong about jet propulsion. He was telling colleagues that it was time for him to go to Lutterworth and say so. He was as good as his word, and accompanied Roxbee Cox and Tobin up to Leicestershire two weeks later, when Whittle and Lance Whyte were treated to an unexpected but nonetheless welcome confession:

> ... Major Bulman stated that his views on the whole project had changed completely in the last few days. He said that he had been very sceptical about the whole project but that we had made some remarkable advances recently which had quite changed his outlook and he proposed to take a close interest in the future.[13]

January brought another change at MAP, too, with the departure of Lawrence Tweedie, though this was almost certainly a coincidence. (While his attitude to jet propulsion had scarcely endeared Tweedie to the team at Lutterworth, he had earned some distinction as an authority on aviation fuels. But he had succumbed since October to serious illness, attributed by Tizard to overwork, and he was being posted to a fuel-research station in Trinidad where he could work as a part-time consultant while restoring his health.[14])

Bulman linked his change of heart to significant advances made in recent weeks. Power Jets had just begun testing the W.1X engine – in all respects a duplicate of the W.1 destined for the E.28/39, except for its inclusion of some components not deemed flight-worthy – and it was true that its performance marked a huge advance on that of the experimental WU engine in all its permutations. The real explanation, though, probably had far less to do with the latest tests at the Ladywood Works than with Bulman's realisation that his Engines directorate was in danger of losing control of the jet project. Tizard's bid to leapfrog into full production tooling for the W.2B ahead of any engine testing at all had obvious echoes, for him, of that lurid ABC Dragonfly episode of 1917. So he had decided to profess a revised and much more sympathetic attitude to Whittle's jet while actually taking steps, just as he had done one year earlier, to undermine Power Jets' role – as would soon become evident – and to shift control of the project over to his friends at Rover.

The build-up of men and machinery at Lutterworth since the autumn had left Bulman bemused. The decisions taken at the BTH conference on 2 January had been even more alarming – not least because of the way that Power Jets had construed them as an endorsement of its own expansion plans. The Ladywood Works was already bigger than the entire RAE establishment at Farnborough, but apparently Whittle wanted it to become three times larger. Bulman learned early in January that Dudley Williams was drawing up a proposal to multiply the Works' floor space several times over, to accommodate an increase in the workforce – currently standing at 140 men – to several hundred by the end of 1941. An alternative proposal from Williams was that Power Jets should move to another site altogether. A suitable fresh location, he had suggested, might offer as much as 70,000 square feet. This compared with a mere 14,000 square feet at Lutterworth. And Power Jets' expenditure was meanwhile rising rapidly. It had totalled £96,500 since the launch of the company in March 1936, of which £75,000 had been spent in 1940. It was already obvious that expenses in 1941 were going to be of a different order: the government was now committing itself to significant expenditure on the jet. (Expenses would reach £200,000 by the end of the year, equivalent to £10 million today.) It was all part of transforming the makeshift operation set up at the end of 1937 into a facility for assembling and testing experimental engines, as well as designing them.

And to Bulman's mind, it was madness. In his memoirs, written largely in the 1960s, he offered a colourful depiction of his tactics in opposing Whittle's plans. He described how, at the Farnborough conference chaired by Lindemann in October 1940, he had spoken out against Whittle's 'box of black magic' to such effect that he had killed off Lindemann's interest on the spot:

I pointed out quietly that, incalculable as was the ultimate value of the jet, it was still only in its earliest experimental stage.... [It] might seem to be delightfully simple, straightforward and attractive to other than hard-headed, experienced engineers. But, in fact, the very novelty of the concept brought with it a host of entirely new and vital problems... The Prof looked hard and long at me... [then] got up and drove back to London... [N]othing more came of that meeting from Number 10.[15]

There is no contemporaneous record of this speech ever being made – and Lindemann was far from deterred by the conference, as noted – so Bulman in old age had let his imagination roam. This was certainly a speech, though, that he would like to have delivered. It was a polished articulation of his lifelong disdain for 'Wild Inventors' and too-clever-by-half scientists. All but overwhelmed in 1940–41 by MAP's responsibilities for the very survival of the RAF, Bulman resented having to cope with an obsessive individual whose pursuit of an uncompromisingly novel technology plainly struck him as slightly crazed. Indeed, he thought Whittle was showing signs of clinical paranoia, and perhaps he was right: paranoia would later come to be seen as a common side effect of addiction to Benzedrine. (Whittle, recalled Bulman years later, 'was quick to invest every discussion with the venom of suspicion, scavenging through letters and minutes of meetings for odd words or phrases which he could pick on to suggest that they were deliberately ambiguous and revealing of a sinister influence...'[16]) The MAP man, steeped in the business of equipping the RAF with piston engines for almost thirty years, thought it his duty to minimise the jet project's disruptive influence. The combination of Whittle and Tizard was in this sense even more of a challenge than the tacit alliance between Whittle and the Air Marshals that he had faced over most of 1940. The pressure of events through the Battle of Britain and its aftermath meant there had never been time to address the issue properly. Bulman set out in January 1941 to make amends, taking full advantage of the departure of Freeman and Tedder.

There was never any prospect of Tizard offering much resistance. Bulman was an assertive character with a confidence in his own authority that had grown immeasurably in recent times. His central role in the setting up of the shadow-factories scheme in 1936–9 had left him with a strong network of associates across the aero-engine industry, and the scheme's proven success had greatly enhanced his standing within the Ministry and beyond it. By the start of 1941 he was also basking in reflected glory from Fighter Command's performance in the Battle of Britain. Tizard by contrast was working as an unpaid, unofficial adviser whose lack of formal authority was increasingly onerous to him. Bulman grossly overstated this point in his memoirs – 'in his new role Tizard had no real power and his advice was little enough invited, or encouraged when offered...'[17] – but it was evident within weeks of that dramatic conference at BTH in January 1941 that Tizard was not going to have the impact that both he and Whittle had hoped and expected. He could offer Whittle plenty of rhetorical support. 'Difficulties you are bound to have, of course, but I want to make them as light as I can', as he wrote to him early in March 1941.[18] On policy matters of real substance, though, Tizard was going to be overruled by Bulman or simply persuaded to accept MAP's line as a practical necessity. The consequences were to leave Whittle increasingly dismayed.

The opening confrontation that flagged up Bulman's adversarial stance – and Whittle's future reaction to it – came on 14 February 1941. Following a meeting earlier in the day at the BTH plant, Bulman drove to Brownsover Hall for the first time. He was accompanied by Roxbee Cox and Tobin, both of whom were well aware of an underlying tension over Power Jets' attempts to expand the Ladywood Works significantly. (Tizard had been obliged to turn down a string of requests for extra resources, prompting Whittle to suggest that, given their lack of space, he 'should be very surprised if the project is not abandoned in about six months' time, if not before'.[19]) The main item on the agenda for this occasion was far broader. Since his first conversations with Tizard in November 1940, Whittle had been pressing hard for the establishment of a dedicated state organisation for the jet project. He had recently explained his position to a visitor at the

Works: 'in my view no one firm was fitted to take over the quantity production of this job and... a controller should be appointed, and a special organisation created, by the temporary borrowing of high grade personnel from several firms'.[20] Round the table in his study at Brownsover, Whittle urged this case strongly again. There was a heated discussion – and Bulman declared himself 'generally opposed to the scheme'. He would not accept the need for a controller, nor would he support the idea of a state-owned venture. Privately owned commercial firms would have to compete for MAP contracts, in line with the established practice over which he himself had so long presided. Whittle seized on this reference to the private sector as a cue to impress on Bulman the acute reservations that Power Jets felt about dealing with one commercial firm in particular:

> I gave it as my opinion that the outlook and conduct of the Wilks [brothers] in the past was not such as to make me feel optimistic about the outcome of the production with them at the head of it, giving as my main reason that they were actuated far too much by their concern for the interests of the Rover Co and that they had been very obstructive in general up to the present.[21]

This was acutely awkward for Bulman. He had decided twelve months previously that the best way of asserting MAP's close control over the jet project was to shift the management of the whole business as far as possible to Rover – and he was now more determined than ever that this should be MAP's official line.

As someone allergic to talk of visions and new beginnings, Bulman still saw the policy as a sensible compromise. Whatever the ominous parallels with the Dragonfly episode, the excitement over the project had reached a pitch that made its outright cancellation politically impossible. Besides, he had to acknowledge the positive stance towards the jet being taken by men like Halford and Ricardo, individuals he had known and respected since the First World War. (He and Halford had been joint assistants to the RFC's Chief Inspector of Engines, sharing an 'amazing and adventurous comradeship', as Bulman remembered it.[22]) And some allowance had also to be made for the possibility, however remote, that the jet engine might after all emerge as a genuine breakthrough. Standing alone against Nazi-occupied Europe, and with little prospect, it seemed, of the United States abandoning its neutrality, Britain was in no position to ignore any prospect of a powerful new weapon. All the more reason, then, to insist that any future production be handed comprehensively and unambiguously to the kind of engineers and businessmen with whom Bulman had been cultivating relationships through a long career – as exemplified by Spencer and Maurice Wilks, whom he thought 'always most patient and likeable men'.[23]

Just a week later, Bulman was powerfully reminded of another reason why the jet engine could not be ditched altogether. He and Tobin were summoned by Beaverbrook for a grilling over the status of the project. Churchill had asked for a monthly report on its progress, and a very annoyed Beaverbrook wanted to know why the engine's development had not been more rapid. Tobin telephoned Whittle later to tell him what had happened. Bulman had confessed, according to Tobin, 'that part of the trouble had been that the Ministry had lacked confidence in the scheme until recently'.[24] How far this placated Beaverbrook is unclear – but those monthly reports never materialised. As for Bulman's avowed intention to take 'a close interest' in the scheme, he gave no further indication to Power Jets of viewing it sympathetically. He either looked askance at Whittle's repeated pleas for help or ignored them altogether. He declined a request from Whittle's production manager for a MAP letter that could be sent to all sub-contractors, stressing the need for Power Jets' orders to be delivered as urgently as possible. And he spiked a succession of increasingly desperate notes from Whittle asking for clearance to hire additional workmen.

A clash was inevitable, and came early in March 1941. Whittle explained in another phone call with Tobin that the staffing shortage at Lutterworth was becoming critical. 'I said that we had felt this need for so long and the action taken had been so ineffective that I was not willing to put up with the situation any longer, and asked Tobin to try and arrange that I should see the Minister.'[25] No audience with Beaverbrook could be fixed. Instead, Whittle was invited to a meeting at Rover's Chesford Grange plant near Kenilworth on 5 March. Bulman took the chair in the absence of Tizard, who had fallen ill late in February with erysipelas, a nasty skin infection.

According to his own minutes, Bulman began by noting that some crucial deadlines loomed. 'It was agreed that... drawings for the production of the initial batch of 30 [W.2B] engines must be finalised within the next few weeks...'[26] Rover had cleared space on the factory floor to begin tooling up. Spencer Wilks confirmed plans to have finished engines for the Gloster Meteor rolling off the line at the agreed rate of eighty a month as soon as the experimental flights ended – not quite by October 1941 but surely by the spring of 1942. The net result of all this enthusiasm was a significant concession by Power Jets. Whittle felt it had no option but to send all its detailed and General Assembly drawings for the W.2B off to Rover (just as he had handed them the W.1 drawings in April 1940). They were despatched a week later. At the time, this seemed a milestone of some importance. The proceedings on 5 March, though, also encompassed a significant clash of views over Rover's terms of reference.

Tizard had recently conceded that manufacturers might make 'minor mechanical adjustments' to Whittle's drawings. With Bulman's obvious complicity, the Wilks brothers made it clear that in their view Rover would be 'substantially free' to make whatever changes it wanted to the mechanical design of the engine. (Inevitably there were sharp differences over several 'mechanical' issues, notably over what kind of gearbox should be employed on the engine – emphatically not a minor adjustment.) Whittle warned the meeting that 'the Ministry was proposing to jettison completed designs, in favour of design proposals which were far from complete, and untried'.[27] It particularly upset Whittle that the Wilks brothers were able to present the meeting with a letter from Tizard, giving their proposed approach his blessing. He wrote a few days later to the convalescent Tizard – recovering at his home in North Oxford – to register his 'great shock' over this and to list various damaging consequences.[28] Over the next three weeks, awaiting Tizard's response, he received a string of visitors at Brownsover Hall, including Roxbee Cox and Tobin, who were all forthright in their support for his position. Hayne Constant was especially indignant about the extended dispensation offered to Rover: he 'gave his opinion that one man should be responsible for design of the production of the W.2B,' recorded Whittle, 'and that man should be me'.[29]

Constant was right. He and Roxbee Cox both had a far keener appreciation than Tizard at this point that drawing a false parity between Rover on the one hand and Whittle on the other was to put the future of the whole jet project at risk. Of course Whittle could be almost impossibly demanding at times. He was often strident in his views and rarely open to even discussing a compromise where the integrity of his design work was at stake. This intransigence, though, had nothing to do with personal or professional rivalry let alone a mere quirkiness of temperament. As Constant and the RAE staff well understood by now, Whittle was pioneering a new field of aero-engineering – a truth never properly acknowledged by most of those engaged on the contract work at Rover and BTH. The mathematics that covered page after page of his Workshop Note Books might as well have been Egyptian hieroglyphics as far as their engineers, or Bulman's staff at MAP, were concerned. In one technical conference after another, assembled to review test data on the latest engine under development, Whittle's approach was informed by a grasp of the underlying science that barely troubled others around the table. 'They don't even understand Bernoulli's theorem!' protested Whittle to Tizard after one especially exasperating meeting with some of his supposed peers at Rover – a gap in their knowledge that in his view virtually disqualified them as engineers fit to run a finger over his designs. The unfamiliar demands of the jet engine also led Whittle to challenge many of the basic mechanical decisions being made by BTH and Rover, and with good reason. Interminable wrangling over ducts and bearings, shafts and spill valves, scavenge pumps and exhaust pipes, blade angles, aperture widths, nozzle rings, flame tubes and a thousand other topics, all vital to eventual success, almost always ended with those around the table deferring in the end to Whittle's judgement over what would best meet their needs. Reaching accord, though, was all too often a fraught business.

The resulting tensions, manifest in a torrent of notes penned at Brownsover Hall as well as official minutes recorded by MAP, underpinned Whittle's constant plea for the Ministry's support to be all but exclusively focused on Power Jets. Tizard now seemed more eager than ever, though, to draw other firms into the frame where possible. This strategy – and his apparent readiness to appease the Wilks brothers – was in Whittle's view wholly mis-conceived, a bad case of inviting too many cooks into the kitchen. With no 'chief executive' figure in place, confusion was inevitable. Spreading development work across more firms would also entail a costly dissipation of the meagre national resources at Power Jets' disposal. It would overstretch the few supply companies capable of making components to the jet engine's demanding specifi-cations, while encouraging a wasteful duplication of test work. And for Whittle personally, it would mean ever more demands on his time when he was already working unconscionably long hours. On most mornings, Whittle would start at the Ladywood Works by eight o'clock and return to Broomfield only at the end of the afternoon. After supper was finished, he generally toiled over his work papers for several more hours. Bob Feilden later recalled: 'Many is the time I took over test results [from Lutterworth] in my ancient car to his home in Rugby, and went back to bed about midnight – leaving him to analyse the results into the small hours.'[30] It was a relentless schedule, sustained week after week without a break. Whittle thought Tizard too little appreciative of the burden on his shoulders – and had no doubt it would weigh heavier still if new third parties were brought within the project's scope. (He was right about that: when Frank Halford set about building his own jet engine at de Havilland, he sought advice from Whittle on several aspects of its design – and Whittle even found the time to meet his request for drawings of an innovative impeller rotor.)

Most damaging of all, Tizard's expansive approach exposed the project to outside parties with little or no real understanding of the difference between building piston engines on the one hand and jet engines on the other. One of the newcomers introduced by Tizard as a potential partner/supplier was Vauxhall Motors, based in Luton. They were already backing out of the project by March 1941, confessing they lacked the basic skills to match the jet engine's demands. (It vexed their engineers that Whittle would not simply change the shape of his turbine blades at their bidding to make them easier to mass produce.[31]) As for the calibre of all but very few of the BTH and Rover engineers – Whittle began to despair, through the early months of 1941, at Tizard's refusal to distance himself from Bulman's support for the two firms. Tizard had told Tobin in November 1940 that he was 'very favourably impressed by M. C. Wilks as an engineer' and he stuck to this view. Whittle thought Wilks was a good automotive engineer but (as he had told Tedder in 1940) 'like a child' in front of the jet-engine challenge.

Nor did Whittle share Tizard's readiness to trust the Wilks brothers. Indeed, he regularly impugned their motives in private correspondence and had little doubt they were secretly pursuing their own commercial agenda. His suspicions were fuelled by the zealous regard for security that he encountered at Rover's sites. It affronted Whittle early in February 1941 when he first visited their factory at Chesford Grange near Kenilworth. Their 'Whittle work' was briefly housed there, having been temporarily relocated from Coventry in the wake of the November blitz. For two hours, Rover's men under their project leader Dr Robert Boyle plied him with technical questions ('they admitted they were new to the job and appeared a little frightened about starting up') which he answered in great detail. Whittle made a careful note of the sequel:

> I then asked Dr Boyle if I... could see their Engine Room and [W.2] engine. He stated that they were keeping this very, very

secret and that only three people were permitted into the room and, as he was fully occupied in the meeting and the other two people were not available, he would like me to go over on some other date.... On the way out, however, I met Mr Wilks in his office. He did not appear to be very busy and after a few minutes chat I left the premises...[32]

There were to be many more incidents of this kind in the months ahead.

Tizard was back at his desk by late March. Aware of the tension that had built up in his absence, he tried to dispel it at a roundtable conference in his office at MAP on 25 March 1941. It was almost exactly a year since the ill-fated meeting chaired by Tedder at Harrogate in 1940. Whittle by now was growing accustomed to losing battles that he wrongly believed had been fought and won weeks or months earlier. He was nonetheless bewildered by the discussion that followed. Roxbee Cox and Constant were there and voiced their full support for him as he rehearsed again the arguments against allowing Rover 'to have a free hand on mechanical design'.[33] All to no avail. Tizard sided entirely with Bulman. The two men insisted together 'that Rovers had to be responsible for the engine'. Whittle asked why anyone could think it reasonable for him, 'having been through all the agony of designing the W.2B', to have to go and stand over the Rover engineers 'making sure they did not make any silly mistakes'. Tempers ran high. Tizard at one point accused Whittle of putting his own interests before the country's and of 'trying to monopolise the design so that nobody else should get the credit'. Both jibes hurt Whittle deeply, coming from someone as well placed as Tizard to know how much he had sacrificed for the project.

Tizard soon made amends for his remarks but his obvious annoyance on this occasion, presenting such a contrast with his steadfast support in the past, is probably a fair measure of the demands that Whittle was now making on even those who were disposed to help him. He had no stouter ally than Tizard. But this seasoned Whitehall campaigner had begun to tire of constant notes protesting over one aspect or another of Rover's behaviour or MAP's attitude to Power Jets. Tizard had confessed as much in a memorandum to Beaverbrook in the middle of February – 'The troubles are mainly human not technical'[34] – and in his correspondence with colleagues he was increasingly inclined to suggest that the personality clashes afflicting the project were, as he told Beaverbrook, 'six of one and half a dozen of the other'. In short, Whittle's vehement advocacy of his own cause was becoming counter-productive. What he badly needed at this point was a coup for the jet engine that might make absolutely clear to the world just how much was at stake. With happy timing, Power Jets and Gloster were about to provide it. They had been liaising closely for a year on the W.1's installation into the E.28/39. Now the E.28/39 was all but ready to fly.

iii

George Carter and his Gloster team had completed building the E.28/39 at their factory in the Cotswolds several weeks earlier. Custom-designed for the gas-turbine engine, the plane had the shape of a short cigar with a tubby midriff. It was no Spitfire look-alike. Whittle and his team had taken to calling it the 'Squirt', which seemed to suit its rather squat appearance (*Fig. 17*). Its wings were low-slung and they sat oddly close to the ground, for the very good reason that this plane had no need to lift a propeller clear of it. The plane sat on a novel 'tricycle' arrangement of three wheels as proposed by Whittle in October 1938, with a third wheel under the plane's nose to leave the fuselage horizontal, and an extremely short undercarriage for the two wheels under the wings. To keep it away from prying eyes, Gloster had stored it in a commercial garage in the centre of nearby Cheltenham, where its hiding place was signalled only by the round-the-clock presence of a solitary armed policeman on the pavement. On the last day of March 1941, its Chief Designer supervised the return of the plane from Cheltenham to Gloster's flight-test airfield eight miles to the south beside a village called Brockworth. Carter was

Fig. 17. The mint-condition Gloster E.28/39, ready for its maiden flight

still as enthused by working with Whittle as he had been from the outset. 'We all look to you with undiminished confidence,' he wrote to him now, 'to maintain and fully exploit the unique and exceptional experience which you alone have, for the benefit of all concerned.'[35] He was in no doubt they were on the brink of a momentous event.

On the morning of 1 April 1941, a lorry arrived at Brockworth from the Ladywood Works bearing an engine ready for installation. This was not the W.1, which had yet to be ignited for the first time. It was the W.1X, the non-flight engine built to an identical aerodynamic design but with components that had not been cleared as flight-worthy. Bob Feilden accompanied it. (Whittle had invited his top engineers to draw straws a few evenings earlier, to decide which of them would have the glory of actually installing the engine. Feilden won the Brockworth job; his colleague Geoffrey Bone would have the same role at Cranwell later, for the W.1's installation.) The W.1X had been undergoing constant bench tests since Christmas. These had involved a couple of serious setbacks as recently as mid-March, but now it was believed ready at last to be used in taxiing trials that would mark the first step towards putting a jet engine into the air. Another week was spent installing the W.1X into the airframe and making final adjustments under Feilden's supervision. Then Carter telephoned Brownsover Hall to let Whittle know they were ready for him. He drove over the next day, 7 April.

The man preparing to handle the maiden flight was perhaps the best-known test pilot of his generation, Gerry Sayer, who had been head of Gloster's small team of test pilots since 1933 and had already visited Lutterworth to familiarise himself with the W.1X's controls. No doubt Whittle would have been eager to fly it first himself, if allowed to do so – but as William Farren had remarked to him at a Farnborough conference in 1940, there could be no question of ever letting him do anything 'that might end with you going up in smoke'. Whittle was not to be denied altogether, though, and Sayer gallantly agreed to step aside at the outset so that the engine's inventor could be the first to power up the E.28/39 and taxi it across the airfield. Even so, Whittle would have to comply with detailed instructions from MAP over the amount of throttle he could use. This proved slightly unfortunate when the little plane was rolled from its hangar on the evening of the 7th for its first trial. The grass airfield was so sodden underfoot that the maximum permissible revs were only enough to move it along at less than 20 mph.

Calls were made to London the next morning and Denis Tobin prevailed on Bulman's deputy, Major A. A. Ross, to sanction a bolder run. Whittle tried again. And for the very first time, the jet engine gave a real glimpse of its potential. Engineers measure the power output of any aero-engine by multiplying its thrust by its velocity. A stationary engine on a test rig has zero velocity so can have no power, whatever its measurable thrust. Only at Brockworth on the morning of 8 April 1941, as he opened the throttle and let the E.28/39 accelerate up to 60 mph across the grass, could Whittle finally sense the power of the jet-propulsion concept he had first captured with a physical engine at BTH's plant almost exactly four years earlier. Speeding along, he made a mental note – as the test pilot he had once been – of the advantages to this new way of powering an aeroplane that had been scarcely considered in the workshop: 'the complete absence of vibration, the big reduction in noise compared with conventional aircraft, the excellent view from the cockpit, and the simplicity of the controls...'[36] It was less pleasing to the eye than the Spitfire but might yet prove easier (and much more comfortable) to fly.

After a break for lunch, Whittle and Carter handed the plane over to Gerry Sayer. They and their two teams stood watching as Sayer taxied slowly away to the end of the airfield, passing an RAF Stirling bomber at the side of the field on which Gloster mechanics were busy with their maintenance routines. Then Whittle saw the E.28/39 turn and gather speed towards them, with the whine of the jet suddenly much louder. He knew immediately what Sayer intended, for he had deliberately taken off directly into a brisk wind. Sure enough, an instant later, the E.28/39 rose six feet or so into the air and flew for a couple of hundred yards. The sight sent a frisson through all the spectators. 'That was one of the most marvellous moments of my life,' recalled Bob Feilden many years later.[37] It was probably long remembered, too, by the Stirling mechanics who knew nothing of the plane with no propeller but had just seen it doing the impossible. (Whittle never forgot the sight of one of them, an American, losing his footing on the bomber's wing and almost falling off it in shock.) Sayer made two more runs, each with a short flight and a perfect return to the ground. It was a flawless performance by the W.1X. When they all gathered in the hangar shortly afterwards, Sayer told Whittle he would have felt quite happy 'making a continued flight'.[38] In fact they had all seen and heard enough to know their next move. It was agreed that Power Jets would push ahead with the bench testing of its W.1 flight engine as quickly as possible. Then it would be sent straight over to Brockworth for installation. Gloster would truck the reassembled aeroplane on a 'Queen Mary' trailer across England to the wilds of Lincolnshire – to RAF Cranwell, indeed, where arrangements had been made for Sayer to make the first proper flight. Whittle and his colleagues headed straight back to Leicestershire that day. Tobin joined them at Brownsover Hall on 9 April for a debrief and to plan the next steps. 'We then went to Lutterworth,' recorded a plainly relieved Whittle, 'for a mild celebration.'

The W.1 flight engine was run on its bench at Lutterworth for the first time on 12 April 1941 – by chance, the fourth anniversary of the WU1's ignition. It then had to undergo rigorous testing for twenty-five hours, at MAP's insistence. Cleared for ten hours' flying time after a flawless bench performance, it was despatched to Gloster at the start of May. The scheduling of a test-flight programme prompted Pat Johnson to approach MAP's Engines directorate about the desirability of having an official film unit at Cranwell for the first flight. No one at Thames House could be induced to back the idea, however, and Johnson – who was not afraid of drawing some colourful parallels with the Wright brothers' breakthrough at Kitty Hawk – wasted many hours over the next four weeks trying in vain to persuade Bulman's team of the historic importance of the event. (MAP had similarly ignored an appeal two months earlier to rescue the WU3 for posterity when its working days finally came to an end: an engine that might justly have been treated as a precious relic of aeronautical history stirred no interest at all, and eventually went for scrap.) Fortunately, the RAF personnel alerted to Gloster's plans for the E.28/39 were rather more helpful. In particular, the Commanding Officer at Cranwell, Air Commodore Harold Probyn, knew all about Whittle's RAF career and had heard the stories about his youthful exploits with Cranwell's Model Aircraft Society. The prospect of Boy Whittle returning to the airfield he had once graced with his elaborate models, bringing with him a wholly new kind of aircraft, had a certain magic that was not lost on Probyn. He ensured that enough rooms would be made available for all their visitors. Two dozen came in the end, including twelve from Gloster and six from Lutterworth – though not a single senior official from MAP – and Probyn laid on all the logistics for their stay.[39] They and the plane itself arrived safely on 12 May. Whittle turned up the next day and made a last-minute arrangement for Mary Phillips to have a room in the WAAF block at Cranwell so that she, too, could be there for the first flight.[40]

Low cloud and driving rain made flying impossible for two days. They all sat around the station, reading reports in the newspapers of the House of Commons' destruction by German bombs over the night of 12 May (and debating together the significance of the bizarre arrival in Scotland by parachute over the weekend of Hitler's deputy, Rudolf Hess). Early on the morning of 15 May, waking to yet more filthy weather, Whittle foresaw a third frustrating day and decided to drive the seventy miles back to Lutterworth. After arriving there in the late afternoon, he took a call from the Cranwell control tower to say the cloud base was lifting. A young naval pilot had completed a weather test and found that visibility was rapidly improving. (This was Eric 'Winkle' Brown, later a world-famous test pilot, who had landed at Cranwell halfway through a long flight from Scotland to southern England and been puzzled to find the station so full of civilians. He had shared a room overnight with Whittle's chief installation engineer, Geoffrey Bone, but had gleaned nothing whatever from him about the contents of a closed hangar on the airfield that was roped off and under police guard.[41]) Whittle jumped in his car and drove straight back to Lincolnshire. He found Sayer and the Gloster team standing with the E.28/39, awaiting his return. At 6.40 p.m., the plane was cleared to take off, and Sayer started up the W.1. The moment had arrived for the first flight. Whittle would recall:

> He ran the engine up to 16,500 rpm against the brakes. He then released the brakes and the aeroplane quickly gathered speed and lifted smoothly from the runway after a run of about 600 yards. It continued to the west in a flat climb for several miles and disappeared from view behind cloud banks. For several minutes we could only hear the smooth roar of the engine. Then it came into sight again as it made a wide circuit preparatory to landing. As Sayer came in it was obvious that he had complete

confidence in the aeroplane... Those of us who were pilots knew
that he felt completely at home.[42]

All on the ground were exultant. In his *Jet* memoir Whittle
claimed to have been nervous only on George Carter's behalf, and
to have felt no anxiety at all about his engine. As he pointedly
recalled, 'I was not one of those who needed convincing that it
could fly'. But everyone in attendance on that chilly May evening
at Cranwell knew how much was at stake. Pat Johnson slapped
Whittle on the back and exclaimed, 'Frank, it flies!', to which (by
his own account) he could only reply: 'That was what it was bloody-
well designed to do, wasn't it?' The absence of an official cinema-
tographer was a shared regret among them all, but fortunately one
of the Power Jets men had his own cinecamera. At considerable
risk to himself – he might have ended up in prison – he filmed
an illicit record of the first take-off which has survived.[43] After
Gerry Sayer landed and began taxiing the plane back towards the
waiting crowd, his deputy Michael Daunt brandished a camera in
the air. He was shepherded to the front, and so caught the moment
when a beaming Whittle reached up to the cockpit of the plane
and shook Sayer warmly by the hand (*Plate 7a*). It was the only still
photograph of the occasion that anyone thought to preserve.

MAP had authorised ten hours' flying time for the new plane.
Sayer completed these in fifteen separate flights over the following
twelve days. The performance of the W.1 engine matched Whittle's
mathematical predictions with (to the layman) uncanny precision. Flying at 25,000 feet, the E.28/39 reached a top speed of
370 mph. So this little plane, despite its dumpy appearance, was
actually faster than any Spitfire or Me 109 of the day. Carter and his
chief test pilot had been together through many inaugural flights
of new planes and engines in the past. Both agreed the flawless
success of this jet-propulsion aircraft was quite unprecedented.
One unique feature in particular made a lasting impression on
the Gloster ground crew. The morning after the first flight, all
the Power Jets engineers packed their bags and left, saying they
had seen enough to know their services would not be required

again. The Gloster men, assuming the W.1 would require plenty of mechanical attention just like any fledgling piston engine, watched their departure in disbelief – only to find the optimists from Lutterworth proven entirely correct. The cowling over the W.1 remained in place from start to finish of the test flights, with no need whatever to make a single further inspection of the engine. When it came to maintenance, though MAP had yet to grasp this, the jet engine enjoyed a massive advantage over all its piston rivals.

There followed some unforgettable days at RAF Cranwell. The station received a steady stream of VIPs, all anxious to see for themselves this new technology that had been miraculously produced on a shoestring budget by a tiny company outside the established aircraft industry. Lord Beaverbrook would surely have loved it, but had resigned from MAP at the end of April. Almost everyone else of any consequence – with the conspicuous exception of George Bulman and his deputy, Major Ross – made the trek. When the electrifying news of the first flight reached Tizard in his office at Thames House, according to his scientific assistant at the time, he sprang up from his desk and exclaimed 'History has been made!'[44] He raced up to Cranwell at the first opportunity and arrived in the middle of the E.28/39's sixth flight on 17 May. Evidently the sight of the plane dispelled all those doubts in his mind that had led Tizard to be so critical of Whittle only a few weeks earlier. That night, after a late dinner, he sat talking with Whittle and Whyte into the early hours 'about future action'.[45] His considered reflections, penned in an official minute of 20 May, captured the sense of urgency that was about to take hold among his peers:

> In my opinion we have now reached a stage when the odds against the jet propulsion engine of the Whittle type being developed to a successful issue in the near future have disappeared. With real energy we ought to be able to look forward to getting reliable engines in production in a year's time... I believe that the difficulties ahead, which are no doubt many, not only can be solved, but must be solved, and will be solved if a real effort is put into it, and if the sceptics will cease to be sceptical.[46]

The climactic day was 21 May 1941, when the guest list included a virtual rollcall of the key players in the jet's story to date. Dudley Williams and Coll Tinling were there to see the fulfilment of the vision they had sold to Whittle round his kitchen table at Trumpington in 1935. Harry Sporborg and Bob Collingham came from BTH, alongside the Wilks brothers from Rover. Tobin and Roxbee Cox headed a small team of officials from MAP, accompanying the Deputy Minister, Patrick Hennessy. Geoffrey de Havilland and his son flew up from Hatfield, bringing Major Halford with them, and Tommy Sopwith arrived from Coventry with a group of Hawker Siddeley directors. For the government, an RAF plane brought up the Air Minister, Sir Archibald Sinclair, and his Under-Secretary Harold Balfour. Early in the evening, Sayer gave them all a spectacular demonstration of the E.28/39's grace and power, landing just in time to let everyone run for cover as another heavy rainstorm swept the airfield.

Whittle noted modestly for his diary that Sinclair 'was apparently very impressed'. This hardly captured the drama of the occasion. Some grand claims had been made for the jet engine over the years. Who now could dismiss its potential? The extraordinary sight of this stubby-nosed plane with no propeller, sweeping over the airfield at a thousand feet and then climbing steeply up into the clouds and back again, left many of those watching from the ground feeling simply awed. None could doubt Whittle had defied all the naysayers and pulled off a tremendous feat. Among the engineers who now rushed to offer him effusive congratulations, probably few had been wholly free of a secret suspicion that the gas turbine might linger for a few years yet on test benches. Most of the politicians and officials, many of them only briefed quite recently about an engine that sounded distinctly futuristic, were startled to discover the jet aeroplane was actually a reality. Sinclair, despite having been Air Minister since May 1940, had arrived at Cranwell not knowing whether Whittle was responsible for the aeroplane or the engine.[47] In less time than it would take them all to return from Lincolnshire to London, most of these men were beginning to ask themselves how and when some version of it might be delivered to the RAF as a serviceable aircraft.

A widespread belief that jet fighters would soon be attainable took hold, in fact, with dramatic suddenness – all the more surprising, since the jet engine's existence was shrouded in the utmost secrecy. (All documents had to refer to the engines as 'superchargers'.) No doubt the RAF's current requirements heavily influenced this reaction: relentless German bombing since the start of the London Blitz had exposed the lack of night fighters as a serious weakness. Fears were also growing that interceptor fighters might soon have to combat German bombers flying at much higher altitudes. (A reconnaissance aircraft, the Junkers 86, had been detected flying over England at 42,000 feet in 1940. Its flights seemed to have been discontinued by the summer of 1941, but the prospect of it returning as a high-level bomber was cause for serious concern.) The aero-engine industry for its part was ready to respond immediately: its company bosses, some of them privately dismayed by the sight of the E.28/39 in flight, needed no second viewing to grasp the case for engaging with gas-turbine technology. Even the directors at BTH woke up to the mistake they had made: it took them less than a month to reverse their earlier decision to withdraw from the project.

Whether it could also look forward to Churchill's active support would of course be even more important. The Prime Minister's personal interest in the jet was not in doubt. His scientific adviser, though, had not appeared at Cranwell. A few days after the first flight, Tizard received a letter from Lindemann enquiring about the status of the project. He sent him a short reply confirming 'some very satisfactory flights' which he thought ought '[to] silence some of the sceptics, and to encourage everyone to go full speed ahead'. He readily confessed, though, that it was an aircraft programme quite unlike any other:

> We are gambling, I think rightly, on the production of an aircraft [i.e. the Meteor] with engines the design of which is not yet settled... I am sure the outstanding problems can be solved – the

great thing is to solve them in time. I have just been making arrangements for still further extension of the development work...[48]

It would be several weeks before this report detonated in Downing Street.

iv

Unknown to any of the E.28/39's dazzled spectators at Cranwell, however, Whittle by May 1941 was harbouring a secret worry over the whole future of his engine. A couple of weeks after the party in April to celebrate the E.28/39's initial taxiing, Whittle had led his engineering team to the test bed at the Ladywood Works for the first of several runs scheduled for the newly completed W.2 engine, recently received from Rover. He had designed it to produce almost twice as much thrust as the W.1 engine: the most significant change had involved adding many more vanes to the diffuser in an effort to improve its efficiency. This had undoubtedly left Whittle feeling apprehensive, though. By his own calculations, the W.2's components were likely to fall short of their efficiency targets. He therefore had low expectations of the new engine as they prepared it for a first run up to full power on 25 April 1941. What happened next nonetheless came as a shock. Just as it was approaching its operating speed, at around 11,000 rpm, the engine gave a series of terrifying bangs and began to shake violently in its test frame. To Whittle's consternation, it had effectively gone into reverse, forcing compressed air back from its combustion chambers and out through the front of the engine. Flames shot out of the air intake and all the instruments attached to the engine went wild. A moment later they settled back to normal, only for the cycle to repeat itself. He hastily shut the engine down, and the runs scheduled for the rest of the day were postponed. Whittle retired to Brownsover Hall and his slide rule, to begin a careful analysis of what had gone wrong.

This was an entirely new phenomenon: neither the WU, in any of its three permutations, nor the W.1 had ever run into it. (Sheer luck, as would soon become clear.) Various experimental cures were applied over the next several days, but it was quickly apparent to Whittle that they had encountered a fundamental problem. The normally steady flow through the compressor was becoming destabilised, triggering the convulsions of the engine and sending the air 'surging' backwards. With the combustion chamber emptied of air, the compressor was able to reassert itself – but the process would then be repeated. No matter how they varied the acceleration of the engine, it could not be taken past a 'breakdown speed' in a range just short of 12,000 rpm. This diagnosis, though, stopped short of an explanation. Whittle had no idea what was causing the surging. Nor was there a test rig at Lutterworth – or, indeed, anywhere else – with sufficient power to run the W.2's compressor on its own, for a methodical study of the problem. It was deeply vexing.

By the day of the E.28/39's triumph at Cranwell on 15 May, Whittle knew that surging posed a mortal threat to the entire development programme. The solution might involve redesigning every major component of the engine. It was impossible to know how many remedial changes might be required. A serviceable version of the jet engine might be far more difficult to attain than either he or anyone else had envisaged. Mulling this awful truth even as all those around him were rushing forward with their congratulations evidently made Whittle acutely anxious. Some of the more boisterous reactions to the E.28/39's performance – there was talk in Whitehall of a jet fighter taking to the air by Christmas – caused him further alarm, and made it no easier for him to share his secret. In the hours after seeing it fly on 17 May, even Tizard was so elated over the engine's future prospects that Whittle could not bring himself to break the news. (Hence Tizard's jubilant note on 20 May, quoted earlier.) At a roundtable conference in Tizard's office in Thames House on 22 May, though, Whittle could hold back no longer. He expounded on the surging phenomenon at some length, and it prompted a sobering discussion about 'the poor behaviour of the W.2'.[49] To judge by subsequent events, Tizard took the implications to heart and began immediately to think about ways of boosting Whittle's resources.

Two days later, on 24 May, he visited Lutterworth to see the W.1X running. Whittle took him aside at one point for a further talk about the W.2. ('We told Tizard that we thought the poor blower [i.e. compressor] performance was due to interference between the diffusers and the corner vanes.') Power Jets was thinking of suspending work on the W.2 altogether. Tizard's reply led to an exchange that would later assume rather more significance than Whittle allowed it in his diary at the time:

> Tizard suggested that Rolls-Royce were likely to be called in to assist in the development. I said they could undoubtedly give us a lot of help if they would make things exactly as we wanted them. He said he would arrange a visit of one of their representatives, with a view to getting them to work as soon as possible.[50]

In fact the notion of recruiting Rolls-Royce to assist with the project had been under review inside MAP for a little while. In all probability Tizard had merely been awaiting an opportunity to pitch the idea as elegantly as possible. Whittle's reaction was all he could have hoped for, and went down well within the Ministry. A formal letter was promptly despatched to Derby on 5 June 1941. It was suggested to Rolls-Royce that it set aside Arnold Griffith's work on his contra-flow axial compressor and switch the unparalleled resources of its Experimental Shop over to the more immediate development of an engine along the lines of Whittle's design.[51] A second letter went off the same day to Coventry Gauge and Tool Company, another large company yet to be recruited to the cause.

The next day, 6 June, Tizard chaired a meeting at MAP to discuss the prospective integration of these two heavyweights into the post-Cranwell strategy. He had partly called the meeting because he was so concerned about the antagonism between Power Jets and Rover to date. He had taken an optimistic view of the agreements reached in March and had been disappointed by

Rover's failure to meet its obligations towards Whittle. Spencer Wilks and Whittle were given only a day's notice of the meeting, for which they both had to travel down from the Midlands. Tizard insisted they attend, so that he could appeal in person to them 'to get together and decide in common how best to use the facilities of these two [Derby and Coventry] firms...'. The immediate sequel to the meeting so incensed Tizard that on 12 June he wrote a long note for Beaverbrook's successor, John Moore-Brabazon, about Spencer Wilks' behaviour. An explicit accord had been reached, he suggested, and yet:

> Mr Wilks nevertheless goes entirely independently to the Coventry Gauge and Tool Company and Rolls-Royce without taking Wing Commander Whittle with him, orders from these two firms parts to the Rover Company design, and gives no indication to them at all of his desire to collaborate with Wing Commander Whittle.
>
> This really is a hopeless position, both from a human point of view and from a technical point of view. From the human point of view it tends to produce the maximum amount of friction with an extremely able, enthusiastic and naturally rather temperamental inventor... [who] is the only person who has, in fact, produced a design of a jet propulsion unit which has worked in the air...[52]

Tizard had no thought of abandoning Rover as their large-scale producer, but he now decided that Whittle had been right about Spencer Wilks after all. He could not be trusted, and Rover had been left far too much discretion over the development stage of the engine. In light of Wilks' treatment of Whittle, Tizard told Moore-Brabazon, Rover 'are not, in my opinion, a firm that is good enough for deciding what to produce. Their freedom of action in this way should therefore be curtailed.' He could only see two ways of doing this. One would involve appointing a powerful overlord for the whole project – and, as ever, he could think of no one for the role. The other would involve reviving an old idea, more than once floated in Tedder's day. They would set up an executive committee. Wilks, Whittle and officials from

MAP would all have to be on it – plus, if possible, a representative from the firm long seen by most aero-engineers as the best in the business, Rolls-Royce.

There was only one man who could speak for Rolls-Royce at this level – Ernest Hives. His official title was plain 'General Manager', but Hives embodied the company that he ran to an extraordinary degree. Everyone knew the stories about Charles Rolls and Henry Royce, but it was really Hives who had created the engineering powerhouse that still bore their names. His own career had already spawned any number of colourful stories that all added to the mystique of the Rolls-Royce brand. (He had begun life as a humble bicycle mechanic in Reading. Charles Rolls, driving through the town in 1903, chanced to break down outside the garage where he worked. The seventeen-year-old Hives was the only man willing to try fixing the car. He succeeded so ably that Rolls hired him on the spot, as his chauffeur.) Hives' great achievement as General Manager since 1936 had been the transformation of Rolls-Royce from a struggling manufacturer, turning out beautiful but extraordinarily expensive motor cars in their hundreds, into a re-energised producer of top-quality vehicles priced to sell in Britain and overseas in their thousands. Far more important in the context of the company's wartime role, though, Hives had also set Rolls-Royce on the trajectory that was to see it become easily the country's most important wartime producer of aero-engines.

It was not yet the industry leader by 1939 – the Bristol Aeroplane Company was still rather larger – but Rolls-Royce had the Merlin, derived from the R engine which had been built in six months in 1929 under Hives' own personal supervision. Its superb design, never really superseded by any other piston engine, had sprinkled the Derby firm with stardust. The Merlin production lines at the company's multi-shop factory on Nightingale Road had effectively won the Battle of Britain: for all the bravery of The Few, it had been the RAF's evident ability to rely on a seemingly inexhaustible supply of new engines for replacement aircraft that had eventually forced Goering to call off the Luftwaffe's offensive. By mid-1941 production rates for the Merlin were still rising steadily, with huge numbers now needed for Bomber Command's rapidly expanding fleet of Avro Lancasters. Every inch of the Nightingale Road premises had been developed accordingly. Rolls-Royce – or simply Royce's, as the company was invariably called by all Derby locals – had also acquired a suitably impressive block of redbrick executive offices along the front of its expanded factory. A stylish new entrance ('the Marble Hall') had been added: a three-storey art-deco embellishment, built of stone and adorned inside with marble columns and polished limestone floors. A double staircase from the entrance doors led up to a brass-railed balcony on the first floor, where one door led to a boardroom and a second announced the General Manager's office, half-panelled in oak and complete with an open fireplace. Behind his desk opposite the fire sat Hives, as Wilfrid Freeman was once heard to remark, 'like a great Buddha presiding over his men'. Freeman knew better than anyone how the unfolding crises since 1936 over Britain's readiness for war had brought out the best in Hives as a formidable captain of industry. The understanding between them had been vital to the nation's survival. (It is a measure of the high regard that the two men had for each other that Hives, towards the end of the war, would manage to persuade Freeman to sit for a portrait which Rolls-Royce commissioned as a gift for his wife, Elizabeth. She told Hives that neither she herself nor their children could ever have persuaded her husband to agree to the idea.[53]) By the summer of 1941, few if any other individuals in civilian life were as important as Hives to the war effort – as Tizard, too, was well able to appreciate.

The moment Tizard heard of Spencer Wilks' antics after the 6 June meeting, and his devious approach to Rolls-Royce, he sent Hives an invitation to meet him urgently at Thames House. Hives was notoriously averse to hobnobbing with civil servants. (In a letter this same month, he wrote to Freeman with his character-istic bluntness: 'I've never yet attended a meeting at MAP that I have not left with a stomach ache and a feeling that it has been a waste of time... We have a saying here that Hitler goes half way across Europe while we are trying to get one contract through the MAP.'[54]) But he accepted Tizard's invitation and joined him for lunch on 10 June. Tizard made a detailed note of the outcome:

> I told him about the Whittle position and said that I was anxious for him to make up experimental parts for test by Whittle, as well as parts to Rover's design. Hives said he was quite willing to make up anything that was wanted, but that he wanted to put the ideas of his own firm into the project. He agreed that in the past they have paid too little attention to Whittle's work and that they have made a mistake. I said we were only too anxious that he should develop on these lines, making as much use as possible of Whittle's goodwill and experience.[55]

A week later, they sat down again for a meeting in the Nightingale Road boardroom to which Hives invited several of his most senior engineers. They included the man in charge of Rolls-Royce's supercharger department, Stanley Hooker.

Tizard and Whittle had driven up from London together, having met the day before to discuss the background. Of course Whittle knew of Hives by reputation, but the two men were now to meet for the first time. Tizard had told Whittle about Hives' remorse that Rolls-Royce had shown little or no interest in his jet project until May. In Tizard's view, this neglect was at least partly due to the fact that – inexplicably, to many people – the firm had hired A. A. Griffith in 1939. Hives had watched him labouring over his CR1 with mounting scepticism that anything would ever really come of gas turbines. The Cranwell flights, said Tizard, 'had made them sit up'.[56] It is quite possible that Hives had heard Freeman talking enthusiastically about Whittle's work at some point, but if so he had assumed that ample notice would be given of any breakthrough event. He must have been shocked to hear the news from Lincolnshire, and his reaction ensured a change of heart at Derby more or less overnight. Within days of the last test flight, Hives and a senior colleague had been to see the Wilks brothers at their Kenilworth plant. It had been agreed in principle that Rolls-Royce might take on work for Rover as a subcontractor. Then Spencer Wilks had made his ill-judged trip to Derby that had so annoyed Tizard. Since then, and following his lunch at MAP, Hives had confirmed that the resources at Derby would be just as available to Power Jets as to Rover, to advance the W.2B's progress as quickly as possible.

Of stocky build, with a cleft chin and heavy rimmed glasses – he bore a passing resemblance to Churchill's ministerial colleague Ernest Bevin – Hives chaired the meeting on 17 June 1941 with his customary charm and directness. Whittle was delighted to hear him confirm everything Tizard had said, though Hives was quick to make clear that he had no interest in joining any industry committee. What must have made it an especially memorable occasion for Whittle was the presence at the table of A. A. Griffith. No one appears to have been impolite enough to remark on the irony of what followed, but Whittle himself can hardly have missed it. The General Assembly drawings for the CR1 were laid out for him to inspect, rather as his own youthful ideas had once been laid across another table in South Kensington twelve years earlier. Some considerable time was devoted to the ensuing discussion, with Whittle poring over every detail and subjecting Griffith to a barrage of searching questions.

They then moved on to consider what might be done at Derby in support of the work at Power Jets. Again, Whittle chose not to say anything about his mounting concern over surging. He only suggested that he provide Rolls-Royce with a specification for the W.2B turbine, so that the firm could design its own version which ought to be 'completely interchangeable' with his own. This met with some equivocation, as he noted later:

> Dr Griffith was hesitant about this, saying that he would prefer to do cascade tests first. I suggested that he should do as we had been compelled to do – namely, make an intelligent guess, but he appeared to be reluctant to do this.[57]

The others at the table, though, gave Whittle a warmer hearing. The longer the discussion continued, indeed, the more apparent it became (to judge by his own typically detailed record, at least) that he was revelling in an instant rapport he had discovered with these Derby men at the helm of the finest engineering firm in the country. They were avid to hear his views on every aspect of the gas-turbine plant. Griffith chipped in from time to time, reminding them of his own diligent workings to date. But the CR1's designer, whose bench-bound engine was still languishing in the experimental workshop after two years' work, must surely have felt a twinge of angst on hearing Hives proclaim at the end of the morning that he was offering neither Rover nor Power Jets any assurance 'that there would not be a Rolls-Royce-Whittle unit making its appearance presently'. By Whittle's own account, this exchange soon led to 'a fruitful technical cooperation' between the two companies, with the Experimental Shop at Derby turning out various components for test engines to be assembled at Lutterworth.[58]

One especially notable outcome was an offer by Rolls-Royce's supercharger boss, Stanley Hooker, to help Whittle in his struggle to conquer the surging problem. A few days after the roundtable discussion at Derby on 17 June, Hooker turned up at the Ladywood Works one morning with a young Rolls-Royce colleague called Geoff Wilde, who had organised and run numerous Merlin supercharger tests for him. Wilde, predictably 'Oscar' to his colleagues, had joined the company only three years earlier as a twenty-year-old, but Hooker knew him to be a highly innovative engineer and had been impressed by his acute reading of test results. After a lengthy discussion with Whittle and Leslie Cheshire, Hooker suggested that Rolls-Royce should arrange a rig test for the W.2B's compressor. Whittle was by now seriously disturbed at the possibility of a fundamental flaw in his jet-engine concept. He gratefully accepted Hooker's offer, well aware that designing an appropriate rig would be no light undertaking. No doubt Hooker expected it to be arduous business – but on the journey back to Derby his protégé pleasantly surprised him. While doing the driving, Wilde outlined exactly how a rig might be built to spin the compressor at the high speeds they would require. But he would need a 2,000 hp engine. Hooker had no hesitation offering him a Vulture unit for the job, the 24-cylinder monster that had proved so disappointing on the Avro Manchester aircraft and been effectively shelved. So that was settled, though Wilde was sensible enough to suggest he would need some months to reach a result.[59]

On 29 June, the Ladywood Works had another visitor from Rolls-Royce. Ernest Hives wanted to see Whittle's operation for himself. He drove down from Derby in his personal Rolls-Royce, bringing Hooker with him. Whittle made a dry note of the occasion, as usual, but must have taken some pride in his guests' reactions: 'Saw test run of the W1X and had a look round. Were very impressed by the test run, particularly the absolute steadiness of all the instruments.'[60] The aura round Hives often ensured that he left a trail of good stories behind him, some no doubt apocryphal, and his quick survey of the Ladywood Works spawned a few more. The engine they watched perform in the test shed gave a measured thrust of 800 lbs. Hooker would later recall that Hives had at first been underwhelmed by this figure – 'It wouldn't pull the skin off a rice pudding, would it!' – until it was pointed out to him that this was very nearly the same as the thrust achieved by the latest Merlin powering a Spitfire at 300 mph.[61] Whittle remembered Hives asking why Power Jets had only one finished unit to show them. Told of the problems encountered with Rover and BTH, Hives immediately offered his own firm's assistance: 'Send us the drawings to Derby, and we will make them for you.' Whittle made a special point of explaining to him the simplicity of his engine – to which Hives memorably replied, 'We'll bloody soon design the simplicity out of it!'[62] A few days later, Whittle wrote to Hooker confirming that Power Jets would happily send Rolls-Royce 'such drawings as you may require' to begin a collaboration together on the development of the W2.B.[63]

In the weeks after his reaching this accord with Rolls-Royce, the stars presiding over Whittle's jet engine slipped suddenly into alignment. If there was a climactic moment when the jet might have taken a giant step towards realising the 'potential war-winner' promise identified by Freeman early in 1940, it was surely July 1941. The notion of a jet fighter had been given a new level of credibility by the triumph of the Cranwell flights. The interest shown in the idea by the engineers at Derby promised to make it a far more practical proposition. And open support for the project from Ernest Hives suggested that the formidable organisational skills employed at Rolls-Royce might now be available to harness Whittle's genius properly at last. There was no time to lose. George Bulman and his colleagues had begun to despair of their relationship with him. Whittle's fierce determination to remain in charge of the jet engine's development had all but wrecked his personal relationship with several Ministry officials and Bulman in particular. The animosity between them was entirely mutual, as Bulman later acknowledged in his own memoirs: 'I told him one day in a moment of exasperation that he was the most impossible man I'd ever had to deal with! He never forgot it.'[64]

True, surging remained a serious obstacle yet to be surmounted, but it had just become clear in June 1941, with fortuitous timing, that Power Jets had another engine in the pipeline that offered a formidable alternative to the W.2B and an apparent immunity to surging. This was the W.1A unit. It had been designed by Whittle in February 1940 as a modification of the W.1, incorporating several features intended for the future W.2 which he wanted to try out in advance. At its first run in May 1941, the results had been disappointing. Whittle had added to the structure of the impeller to improve the flow of air into it and expected this to yield a useful boost to the engine's thrust. He had also agreed, though, to accept a redesign of the turbine by the RAE's engineers. Faced with the poor outcome, he soon dropped the RAE turbine and restored its predecessor. At the next run, his improved compressor operation produced a dramatically better performance. The engine's thrust was increased by no less than 40 per cent, a huge gain, made all the more impressive by a significantly lower rate of fuel consumption.[65] This was a scarcely believable advance. The W.1A opened up exciting possibilities for the E.28/39. Gerry Sayer's written reports on his test flights at Cranwell had left no doubt by the end of May that, notwithstanding its stubby shape, the E.28/39 was a superb aeroplane easily capable of operational service. George Carter at Gloster had always intended as much, and had made allowance for the installation of more than adequate guns. All that was needed, by July 1941, was someone of real influence to step forward and propose an immediate production schedule for the E.28/39 powered by the W.1A. Someone unafraid to promote the taking of risks regarded by their peers as unacceptable.

Churchill, of course, was that person – and, indeed, he seized the idea of the jet plane with characteristic bravura. How far he had been briefed by Lindemann (now Lord Cherwell) since early June – and how much, if anything, he really understood about the W.1A's test performance – is tantalisingly unclear from contemporary records. Churchill's dramatic intervention, though, is not in doubt. On 13 July 1941, the Minister at MAP, John Moore-Brabazon, received an 'ACTION THIS DAY' minute from Downing Street. Churchill wanted MAP to consider throwing caution to the winds:

> Will you convene this week a meeting of the necessary authori-
> ties, including the S. of S. for Air and C.A.S. [Chief of the Air
> Staff] and Lord Cherwell, and report to me whether in the
> circumstances we ought not to proceed forthwith in the pro-
> duction of the Whittle aircraft without waiting for a pilot model
> of Mark II. If this latter course is adopted we shall be delayed
> till January or February, and very high level German bombers
> may well appear over Britain in the interval. I am assured that
> the production of, say, 1,000 WHITTLES would not cut in upon
> the existing types of aircraft to any serious extent.[66]

The 'Whittle aircraft' referred to by Churchill can only have been the E.28/39. (The 'pilot model of Mark II' was the prototype of the F.9/40 Meteor, which he had been told would be available in due course.) The Downing Street minute suggests someone, almost certainly Cherwell, had pointed out to Churchill how easily and cheaply the E.28/39 could be turned out in large numbers, given the political will. The prevailing expectation in Whitehall was that jet aircraft could be available by the summer of 1942. Churchill wanted results much sooner than that. Britain was in desperate straits in the summer of 1941. Hitler had broken his pact with Stalin and invaded Russia in the last week of June, but many doubted whether the Soviet Union could survive for long as an ally. If it were to be crushed by the Wehrmacht before the end of the year, Hitler would surely turn back to his unfinished business in the West. Renewed heavy bombing of Britain's cities by the Luftwaffe seemed all too likely.

This was a critical moment in Whittle's war: had these '1,000 Whittles' been authorised, it might have been the realisation, in effect, of the 'Jet Interceptor Fighter' as proposed by him a full year before the war had begun. But the authorisation never came, and the E.28/39's potential as a jet fighter gained no traction at all. (In old age, Whittle claimed never to have heard a word about Churchill's July minute at the time.[67]) With minimal funding available from MAP, and no spirited leadership of the kind that Churchill had envisaged, a W.1A engine was not even cleared for flight tests until six months later, in December 1941. The E.28/39 did not fly again until February 1942, fully eight months after the end of the Cranwell series. The W.1A did prove itself an exceptional design in the end: it was actually the first jet engine ever to pass the '100-hour test', which it did late in 1942 with more than half the continuous running time achieved at almost full speed.[68] But it lived out its days as an experimental engine – rather as the E.28/39 itself was left to become an experimental plane and a curiosity, shipped into London's Science Museum as an exhibit in 1946. Full-scale models of the E.28/39 were eventually to be erected in various out-of-the-way locations as memorials to Whittle – though they might equally be seen today as reminders of the potential 'war winner' that was never given the chance to prove its true value. Had the British government pursued the jet plane at this point with anything like the desperation shown in Germany later in the war, an E.28/39 memorial might today have graced one or two of the finest squares in London.

The inescapable conclusion must be that Churchill's appeal to Moore-Brabazon fell on deaf ears because nobody inside MAP could contemplate switching away from the W.2B development programme to which the Ministry – notwithstanding all Bulman's dire warnings and machinations – was now so heavily committed.

Neither Tizard nor even Whittle himself managed to see the W.1A at this point as anything but an awkward distraction from progressing with the W.2B. (Ironically, the W.2B was soon to prove as vulnerable to surging as the W.2. First run in October 1941, its development programme was seriously impeded at both Rover and BTH as well as at Power Jets by the surging phenomenon – and Whittle's preoccupation with resolving this problem probably helps explain his own relative neglect of the W.1A's potential.) Churchill's minute could not be simply ignored, and a meeting of all the key decision-makers was duly held in Moore-Brabazon's office at MAP on 18 July 1941. The minutes made not a single reference to either the E.28/39 or the W.1A. The progress of the Meteor dominated the whole discussion. It was noted that component parts for 400 W.2B engines had already been ordered, which represented jigging and tooling for eighty airframes a month. The pace would be stepped up. 'It is desirable to take all practicable preliminary action now to secure increased output rapidly if necessary, and a second set of jigs and tools should be ordered.'[69] With Rover, BTH and Power Jets each contracted to build two prototype units of the W.2B, it was easy enough to finesse any consideration of the Prime Minister's allusion to '1,000 Whittles'. Both Cherwell and Freeman were present at the meeting, and neither seems to have raised any objection. Everything possible, after all, was now going to be done to achieve line production of the W.2B within a year: 'output [of the Whittle aircraft] in quantity next summer would probably be acceptable to the Air Staff in place of a proportion of planned fighter output.' So equipping the RAF with jet fighters was now a strategic priority, if not quite as Churchill had urged. They could forget the W.1A. Senior officers would be asked to begin submitting logistical information immediately for deployment of new jet planes powered with the W.2B by July 1942.

This conclusion was grudgingly accepted in Downing Street, with Churchill making clear his impatience in a minute sent directly to Moore-Brabazon at the end of July: 'We must not allow the designer's desire for fresh improvements to cause loss of time. Every nerve should be strained to get these aircraft into squadrons next summer...'[70] Churchill was not alone, though, in worrying that some kind of high-water mark was being passed. Just before the end of the month, a devastating paper emerged from the research station at Farnborough. It was written by Hayne Constant. 'The introduction of a completely new type of aircraft power plant is an event which has never occurred before and is unlikely to occur again for a considerable time', began his four-page memorandum.[71] Then he set down the many ways in which he believed this 'unique opportunity' was in danger of being wasted. He bemoaned a 'superfluity of projects' – in other words, the encouragement of several parallel projects, as now espoused by Tizard. Constant feared this approach to the jet engine had been rendered potentially fatal by a failure to define 'the responsibilities of the various bodies and individuals concerned' and the absence of any effective coordination between them. Whittle's engineering prowess was not in doubt. Their main problems were 'organizational and psychological'. If they could only devise 'a sound organisation' with clearly defined responsibilities and functions, then the remaining technical problems would quickly be overcome.

In other words, the bungling had to stop. As if to illustrate his thesis, the alternative and much more rigorous approach pressed by Hayne Constant was in fact about to be adopted – allowing one focused effort to go forward under clear leadership in pursuit of a finished jet plane, to be completed within a spectacularly short timeframe. The Americans were going to show how it was done.

8

The Cherry Orchard

July 1941 to May 1942

i

Across the vast continent of America, by the start of the 1940s, civilian airlines operated on a scale unimaginable in the Old World. They were flying more than a million passengers a year and most large cities had their own metropolitan airport. In a fiercely competitive marketplace, the leading names were constantly in search of technical upgrades that might offer them (briefly) an edge over their rivals. Plane makers like Boeing and Douglas Aircraft responded with a stream of successful designs – none more fêted than the Douglas DC3 Dakota, launched in 1936 – powered by ever larger piston engines that were mostly designed and built by two dominant manufacturers, Wright Aeronautical and Pratt & Whitney. Aero-engineers who followed the development of US aviation from the other side of the Atlantic had watched a series of exciting innovations arriving over the years – from all-metal fuselages and radial engines with enhanced air-cooling to variable-pitch propellers, cantilever wings and pressurised cabins for flying at high altitude. On 25 March 1940 it was reported in *The Times* that Pan American Airways had taken delivery from Boeing of the 'Strato-Clipper Flying Cloud', a four-engined airliner capable of carrying thirty-three passengers across the Atlantic in twelve hours. Whittle, with his enduring vision of long-distance flight, had long been fascinated by the Americans' progress. One aspect was of special interest to him. Engines built for the latest additions to the Boeing and Douglas catalogues, like the Flying Cloud, were being fitted with turbo-superchargers, incorporating turbine blades as sophisticated as any so far manufactured in Britain. He was keen to learn more about them, as he explained to Henry Tizard in the early summer of 1940. It happened that an RAF officer with a good knowledge of the US, Wing Commander Anderson, was just leaving London to join the Air Attaché's staff at the embassy in Washington. Through Tizard, Whittle asked him to collect as much information as possible, during his first weeks, about American turbines. Naturally, Whittle was also anxious to know whether anyone in the US had yet made the leap from turbo-chargers to jet propulsion.[1]

Anderson had made a tour of the country's military airfields early in 1939, travelling with Arthur (one day to be 'Bomber') Harris from the embassy, and had good contacts in the US Army Air Corps which was effectively the national air force. He turned to his assignment on Whittle's behalf as soon as he arrived at the embassy. In response to his queries about the status of gas-turbine engines in the US, he picked up only historical traces of a topic that had apparently been neglected for many years. Early in the 1920s, the Air Corps had looked into the possibility of such an engine and reached a gloomy verdict: its official report, *Jet Propulsion for Airplanes* (1923), had deemed the whole concept 'inefficient and impractical'.[2] The country's leading manufacturer of steam turbines, General Electric (GE, not to be confused with Britain's GEC), had reportedly given up on the gas-turbine as the basis of an engine even before the First World War, though it had much later managed to turn centrifugal air compressors into a new product line. Under an inspired engineer called Sanford Moss, GE had used his knowledge of compressors in the interwar period to build a range of turbo-superchargers, boosting the performance of piston engines at high altitude. Anderson seems not to have met anyone from GE, however, and he assumed (wrongly, as it turned out) that the company's interest in a gas-turbine engine was still dormant. Washington's view of jet propulsion, anyway, had remained unchanged since the 1920s. Only days before Anderson took up his full-time posting to Washington in June 1940, a paper emanating from the US National Academy of Sciences had declared: 'In its present state, and even considering the improvements possible... the gas-turbine engine can hardly be considered a feasible application to airplanes...'[3] Little if any note had been taken of Power Jets' progress. It did not take Anderson long to pen his findings for Whittle. 'I have been making discreet enquiries on all possible occasions,' he wrote to him at the start of July, 'and find that it is most unlikely that there is anyone in this country who is working on the same lines as yourself...'[4]

While this discovery may have gratified Whittle's competitive streak, it struck Anderson as a matter of real concern. The Phoney War was over and the future grimly uncertain. If any disaster befell Whittle's project, then all progress on jet propulsion might be lost for years (unless the Germans were at work on it, which would be even worse). In the wake of the recent calamitous retreat from Dunkirk and the fall of France, the embassy staffers in Washington were watching events at home with real alarm. In his July 1940 letter to Whittle, Anderson went on to spell out a logical conclusion: 'I wrote to Sir Henry Tizard shortly after arriving here and suggested that it was a matter of considerable importance that your work should at least be duplicated on this side of the Atlantic, if you were not transferred here altogether.' (Personally, admitted Anderson, he preferred the latter option.) Arranging for Whittle's work to be cloned in the US would obviously mean sharing the gist of it with the American government, so Anderson's letter to Tizard touched on a highly sensitive matter that had been under debate in Whitehall for several months: on what basis ought Britain, fighting for its life against Nazi Germany, to contemplate an exchange of its most precious scientific secrets with the US, where most people in public life were fiercely committed to neutrality and where historic ties with Germany lingered still?

Whittle's interest in the state of American research into gas turbines may in fact have been prompted by hearing of this debate's latest turn. Those in favour of a cautious approach based on a quid pro quo bartering of individual items of information – and they had often included Churchill himself – were fast losing ground, by June 1940, to those arguing for a comprehensive pooling of technical secrets, with few if any restrictions. Service chiefs in Washington, too, were rallying to this latter idea. (The US embassy in London reported to General Marshall, head of the US Army, that 'Great Britain is a goldmine of information of a technical nature which should be worked to the limit'.[5]) The Air Ministry had preferred the hold-nothing-back option from the start and Tizard himself had been one of its strongest advocates. Before the end of July 1940, Churchill closed the debate by deciding in favour of the broadest possible exchange – and he invited Tizard to lead an initiative to this end. Given just a few weeks to prepare for extensive talks in the United States that would mark an episode of seminal importance to the future of the war, the 'Tizard Mission' was under way.

The Mission's many distinguished scientists were split into eight speciality groups. Tizard himself took on the responsibility for aircraft and aircraft engines. As he prepared for his trip, he sought Whittle's thoughts on how to handle any disclosure of the jet engine's secrets. The response from Lutterworth was that the Mission posed a dilemma. On the one hand, suggested Whittle, Anderson's findings in June had been quite surprising and a jet programme ought indeed to be urged on the Americans at the earliest opportunity. If this required that Britain's leadership in the field be shared, and perhaps even surrendered, this was surely an unavoidable strategic necessity. As for concerns over security, they paled in comparison to the more immediate risk that all would be lost if Britain should succumb to Hitler's Third Reich. On the other hand, Whittle was far more aware than most of his contemporaries of the potential commercial implications of full disclosure. He had spent over a decade, after all, arguing that a successful gas-turbine engine would change the future of flight and launch both military and commercial aviation into a new era. This outcome might offer Britain's aerospace industry a handsome advantage over its foreign rivals for years to come. It was a heady prospect, not to be lightly sacrificed. Power Jets had had little option but to share its secrets with other British firms, at MAP's behest. But handing the jet's technology over to the Americans would take disclosure to another level altogether. Whittle was duly nervous about proceeding before the patent lawyers had done their best to shore up Britain's ownership, vested either in Power Jets or in Her Majesty's Government. He had little personal stake in the outcome – having lost his patent rights to the state and handed over much of his equity in the Lutterworth business to the Treasury – but he was convinced of the jet's value as 'a source of revenue to this country after the war'.[6]

Tizard broadly agreed: there were two priorities, and they clashed. Prior to the Mission's departure in August 1940, at the very height of the Battle of Britain, some vague understanding was therefore reached in Whitehall that detailed information on Whittle's work would be withheld. 'Jet engines', according to one history of the Mission, 'were to be discussed in only the most general terms.'[7] This line, though, did not hold for long. Soon after arriving in Washington, Tizard and his colleagues found themselves under far more pressure from their American counterparts than they had expected. This was at least partly attributable to the British party's disclosure of its most jealously guarded secret. It was a device that had only been assembled for the first time in July. The prototype had been carried to America in a leather suitcase – the most valuable object, it was later said, ever to have flown over the Atlantic – and was stored in Washington under the bed of one of the Mission's secretaries, who had no idea what the suitcase contained until well after the war.[8] It was called a 'cavity magnetron', a fiendishly clever device that would open the way to using short wavelength radar, so allowing detection sets to be miniaturised for installation in ships and planes. Deeply impressed that British scientists had pulled off this invention, the Americans began pressing for as much information as possible on every front – including aero-engines. On 19 September, Tizard met the head of the US Army Air Corps (USAAC), General Henry H. ('Hap' – short for 'Happy') Arnold for a private talk; and eight days later Tizard and two colleagues were quizzed on aircraft matters at a meeting of the recently established US National Defense Research Committee.[9] A recent paper from the US National Academy of Sciences had discounted the feasibility of a jet engine. It seems Tizard relished explaining that he himself had seen one running nine months earlier, and it had worked. So Whittle's secret was out. Towards the end of the Mission, a formal summary was drawn up of all the information that had been handed over in Washington and this was Item No.6:

6. **Engines** (Aircraft)

Particulars have been supplied to the NACA [ie, the National Advisory Committee for Aeronautics, a Federal agency] of our experimental work on:-

    a) Two-stroke internal combustion engine
    b) Internal combustion turbines
    c) Jet propulsion for aircraft

Reports on these subjects have been handed to the NACA.[10]

Who had written the jet-propulsion report, and what it contained, went undisclosed in the Mission's records. But it seems evident that all qualms about revealing the jet project to the Americans had been abandoned by the time Whittle found himself working closely with Tizard, from November 1940.

The mystery by early 1941 was that no request had yet been received for further briefings on the subject. The officials at MAP were slightly bemused, as Roxbee Cox noted on 8 March. 'The NACA... are aware of the general principles; they also know of our interest in the Whittle engine. They do not, however, appear to have asked for detailed information although they have had some months in which to make a request.'[11] Roxbee Cox and his team might have been even more puzzled, had they known how close some of the engineers at GE had already come to conceiving a jet engine of their own. (Sanford Moss had heard in 1937 of some kind of jet engine being ignited at BTH.[12] He had immersed himself in theoretical calculations, rather as A. A. Griffith had once done, without ever quite breaking free of the turbo-supercharger mind-set. Asked some years later how he had managed to fall short of inventing the jet for himself, Moss is said to have replied, 'Just dumb, just dumb'.[13]) Six months after Tizard's confirmation to the NACA that the jet engine was no pipe dream, the American military still seemed content to explore its own way forward independently of any work done in Britain. The head of the US Navy's Bureau of Aeronautics, Admiral Towers, asked the NACA in March 1941 to set up a committee to this end and the country's three largest turbine manufacturers – GE, Westinghouse and Allis-Chalmers, all of them conspicuously *not* stalwarts of the existing US aero-engine business – were invited to submit separate development proposals.

The USAAC's General Hap Arnold arrived in England on 12 April for two weeks of introductory meetings with ministers and RAF personnel. By this point, the British government was ready to accommodate almost any request from visiting US service chiefs. On the day before Arnold landed, Beaverbrook told Churchill that nothing would be held back from him:

> We would even allow him to see the Whittle engine, which has just made its first jumps. We have not shown it to a soul yet. Indeed we have even flown it on a cloudy day so that the angels could not see it. But what is forbidden to the angels shall be permitted to the General.[14]

It was a typically colourful promise from Beaverbrook – and nothing came of it. The E.28/39 had indeed made 'jumps' but had yet to fly, for the angels or anyone else. Nor was it about to be shown to the General. Indeed, Arnold seems to have been told nothing whatever of the project at Lutterworth – perhaps an indication of how little real significance was attached to it in most quarters, prior to the first flight. He had long conversations with dozens of senior RAF men and an impressive list of dignitaries that included not just Beaverbrook and Tizard but even – to his amazement – Churchill and the King. ('He was the kind of man I always imagined the British King would be.'[15]) He saw and heard much that made a great impression upon him, warranting a detailed nine-page chronicle of the visit when he came to pen his autobiography. To judge by his own account, though, he flew home on 27 April without having heard one word about Whittle or the jet engine.

It was during his absence from Washington, ironically, that the NACA's curiosity about the British jet programme finally prompted its members to begin asking MAP directly for more information. Reports of the work at Lutterworth were probably already reaching the US from a GE engineer called Ray Shoults who had been in residence at BTH since the start of the year. (He was in Britain as GE's technical representative. Part of his duties involved supervising maintenance work on turbo-superchargers at Rugby but he soon heard about the plant's other, more glamorous workload. 'As I went about my supercharger work,' as Shoults recalled in old age, 'I was gradually made aware of the details of the Whittle engine.'[16]) How best to respond to the NACA members' requests was a question apparently left to Tizard, and he was juggling with it when he travelled up to Cranwell to see the E.28/39 fly on 17 May 1941. He talked of it to Whittle, who thought it 'very desirable to get a parallel development going in America' and suggested 'the best way to do this would be to send over a nucleus to form a branch of Power Jets over there... possibly taking one of the W.1s with them'.[17] Whittle made no mention of Tizard's reaction to his radical proposal. This, though, is essentially what now happened – except that Power Jets never had the remotest chance of setting up shop alongside some of the behemoths of American heavy industry.

While most of those privy to news of the Cranwell flights heard of them with considerable surprise, few can have been as astonished as the military attachés at the US embassy in London. It was suddenly apparent that the itinerary arranged for General Arnold's visit in April had fallen short in rather a critical respect.

How Arnold himself reacted is not hard to imagine. A forceful character, even by the standards of the US military, he informed the British government in June that it was his intention to see a jet-development programme pursued equally on both sides of the Atlantic, in the spirit of the Lend-Lease agreement between London and Washington that had just been signed in March. He asked accordingly for USAAC officers to be given full access to the work that had been done in Britain to date.

This abrupt demand for a total pooling of knowledge, after the mere trickle of requests that preceded it, seems to have prompted a brief spasm of doubt in Whitehall. Beaverbrook had resigned at the end of April and his successor, John Moore-Brabazon, was a patrician Tory who had his own distinguished record as a brave aviation pioneer – he had been the first man to qualify as a professional pilot in Britain, in 1910 – but was slow off the mark in dealing with the Americans. He initially sent Arnold a desultory response that described the workings of the jet in a handful of skimpy paragraphs. This misjudged the situation and drew a scathing response from the General. After a brief stand-off – made more complicated by an untimely row over security measures – the new man at MAP came to terms with reality. He sent a cable on 15 July 1941 to the British Air Commission in the Washington embassy with a momentous message: 'we agree to release of information on the Whittle [sic] to US Government, subject to special care being taken to safeguard its secrecy.' Thus did the jet engine join a cluster of notable British innovations in the world of science and technology – including penicillin, which had just been given its first clinical trials in Oxford by scientists desperately short of resources – that found their way over to the US around this time. Another followed a few weeks later when the British government decided, after another scare over security, to share with the Americans all its research into the possibility of a nuclear bomb. The so-called MAUD Report by a committee of Britain's top nuclear scientists was handed over in September 1941, on almost identical grounds. Like the jet project, the bomb was another possible war-winner that demanded greater industrial resources than Britain could possibly muster in wartime – and needed to be pushed ahead as a priority, just in case the Germans were engaged on a parallel programme. (The pooling of knowledge on the bomb led to the Manhattan Project, though, which was research on an incomparably larger scale than any wartime commitment made on either side of the Atlantic to the development of the jet engine.)

At the Washington embassy's behest, Moore-Brabazon's message to the Americans in July included a recommendation that they turn to General Electric, and suggested that 'a suitable [GE] representative be sent to this country to discuss development on the spot'.[18] Those at BTH and elsewhere who had hinted in the past about Whittle's prima donna tendencies might have supposed that American engineers turning up at Lutterworth would soon lead to trouble. In fact, the opposite was true. The early stages of bringing the Americans up to speed lasted several weeks and Whittle found the whole business immensely gratifying. As rewarding, it might be said, as his dealings with Rover had been dispiriting. The GE engineer from Rugby, Ray Shoults, and the USAAF's man from the US embassy, Colonel Al Lyon, arrived at Lutterworth with Roxbee Cox and David Pye on 25 July to begin their detailed appraisal of the project. (The USAAC had become the US Army Air Force in June 1941.) Roxbee Cox had given them a briefing at MAP four days earlier on what to expect. This seems most unlikely, though, to have prepared them adequately for the shock of what awaited them at the Ladywood Works.

Its rapid growth in 1940 had been overseen by Whyte, Williams and Tinling without much recourse to a formal management structure. Even as the company had almost doubled in size over the first half of 1941, from 130 to 250 employees, the Works had retained the air of a slightly anarchic laboratory full of clever young men dashing in and out on mysterious errands. The designers at Gloster Aircraft, who were frequent visitors to the site for a while, had nicknamed it 'the Cherry Orchard' after Chekhov's play in which, as they explained to a puzzled Whittle one day, 'various characters would appear on the stage, say something quite irrelevant and then disappear again'.[19] The Works had nonetheless flourished, on the back of small engineering teams that had essentially managed themselves. Their work was orchestrated by a band of highly motivated star graduates, inspired by Whittle and the ground-breaking nature of the jet venture.

If they were disconcerted by the modest scale of the Cherry Orchard, the Americans were too courteous to show it. (Or too savvy: they could hardly believe their luck that a technology with such tremendous potential for the future was being treated as a relatively minor matter in Britain. There was no reason for them to spur London into treating it as a more precious national asset.) Over the course of their first visit and others that followed into August 1941, Whittle found their ready enthusiasm and straightforward professionalism hugely appealing. He had, of course, never been to the US, and had scarcely met any Americans except BTH's Harry Sporborg, whose bombastic style he had always found vaguely irritating. After Shoults returned to Washington to brief General Arnold in person, another USAAF officer with a background in engine research, Major Don Keirn, took up the running. He spent four whole days at Lutterworth from 28 August. Whittle was once again struck by an openness and geniality that he found much to his liking. Keirn made a particularly strong impression, as Whittle would later record: 'His ability and pleasant personality fitted him very well for the task, and the smoothness of the transatlantic collaboration owed a lot to his good work.'[20] And indeed, as he might have added, to his own growing affinity with these American engineers.

As the technical men reported back on their findings, Washington's serious interest in the jet project became more evident. After the first protracted round of talks with Whittle ended on 13 August, the USAAF's Colonel Lyon called at MAP to talk about future cooperation. 'During the discussion', as an official British report on the whole episode recorded after the war, 'it was felt that America's best contribution to the provision of jet-propelled aircraft would be the provision of engines.'[21] General Arnold had in mind a broader US remit by far. After Major Keirn left Lutterworth, Colonel Lyon paid MAP another visit. This time he brought a shopping list from the USAAF, which included a request for 'one complete engine now in being and one of the single engined test bed aircraft'. Arnold had decreed that 'a jet-development programme' in the US would mean building aircraft as well as engines. They would be developed together.

By early September 1941 Arnold was ready to confirm the selection of GE as America's first jet-engine manufacturer. His award of the contract at a personal meeting with the company's executives gave rise to a story endlessly repeated in the US aero-space industry for years to come:

> In the corner of his office Arnold had a small safe with a combination lock from which he took out a sheaf of Power Jets' drawings and other reports. After some discussion he handed the documents to [GE's corporate vice-president] Roy Muir, saying: 'Gentlemen, I give you the Whittle engine. Consult all you wish and arrive at any conclusion you please – just so long as GE accepts a contract to build fifteen of them'.[22]

And accept it they did. As if to underline the contrast this presented with the interminable wrangling over MAP's contracts for Power Jets, BTH and Rover over the past eighteen months, Arnold there and then agreed with GE on the choice of an airframe designer. They went for Bell Aircraft, based in Buffalo, New York. The company's founder-chairman, Larry Bell, was summoned to a meeting in the capital the next day and given a contract to supply three prototype jet fighters.

A few days later, the British government accepted the full list of Washington's demands 'with the exception of the aircraft'. The US engine would be based on the W.2B design, modified as necessary to accommodate American accessories, and the W.1X engine (as used in those first taxiing runs by the E.28/39) would be despatched by air to the US immediately to help GE begin its work. It was even agreed at a meeting in Thames House chaired by George Bulman on 9 September that, in addition to those travelling as custodians of a Power Jets engine, 'further personnel should go [to the US] as a small mission and that this should include W/c Whittle'.[23] The Americans were effectively being given carte blanche for the development of their own jet aircraft industry. They were mindful of this goal from the start, insisting that 'the US Government be given definite authorisation in writing transferring complete production rights'. As Lyon wrote to Arnold on 20 September: 'England does not have the money to put into adequate Jet Propulsion and Gas Turbine Laboratories. We have.'[24] Assembling a Whittle engine would be 'purely a stopgap measure,' he suggested, en route to a complete 'turbojet' programme that would soon leave Britain's far behind.

The way ahead was formally cleared by the Washington embassy's British Air Commission on 22 September, with an almost wistful legal proviso that was scarcely ever referred to again ('permission to manufacture has been given, in order to assist the joint defence plans of our respective Governments, [and] it is agreed that its use will be limited to such purpose...'). The complete drawings for both the W.1X and the W.2B had just been despatched, and on 29 September Major Don Keirn arrived at the Ladywood Works to collect the physical engine. It was packed into three large crates and given a three-man escort comprising Whittle's Chief Engineer, Dan Walker, an RAF Warrant Officer, James King, and one of the most popular men in the company, a London-born son of Italian parents called Bruno Bozzoni (known to all as Old Bozzi). Taken by road to Prestwick, the engine was flown over the Atlantic in the bomb bay of a B-24 Liberator of the USAAF with its three minders from the East Midlands seated shivering beside it. It was a momentous transatlantic shipment to set beside that of the cavity magnetron – with less immediate impact, as it turned out, but rather more sweeping consequences eventually.

Whittle heard no more until a cable arrived at Brownsover Hall from the British Air Commission late in October. It confirmed that GE would be working to the W.2B design, with minor amendments. The company planned to have its first engine, a 'Type I' (as in 'eye'), running within six months.

ii

Whittle's own operations at Lutterworth, meanwhile, had been faring less well since the mid-summer of 1941. The development of a revised W.2 engine, the Mark IV, had run into a spate of embarrassing delays. The W.2B was also behind schedule: Whittle had decided he wanted to fit more blades into its turbine, all of them to be a full inch wide instead of 4/5ths of an inch.[25] Hovering over all their work, meanwhile, was the problem of surging to which there still seemed no practical remedy. Whittle had to suppress his deep anxiety over this, in the face of government ministers arriving at the Ladywood Works to congratulate him on the success of the E.28/39's trials. The subterfuge involved in feeding their new-found enthusiasm for his project was visibly draining. In a photograph of him welcoming the MAP Minister John Moore-Brabazon to the site in July, he appears almost haggard in contrast with his visitor's portly figure (*Plate 7b*). He evidently rose to the occasion as usual. After returning to London, Moore-Brabazon wrote back with an effusive note of thanks: 'my short visit gave me more interest and enjoyment than any which has fallen to my lot since joining this Ministry.'[26] This only exacerbated Whittle's problem, though. Moore-Brabazon asked Roxbee Cox to give him daily reports on progress, and even began calling Whittle directly for news of the latest test results. Whittle confessed to Roxbee Cox that he was 'beginning to feel like a hunted man'.[27]

Perhaps it added to his sense of vulnerability that he had now parted company with the 'scientist, philosopher and banker', as Whittle liked to describe him, who had been by his side since 1936. He and Lance Whyte had never been personally close; but as Whittle's business manager, in effect, Whyte had always played an important supporting role. Having deprived him of the chairmanship nine months earlier, Whittle had suddenly dismissed him as the Managing Director on 2 July. It was a revealing episode, though neither Whittle nor Whyte were to say much about it in their respective memoirs. Whittle looked back on it as 'the culmination of a long period of disharmony', asserting that Whyte had resigned. 'Difficulties had accumulated' was Whyte's own brief verdict, 'and the task I had set myself was accomplished.'[28] In fact Whittle's letter of dismissal seems to have quite disconcerted him. It was wholly unsentimental, giving only the slightest nod to Whyte's pivotal role in the corporate story and the fact that the two men had worked together side by side for almost six years: 'I freely acknowledge that you are a man of very considerable ability,' wrote Whittle with a rather chilly remoteness, '... but unfortunately your particular abilities do not seem to be of the right type for the efficient management of the affairs of a rapidly growing engineering organisation such as Power Jets'.[29] It was also Whyte's misfortune that he had had to deal 'with individuals whose motives and business morals leave a lot to be desired'. (Whittle was by this time totally disenchanted with the Wilks brothers.) Much of the letter was devoted to tittle-tattle about Whyte's private life. He had been renting a beautiful Georgian rectory outside Rugby with his Austrian wife, Lotte, and Whittle had been perturbed by gossip about 'aliens' seen on the premises – probably refugees from Nazi Vienna given a roof by his wife.

The real reason for Whyte's dismissal, only obliquely cited by Whittle in his letter, was a clash of views over the practical sense of pressing on with the expansion of Power Jets. By the late summer of 1941, the Cherry Orchard had more than two hundred men on stage. It had been given clearance by MAP to plan for the making of twelve experimental engines a year. The shortage of space was becoming a serious limitation. The proposal for a large new factory had finally been approved by Tizard, and Dudley Williams was finalising plans for its construction on a greenfield site nine miles north of Lutterworth, next to a small Leicestershire village called Whetstone. Whyte regarded this whole scheme as an ill-considered extension of their original objective. He thought Power Jets had achieved enough to warrant a buyout by the state that would properly reward the original private shareholders (though in fact the Treasury was shortly to reject this idea). Building experimental engines from the W.2B onwards could then be handed over to established engine manufacturers, while Whittle could either consolidate Power Jets as an independent research body – a 'small design unit', indeed – or agree to see it merged into a larger parent company. Either way, Whittle's inspired vision now seemed to Whyte assured of its future. A few days later, Whyte sent Roxbee Cox a thoughtful letter, urging that a majority stake in the company be acquired by the Treasury as soon as possible. This would properly heed 'the great importance of the Company's contribution to the war' and enable the engine's development to be promoted more effectively.[30] But Whyte took his recommendation no further. His wife Lotte died suddenly on 17 July and he moved back to London and another role in the war effort, severing all links with the project.

Whittle had been affronted by the suggestion that he should go along with the possibility of a merger – especially coming from Whyte, who knew how strongly he had resisted the idea from the very start. Leaving aside his socialist beliefs and suspicion of large companies' predatory ways, Whittle was opposed to surrendering Power Jets' autonomy out of a steadfast conviction that it would retard the development of the engine. His confidence on this score sometimes startled his peers. Late in July 1941, he was visited at Brownsover by a senior man from Farnborough, A. H. Hall, who was just retiring as the RAE's Chief Superintendent. When they began discussing the progress of the W.2B, Hall had to listen to a familiar litany of complaints about BTH and Rover. Whittle had some much more complimentary things to say, though, about his new friends at Rolls-Royce and the assistance that the Derby firm had agreed to provide. They talked of the need for a fully resourced business dedicated to the future of the jet engine – which prompted Hall to muse that a Rolls-Royce operation 'might be the ultimate form this kind of unit might take, and he did not want to see the E.28/39s eventually drop into the background'. No fear of that, retorted Whittle, not least because 'Rolls-Royce were likely to find that they were anticipated by us in most respects'.[31]

Fig. 18. The W.2B engine, given its first run in October 1941 at Power Jets

Through the autumn of 1941, the men from Rolls-Royce were indeed impressed to discover how much ground he had covered already. The first version of the W.2B was finally given its initial run in October (*Fig. 18*). Whittle's principal contact at Rolls-Royce remained Stanley Hooker. A tall man with a slightly stooping posture, Hooker was almost exactly the same age as Whittle and had trained as a mathematician before developing a passion for the aeronautical sciences. This had led him to Rolls-Royce in 1938, where he had immediately begun work on improving the efficiency of the Merlin's supercharger – a unit essentially the same as the centrifugal compressor on Whittle's jet engine, though much smaller. Hooker and Whittle hit it off from the start. (In their very first conversation, by his own account, the Derby man had quickly steered the discussion round to centrifugal compressors on which he genuinely believed himself to be the world's living expert. 'But I soon realized that I was talking with my master.'[32]) Hooker was genuinely keen to assist the team at the Ladywood Works wherever help was needed. He drove over to visit Whittle on several occasions through the autumn of 1941, bringing with him a succession of other colleagues to advise on possible joint ventures and updating Whittle on the progress being made by Geoff Wilde in Derby on the test rig for the compressor work. In one significant conversation, on 21 October, Whittle told Hooker and two of his colleagues that he had himself arrived at a hypothesis for the surging phenomenon. Its cause, he suggested, might be the switch they had made with the W.2B to a design incorporating many more vanes in the compressor's diffuser. The W.1A only had ten vanes and had had no problem with surging. Perhaps Wilde might explore this further? Whittle noted: 'Hooker and company thought that our scheme with ten major diffuser vanes with sub-divided channels was well worth trying.'[33]

It did not take long for Hooker to become aware of the mounting tension between Power Jets and Rover. After they agreed to manufacture three hundred turbine blades for Whittle, Rolls-Royce was informed by MAP that the raw metal would have to be sourced via Rover. On this basis, and because Rover tried to interfere with some tests being offered by Rolls-Royce, Hooker inferred that Rover and Power Jets were effectively joint developers of the jet. His misunderstanding drew a sharp correction from Whittle ('I disillusioned him...') and the whole complicated background to the project was very soon apparent to Hooker – who wasted no time alerting Ernest Hives to it in August. This was timely, for Hives was in the process of reconsidering the best approach for Rolls-Royce to take. It was about this time that he caught wind of the accord reached between MAP and the US government. (The news had just broken, too, of Churchill and President Roosevelt meeting for a conference with all their advisers somewhere in the Atlantic on 25 August to talk about 'deep underlying unities', as *The Times* had reported.) So when Roxbee Cox visited Derby late in August, Hives had a proposal to make. With so much information about to be shared across the Atlantic, said Hives, perhaps it was time for 'a bit of collaboration at home', too.[34] Presented so innocuously, it might almost have been a casual aside if coming from anyone else. Coming from Hives, it was a canny indication that Rolls-Royce intended to play a significant part in the future of the jet engine – and Roxbee Cox appreciated as much. He promised Hives that he would give the collaboration idea serious thought.

Back in his office at MAP, Roxbee Cox began devising a scheme to provide the aero-engineering industry with an appropriate platform. He suggested the Ministry should invite all those involved in the jet project to appoint technical representatives to a committee, which would act as a kind of data-clearing pool. Information and experience gathered by the firms could be exchanged via this committee, free of legal and financial barriers. All patent questions would simply be shelved, for consideration after the war. It was a truly radical plan, and it elicited a mixed response. At Freeman's behest, a new senior officer, Air Vice Marshal F. J. ('Black Jack') Linnell, had been brought into MAP and formally appointed as Controller of Research and Development in June 1941. Linnell, a lean RAF officer rather in the Tedder mould, thought the Roxbee Cox scheme made sense. The jet was an experimental venture, so in Linnell's view warranted an experimental procedure. George Bulman, though, opposed it. No successful piston engine had ever been the result of a collaborative venture, he insisted, and he could see no reason why the jet engine needed one. Neither Tizard nor Moore-Brabazon had yet sought to overrule Bulman on a matter of any significance and it was only with some difficulty that Linnell eventually managed to persuade him to accept this initiative. (Much later, Linnell would express regret that he had not relieved Bulman of all authority over the jet at this point; but that is to jump ahead.) Whittle, too, had strong reservations about the committee idea at first. It struck him as an unwelcome boost for Tizard's strategy of engaging the wider aero-engine industry. For this same reason, Tizard himself gave it his warm support.

This was in fact Tizard's last significant contribution to the jet project. He had never been officially appointed to the Research and Development job at MAP, and Linnell's arrival – added to Cherwell's pervasive influence in Downing Street – had rapidly curtailed his role within the Ministry (though he was to remain an adviser there and a member of the Air Council until September 1943). He had many other interests wearing his scientific-adviser hat. He was increasingly preoccupied, for example, with a debate in Whitehall over the future deployment of Bomber Command. Having helped to bring Whittle and Rolls-Royce together in June, Tizard seems to have felt that he had honoured his commitment to the jet engine's future – even though it must have been apparent to him, as to others, that his January gamble on fast-tracking the development of W.2B prototypes straight from the drawing board was now most unlikely to come off. It is hard not to suspect that he had also been worn down by the strain of trying to mediate between Whittle and Bulman, and by his disenchantment with Spencer Wilks' behaviour. On all counts, anyway, he was content to step back and leave an industry-wide committee to resolve the continuing problems over Rover's status as MAP's prime contractor for the jet. He had done his best since 1936 to boost its prospects. (Whittle viewed his contribution less positively. In an interview for a BBC television programme in 1976, Whittle recalled wanting to cooperate with Rolls-Royce 'from the very earliest days that we'd started practical work but Sir Henry Tizard… wouldn't agree to it on the grounds that Rolls-Royce were already pursuing their own particular work'. The resulting delay to the project, exacerbated by Rover's involvement, was a calamity: 'It would have been possible to have had [jet fighters] two years earlier than we did.' So, asked his interviewer, was Tizard to blame? Whittle replied: 'I think so.'[35])

When Linnell finally announced the formation of the 'Gas Turbine Collaboration Committee' (GTCC), he made Roxbee Cox its first chairman. If this riled Bulman, it delighted Whittle and persuaded him to drop his initial reservations. The GTCC convened its first meeting early in November 1941. It would later become a body of considerable importance to the emergence of a jet-engine industry in Britain and the success of its early proceedings owed much to Whittle. With his usual disregard for the prodigious effort entailed for him personally, he wrote two long papers for the GTCC's founding members. One set down a comprehensive review of the jet-engine project's history to date.[36] The other comprised a quite brilliant seventy-four-page study of the surging phenomenon that was continuing to plague all their work.[37] The latter was another measure of Whittle's distinction as engineer and aerodynamicist. Sadly, some members of the GTCC may have needed reminding of this, given how worryingly the development of the W.2B had slowed down since the summer. Whittle closed his paper on surging with a veiled plea for patience: '... the period of apparent lack of progress has largely been a period of gestation, and the moment now appears to be ripe for a big step forward.'

He had warned on several occasions since May 1941 that many issues yet remained to be resolved. The heat-resistant quality of the engine's steel components, for example, turned out to be less dependable than expected. The 'Rex 78' steel from Firth Vickers needed replacing, and various possible substitutes had to be tried and discarded – including one, 'Hastalloy B', used successfully by American firms for exhaust valves in piston engines – before Whittle settled on a winner, a nickel-chrome steel called 'Nimonic 80' from the Mond Nickel Company. Again, combustion problems were still bedevilling matters, prompting many late changes to the very core of the engine where fuel met compressed air. The Lubbock atomiser adopted in July 1940 was a proven success, but the impact of the burning fuel on the 'local' metals of the 'flame tubes' remained problematic. Only now did Whittle come across a design that fully satisfied him – an ingenious perforated tube, nicknamed the 'colander' and invented by an engineer at the Burnley factory of Joseph Lucas Ltd., one of Rover's main sub-contractors (and the manufacturer of the atomiser). And as the participants in the meeting at MAP on 18 July 1941 had been warned, he was still working his way through revisions of the basic turbine blade, devising four of them in turn before amalgamating their subtly different shapes into a fifth, henceforth known as 'No.5'. All these were fundamental steps in the development process, not just pragmatic adjustments aimed at making quantity production easier. They showed, in Cynthia Keppel's words, 'how fluid the design of the important components remained until a comparatively late stage and how, where this fluidity was due to insufficient knowledge of the behaviour of the gas turbine, it was unavoidable'.[38] This, after all, was a radical new technology in its very earliest stages.

Reactions to the apparent lack of progress were mixed. For

those hoping to see jet fighters in the air by mid-1942, the autumn of 1941 brought keen disappointment. The September target for thirty experimental W.2B engines was soon abandoned, the first in a long sequence of aborted deadlines. For others, including some of the RAF's senior officers, the rescheduling came as a relief. Sir William Sholto Douglas, Dowding's successor as head of Fighter Command, was the man tasked with rebuilding the RAF's depleted squadrons. He had been perplexed in the summer at the sudden excitement over jet aircraft, and thought the Air Ministry's plans to introduce the Gloster Meteor across the service in 1942 were dangerously premature – not least because he himself had had no chance to offer an opinion about it. ('I strongly object to having an aircraft foisted upon me on this scale in whose design I have had no voice.'[39])

Between the disappointed on the one hand and the relieved on the other were those who responded to Whittle's travails with a philosophical shrug, pointing out to less worldly colleagues with little or no experience of aero-engineering that gas-turbine engines were, after all, not so very different from piston engines. Or as George Bulman would put it in his memoirs, 'There is the irreducible period of gestation in the creation of a new aero engine, fit for use, which even the scientists must come to realise.'[40] It was time, as Bulman suggested to Jack Linnell in October 1941, to reassert MAP's responsibility for the jet project, notwithstanding the highly unusual goings-on that had been sanctioned at Lutterworth since the start of the year. In practice this meant reminding Rover that it was still trusted as the Ministry's principal contractor, and strengthening the ties between Rover and MAP's Engines directorate.

Linnell wrote to Spencer Wilks accordingly. On the surface, his letter might have seemed unexceptional. It restated the understanding struck by Tizard between MAP and Rover in January 1941. Whittle was to be consulted along all the familiar lines (on 'changes affecting the thermodynamics and aerodynamics'), while Rover would have final responsibility for the production-design and output of the engines. Given all that had happened since January, however – the extraordinary growth of Power Jets, the triumph of the Cranwell flights, the intervention by Churchill himself to force the pace and the tireless efforts made by Whittle and his team to master the unforeseen challenges of the jet engine – the Linnell letter's determination to cast Rover as the driving force behind the W.2B amounted to a woefully culpable, bordering on scandalous, folly. Another senior officer with no engineering background whatever, Linnell showed no awareness of the implication of his edict. Rover was to work with Whittle's design ('presuming... [it] meets requirements') but could make changes 'in the interests of ease of production and of increased reliability in service'. The motorcar manufacturer would also be entitled to 'experiment yourselves along lines which you believe to be profitable... having in view improvement of the W.2B engine or advancements leading to another Mark'.[41] It seems most unlikely that Whittle ever saw this letter, which would surely have triggered another almighty row. But he was quickly apprised of an organisational change at MAP announced in the letter. Linnell acknowledged Spencer Wilks' request for there to be a single official at MAP answerable 'on all questions concerning development, and the design for production...' Linnell's nominee for this post was not Roxbee Cox, who had effectively filled just such a role since mid-1940, but Major A. A. Ross – the deputy head of Engines who reported directly to Bulman. 'I think we shall find', as Linnell confided to Wilks, 'that the majority of present day problems fall directly within Ross's province...' It was yet another mark of Bulman's extraordinary influence over the Ministry's affairs. Linnell, like Tizard and Tedder before him, had felt obliged to accept that, with so many years of experience behind him, Bulman knew best.

One of Ross's first assignments involved a trip to Lancashire in November 1941. Even before the devastation of Coventry by the Luftwaffe a year earlier, many Midlands manufacturers had begun to relocate plants critical to the war effort. With MAP's blessing, Rover had acquired in September 1940 a defunct cotton mill on the edge of the Pennines at Barnoldswick (pronounced 'Barlick' by the locals).* Here it had housed a new production facility, the 'Bankfield Shed', for manufacturing its jet engines.⁴² A second, smaller site called Waterloo Mill was acquired shortly afterwards in the nearby town of Clitheroe, to serve as a design and development centre. Whittle had good reason to be intensely suspicious of Rover's intentions. His combustion expert, William Hawthorne, had visited Clitheroe in the summer of 1941 and returned with an ominous report: 'It appeared to me that Waterloo Mill was a Rover version of the Power Jets' set-up...'⁴³ Rover's leeway for development was supposed to have been kept to a minimum, yet Maurice Wilks had moved up to Clitheroe with a team of Rover engineers. It only added to Whittle's concern that he received no invitation to see the new premises or to offer advice on what to put inside them.

And now, at precisely the same time as Ross was expressing his satisfaction over Rover's progress at Clitheroe and Barnoldswick, Power Jets was denied the funding for a full-scale test rig for compressors at Lutterworth. Whittle insisted this expensive item was essential to run the component parts of his engine in isolation from each other, for the diagnosis of persistent problems. He was at first supported by the Minister, Moore-Brabazon, who declared himself 'very enthusiastically in favour of separate testing of compressor, turbine and combustion assembly'.⁴⁴ Separate rig-testing was indeed indispensable (as it remains to this day, for the development of any gas turbine). Bulman refused to go along with it. Though Power Jets had been given permission months earlier to plan for the production of experimental engines, he rejected the test-rig request and Moore-Brabazon – as usual –

---

* Barnoldswick was actually located in the West Riding of Yorkshire, and proud of it. Only in 1974 did it become a Lancashire town, following a redefinition of local boundaries in the wake of Edward Heath's 1972 Local Government Act. Clitheroe was always a Lancashire town. To keep things simple, Rover's two plants in the area will both be referred to below as Lancashire-based operations – which is how they were generally described by MAP officials at the time, though probably not in conversation with any Barlick locals.

accepted his decision. The stream of design changes to the W.2B over recent months had induced Bulman to take a stronger stand against Whittle's endeavours. Tizard's decision to sanction a new factory for the company at Whetstone had left him baffled. Now that established firms like de Havilland and Metro-Vickers were making progress with their own jet-engine programmes – encouraged (ironically) by the GTCC initiative that he himself had opposed – Bulman saw even less reason to countenance helping Power Jets to turn itself into a production plant.

For Whittle, by far the most important of the other firms was Rolls-Royce. He was delighted at its willingness to make parts for him – and valued almost as much the start of a broader association, as exemplified by Geoff Wilde's continuing investigation into surging. Whittle desperately needed opportunities to air his latest thinking with like-minded engineers. His many problems with the W.2B – the first order for experimental units had now been reduced to just four, deliverable by the end of the year – were causing him real anguish, which he could share with few others. He was seeing very little of Tizard any more. His Chief Engineer, Dan Walker, had gone to America with the W.1X and Hawthorne, soon after returning from his trip to Lancashire, had come to the end of his secondment to Lutterworth and had returned to Farnborough. So his burgeoning relationship with Rolls-Royce meant a great deal to him, by the middle of November 1941.

Wretchedly, it was now suddenly cast into doubt. The Derby giant had development challenges of its own. Combat reports over the autumn of a powerful new German fighter, the Focke-Wulf Fw 190, left no doubt that this aircraft could outperform the RAF's front-line fighter, the Spitfire Mk V flying with the latest Merlin. Hives was under constant pressure to deliver a yet more powerful version of his totemic engine. He also had to contend, as noted already, with an unprecedented volume of orders for the Merlin from Bomber Command. Hives ordered a halt to all non-essential tasks in the development shop at Derby, effectively shelving work on turbine blades for Power Jets. Whittle appealed to him to change his mind:

You have already given us very valuable help but recently we have been informed that the load on your development shop is so heavy that you cannot do anything more for us for the present. This has hit us very hard and we hope very much that you can be persuaded to relent. The development has already suffered severely from lack of manufacturing facilities and in my opinion there is little doubt that most of our troubles would have been over long ago if we had at our disposal resources comparable with your development shop.[45]

Whittle did not mention it to Hives, but his team had just had to resort to using a diffuser with vanes made of wood in their current test engines. It was a graphic illustration of their lack of resources – the *reductio ad absurdum* of building a whole jet-engine project on a shoestring budget. (To no one's great surprise, the wooden diffuser parts quickly splintered on 2 December – though not before serving their purpose: '... though they only survived for about ten minutes of high-speed running, they provided the vital information required to cure surging.'[46] How this fed into Wilde's work at Rolls-Royce is unclear.)

It was certainly not Hives' intention to signal any loss of interest in the jet engine – on the contrary, he was actively mulling the case for taking a much bigger stake in its future – but Whittle by this time was in no shape to cope with any fresh adversity, let alone the loss of his cherished link with Rolls-Royce. There seemed a real possibility that the jet project might soon be abandoned: Whittle knew there were those in MAP's Technical Department who believed it had fallen between two stools, being neither a production job on the one hand nor a 'normal prototype procedure' on the other, involving multiple aeroplanes.[47] The prospect of failure, despite all that had been achieved in 1940–41, and despite all the encouragement offered by the engineers at Rolls-Royce over the summer, was almost more than he could bear. His natural intensity, hitherto appealing and often charismatic, was frequently apparent now as a brittle irascibility: he was drawing ever closer to a nervous breakdown. The list of symptoms that he cited in *Jet* was candid up to a point, though he stopped short of mentioning his addiction to Benzedrine: 'Exhausted by a four-and-a-half-year struggle with formidable engineering problems, and depressed by pessimism about the outcome of MAP policy, I began to suffer from insomnia, irritability, lack of appetite and other symptoms of nervous strain.'[48]

The news on 7 December 1941 of the Japanese attack on the American naval base at Pearl Harbor did nothing for his peace of mind, triggering much speculation at Lutterworth about the possible implications for Power Jets with its new ties across the Atlantic. Three days later, Whittle was in the large study at Brownsover Hall, working at his desk as usual. There was a sudden commotion in the hallway and Leslie Cheshire burst into the office with some desperate news. Japan's entry into the war had prompted the Royal Navy briefly to deploy two of its biggest ships off the east coast of Malaya. On their way back to Singapore, both had been sunk by enemy bombers. Whittle, who had experienced the intimacy of life aboard a big ship during his time as a test pilot with the Royal Navy, was totally overwhelmed. He leapt to his feet and lost control of himself, shrieking at Cheshire to get out of the room and hurling a chair after him. As Cheshire retreated in dismay, Mary Phillips called George Lees to come immediately and drive Whittle home to Broomfield. This was the collapse that so many had feared might overwhelm him. (Recalling the episode, he himself suggested: 'The thing to be wondered at is that it had not happened before.'[49]) He took to his bed, and arrangements were hastily made at MAP for the RAF's top neurologist, Group Captain Symonds, to visit him at home. Symonds, already renowned within the service for his work on what he called 'flying stress', seems to have prescribed merely a period of rest. If so, this took too little account of Whittle's obsessive need to keep working. For several days, papers flowed to and fro between the house and Mary's desk at Brownsover Hall. Another crisis then ensued over Christmas, and on 27 December he was admitted at Symonds' insistence to the Military Hospital for Head Injuries installed at St Hugh's College, Oxford. His admission notes recorded: 'Working 7 days a week for last 4 years, without holiday [for] 2 years, has become depressed, irritable, inability to concentrate and [has] suffered from insomnia.'[50] He was diagnosed with neurasthenia, with 'recurrent crops of boils and furunculosis of ears'.[51]

Whittle found his enforced idleness within the hospital 'extremely depressing' and was probably an insufferable patient. He seems to have been given electro-convulsive therapy, which in those days was still highly experimental – and came much later to be used for cases of depression rather than acute stress, which was Whittle's problem. By one account, Roxbee Cox visited him in hospital and appealed to the doctors to have the therapy stopped. When told it was the only way to get Whittle back to normal, he objected that Whittle 'never was normal'.[52] After eight days Whittle prevailed on Symonds to let him recuperate at home, under Dorothy's care. Two weeks later he was back at work. Without doubt a much longer period of convalescence would have served him well, but he had pressing reasons to return.

iii

Over the Christmas and New Year period of 1941–2, Bulman and Ross took advantage of Whittle's absence to push back hard against Power Jets' expansion plans. They persuaded both Moore-Brabazon and Linnell that the time had finally arrived to relegate the company to a minor supporting role. The Ministry's change of stance was signalled at one of the enormous roundtable conferences to which MAP seemed partial. Speaking to more than thirty delegates, assembled at the main Joseph Lucas plant in Birmingham, Ross said it needed to be clear to all that 'the position of Power Jets was simply that of consultants'.[53] This remark was made in the context of installing engines into the Meteor, but the drift of Ross's comments from the chair thoroughly alarmed Pat Johnson and the rest of the Power Jets team in the room. Back at Lutterworth, Johnson agreed with Williams and Tinling that the three of them could not afford to wait on Whittle's recovery and should seek a meeting immediately with Linnell. They travelled down to MAP on 30 December 1941. The Air Marshal was called away at the last minute, so it was left to Denis Tobin to confirm to the three visitors that a change of approach had been agreed 'literally overnight'. Power Jets had hitherto formally reported to the Director of Scientific Research, which had at least assured it some slim measure of independence from Bulman's Engines directorate. This reporting line was now scrapped, leaving Bulman and Ross effectively in charge – insofar as Rover would have to answer to anyone in government at all. Power Jets would be 'responsible for such Research and Development as may be put upon them', at Rover's discretion.[54] When Moore-Brabazon then gave the Lutterworth party a brief audience, he airily waved aside their objections. Designers in the aircraft industry, he said, always squabbled with production people. Power Jets had no capacity to manufacture anything. So the project would go forward under Rover. Bulman and his deputy had everything in hand.

Behind this fateful decision, largely driven by George Bulman himself, lay several considerations from MAP's perspective. Rover claimed it would soon be in a position to deliver its first finished W.2B engines. The Meteor prototypes could therefore be launched in the spring of 1942, albeit a little behind schedule. Endless design amendments pushed at them by Whittle had begun to exhaust everyone's patience. The project would surely make better progress by distancing him from Rover's work. This would also allow MAP officials to revisit what they regarded as an eccentric decision by Tizard to let Power Jets build a new factory from scratch. This scheme had been vehemently opposed by Bulman from the start. Indeed, the whole arrangement whereby this privately-owned company was being bankrolled by the Treasury from one month to the next was simply anathema to most of the officials. True, the established aircraft companies working to Treasury contracts were also privately-owned. Their shareholders had invested pots of capital, though, that in Whitehall's view made them more truly partners with government. (They were also run by men whom Bulman had counted as personal friends for twenty years or more.) Power Jets was effectively a state-owned concern, yet the state had no control over those who were running it – none of whom had any track record of management in the aircraft industry.

Misconceived in principle, Power Jets had also given rise to much vexatious behaviour in practice. Johnson, Williams and Tinling – as Whittle's triumvirate on earth, according to one Ministry wag – had pestered Whitehall officials for months over Power Jets' financial and contractual position and the post-war status of its patents. Their preoccupation with these matters, prompting endless meetings and a stream of indignant memoranda, had become a serious irritant. As for Whittle's own conduct over the course of the past year or so – it was apparent to all inside MAP that it had led to a considerable degree of personal animosity between him and Bulman, which really could not be allowed to fester much longer. His illness was a sad business, but at least allowed MAP to make a timely break with his services. Few believed he could make a quick recovery from his crisis in December. (At one meeting early in the New Year, when someone cited Whittle's views on the topic under discussion, 'a senior MAP official… said "it's no use taking any notice of Whittle – he's gone round the bend"'.[55]) And there was one other aspect of the situation that weighed heavily with Bulman in January 1942, though it would not become apparent to others in the Ministry for a few months yet. Maurice Wilks had drawn up his own design for a jet engine that Rover was secretly developing at Clitheroe in parallel with the W.2B. Extraordinarily, Bulman and Wilks had reached a private agreement over this shamefully duplicitous arrangement. For both men it was convenient to see Power Jets distanced from all future production tasks.

For several days Johnson and his colleagues withheld news of MAP's latest move from Whittle. They were anxious not to involve him in yet another stressful quarrel, so the long and angry papers fired off from Lutterworth over the following days were written by Tinling and Johnson himself. They plainly hit their mark, for on 13 January Linnell travelled up to the Ladywood Works to talk to them, accompanied by Ross. Whittle was still recuperating at

Broomfield, but the rest of the team pitched the Power Jets' case against Rover with a conviction that plainly impressed the Air Marshal. When he invited his hosts at one point to speak candidly about the personalities involved, they were happy to oblige. Dudley Williams expressed 'horror' at the idea of having to report directly to Bulman. Just a hint of impropriety was allowed to float in the air: 'if we were to be quite frank, we considered Rovers had some unexplainable influence with Major Bulman...' By the end of his visit, just like Tedder before him, Linnell was starting to waver over the policy being pushed at him by his officials. According to Tinling's record, Linnell 'said he could well understand some of our points of view and that he had inherited a lot of unfortunate decisions and would do his best to straighten matters out'.[56] Next day, at Linnell's suggestion, Johnson wrote a comprehensive review of Rover's dismal performance to date and the reasons why Power Jets regarded the company as fundamentally inadequate for the job. His paper urged that Rover be ditched altogether – or else 'be put under close technical supervision... as manufacturers only'.[57]

Whittle returned to his desk at Brownsover Hall on 14 January 'on light duty' and began reviewing papers on several technical discussions with Hooker and his Rolls-Royce colleagues that had been held in his absence. A memo from Leslie Cheshire drew his attention to an especially interesting meeting of 9 January. The ostensible purpose of a visit from the Derby men had been 'to discuss certain problems in connection with the blower test rig...'.[58] Their subsequent conversation, though, 'covered much wider ground as it appeared that RR are seriously considering constructing the Whittle type unit'. More precisely, it seemed they were intending to build an engine that would be closely based on the W.2B while being unmistakeably a Rolls-Royce version of it. Later the same morning, a letter from Hives himself landed at Brownsover Hall. It confirmed what Hooker had suggested to Cheshire. Rolls-Royce proposed to make a jet engine of its own. Hives wanted Whittle to know the decision had been reached 'with the sole desire of helping with the national effort'.[59] There was no question of competing with Power Jets: 'We want you to look upon our contribution as an extension of your existing facilities for development, both as regards technical assistance and facilities for producing the pieces.' Whittle was elated and replied by return of post in effusive fashion: 'We are very pleased to hear that you wish to go ahead with a Rolls-Royce version of our unit, and you can count upon us to give you all the assistance in our power.'[60] As for the pernicious talk in some quarters about Power Jets resenting competition from others, Hives need pay it no attention whatever: other firms, promoted as partners for the project, had generally been as unsuitable as Roll-Royce would be ideal. Power Jets had no misgivings at all 'in respect of any contribution you may wish to make'.

It was fully six months since their initial meeting under Tizard's auspices back in June 1941. Power Jets' ties with Rolls-Royce had been slower to jell than Whittle had hoped and expected. Nonetheless it seemed his dream of working in partnership with the Derby firm might become a reality after all. Even as he was penning his reply to Hives at Brownsover Hall, Stanley Hooker was back at the Ladywood Works for more discussions. With him had come Rolls-Royce's Chief Designer, Albert Elliott. Next day George Lees sent Whittle a record of their visit, relaying fulsome compliments from Elliott for everything they had achieved. Coming from a man who had joined Henry Royce's team in 1912 and personified the history of the piston engine, it was no small praise. 'He said that in his opinion, in ten years' time the reciprocating engine would be a back number as far as aviation was concerned... [the jet engine] represented a tremendous step forward, and this was why they were so anxious to participate.'[61]

Almost certainly Elliott had a particular reason to voice such optimism. He must surely have heard the news that Geoff Wilde – having completed the building of his test rig in October 1941, widely seen as a considerable feat in itself – had just proposed a definitive solution to the surging phenomenon. Working with Leslie Cheshire from Power Jets, Wilde had been testing the compressor with various diffuser designs. Most incorporated eighty vanes, as designed by Whittle in an attempt to improve the diffuser's efficiency for the W.2B. A surviving record from January 1942 shows that by the middle of the month Wilde had also begun testing an experimental 'No.13 diffuser' which sported just ten vanes, in line with the hypothesis Whittle had put to Hooker three months earlier.[62] In the space of a few days, he had been able to demonstrate that switching from eighty vanes to ten for the W.2B would rid the engine of its surging curse.

This was not some arcane engineering detail, as any layman might have supposed. It lifted a dark cloud that had hovered over Whittle and his whole project for more than six months. After Wilde's No.13 diffuser had been fitted to a W.2B and the engine had been run at full speed without a hitch, Whittle sent a triumphant letter off to Jack Linnell at MAP on 20 January 1941:

> [The test results using the experimental No.13 diffuser] were such that we regard them as highly satisfactory and constituting an important landmark in the development – I will go so far as to say that the most serious aerodynamic and thermodynamic troubles which were limiting the development have now been overcome, and the main purpose of this letter is to put this opinion on record.[63]

Here was a tonic for the convalescent patient more potent than anything that Dr Symonds could have prescribed. Strikingly, Whittle agreed with his team that the new redesign of the diffuser was so important that it would have to be shared immediately with Rover. George Lees wrote to Maurice Wilks to notify him of the development on 28 January: 'we are sending to you under separate cover drawings giving the essential features of this [No.13] diffuser.'[64]

The next day Whittle travelled to Derby with Pat Johnson and Dan Walker (freshly returned from Massachusetts) to meet their counterparts. Presided over by Hives, 'quite a large conference developed' and the visitors from Lutterworth were accorded more flattering attention in a day than had come their way in years. Hives set the tone by declaring Rolls-Royce's determination 'to develop a unit which could be of use in this war... [and] to do this practically speaking whether or not they get MAP backing'.[65] Whittle and Hooker shared their notebooks and impressed all present by 'talking identical language...'. Hooker also allowed himself a cryptic reference to the recent breakthrough with Wilde's test rig: 'some results obtained on the Vulture rig... had taught them a lot...' No doubt it was especially gratifying for Whittle to hear that 'RR had satisfied themselves that a Whittle unit was now equal to, or slightly better than, a Merlin 61, which engine was virtually the peak of RR achievement'. Hives spoke warmly of 'the very strong appeal of simplicity in a Whittle type unit' – so very different from that other jet engine sitting in the Derby workshop – and 'wanted it to be understood that they would put themselves in Whittle's hands' in deciding on the design eventually selected for production. Nightingale Road's resources would be at the disposal of the tiny Lutterworth operation for 'the detailing and manufacture' of its engine.

This *entente cordiale* marked an extraordinary coup for Whittle. He decided to bank it immediately and arranged an audience with Linnell for 24 January 1942. It was little more than three weeks since Moore-Brabazon had given the Engines directorate his blessing to banish Power Jets to a consultancy role. Even by MAP's standards, the confusion that now swirled round the Ministry's handling of the jet project was quite extraordinary. Following his trip to Lutterworth nine days earlier, Linnell was still feeling perturbed over the contrast between his officials' disdain for Power Jets and the evidence he had seen of its progress on the ground. Whittle now added royally to his discomfort, presenting him with the momentous news that Power Jets and Rolls-Royce were to launch 'a joint effort' in pursuit of an engine based on the W.2B.[66] In a bid to restore a more consistent approach to policy, the Air Marshal had set up what he titled his Jet Engine Advisory Panel, bringing together officials including Bulman and David Pye with various senior RAF officers. After he had listened to Whittle's fulsome account of the conference at Rolls-Royce, Linnell took him straight into a meeting of the Panel which happened to be underway at the time.

Whittle treated them all to another summary of 'the Rolls-Royce proposals'. For good measure, he also presented them with graphs detailing the superior thrust available from the prospective W.2B engine as compared with the latest Merlin. His announcement that Rolls-Royce would be working as a subcontractor to Power Jets raised eyebrows round the room, but only Pye spoke out against it. Whittle's note also recorded that 'the members were nervous of the reactions of the Rover Co'. The allure of securing Rolls-Royce's backing for the jet nonetheless carried the day. By the time Whittle left for his train home, he had been promised by an admiring Roxbee Cox 'that we should get a contract for the Power Jets/Rolls-Royce scheme'. He felt confident enough to send Linnell a note on 27 January about the future system for naming the engines that Power Jets and Rolls-Royce would turn out together. (Some wanted to keep his own initial 'W' in the frame, others wanted to hark back to British history and legend: 'to meet both requirements, a good start might be "Welland", the legendary Smith of Kent, or "Wyvern".'[67] They settled in the end on 'Welland' – a name also familiar to Derby men as a river flowing from the East Midlands to the Wash.)

Meanwhile technical discussions were already beginning with Rolls-Royce – and another significant move beckoned. On 30 January 1942 Hives came down to the Ladywood Works bringing his Managing Director Arthur Sidgreaves with him, to tour the site and to broach with Whittle the need for a commercial agreement as the next step. At Brownsover Hall in the afternoon, Hives suggested 'it was essential for the smoothness of future cooperation that there should be some kind of link up' between the two companies.[68] Whittle offered a slightly arch response – Power Jets was not opposed to the idea, but had always been clear 'that any alliance that might be formed would have to be with a very respectable concern' – and stressed how vital it would be for his whole enterprise to retain its independence. Hives and Sidgreaves concurred enthusiastically. Any concrete proposal coming from Derby, they said, would naturally respect this condition. In exchange, Whittle 'set their minds at rest' that no other scheme would be pursued without giving Rolls-Royce 'first refusal'. Next day, 31 January 1942, Whittle was at Derby and had a brief further talk with Hives. A purchase of Power Jets' remaining 27,000 'B' shares was contemplated – Whittle carefully pointing out to Hives that he 'was not to assume… [they] could be purchased for £27,000' – and with equal candour Hives acknowledged the key business motive that he and Sidgreaves had in mind:

> A factor operating powerfully with them was that they realised that at the end of the war there would be an absolute glut of Merlin engines which threatened absolute stagnation in their aero engine business unless they were on the go with something which rendered the Merlin obsolete.[69]

On a piquant note, Whittle closed with a reminder to Hives of Arnold Griffith's personal history with the jet engine since 1929 – 'adding that it was rather important that, if possible, Dr Griffith and I should be on the same side of the fence'. Having Rolls-Royce and MAP on the same side of the fence might have been even better, as was soon to be apparent.

iv

The Derby firm under Hives was now poised, in effect, to provide the leadership sought in vain by Tizard in 1941 and Tedder in 1940 before him. As for the engineering challenge, many difficulties were still to be resolved; but none could doubt the potency of the resources and capabilities that Rolls-Royce would put at Whittle's disposal. Elliott and Hooker expressed confidence that, 'assuming the design data to be at hand', they would be able to produce a first complete engine 'in about four months'. (Rover had so far been nominally in charge of the production effort for twenty-two months, without producing a single flight-worthy engine.) It was much too late to hope that jet fighters might be in service with the RAF by the summer of 1942, but a late 1942 delivery date might yet prove achievable. Dudley Williams, ever the optimist, told the Air

Ministry's Contracts section to expect at least a hundred units by the end of the year. As hardly needed spelling out, success on that scale might have momentous implications for the war effort, giving the RAF a fighter 100 mph faster than the Spitfire.

George Carter and his team at Gloster were also beginning to scope the potential for heavy bombers powered by jet engines. They had first mooted the idea several months earlier. A secret paper submitted to Downing Street in August 1941, 'Gloster Jet-propelled Bomber Aircraft', had suggested that four-engined planes could be designed to fly at 40–45,000 feet and speeds of around 440 mph, so making them immune to flak from the ground as well as the Luftwaffe's best fighters. 'The proposal may be regarded as a rational development of the Gloster F9/40 fighter...'[70] Now the notion of a jet bomber had taken on a new significance. The debate over RAF Bomber Command's future tactics had just come to a head: the RAF announced its 'Area Bombing Directive' in February 1942, adopting a strategy based on night-time raids by massed formations of bombers on Germany's cities and industrial centres.

In aspiring to a partnership that would take their companies beyond mere technical cooperation, the peculiar nature of Power Jets posed some delicate issues for both Whittle and Hives. As a serving RAF officer on secondment to the company, legally speaking, Whittle wondered whether he even had the right to embark on commercial negotiations about its future. Hives for his part was unsure how to broach the notion of acquiring all or part of Power Jets, given its total reliance since 1940 on Treasury funding and the fact that its patents had effectively been consigned to the government. We know of their exchanges through the second half of January because Whittle, as ever, kept a contem-porary record of them. When he came (after the war) to compile a digest of all his wartime dealings with Rolls-Royce, it is striking that he chose to omit any items dated between November 1941 and June 1942.[71] Perhaps the memory of this episode was too painful to chronicle in detail – for nothing, in the end, was agreed. The two sides circled each other for weeks but failed to reach any kind of financial accord. For his autobiography, Whittle managed a succinct summary:

> At a later date... it transpired that there had been a most unfortunate misunderstanding... [and] that each party was under the impression that the next move lay with the other, so both Power Jets and Rolls-Royce waited for a move which never came and a golden opportunity was lost.[72]

Put another way, the two sides had been in need of a government intermediary, capable of resolving their uncertainties and encouraging some kind of merger in the national interest – but in Wilfrid Freeman's absence, MAP had lacked any individual with the authority and imagination to fill this role. George Bulman and his colleagues still saw jet propulsion as just an incremental advance on existing piston engines. This dictated a cautious approach, so they stuck resolutely to their faith in Rover and simply refused to contemplate disruptive second thoughts. The government had made a worthwhile investment in Rover's Shadow Factory No.6, under construction at Barnoldswick. The company had assembled a local workforce, forged ties with leading suppliers like Joseph Lucas and laid out cash for jigs, tooling and raw materials. By comparison with the massive expenditure on Bomber Command's growth, it was small beer. It was nonetheless an industrial commitment by the state that could not be lightly set aside.

By the same token, MAP's backing for Rover was now becoming seriously problematic. The working relationship between the Wilks brothers and Power Jets had effectively collapsed. Jack Linnell told Whittle on 24 January that he had been 'horrified by the atmosphere of distrust and suspicion that he had found to exist' during his visit to Lutterworth earlier in the month. Whittle's team were no longer prepared (if they had ever been) to set any store by Rover's theoretical research, technical skills or manufacturing capabilities – let alone its handling of aircraft matters. Towards the end of January, Rover announced that it was planning a test flight in March 1942 for one of the initial W.2B engines that was almost ready for despatch. They planned to fly it in a Meteor after just ten hours of testing on the bench. (The E.28/39's W.1X had had fifty hours.) MAP officials thought Rover had done well in the face of an often exasperating stream of design amendments. Whittle was appalled and rang Bulman's deputy to denounce the flight plan as 'extremely dangerous'.[73]

The Wilks brothers, meanwhile, had been carefully following reports of the strengthening Derby/Lutterworth rapport. It only confirmed to Spencer Wilks and his brother that in the jet engine they were backing a potential post-war winner. They still enjoyed Bulman's confidence, and MAP remained intent on a timetable that called for twelve prototype aircraft to fly before the end of June with Rover W.2Bs, leading without a break into higher production numbers, month by month.[74] While not prepared to abandon these plans, the brothers were almost as disenchanted as Whittle himself with the Rover/Power Jets relationship. The logic of the situation, decided Spencer Wilks, dictated an obvious commercial outcome. Rover should form its own partnership with Rolls-Royce. He and Hives were old sparring partners in the Midlands business world. Their two firms were well acquainted. They could pool their complementary skills, and their relations with the hypercritical Wing Commander of Lutterworth could then be placed on a more arm's length basis. Surely with MAP's knowledge if not its connivance, Wilks invited Hives to a meeting on 7 February and made his pitch. Hives heard him out and promised a written reply. The letter that followed, dated 11 February 1942, was worthy of Rolls-Royce's proud reputation for integrity, in commerce as in engineering:

> I have discussed with Mr Sidgreaves the proposition you put forward last Saturday. The decision we have arrived at is that it would be impossible to take advantage of your offer. As I pointed out to you, in agreement with MAP and Power Jets Ltd, we are producing a Whittle turbine to Rolls-Royce designs [sic], and we have undertaken the development work. In connection with this project we have agreed to act as sub-contractors to Power Jets Ltd. I am sure you will appreciate the impossible

position, which would arise if we [were to] have any link-up
with the Rover Company.[75]

In the aftermath, however, as a corporate history of Rolls-Royce
notes cryptically enough, 'not much happened...'.[76] The firm's
dealings with Whittle shrivelled. Rover, by contrast, resolved to
press ahead. The consequences were to prove deeply unfortunate.
Two unhappy episodes within the next couple of months persuaded Hives – always concerned not to be seen as 'a trespasser'
– that Rolls-Royce needed to keep its distance, for the moment at
least, from a project in danger of becoming terminally messy.

The first involved disclosure of the engine developed on the sly
by Rover since the autumn of 1941. Known within Rover's design
unit at Waterloo Mill as the STX (for 'Straight Through Experimental') engine, it was given the official specification 'W.2B/B.26',
or plain B.26. In place of combustion chambers involving two
reversals of the airflow, it had 'straight-through' chambers that
gave the airflow an unimpeded run between the compressor and
the turbine. (Whittle had considered this variant on his basic
design and had even accepted a contract to build it – naming it
the W.2/Y – but had rejected it in favour of sticking to his reverse-
flow design. This meant he could keep the turbine shaft as short
as possible, and so avoid the risk of the shaft 'whirling'. The STX
design required the engine to be significantly longer – but a gifted
young designer at Rover called Adrian Lombard came up with
a novel kind of coupling which enabled the shaft to be divided
into two, with three lots of bearings. This 'Lombard coupling'
averted the whirling danger.) Whatever the B.26's undoubted
merits, there was no disguising the extent of the departure from
Whittle's original design. The whole scheme, as even a sympathetic history of the Lancashire operation has put it, was bound
to incur Whittle's wrath and 'great pressure would be brought to
bear to stop such a development'.[77] Yet, as experienced engineers,
the Rover design team felt certain that this should be the way
forward. Accordingly the modification to the design was carried
out in absolute secrecy in the Waterloo Mill design office.

Unveiling it was inevitably going to be a delicate matter. On 11 February, Lees, Johnson and Walker were just leaving a technical discussion they had attended as Power Jets' representatives at the Bankfield Shed, and 'were literally putting their coats on to depart', when the eight-man Rover team tabled a General Arrangement drawing for 'a re-arranged W.2B'.[78] This suggested work on some putative engine was still at a preliminary stage, and the item was minuted with no discussion at all. Actually the B.26 engine was almost complete. MAP's Major Ross presided over this mendacity even though, as Whittle much later observed, he 'must have known the position'. (Had there been a Minister in post at MAP, he would surely have taken a keen interest in the affair. The post, though, was empty: Moore-Brabazon had just disgraced himself with a public observation – eight months after Hitler's launch of Operation Barbarossa – that the Soviet and German land forces might, with any luck, destroy each other. Churchill had sacked him.)

Linnell's Advisory Panel only discovered at the start of April 1942 that a finished B.26 had been run three weeks earlier, on 7 March. According to an RAF officer at MAP who kept Whittle and his colleagues updated with several calls a day, Linnell as MAP's Controller of Research and Development 'expressed amazement at the state of affairs...'.[79] He was assured the B.26 was 'a private venture'. Even so, launching a covert programme at this point struck Linnell as highly improper – 'a pretty grim business', as he admitted to Johnson and Williams at a meeting on 9 April. With Whittle fulminating on full throttle at Lutterworth ('a gross discourtesy to myself personally in my several capacities'), Linnell gave Bulman and Ross a dressing down over the affair and summoned Spencer Wilks to London to explain Rover's behaviour. Just half an hour before Wilks arrived at MAP, Bulman admitted to the Air Marshal that his department had in fact given official authorisation for the B.26 'experiment' some months earlier. It was an astounding confession, and the implications reverberated inside MAP for months. Those kept in the dark by the Engines directorate – including Linnell, Pye and

Roxbee Cox – were severely embarrassed. In effect, MAP was party to a transgression against the 'pooling' agreement between the member firms of the GTCC which had otherwise proved such a notable success since November. Whittle himself turned surprisingly quickly to a meticulous appraisal of the B.26's strengths and weaknesses, but not before castigating the whole episode as an utter betrayal of the collaboration that Power Jets had been enjoined to support through more than two harrowing years of discord. It was 'the culminating act' in Rover's long-running display of bad faith. In concluding a 'somewhat lengthy' and forensic post-mortem for Linnell, Whittle suggested in effect that the two companies should now go their separate ways.[80] Many others, including Hayne Constant at the RAE, thought Rover should be dropped by MAP altogether.

The second heavy setback to befall the project in 1942 had meanwhile made a mockery of its delivery timetables. Not least because of their extracurricular activities at Clitheroe – 'the B.26 bee in their bonnets', as Whittle later put it – Rover left it until the last minute before shipping a first mock-up of the W.2B to Gloster's for installation into an F.9 Meteor airframe. Originally scheduled for delivery in November 1941, the engine finally arrived in the second week of March for a 'mock-up conference' organised by the RAF. Invitations had gone out to various service personnel to have their first sighting of the proposed fighter. When the Rover engine came off the lorry, it made such a poor impression that many invitations had to be hastily cancelled. One of those who did attend the event was dismayed by what he saw:

> At a further view of the mock-up on the second day, Squadron Leader Welles Coates revised his opinion of the mock-up which he had expressed the first day as a 'dog's breakfast', and he now called it a 'rat's breakfast'. He had observed for himself that the general arrangement was extraordinarily short-sighted and inefficient... The S/Ldr was seriously concerned with the whole position and the fact that Gloster cannot conclude their designs for possibly a further six months...[81]

This prediction seemed overly pessimistic to the Gloster team (though in fact it would prove to be not far off the mark). But there was no disguising a serious slippage in the schedules. In the first week of April, Ross and a colleague visited Rover to review its plans – and made an unnerving discovery. The Lutterworth team, as noted, had sent Rover drawings of the No.13 diffuser at the end of January with a clear indication of the design's crucial importance for the avoidance of surging. Ross was now informed that Rover intended, in effect, to disregard the new design. The official minutes recorded: 'experience had shown that Rovers could not now introduce the new diffuser (type 13) into any of the thirty prototype engines, and that there was little prospect of its immediate introduction into the first batch of 50 production engines.'[82] Ross, to his credit, refused to accept this. Any Meteor flying with two of those batch engines, after all, would be at serious risk of engine failure. Returning to MAP, he told a scheduling conference on 8 April 'that considerable trouble was being experienced in engine development and that even the best [delivery-date] estimates... were liable to very serious amendment'.[83]

So much for having twelve prototypes flying by the end of June. Lord Cherwell visited Power Jets in May, intent on pinning down for Churchill a firm date by which he could expect to see jet fighters on active service. He pressed Whittle and his whole senior team at a roundtable discussion in the big study at Brownsover Hall – 'and he was visibly critical of the position when we told him that it was unlikely that F.9s would be available operationally before the summer of 1943'.[84] Whittle had warned many times of the mechanical flaws in Rover's work. As so often in the past, events had borne out his comments. He had now begun work on the drawings for a new engine – to be called the W.2/500 – that he was confident would mark a significant improvement on the W.2B. It infuriated him to think that neglect of the W.2B might prompt some to look askance at any successor engine. He was openly scornful of Rover's efforts – and this unhappily prompted an official at MAP to suggest to his face that perhaps production engineering was 'not his bag'. Whittle erupted in fury – then sat down immediately afterwards to pen a fierce letter to Linnell, decrying those who seemed intent on casting him as some kind of wild-eyed boffin, a visionary designer hardly to be trusted with a spanner:

> Perhaps owing to a certain diffidence on my part I have never urged with any great emphasis the fact that I am as well equipped to direct matters of production as I am to deal with academic questions [of design]…
>
> It has been the custom of certain individuals to treat me as a 'gifted amateur', inventor, etc, and to talk of 'taking my child and sending it away to school'; to say I have no production experience, etc, and, I believe, to represent me as a somewhat difficult and temperamental individual. On the one hand a good deal of lip service has been paid to my achievements, but on the other it has been implied that I am fit only to have 'bright ideas', with the result that, as it seems to me, I have been regarded as being either too biased or too incompetent to make a good judgment or to give good advice on major matters of policy…[85]

This bitter complaint struck the Air Marshal as a persuasive appeal that deserved their full sympathy and understanding. He showed the letter to Roxbee Cox, who agreed they urgently needed to find some way of reassuring Whittle that his special gifts were still appreciated.

It happened in the middle of May 1942 that Roxbee Cox heard intriguing news of the jet project on the other side of the Atlantic. Only six months after receiving the W.1X, General Electric had almost completed assembling its own version of the W.2B. Talking to Dudley Williams on 15 May about the idea of putting Whittle's name to a future aeroplane, Roxbee Cox suggested 'that in view of the fact that the Americans hoped to have an aeroplane flying very shortly, it was probable that a certain amount of publicity would in any case be attached to Whittle'.[86] Thinking about this later, Roxbee Cox was inspired to call the US embassy and ask whether the idea of having Whittle follow his W.1X to Boston was still of interest. Two days later he had his answer. Both General Electric and the US Army Air Force would welcome a visit by Whittle

– and hoped he could arrive before 1 June. By chance, a glowing report by Dan Walker about his months in America landed on Whittle's desk on 23 May. By the time he had read it, Whittle was more than ready for Roxbee Cox's phone call. By the evening of 27 May he was on an evening train from Paddington to Bristol to start the first leg of a transatlantic crossing.

9

Reckoning with Rolls-Royce

May 1942 to May 1943

i

After the short hop from Bristol to Ireland, Whittle spent almost a week at the end of May 1942 holed up in the Royal George Hotel in Limerick waiting for the weather to allow his RAF flying boat to take off for the Atlantic crossing. He had much to look forward to. Just a month or so earlier he had been given the news that General Electric had pulled off the feat of completing its own jet engine, basically a copy of the W.1X, in less than seven months after taking delivery of the original. Their 'Type I' unit had been given an initial run on 23 April and was now undergoing intensive tests, so he was assured of some interesting technical discussions. The general background to his visit also promised to ensure an intriguing agenda. He would be travelling – in RAF uniform for most of the time – as a representative not of Power Jets but of Churchill's government. In effect, he would be another envoy for the historic transfer of British scientific and engineering know-how to the US instigated by Tizard in 1940. He had been made well aware of this development's importance for both countries – now, at long last, allies together in the war against the Axis powers – and he knew that officers in the British Air Commission (BAC) in Washington DC were hard at work arranging appropriate introductions for him. And then there was the personal dimension to his trip. He had never yet strayed far from his modest roots in the Midlands and had certainly never been abroad before. The prospect of escaping Britain's wartime austerity was alone enough to lift the spirits, and the letters home from Dan Walker and the W.1X guardians a few months earlier had given him a glimpse of the well-fed days to come ('The food here is very fancy & all messed about until one can hardly recognize it, but there's plenty of it…'[1]). It seemed unlikely there would be much room for a holiday in his crowded itinerary, but Whittle could relax in ways that few of his RAF peers could imagine. He had purchased a small black leather-bound notebook in which to scribble his daily notes.[2] Sitting alone at the Royal George and liberated from the daily travails of the Ladywood Works, he covered its first eight pages with a blizzard of mathematical equations (*Fig. 19*). He was starting to enjoy himself.

He finally reached Washington on 6 June 1942, nursing a terrible hangover thanks to a stopover in New York that had included a welcome party and several Manhattans too many. ('Next morning very ill.') The embassy and BAC personnel led him through a busy round of introductions in the capital over his first weekend, then put him on a Pullman sleeper to Boston. There on the Monday morning he was reunited at the Statler Hotel with Major Don Keirn, the USAAF officer who had supervised the W.1X's shipment from Britain and who would now accompany him on his travels. It soon dawned on Whittle that these had been carefully choreographed by the US government, with much trouble taken to keep them secret. His room, for instance, was equipped with its own telephone switchboard and the staff in attendance on him watched over his comings and goings with an unsettling diligence. (Not until much later was it explained to him that most of them were FBI agents.) He was even required to adopt a false identity – though since 'Mr F. Whitely' continued to sign his room bills as Frank Whittle, this disguise may not have been impenetrable.[3] On the Monday afternoon, with these curious preliminaries settled, it was time for his visit to start in

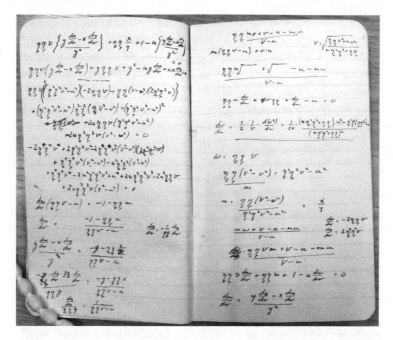

Fig. 19. A two-page spread from the pocket notebook
kept by FW on his US tour in 1942

earnest with a first scheduled meeting at General Electric. Their
fledgling Type I engine awaited his inspection at the company's
River Works in Lynn, a short drive up the coast from Boston.

So began an extraordinary couple of months. Quite how lasting a mark they made on the initiation of America's jet-engine
business is hard to say – but they made a deep impression on
Mr Whitely. In addition to spending many hours with the
engineers at Lynn, he was taken by Keirn to meet teams working
on superchargers at a couple of other GE plants in New England,
one at Schenectady, NY and the other at Everett, near Boston.
(They had to work independently of the Lynn project, and of
each other, in deference to Washington's stringent security rules.)
The two men also flew upstate together to Buffalo, to talk to Bell
Aircraft where the first jet plane (the 'XP-59A') was being built to

fly with two Type I engines. And Whittle made the long overnight trip on his own to the West Coast to visit Northrop Corporation in a suburb of Los Angeles, where an alternative jet-engine design was under consideration. At all these venues, and in other meetings with government officials and serving officers in the USAAF, Whittle was asked for an extensive debriefing about his own work in Britain. Most of his listeners were astonished at his achievements and could scarcely believe the way these had so far been treated in Britain: 'The Americans generally were astounded at the parsimonious attitude of the MAP towards the work of Power Jets.'[4] They registered their incredulity by deferring to his expertise in a manner that Whittle had seldom encountered in the past. He had become accustomed in England, at countless technical conferences, to having his say on most agenda items treated as just one opinion among many, until he backed it with forthright explanations. Here in America it was different. Wherever he met his working peers, he soon had their rapt attention. Whittle relished their professional curiosity. 'I get on very well with the engineers over here,' he wrote home to George Lees a few weeks into the trip, 'because they have both enthusiasm and ability, which is a pleasant change from some we know of, and… I think my efforts are appreciated.'[5]

Where he was allowed to mingle with ordinary employees in the workplace, line managers and machine-tool operators talked to him (in the American way) as their social equal. It thrilled Whittle to find himself immersed in a classless world so remote from the stratified society that was all he had ever known at home. He was just as comfortable, of course, meeting some of the leading figures in US aviation – and as word of his polymathic grasp of aircraft matters spread, they were anxious to make time for him. At Bell Aircraft, 'Mr [Larry] Bell had rushed back especially to meet me'. At Northrop he was taken through the works by Jack Northrop in person. On a visit to Wright Field, the US Air Corps' technical centre outside Dayton, Ohio, this mere thirty-five-year-old Wing Commander in the RAF was led around by the Commanding Officer, General Vanaman. When Whittle told him that the problems so far encountered in the development of an American jet engine were all replays of those experienced by Power Jets in England, and therefore could certainly be resolved, the General replied: 'In that case, he would press for an extension of my stay in the States until the development had caught up with corresponding work in England.'

As Vanaman may well have been aware, GE's progress had in fact slowed abruptly since the ignition of its first engine in April. As Whittle later wrote home to Roxbee Cox with a suitably transatlantic turn of phrase, his GE friends 'were running into a heap of trouble' by the time he arrived at Lynn. 'I have seen the GE engine running under conditions which made my hair stand on end...'[6] He watched them struggling with bearing failures, a host of minor mechanical problems and that old familiar bugbear, the combustion system. He did his best to convey the many lessons learned at Lutterworth ('for the most part the answers were easy to supply') while reining back any less generous observations. Whatever his reservations, anyway, Whittle was constantly delighted to hear the jet engine's praises sung with a passion he had heard all too rarely in England. When he and Keirn were entertained to dinner by their GE hosts on 15 June, the Major (soon to become a Colonel) suddenly exclaimed 'that the important thing was to get the thing into the air at the earliest possible moment even if with a de-rated performance...' Not to be outdone, Whittle urged them to plan for the sequel: 'in my opinion, the combined experiences of ourselves and the General Electric were such that it ought to be possible to go into production practically straight away... [and] the moment had now arrived to press for it.'

It all left Whittle totally exhausted. Many days involved him in discussions that quickly took on an inquisitorial flavour – with this small, frail figure standing at the blackboard or seated at the head of the table, answering questions from a dozen or more engineers anxious to hear him spell out every nuance. In dealing with Rover and BTH or with many of the officials at MAP, Whittle had often been made to feel that he was pitching an idea ahead of its time – like someone walking into the royal dockyards of Chatham in the days of Nelson to propose a ship made of iron, as Tedder had once put it, and encountering only men wedded to the virtues of good, solid oak. None of his transatlantic hosts seemed in the slightest bit fazed by the notion of a radical new start for aero-engines. They wanted simply to make sure they were not left behind, and they pressed Whittle accordingly. He spent his days urging them ahead, then turned back on most evenings to the business of keeping a detailed written record. Secretaries were generally at hand in the mornings, to take dictation from him or to type up the notes that he had painstakingly made in longhand. He pored over the finished typescripts afterwards like a medieval monk, illustrating them with miniature drawings where appropriate before sending them off to be filed at the BAC in Washington.[7] (Where the handwritten notes were critical of his hosts, he thoughtfully packed them away, to be handled by Mary on his return.)

In the second week of July, Whittle emerged from his meetings at Northrop even more drained than usual. He had felt obliged to tell his hosts – with more than usual candour – that they were a long way back from the start line and this had made it one of his more stressful visits. (A short while later, largely on the strength of what he had told them, Jack Northrop sacked the executive in charge of their jet-engine project.) Fortunately the BAC officers in Washington had already decided that Whittle needed a holiday, and that California was the best place for him to take it. The BAC's first proposal, though, was a few days' rest in a hotel on the shoreline at Santa Monica. After a single night there, Whittle's little black notebook had acquired some more equations but the place struck him as scarcely more fun than the Royal George in Limerick. Next day he asked the BAC office in Beverly Hills for a plane ticket back to the East Coast. The resident officer, Group Captain Adams, persuaded him to give the Los Angeles area one more chance. If it still seemed boring after another twenty-four hours, then a ticket would be provided immediately. Whittle gave way – and the Group Captain took care of the rest:

Adams suggested that I should go to the Beverly Hills home of Edward Hillman, Jr there and then, and remain on for a barbecue party that was to be held there that evening... On arriving I was greeted warmly by Eddie Hillman (who was dressed only in bathing trunks) and told to 'relax'... [Thereafter] though there were always several people present – some of them well known in the film world – there was a continuous going and coming, with my host as the only element of continuity in an ever-changing scene... He repeatedly told me to relax and, presumably to assist me to do so, ordered his secretary to bring me a bowl of chicken noodle soup (which I did not in the least want at that time of day). The sight of a strange RAF officer [in uniform] sitting in the corner with a bowl of chicken noodle soup appeared to excite no surprise or comment from the new arrivals...

In the course of the party that night I succeeded in 'relaxing' to such an extent that at about 3 am I was induced to join three others in the swimming pool and ruined my wrist-watch which I had forgotten to remove.[8]

He made it back to Adams' apartment eventually – and then gave himself up to some quite serious relaxing that lasted another ten days.

The barbecue host and his British wife Jean, a celebrated dancer, took Whittle under their wing and whisked him off to their beach house at Santa Barbara. He probably had little need of his RAF uniform for his daily routine after that. It typically began with lunch round the pool, followed by an afternoon excursion to the beach (*see Plate 8b*). It then progressed via evening cocktails to a long dinner at one of the top hotels in Santa Barbara or Beverly Hills, after which came a trip to one of the nightclubs where Whittle's new friends liked to drink and dance into the early hours. He quite possibly went to more parties in a week than he had attended in his entire life to this point, and certainly partied with more women than he had encountered in the past twenty years – including two stars of the silent movies era, Mary Pickford and Dorothy Gish. Never hitherto much of a drinker, he developed a taste for vodka cocktails and the way they lightened the burden of his customary shyness in mixed company. On five consecutive nights he ended up at the Mocambo, a nightclub on Sunset Boulevard that had opened the year before and was now one of the most fashionable all-night watering holes in Hollywood. The equations in his notebook gave way to a comically meticulous record of his dancing partners ('Tuesday 14 July... Dance with June, Lee & Mrs Joyce. I learn the Rhumba. Back to hotel at 3.00 am'). A few ladies' names came and went more frequently than others, but none appears to have made any lasting impression. Whittle was just happy to bask in their attention – though for all they knew of his world he might just as well have been an extra-terrestrial being. It was all a long way from Lutterworth.

He returned to earth on 22 July, embarking on ten days of further discussions at GE's Lynn plant and at Bell Aircraft (where he was impressed to see the XP-59A, 'virtually completed and awaiting engines: even the guns were installed, two 37 mm cannon...'). Then he headed back to Washington – and sat down at a desk in the British Air Commission for a week, no less, to take stock of everything he had heard and seen since the start of June. His copious notes fuelled a two-day debriefing with Air Vice Marshal Roderick Hill and his colleagues at the BAC on 4–5 August, as well as subsequent correspondence with them and a further discussion on 11 August. The BAC staffers were well aware of Whittle's reputation at home and had received a stream of complimentary reports about his many engagements from coast to coast. So they had probably prepared themselves for a bracing appraisal of the US jet programme and some radical thoughts about its future. Whittle did not disappoint them.

His verdict on the Americans' progress to date was mixed. 'They did a remarkable job in getting an engine running between receipt of drawings in October 1941 and April 1942, but in the four and a half months since then the development has been far slower than it could have been with the background of experience available as a result of five years of development in England.'[9] From this observation Whittle drew two main lessons. On the one hand, American corporations like GE and Bell could bring massive resources to bear on a properly defined task. In the long term, they would be capable of powering ahead with the jet aeroplane on a scale that would dwarf any rival activity in Britain: 'ultimately the main centres of supply of this type of aircraft will be over here'. On the other hand, left to themselves, the Americans had an alarming propensity for reinventing the wheel and this threatened to delay their progress quite significantly. Reviewing the full range of topics that needed to be properly mastered in pursuit of the jet, Whittle thought the Americans ahead of the British in their knowledge of 'high-temperature materials', but lagging behind in almost all other respects. Unless they took more heed of what had already been accomplished at Power Jets, it seemed to him most unlikely that they could accelerate the jet engine's development much in the short term. He saw this reflected in the test results achieved to date with the Type I engine: as he explained in a letter to Hill, its overall performance looked 'very distinctly inferior to that attained with the W.2B in England'.[10]

Whittle was genuinely vexed by the Americans' reluctance to take more of a lead from the British experience to date, given the enthusiasm they had shown in quizzing him about the work at Lutterworth. He recalled hearing of the same problem in letters from Dan Walker, in the first weeks after Walker's arrival with the W.1X at GE's Lynn plant in the autumn of 1941 ('They had made elaborate plans for testing and despite all efforts on my part are carrying on with their original ideas.'[11]) It had been a slightly troubling feature of his summer tour of the country, notwithstanding all the acclaim he had received:

> I have felt that my own visit has been far less effective than it might have been because I have been rather in the position of a teacher who feels that his pupils are making insufficient notes and has no means of checking whether his instruction has been absorbed until the examination results come out...[12]

As head of Technical Development at the BAC, Roderick Hill had been in Washington just over a year and suggested they take a philosophical view of the matter – 'it was a peculiar factor in America, that we had to allow for continually, that they did not believe anything until they had done it themselves and seen it with their own eyes'.

Whittle, though, advocated a much more forthright response. They should confront the Americans' coyness head-on by making the jet engine an Anglo-American venture. The GE engineers had abundant resources but were short of the know-how that could only be acquired through the experience of working on actual jet engines. The opposite applied in Britain. This was 'a most aggravating situation', in Whittle's view, and 'a far more effective combination... is required if we are to have jet propelled aircraft in quantity production at the earliest possible moment'. He was personally ready to back GE unreservedly: he had shared with them, for example, the design of the W.2/500 engine on which he had been working since March. (It was adopted by GE as the basis for their next engine, to be named the I-16.) He urged that the same line be taken at government level, with the establishment of a British 'advisory organisation' in the US:

> It is suggested that this organisation would be a small scale version of the Power Jets organization; the staff being based on a nucleus of very experienced engineers drawn from the British development. I feel that the importance of doing everything to push the project over here [in America] is such that if necessary we ought to be prepared to weaken the British side of it.[13]

It would help the Americans to broaden their approach, for example by promoting cross-disciplinary skills that were still notably absent – 'None of the GE engineers concerned are familiar with aircraft engineering, especially in the aerodynamic sense, and none of the Bell [airframe] engineers are familiar with turbine design'– and by instilling a better appreciation of the necessary bond between plane and power-plant designs. It might also allow the British to forestall the jet engine eventually emerging as another Great American Invention 'though, of course, this is not an argument we can use with the US authorities'.

Just before leaving Washington for home on the evening of 12

August, Whittle learned a timetable had been set for the inaugural flight of America's first jet: Bell Aircraft's XP-59 and GE's Type I engine were to be transported by train to Southern California within a few weeks, for testing to begin late in September at Muroc Army Airfield (today part of Edwards Air Force Base). The first flight would follow on 1 October 1942. It was going to be a perfect way of celebrating the anniversary of the W.1X's arrival at Lynn, just twelve months earlier. On the long journey back to England, Whittle must have felt hugely gratified to know that his jet-engine concept was now well on its way to transforming the aeronautical world on both sides of the Atlantic. His notion of a joint transatlantic venture looked less assured of fruition, but Air Vice Marshal Hill had at least offered him broad support. Hill had also despatched a report to Air Marshal Linnell at MAP acknowledging the success of his visit in generous terms. 'Whittle's personal relationships with all of those with whom he has met have been of a most cordial nature. He has won great respect from American engineers... [and it] is clearly desirable that as and when he can be spared he should spend as much time in the US as practicable.'[14]

In the event, Whittle fell foul of a broader failure in the US to coordinate their own development activities in this context as effectively as had once seemed possible. He had to wait until the war was over before anyone asked him to return. His strictures on the need for close cooperation across the Atlantic did not go unheeded, though. British and American engineers were to exchange ideas on the development of the jet engine on many occasions over the rest of the war. Indeed, two US officers were invited just a few weeks later to join Whitehall's Gas Turbine Collaboration Committee (for which, conspicuously, there was no American counterpart). One of them was Colonel Keirn, and the other a US Navy commander, P. B. Kauffman. They were to attend their first meeting of the GTCC in Rugby on the last weekend of September – and Whittle would seize the opportunity to walk them proudly round Power Jets' newly completed facility at Whetstone. Other American visitors would follow (*see Plate 9b*).

ii

He had an appointment on 19 August 1942 to see Roxbee Cox, together with an RAF officer who had joined MAP as Roxbee Cox's deputy, Wing Commander George Watt. (A New Zealander, Watt had trained as an engineer before joining the RAF in 1933 and had begun the war as an experimental test pilot at the RAE. He and Whittle were to become good friends.) The MAP men were looking forward to hearing Whittle's impressions of the progress being made in America. In the event, Whittle's impressions of the non-progress in Britain left them little time for any other matters. Having immersed himself for two days at Brownsover Hall in the memoranda and correspondence accumulated by Power Jets in his absence, Whittle arrived at Thames House fairly steaming with indignation. The bad situation he had left behind in May was on the verge, it seemed to him, of becoming a national scandal: 'I expressed considerable disgust at the state of affairs that exist here.'[15] He was not privy to the exact numbers, but could see that large sums were being poured into the W.2B programme. (In fact, the Treasury had invested over a million pounds in plant and machinery for the new Barnoldswick and Clitheroe sites, and Rover was drawing up to £100,000 a month to run them – the equivalent in today's money of £50 million and £5 million respectively.[16] This was now a costly undertaking for the public purse.) Roxbee Cox and Watt told him that Rover's Lancashire workforce had expanded to about 1,600 employees, many of them machine operators with skills that were in short supply across the country. It was rumoured that most were sitting around all day with nothing to do. The entire operation had so far managed to produce just eight prototype W.2Bs. The target rate for monthly production – originally set at 160 engines in January 1941, for achievement by the summer of 1942 – had been cut back repeatedly, even as the projected start date for production had been pushed ever further into the future. Thirty engines a month was the latest objective, for a line that was unlikely to start rolling before some date in 1943. It was a sorry tale, captured a few days before Whittle's return in an episode he had difficulty believing when told of it.

He had warned Rover in January against rushing too quickly into flight tests with the W.2B. Over the intervening months, various problems with the engine – notably with continuing turbine-blade failures – had necessitated changes that had actually diminished its power. This had to be measured principally by the 'thrust' it could deliver. (This same measure is still used today – though the engines used on some modern jets can deliver over 100,000 lbs of thrust where the earliest W.1 was rated at 1,240 lbs.) Three experimental engines built at Lutterworth by January 1942 had each achieved about 1,800 lbs, but the technical changes forced on Power Jets since then had seen its three W.2B engines delivering only about 1,650 lbs each. This reduction had caused much concern and disappointment, not least to Whittle himself. Nonetheless, two engines at the reduced thrust were mathematically equal to the task of powering the first Meteor. Since February, Rover had pursued adjustments to its own engines separately and had reached the same point of readiness – or so it thought. The firm was under some pressure by August 1942 to meet MAP's expectations. Writing to Spencer Wilks with a firm directive that Rover was not to waste time designing new versions of its B.26 'straight-through' unit – there was a war on! – Air Marshal Linnell stressed the RAF's priority: 'the immediate problem is to get the Gloster Meteor aircraft into the air and operational at the earliest possible date.'[17] The plane for the first test flight had been sitting in a hangar at Gloster's Brockworth airfield since the start of June, waiting for some engines. Rover finally delivered them a few days after Linnell's reproof. They turned out to be almost as disappointing as the dud mock-up unloaded at Gloster's factory in March. Each was good for only about 1,250 lbs of thrust. Gerry Sayer, the best and bravest of test pilots for whom Whittle had enormous respect, taxied the plane round the airfield a few times and declared it seriously underpowered. He declined to fly it, and the plane went back into mothballs.

Almost as depressing for Whittle as news of Rover's failure with the W.2B had been his discovery in the files of an acrimonious correspondence between Dudley Williams and George Bulman. It had been triggered by a demand from Linnell in the wake of the B.26 affair that the Ministry should attempt to make a fresh start with Power Jets. After new terms of reference had been drawn up, Whittle's three tireless lieutenants were incensed to find the firm's role had been subtly but fundamentally redefined. Bulman refused to acknowledge any change of policy. It was clear from his own record of a meeting with Dudley Williams and Pat Johnson on 20 July, though, that a very different line was now being taken. They had been reminded by Bulman of the thrust targets indicated by Whittle at the Farnborough conference in October 1940. 'It was largely on that promise of a certain 1,600 lbs thrust and reasonable prospect of 1,800 lbs that the initial decision to plan production including the Rover Company was made' and Power Jets had a 'clear and continuous obligation' to see that these targets were met.[18] In other words, any under-achievement by Rover's W.2B would be tantamount to a breach of promise by Whittle.

Since MAP's Engines directorate had sought repeatedly to freeze Power Jets out of the development process – suggesting a design-consultancy role would be appropriate, as recently as December 1941 – the Power Jets men not unreasonably saw this as deeply disingenuous. Faced with the consequences of his own support for Rover, Bulman was in their view just pre-paring to shift the blame onto Whittle: the jet, it would be said, had never really lived up to all his sanguine claims. Williams had responded with a furious letter, citing chapter and verse on Rover's inadequacies, and on MAP's efforts to distance Power Jets from the development work. 'Fortunately,' ran Bulman's haughty reply, 'my many other correspondents do not regale me with such lengthy epistles, though their matter is frequently of equal moment!'[19] More spirited exchanges had followed.

Whittle read these letters as a foretaste of the recriminations that he knew must follow any serious collapse of confidence in the jet engine. As he had acknowledged to Linnell before leaving for America, his biggest concern over any prolonged crisis was 'the attendant risk that the Whittle engine will come to be looked upon as "a white elephant"....'.[20] Determined to head off this possibility, he turned aside from Rover's travails with the W.2B in order to concentrate on the promising new – and surge-free – engine for which he had begun drawings in the middle of March 1942, the W.2/500. Designed to deliver a thrust of 1,750 lbs, it represented a significant advance on the W.2B. His colleagues at Power Jets had made good progress on the construction of the first prototype during his absence in America. Now he began supervising the final assembly of the engine and its first test run. This was achieved in double-quick time on 13 September 1942, a prodigious feat for a team of engineers with such relatively meagre resources. It was very quickly run up to full speed at Lutterworth – and the performance tests complied almost exactly with Whittle's prior calculations. Perhaps a little unfortunately, in light of what was to happen later in the autumn, a note went off to Linnell at MAP suggesting that 'the design of these engines can now be regarded as almost an exact science'.[21]

To assist the rapid completion of the W.2/500 and its envisaged test programme, Whittle and his team were relying on help from the several engineers at Rolls-Royce with whom they had envisaged joining forces at the start of the year. The Power Jets men had a warm regard for Stanley Hooker and his colleagues, and it was entirely mutual. ('I have often heard it said,' wrote Hooker many years later, '...that Frank Whittle was an awkward and difficult man to deal with. This I absolutely deny.'[22]) The two firms now had a growing list of joint ventures. These included an intriguing, not to say adventurous, project for testing a finished W.2B engine in flight. Whittle had suggested early in May 1942 that it would be entirely possible, for test purposes, to fit one into the rear of a reconfigured bomber. It was a breathtaking idea, but their confidence in Whittle was such that the Rolls-Royce men soon went along with it. They arranged with Vickers-Armstrong for one of that firm's twin-engined Wellingtons to be adapted at RAF Hucknall, an aerodrome near Nottingham owned by the Derby firm and regularly used for test flights. The first jet-boosted

Wellington flew in the middle of August 1942. Unsurprisingly, it caused a minor sensation among the tiny circle of airmen involved. (When knowledge of the project spread further afield, it inspired some colourful stories. It was said that the Wellington, on one early flight, had found itself being shadowed by a Boeing B17 bomber based in Norfolk. The American crew of the four-engined 'Flying Fortress', familiar with the standard Vickers Wellington but entirely unaware of what made this one so special, had spotted it at 10,000 feet and cruised alongside it at 200 mph for a while – then watched in disbelief, it was said, as the Wellington suddenly feathered its propellers and shot off into the distance.)

Most of the factual reports reaching MAP on the W.2B's progress, meanwhile, were less encouraging. In fact, by October 1942 it was evident that Rover's Barnoldswick plant was becoming an embarrassment to the Wilks brothers and the government alike. The company had promised a delivery of flight engines for the Gloster Meteor almost every other week for months past, and not a single one had materialised. Rover had been given all the details of Wilde's research into the surging phenomenon, to help them round that critical obstacle. Yet still the company had produced nothing at all. The chances of the audacious Tizard-inspired production line of jet fighters appearing in 1942 had all but vanished. Sensing as much, Whittle became 'deeply gloomy', as he confessed in a letter to one of his most devoted suppliers in Sheffield: '... nobody is keener than I am to get this [F.9/40] into the fight as soon as possible... [but] I am powerless to do anything about it through lack of adequate facilities and intense opposition – both official and commercial.'[23]

Faced with Rover's ineptitude on the one hand and Rolls-Royce's ready support on the other, Whittle supposed the obvious solution would be evident to all. MAP's February 1942 decision to stick with Rover rather than transfer the whole project to Rolls-Royce simply had to be overturned. Whitehall needed to act with some of the verve he had encountered in America. There was no reason to think the RAF had lost interest in deploying jet fighters. On the contrary. While the immensity of Nazi Germany's struggle on its Eastern Front had clearly lifted much of the pressure on Britain's air chiefs since the darkest days of 1940–41, the Luftwaffe had resumed spasmodic air raids on England over the summer using its high-altitude Junkers 86. This posed an embarrassing threat, given the ceiling limitations of the Spitfire and the Hurricane. (A single bomb killing fifty people in Bristol in late August 1942 had been dropped by an aircraft unseen and unreachable. 'Near-panic ensued in the Air Ministry.'[24]) A compelling case could be made for boosting the jet project, not abandoning it. But would Rolls-Royce still be prepared to take over the leading role? Like the Grand Old Duke of York, Hives had marched his men up the partnership hill and down again twice already, in July 1941 and January 1942. Would he be open to a third approach? On 8 October 1942, Hives and his Managing Director Arthur Sidgreaves paid a visit to Lutterworth for the first time in a long while. Whittle's record of the occasion noted a conversation about the progress of the W.2/500 – 'we [i.e. Power Jets] indicated that we would like RR to produce [it]' – and then he included this brief mention of an even bolder idea:

> There was a hint that Rovers would like to get out of the jet engine field – there has been a suggestion that they should swop over with RR [their] jet engine work for work on [RR's] Meteor tank engines [no relation to the F.9/40 Meteor]. The visitors indicated that they intended to stay in the jet engine field.[25]

Who exactly was doing the hinting and who the suggesting, Whittle did not record. He was evidently left with the clear impression, though, that the notion of Rolls-Royce displacing Rover was once again up for discussion.

Any lingering faith in Rover's efforts disappeared at the end of October 1942, with the failure of a slightly desperate ploy to get a W.2B into the air by fitting one into the E.28/39. (Tragically, Gerry Sayer was not there to fly it: the jet's first pilot had been killed flying a Typhoon some days earlier, colliding with another aircraft on a routine exercise over the North Sea.) An engine was actually installed, at Gloster's, but had to be stripped out again before take-off and returned to Rover, 'it being suspect with regard to impeller blades and may have to be modified'.[26] It was the last straw for Jack Linnell. The Air Marshal called a meeting on 2 November for all the key parties within the Ministry and the RAE – though no one from Power Jets was invited – and the outcome was a foregone conclusion. There was not the slightest chance of Rover providing engines for the F.9/40 Meteor programme in the foreseeable future. It was time to bring the existing plans to a halt. 'It was generally agreed that although a decision to stop flow-production on the W.2B was a most serious step, there was, in fact, no alternative.'[27] Henry Tizard was copied on the minutes. He responded with a philosophical shrug – only confirming, perhaps, how little real power he himself had been able to wield at MAP on Whittle's behalf in 1941:

> The jet position is certainly disappointing, and the gamble of preparing for the production of the W2B engine on a large scale has not quite come off. I am afraid that I am of [the] opinion that this is very largely due to lack of proper collaboration of Rovers with Power Jets. However, even with all the mistakes, human and otherwise, I think the gamble was justified.[28]

Justified or not, the gamble was over. Linnell's decision to halt production plans for the W.2B meant Rover's involvement with the jet had effectively come to an end. MAP's share of the direct responsibility for that 'lack of proper collaboration' was an issue left for another day.

Meanwhile, October 1942 had seen a series of further meetings between the Rolls-Royce and Power Jets teams. Hives and his men had made clear their determination 'to help out the manufacture of any [jet] engines or augmenters which they felt were a realistic contribution to military possibilities...'[29] They had twice visited Whetstone, where – in the teeth of fierce opposition from Bulman – Power Jets had begun installing workmen and tools a few months earlier, albeit at a slightly leisurely pace under Dudley Williams' direction. (It was still operating at less than a third of its planned capacity.) Whittle then heard nothing more from Derby in the first half of November and may have supposed other pressing business had intervened.

In fact, though neither Williams nor Whittle knew it, Hives and Sidgreaves were weighing a fundamental reappraisal of Rolls-Royce's strategic approach to the jet engine. The steadily greater commitment being made by some of their most talented engineers raised an obvious question. If the jet's potential was as exciting as Hooker and his friends – and, indeed, their counterparts in America – believed it to be, could Rolls-Royce afford merely to be engaged from the sidelines, without taking charge and imposing its own formidable disciplines on the project? Hooker had brought back some colourful accounts of the disarray he had seen during visits to Clitheroe and Barnoldswick. These had puzzled Hives, who had enjoyed a friendly and respectful rivalry with the Wilks brothers for years. (When Rover had begun advertising its new models before the war as 'some of the best cars in the country', Hives had been quick to brand Rolls-Royce as the maker of *the* best car in the country.) As for Power Jets' new factory at Whetstone, its scale had come as even more of a mystery to Hives: 'I was astonished at the size of it, and the emptiness of it...' as he confided later in a letter to Roxbee Cox.[30] (The main factory covered about 8,000 square feet.) Walking through its empty spaces may indeed have helped to clinch the matter in Hives' mind. The sight of another potential shambles in the making, coming on top of all the reported chaos at Barnoldswick, was evidently intolerable to him. He had abandoned all the initial misgivings he had felt early in the war – what he called his 'anti-jet' stance, notwithstanding his recruitment of Arnold Griffith – soon after the Cranwell test flights eighteen months earlier and was now openly enthusiastic about the jet's prospects. It was out of the question that its promise should be neglected a moment longer. The time had come for Rolls-Royce to seize the day.

By the time Roxbee Cox turned up at Lutterworth for his next monthly visit, on 16 November 1942, firm views had plainly been exchanged between MAP and Derby. Roxbee Cox asked Whittle and Johnson if they had heard from Hives lately – 'and, on being informed in the negative', as Denis Tobin recorded, 'indicated that an advance by Power Jets at this stage might be viewed favourably by Rolls-Royce'.[31] The Power Jets team agreed to write to Hives accordingly. A fateful letter, penned by Coll Tinling in his usual high-handed style, went off that same afternoon: 'We are prepared to collaborate to the utmost possible extent in this venture and your reactions are awaited with great interest.'[32] It was just the opening that Hives and Sidgreaves needed. Days later, Whittle heard from them again, asking if they might call on him at Brownsover Hall early in December to discuss the jet project's future. As it turned out, their timing could hardly have been better.

iii

Ten days after his return from the US in August 1942, Whittle had gone with Pat Johnson to visit the Gloster men at Hucclecote. Responding to the plane maker's open dismay over the continuing unavailability of engines, Whittle had told George Carter that in his view 'either the USA would become the only source of engines, or an earthquake had to happen in the MAP'.[33] By November the earthquake had happened. On 19 October 1942, after almost exactly two years away serving as Portal's second-in-command at the Air Ministry, Sir Wilfrid Freeman had returned to MAP. Freeman's official title at MAP was to be 'Chief Executive', requiring him to leave the RAF and 'resuming much the same role as he performed between 1938 and 1940, but with wider powers over a larger ministry'.[34] Effectively the pre-war architect of the RAF, Freeman was a towering figure in or out of uniform. Now he replaced others who, as civil servants or as politicians, had nothing like his command of technical and operational issues. Indeed, he had been watching their feeble management of MAP from his lofty position as Vice-Chief at the Air Ministry and had more than once poured scorn on their efforts in official papers. 'MAP appear to be barren of ideas', he had written in May 1942, 'and it is true to say that never before in the history of aviation has so large a staff done so little for technical advancement.'[35] (Whittle would have enjoyed reading that parody of Churchill's salute to The Few in 1940.) Now Freeman wasted no time asserting his effective control over all aspects of the Ministry – and sidelining its Minister, a retired Tory colonel called John Llewellin, into a purely political role. (Just before leaving for America, Whittle had heard Llewellin giving the GTCC a pep talk on 'this jet propulsion business' – a curious harangue, rounded off with a biblical reference: 'Pool your ideas whole-heartedly – do not be like Ananias and Saphira who kept a little bit back and were struck dead...'[36]).

Freeman re-energised the Ministry and demanded briefing papers on a stream of unresolved issues. He had to make critical decisions over the future of problematic heavy bombers like the Stirling and the Halifax, and the timetable for replacing them with the Avro Lancaster as the mainstay of Bomber Command. He had to preside over boardroom changes at several big aircraft manufacturers, including Fairey and Boulton Paul, whose performance as suppliers to the RAF urgently needed strengthening. He had to take stock of the situation at Bristol Aeroplane, which on 21 October announced the sudden and unexplained departure of its Chief Engineer for aero-engines, Sir Roy Fedden (knighted in January). And he faced some critical technical issues, not least a serious problem over the continuing unreliability of a huge 24-cylinder piston engine (Napier's 'Sabre') that powered a recently introduced fighter, the Hawker Typhoon. Nothing in the new Chief Executive's in-tray, however, could be allowed to distract him for long from the files on Britain's jet-engine programme. Taking note of Linnell's decision on 2 November to preside over a cancellation of Rover's W.2B programme, he asked the Air Vice Marshal to review MAP's general policy towards the jet and to submit firm recommendations by the end of the month.

Freeman was in fact determined to find some way of ensuring that the jet engine had a future, despite the *coup de grâce* for Rover's unit. By asking Linnell now to provide him with 'firm recommendations', he effectively suspended the cancellation of the W.2B programme. He had long seen the jet engine as a development of great potential importance. He had been crucial to the survival of Power Jets before the war. Its Air Ministry contracts, however meagre, would have dried up altogether but for his willingness to authorise them in the face of objections from both A. A. Griffith at the RAE and George Bulman inside the Ministry. He had backed Whittle after that tense meeting in his Harrogate office organised by Tedder in May 1940, and he had personally taken steps to shield the project from demolition in those difficult early weeks of Beaverbrook's whirlwind regime. And by late 1942 Freeman knew of other reasons, too, to stand by the jet – on grounds that as yet remained among Whitehall's most tightly guarded secrets.

Intelligence sources had established beyond doubt that Britain and America were not alone in their quest to build an operational jet plane. As some had long suspected, including General Hap Arnold in Washington, German engineers were well advanced with their own work on using gas turbines for jet propulsion. This ought to have been no surprise. Before the war, after all, it had been common knowledge that scientists at Göttingen and several other German universities were leading the field in many aspects of aeronautical research. They had had the use of laboratory resources – notably state-of-the-art wind tunnels – far superior to those available in Britain or anywhere else. They had also, of course, had access to all of Whittle's patents and writings on jet propulsion. As for the calibre of leading engine manufacturers like BMW, Junkers and Daimler-Benz, those pre-war reports brought back from their plants by a stream of visiting British officials – including Bulman and Tweedie – had openly warned of the Germans' prowess at line production. Hard evidence of progress on jet aircraft after September 1939 had at first been sparse, but over recent months it had begun to emerge in rather alarming detail.

The first news of a jet-powered aircraft being built by Heinkel, the He 280, had surfaced in the spring of 1940, as already noted. (Reports of the experimental He 178 of 1939 do not seem to have attracted any attention.) No more had been heard of the He 280

until February 1942, when a report from the relevant intelligence
section of the Air Ministry, a department known as 'AI 2(g)', had
referred to it again: 'Type unknown. Reported to be a jet-propelled
fighter, with two power units in the wings.'[37] This information, it
was noted, 'has been obtained from official German documents…'.
It was corroborated in some style in April 1942. One of the first
cities attacked by Bomber Command, in the new strategic offensive
just launched under Air Marshal (Bomber) Harris, was Rostock.
After four consecutive nights of bombing, pilots from the RAF's
Photographic Reconnaissance Unit (PRU) flew over the city cap-
turing Damage Assessment 'covers' – and these had been forwarded in the usual way to the PRU's interpretation centre at RAF
Medmenham in Buckinghamshire, where highly skilled staff could
pore over the photographs for useful intelligence. The Rostock pictures encompassed Heinkel's Marienehe airfield. The individual in
charge of the aircraft interpretation section, a formidable WAAF
officer named Constance Babington Smith, sat down to examine
them with more than usual interest. She was not to be disappointed,
as she recalled in writing the post-war history of the PRU:

> The photographs were beautifully sharp… At first I lingered over
> the damage, which for those days was considerable, but then
> an apparition suddenly stopped me. Alongside the debris was
> a slim long-nosed aeroplane quite unlike anything I had ever
> seen before. Streamlined and elegant, it… made the bombers
> look like lumbering relics… The image of the He 280, the fighter
> which Ernst Heinkel claims was the first twin-jet aircraft in the
> world to fly, was permanently on record in Medmenham's files.[38]

Confirmation of the He 280's existence was included in an
extensive 'Most Secret' report of July 1942 summarising what was
so far known of the Germans' progress with jet propulsion.

Freeman and Linnell were both on the 'Limited Distribution'
list for this alarming July 1942 paper. It suggested to its select
few readers that, after reviewing all the available evidence on the
He 280, 'it is considered likely that this type is now undergoing
service trials… [although] from information at present available

it is most improbable that jet-propelled fighters will come into service [with the Luftwaffe] this year [i.e. 1942]'.[39] A table in the report specified a rate of climb of 3,500 ft/min for the He 280, with a maximum speed at altitude of 492 mph and a ceiling height of 47,000 feet. This would be a performance capable of winning air superiority for the Luftwaffe, wherever such a plane could be deployed in significant numbers. The belief that its entry into service before the end of 1942 was 'improbable' can scarcely have offered much reassurance. At a meeting of the GTCC on 18 July, Roxbee Cox as chairman told the members 'a report of consider-able interest had been circulated on enemy activities'. He was not able to disclose its contents in any detail, but members needed to know that Britain was in a race to produce a serviceable jet air-craft. 'If an additional stimulus was required to the work of the Committee, this report should provide it.'[40]

Nor was it safe to assume the He 280 was the Third Reich's only effort in this field. Other snippets of intelligence brought news of a second experimental machine, under development by another of the Luftwaffe's main plane makers, Messerschmitt. According to the British Air Attaché in Berne, a valued source throughout the war, it was designated the 'Me 262'. This plane was seen on an airfield at Kiel in the summer and some hair-raising details were coming into AI 2(g) by November 1942: 'Speeds alleged to be about 750 to 800 mph at an unspecified altitude... The rate of climb of this aircraft is much better than that of the Fw 190.'[41] (The Focke Wulf Fw 190, with a performance markedly superior to that of the Me 109, had given the RAF a nasty shock at the end of 1941.) Unsurprisingly, the interpreters of the PRU's aircraft section were on high alert for further clues to the German jet programme well before the end of 1942. In Babington Smith's words, 'The jets were of course much the most interesting thing that was coming along.' The RAF was given a list of fifty airfields in Germany where it was thought likely that new fighter prototypes might appear, with a request for each to be photographed at least once a month.

The ramifications for MAP were stark indeed. To have failed properly to exploit Whittle's great pre-war achievement was bad enough; but to risk finding the RAF suddenly defenceless against jet aircraft flown by the Luftwaffe was simply unthinkable. Some way had to be found of rapidly revitalising the project so badly botched by Rover. Linnell's findings, handed to Freeman on 29 November 1942, were unequivocal (and implicitly damning, it might be said, of MAP's policy-making since 1940). Rolls-Royce, though admirable in many respects, had 'no design of jet engine which looks like becoming a practical job for years to come' (so much for Griffith's CR1). Rover was a manufacturer of whom it was 'unfortunately true to say that [their] basic experience in this field is non-existent [*sic*] and that their limited knowledge has frequently led them to erroneous conclusions'. As for Power Jets, an oddly scathing assessment ('lacks general engineering knowledge') offered one vital redeeming observation: 'Has on hand a promising design in the W.2/500 which… would turn the Meteor into a worthwhile operational type.'[42] Linnell urged a continuation of all the jet-engine projects under way across Britain's aircraft industry – at de Havilland, Metropolitan-Vickers, BTH and Armstrong Siddeley – but his comments on their combined efforts paled beside his central recommendation: 'Rolls-Royce should take over Power Jets and their Whetstone factory and run them as the jet section of Rolls-Royce. This would provide a firm of great standing to complete the development and be capable of producing the Whittle series of engines.' Freeman endorsed the plan without hesitation. Hives and Sidgreaves were invited down to MAP for a conversation on Sunday 1 December.

Four days later, Hives and Sidgreaves went to see Whittle. Within minutes of their arrival at Brownsover, it was evident to Whittle that Power Jets' own overture to Hives in mid-November had been rather dramatically overtaken by events. Hives set out the position with his customary directness. He and Sidgreaves had had an opportunity on 1 December, he explained, to discuss Tinling's recent letter with Air Marshals Freeman and Linnell in person. With their blessing, Rolls-Royce had now firmly decided to build a jet-engine business of its own. All were agreed that the W.2/500 had the makings of a most impressive engine and Rolls-Royce wanted, if possible, to take it through to production with Power Jets' full cooperation. Since the Derby firm's existing facilities were heavily committed to the Merlin, it wanted to propose using the new factory at Whetstone. As this suggested, Rolls-Royce was therefore interested in pursuing not just a technical partnership but also a commercial alliance between the two companies. The possibility had been put to Stafford Cripps, who had arrived at MAP two weeks ago as its new Minister. He, like Freeman, had backed the plan. So what was Whittle's view?

In short, after enduring agonies of delay and procrastination over Rover's programme for almost three years, Whittle was now confronted with a breathless rush to have the management of his project completely overhauled within a matter of days. His own account of the ensuing discussion captured how painfully torn he felt over the proposition, pitched so suddenly that morning. On the one hand, he was delighted at the prospect of working much more closely with the one engineering firm in England that he truly admired. On the other, he was dismayed to hear talk of Rolls-Royce taking over Whetstone and converting it from the outset into a production facility. His anguish soon turned to anger:

> ... Whetstone was destined to be [a] research and development establishment. I thought it was of considerable national importance that it should be preserved for this purpose... I said we had been struggling for our present limited facilities and I should react very strongly indeed to any step which would diminish them. In fact, if that happened I would have nothing more to do with the job...[43]

Hives rose to the occasion with charm and sensitivity, smoothing Whittle's concerns and ceding ground over the Whetstone idea. This was not just a tactical retreat, though: Whittle had pointed out the obvious advantages to Rolls-Royce of taking over not Whetstone but Barnoldswick 'which was both manned and tooled for production of this kind of thing' – and Hives had to acknowledge the sense of this. The only reservation he voiced was that 'before this could happen, it would be necessary to show that

Rover had failed'. It is easy to imagine a yelp of triumph from Whittle. Proving this outcome, he said, would present the two of them with no difficulty at all. And on this note they parted, with Hives only adding at the door that 'he had told Freeman and Linnell that Rolls-Royce got on very well with Power Jets and they wished it to stay that way'. Nothing further had been said in the meeting about the possibility of a commercial deal between them, however. Hives and Sidgreaves returned to Derby with no clue as to how far, if at all, Whittle would go along with that idea.

Hives received a letter from Linnell the next morning. It stressed the urgency that he and Freeman attached to the 'proposal in connection with Power Jets and Whetstone. I do not want to rush you but we are most anxious to hear your reactions to this and do sincerely hope that they will be favourable.'[44] Hives had a lot on his plate: a public announcement was about to be made of the Merlin 61's debut – an engine with a two-speed, two-stage supercharger that would make it twice as powerful as the Merlin III unit used for the Spitfires and Hurricanes of August 1940. Nevertheless, he asked Linnell and Freeman for another meeting and drove all the way back to London again a few days later. When he explained the merits of basing any Rolls-Royce jet programme on the existing plant at Barnoldswick, Freeman backed the idea immediately. The man now running MAP had enormous respect both for Rolls-Royce's capabilities and for its General Manager personally. (Indeed, the close understanding between them was shortly to become a cornerstone of the whole war effort.) As for the terms under which the Barnoldswick site would change hands, Freeman was happy to leave these to Hives. This still left the future of Whetstone unresolved, though, and Freeman pressed anew the logic of merging Power Jets into Rolls-Royce. Hives obviously demurred over this, perhaps sensing more acutely after his latest trip to Brownsover Hall how resistant Whittle might be to losing his independence.

Hives was right to be cautious. Whittle had no intention of seeing Power Jets disappear into the larger company. When Hives telephoned him a few days later to say that Freeman and Linnell 'desired to see something in the nature of a hook-up' between their companies, Whittle waved this aside rather piously: 'I said I hoped they were not going to discuss commercial matters with me because I was a serving officer and did my best to act accordingly. I did everything I could to avoid being involved in commercial negotiations.'[45] Hives probably wondered how long Freeman would put up with this.

In fact, Freeman had already decided to force matters to a head. He invited the serving officer of Brownsover Hall to visit him at MAP on 11 December 1942. For Whittle, already acutely distressed over the collapse of Rover's work and disconcerted by the signals coming from Derby, the resulting encounter was a calamity. While Linnell sat quietly at the side of the room, Freeman strode to and fro 'speaking forcefully and rather abruptly, emphasizing his remarks with vigorous arm movements'.[46] He berated Whittle over the failure of the W.2B and then outlined a fresh start for the jet project that would in future be dominated by Rolls-Royce. He told Whittle there was to be no further role for Rover – nor, indeed, for George Bulman and his staff, whose direct responsibilities for the jet project were now to be transferred to an autonomous department under Roxbee Cox (though Bulman would retain some indirect influence).

Repeatedly left hanging in the air, throughout what amounted to a barrage of criticism, was the future of Power Jets itself. Freeman said he could see no point in retaining either Williams or Tinling – 'He went so far as to say he would have them called up' – but he stopped short several times of spelling out what should happen to the company or its factory at Whetstone. Whittle supposed the whole operation 'was to be handed over to Rolls-Royce, lock, stock and barrel, but that [Freeman] could not bring himself to put it quite as bluntly as that'. Each time Freeman skirted round the issue, Whittle grew more agitated. He had been in an especially fragile state of mind for the past few weeks and Freeman's intensity was simply too much for him. He managed to insist more than once that disbanding his team of engineers at Lutterworth would be a serious mistake; but whenever Freeman asked directly for his view of the best way forward, as happened several times, Whittle struggled to give any coherent reply. Eventually he confessed to feeling too unwell to continue. 'At this point Linnell intervened and asked me what was the matter; I told him very bluntly that I was tired, and sick to death of the whole business.' If Freeman was intent above all on sounding out Whittle's mental state and his eligibility for broader responsibilities in the future – as Linnell, offering Whittle some small comfort afterwards, suggested had been the case – now he had his answer.

Freeman had long regarded Whittle as an engineer of quite extraordinary gifts, but it was plain to him that years of intolerable pressure had taken their toll. Whittle could not reasonably be expected to take on any wider role within the reconfigured jet-engine business that the MAP Chief Executive was determined to see go ahead. By the same token, he decided, it would also be unwise to try coercing Whittle against his will into accepting a merger between Power Jets and Rolls-Royce. They might kill the golden goose. The jet project, as Whittle heard him say with a disarming frankness as they parted on 11 December, 'could not afford to dispense with my brain for some time yet'. So Freeman stopped short of insisting on the merger that Linnell had recommended. Instead, he would depend on Hives to make as much as possible out of a close technical partnership between the two firms. And he would rely on Hives to dictate the exact terms of their liaison over the months to come – just he was leaving Hives to reach a settlement with Spencer Wilks over the transferral into Rolls-Royce's hands of the Clitheroe and Barnoldswick sites.

This latter business was settled with a memorable coup in the remaining days before Christmas 1942. First Wilks was summoned down to MAP for an audience with Stafford Cripps on 18 December. Whittle took an excited call the next day from Roxbee Cox, who told him 'the Minister jumped the hurdle' and a minute had gone round announcing that Wilks had agreed to hand over Rover's entire role to Rolls-Royce.[47] Then Whittle had a call from Hives himself. He had just returned from Lancashire and a meeting with Wilks on 20 December that 'had passed off very satisfactorily and he did not think there was going to be any difficulty'.[48] Hives felt no need to elaborate – but Stanley Hooker had been at his side and much later would provide enough detail to add another page to the book of stories about his boss. They had met Wilks for a Sunday evening meal:

> There were only three of us at the five-bob dinner in that very comfortable old pub, the Swan and Royal in Clitheroe High Street. After dinner Hives turned abruptly to Wilks and said with a twinkle in his eye, 'Why are you playing round with this jet engine? It's not in your line of business, you grub about on the floor, and I hear from Hooker that things are going from bad to worse with Whittle.'
>
> They were great friends, of course, and Wilks, smilingly ignoring the jibe, replied, 'We can't get on with the fellow at all, and I would like to be shot of the whole business.'
>
> Hives then said, 'I'll tell you what I will do. You give us this jet job, and I will give you our tank engine factory at Nottingham.'[49]

It was in fact the rough-and-ready solution that Whittle had heard mooted early in October. By the time they left the pub, Hives and Wilks had shaken hands on the deal. Rolls-Royce would take effective control of the Clitheroe and Barnoldswick sites from the start of the New Year. The Derby company's shareholders would have cause to toast this outcome, a bargain described countless times in later years as the deal of the century.

These closing weeks of 1942 had effectively secured the jet engine's future. No one inside MAP could doubt it. The newly promoted Harold Roxbee Cox, ever the devoted son who sent a weekly letter to his mother in the Midlands, wrote to her just before Christmas about his new position: 'I cease in a day or two to be Deputy Director of Scientific Research and take charge of something about which unfortunately I can say precisely nothing but which will make a damn good tale one day.'[50] Freeman was already seen by many contemporaries as the great unsung hero of the RAF's war. Hives ran the business that had emerged as the single most important arm of Britain's entire defence industry. They had jointly committed themselves to making a practical

Plate 9. Bringing the cast together: when the members of the Gas Turbine Collaboration Committee (*above*) assembled for a meeting in the Spring of 1942, Whittle in his uniform stood out as usual. (Names added by an unknown hand.) In July 1943, Whittle and Dan Walker (*far left*) hosted a tour of Whetstone by US officers – here Lt. Bollay (*left*) and US Navy Cdr Pearson (*right*) accompanied by Major J. N. D. Heenan (*centre*) from the British Air Commission in Washington.

Plate 10. Day of destiny for Power Jets: Minister of Aircraft Production Stafford Cripps (*above, centre*) strides round the Whetstone factory with Whittle and Dudley Williams in tow during his visit on 21 August 1943; Whittle in earnest conversation the same day with MAP's Chief Executive Sir Wilfrid Freeman
(*below, right*) and Harold Roxbee Cox, head of Special Projects.

Plate 11. From state secret to morale booster: after the Allies' announcement of the jet engine in January 1944, officially authorised photographs included (*above*) Whittle celebrating the success of his project with his closest colleagues (*from left to right* Leslie Cheshire, Dudley Williams, Coll Tinling, Dan Walker, George Lees and Pat Johnson); and (*below*) Whittle thanking Dan Walker and the other engineers, all in their twenties, who had joined Power Jets since January 1940.

Plate 12. More photographs for the press: Whittle's team posed round him at Brownsover Hall (*from left to right* Dudley Williams, Leslie Cheshire, Mary Phillips, FW, Pat Johnson, Coll Tinling, Dan Walker, George Lees); at home at Broomfield (*left*) with Dorothy, the 'wife who kept a secret 14 years' (*Daily Express*).

Plate 13. The team that might have been: Whittle with J. P. Herriot (*left*) and Stanley Hooker in the latter's office at the Barnoldswick factory in Lancashire that Rolls-Royce took over from Rover in January 1943. The three men enjoyed close personal bonds, but Whittle had effectively parted ways with Rolls-Royce by the time this publicity photograph was taken late in the war.

Plate 14. Recalling the wartime record: the Power Jets engineering team (*above*) gathers for a first commemorative dinner of 'The Reactionaries' in April 1946 (standing at the back, *left to right*: Coll Tinling, Whittle, Pat Johnson, Michael Daunt, Dudley Williams); and Whittle in America (*below*) making one of many stops on his tour that summer, with WAAF Staff Officer Jill Shepherd always by his side.

Plate 15. Proud moments at home and abroad: an official portrait in 1946 (*above*) had Whittle contemplating fine models of the E.28/39 (rt.) and the Gloster Meteor in his study at Brownsover Hall; while at the US Pentagon in November of the same year (*below*) he was awarded the US Legion of Merit, a rare honour for a non-US citizen.

Plate 16. Aviation's grand old man on parade: with Hans von Ohain (*left*) at La Guardia Airport in October 1980 when both collected awards from the Wings Club of New York; and at Britain's Farnborough Air Show in 1988 (*below*), where Rolls-Royce invited him to compare jet engines ancient and modern.

success of the concept envisaged by Whittle all those years ago. So against all the naysayers, the sceptics and the would-be usurpers of his idea, Whittle had in this sense prevailed. His labours on behalf of the engine had brought him close to physical and mental collapse, as his latest unhappy confrontation with Freeman had confirmed again, but the long-term implications of his work would now be impossible to ignore. A new era beckoned. In the meantime, though, some more immediate issues remained to be settled. As of the start of 1943, it was not clear how exactly the 'liaison' between Power Jets and Rolls-Royce would work. Nor was it obvious where in the new scheme of things a suitable role would be found for Wing Commander Whittle himself.

iv

The Wilks brothers had never allowed Whittle anywhere near their factory at Barnoldswick. He set off there for a first visit in January 1943 at the personal invitation of Stanley Hooker, to whom Hives had assigned the job of turning the Rover site into a Rolls-Royce plant. The journey meant a longish drive – and Whittle, ever conscious of his social status, always prized the chance to arrive at a new venue with a chauffeur – so 'Daddy' Lees took the wheel. They made more than one wrong turn on their way north from Manchester before finding their way over the moors to 'Barlick', on the flank of the Pennines.

While the town was rather smaller and more remote than Whittle had expected, the spread of the engine works installed since 1941 came as a shock to him. Bankfield Shed was the largest of the former cotton mills in the area, most of them hollowed out by the Great Depression, and Rover's sizeable operation now filled it. Hooker greeted them in person and had laid on the arrangements for an immediate tour. He walked them through the manufacturing shops, where Whittle made a mental note of machines standing idle and others poorly placed for a smooth workflow. He had heard many reports of disarray, but it seemed to him that at least a semblance of order had already been established. He was impressed to see dozens of machine tools in use on the honing of forged turbine blades. Most of the operators were young women, brought into Barnoldswick from the surrounding district. (They lived through the week in a large hostel, said Hooker, known to all as Virgin Villas.) Whittle remarked wryly on the size of the workforce in general: with about two thousand employees, it probably outnumbered the entire population of the pre-war town. Hooker told him that Rover had hired sufficient numbers to complete twenty jet engines a week. To date, the site had yet to sign off a single unit of the latest design agreed with MAP, a marginally amended version of the W.2B (complete with the No. 13 diffuser) labelled as the 'B.23' by Rover. But the stockyard was piled to the roof with enough alloy blocks, steel plate and metal tubing for two hundred engines.[51] And no fewer than four test beds stood at the ready, compared with the single makeshift facility employed at Lutterworth since 1940.

The sight of a uniformed RAF officer walking through the workshops caused a predictable stir, and Hooker made little effort to disguise his guest's identity. After the tour, he introduced Whittle to the handful of Rover engineers who had elected to stay with the project – the rest would be going to work at the tank factory in Nottingham – and to those colleagues from Derby who had already arrived to join the new team. At Hooker's request, Whittle gave them all a short talk about his hopes for 1943. A notable account of the occasion can be found in Hooker's autobiography. Part of it certainly rings true: 'His presence amongst us caused great joy and enthusiasm, which was heightened by his personality and his ability to captivate a large audience.'[52] But Hooker also claimed (in 1984) to have played the role of the proverbial Dutch uncle, later in the day warning Whittle off any notion of persevering with a substantial company of his own. Now that Rolls-Royce had taken over, he had to understand, control of the jet engine had 'necessarily' passed to them. 'With the facilities now at our disposal', as Hooker recalled telling Whittle, 'it is no use you trying to compete. On the contrary, you must join with us...'

Perhaps he did indeed express this view – it was widely held by now – but the response that Hooker attributed to Whittle seems highly implausible: 'Though this moment must have been a crucial turning-point in his life, he readily agreed.'

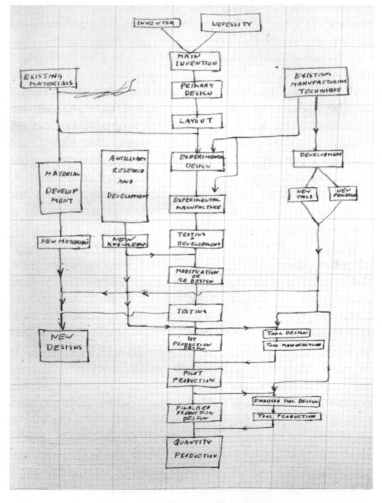

Fig. 20. How Whittle in 1943 envisaged future
pilot-manufacturing at Power Jets

In fact, Whittle agreed nothing of the kind. His warm reception at Barnoldswick seems only to have strengthened his belief that its 'technical liaison' with Rolls-Royce had at last opened the way for Power Jets to realise its full potential. It could now look forward, he honestly believed, to expanding at Whetstone into a formidable research and development company. It would refine engines like the W.2/500 – and Whittle was already thinking of further improvements, to go into a W.2/700 and then a W.2/800 – and it would also build enough of them on a 'pilot production' basis to iron out the early manufacturing challenges. All this could be done in the context of a close entente with a top-drawer manufacturer, open to the task of developing new tools and new line processes. A diagram in his 1943–5 Workshop Note Book shows how much thought he had given to this joint endeavour (*Fig. 20*). It suggests that he was even ready to contemplate turning out engines in larger quantities at Whetstone, though he certainly had total confidence in Rolls-Royce's production capabilities. The Derby firm would be Power Jets' ideal partner. Together they could forge a rare combination of brains and industrial brawn. As it rolled forward, he would rely on Coll Tinling and Pat Johnson to tie up assorted government contracts and patent agreements that would ensure a glittering post-war future for Power Jets. There would be no need, after all, to resort to an Anglo-American joint venture to carry the jet engine forward, as he had conjectured six months earlier. On the contrary, Power Jets would enjoy a worldwide monopoly, no less, on the design of jet engines.

Back in the real world, apparently undetected by Whittle, there had meanwhile been a decisive shift in the wind. However unjustly, Power Jets' reputation in Whitehall had suffered by association with the Rover debacle, and the many twists and turns in the development of the W.2B. Air Vice Marshal Jack Linnell, never as warmly disposed as Tedder towards Whittle personally, took every opportunity to stress that 'lessons had been learned': for instance, as Controller of Research and Development he would entertain no talk of future production for the W.2/500 until prototypes had been tested far beyond normal endurance limits. MAP was now inclined to hedge all bets placed on Power Jets' ability to deliver. Whittle still enjoyed a genuine rapport with Roxbee Cox, but other officials were beginning to take a much more detached view of his endeavours. A Mr Tams, visiting Lutterworth early in February 1943, gently alluded to this change of heart. A year earlier, he told Whittle, the Ministry 'had rated our priority very high but there was a feeling now that there was nothing much to show for it and he thought that in consequence our priority might have suffered'.[53] It was an oblique way of saying the future of the jet engine was no longer to be as closely identified with Whittle and Power Jets as in the past. Nor was this just an acknowledgement of Freeman's intervention and the new role to be assumed by Rolls-Royce. The recruitment of additional firms, initiated by Tizard at the start of 1941 in the face of pained objections from Whittle, was now bearing fruit with the emergence of other engines – and the first of them was just being readied for flight. The reaction in Whitehall would betray the new ambivalence over Whittle's future role.

By the start of 1943, Major Frank Halford's H.1 unit, later christened the Goblin, was starting its final bench tests. Built for Halford by Geoffrey de Havilland's company at Hatfield, the H.1 differed from Whittle's W.2 series principally in its adoption of 'straight-through' rather than 'reverse-flow' combustion chambers, but was otherwise substantially a reworking of Whittle's basic design. Initial contacts between Halford and Whittle early in 1941 had prompted a misunderstanding between them, but this had long since given way to a healthy mutual respect. Whittle had been more than happy for Power Jets to assist Halford's work, and had been generous with his own advice. In July 1941, for example, he had sent de Havilland's Chief Engineer, E. S. Moult, some 'preliminary ideas' on how a straight-through combustion chamber might be built.[54] Later, at Halford's own request, he had designed an innovative single-sided impeller for use in the H.1. All this was generously acknowledged by Moult, who wrote to Whittle with thanks for his help early in January 1943: 'We greatly appreciate the help which your company has given us.'[55]

Whittle refused to see Halford as a competitor, even when told that an inaugural flight of the F.9/40 Meteor early in March 1943 would be powered not by W.2Bs but by two H.1 units. He was distressed, though, to hear that erstwhile supporters of his own project were hailing Halford's engine as a welcome alternative: 'there were powerful influences at work,' warned MAP's George Watt in a telephone call to George Lees, 'boosting the H.1 unit and decrying the W.2B and the [W.2/]500'.[56] (In the event, de Havilland's engineers would struggle over the next two years to achieve the full thrust promised by the design of the Goblin, and its promise was not properly realised until after the war.) When the arrangements were made for the Meteor's debut at Cranwell, Whittle's name failed to appear on the official guest list. Given his contribution to Gloster's design work as well as the Meteor's engines, it was a shameful omission and it caused embarrassment in many quarters. Gloster's test pilot, Michael Daunt, sent Whittle a touching personal invitation, urging him to be there on 5 March '[as] the father and I feel the man who is really responsible for Jet Propulsion being possible today in England'.[57] But he stayed away.

Most officials seem initially to have assumed, like Hooker, that Whittle would soon come to some kind of accommodation with Rolls-Royce. Even among those who knew of his pre-war career – and were vaguely aware of the younger Whittle's fervent socialist ideals and his antipathy towards the big firms in the aero-engine business in particular (those 'wolves at the door') – it was supposed that the logic of joining forces would appear to him compelling in the end. Even Roxbee Cox believed so and was content to let the two parties decide between themselves where to draw the line between cooperation and combination. When it became apparent that Whittle intended to retain a robust independence, there was genuine surprise – which soon turned to exasperation in Whitehall. Roxbee Cox's deputy, George Watt, warned those around Whittle early in March that they should take nothing for granted: 'the whole position has changed… The whole subject of responsibilities, programmes of work etc is under consideration'.[58]

As, too, was Whittle's career. Whitehall's patience with him was now wearing terribly thin. He was startled to hear from Watt one morning that he might shortly be posted away from Power Jets altogether. Pressing other MAP officials for more information, he was incredulous to learn that someone in Whitehall had seen fit to suggest he be assigned to an operational training unit in Scotland 'for engineer duties'. Seething with indignation, he strode into Thames House on 17 March to ask Roxbee Cox what on earth was going on – and drew scant comfort from their talk. 'I said I could not believe that it was an ordinary engineer officer's post, but he assured me that it was.'[59] Loyal as ever to the RAF, he probably surprised Roxbee Cox by saying he would go if ordered to do so. (He never was.) Roxbee Cox thought he would be better advised to resign his commission, 'but he could not suggest any reasonable alternative'. It was a shattering episode for Whittle, whose sense of his own identity had always owed so much to his RAF career.

From his desk in Derby, meanwhile, Hives had been keeping track of developments since the start of the year and had felt no urgent need to intervene. Decades after the war, Roxbee Cox told an interviewer that he believed Hives was patiently waiting through these early months of 1943 to find some way of persuading Whittle to join Rolls-Royce.[60] Certainly this accords with the way that Hives left his senior engineers to work on a steady strengthening of their relations with him. As Chief Engineer, Elliott paid frequent visits to Brownsover Hall. He and Whittle were soon mooting together the notion of regular weekly conferences for their two teams, alternating between Brownsover and Derby. (Notably absent from their deliberations, it might be noted in passing, was any reference to the man hired by Hives in 1939 to build a jet engine. No mention was made of A. A. Griffith at all, nor would meetings at Derby have occasioned any awkwardness on this score. Griffith had been given his own private office at Duffield Bank House, the stylish rural retreat several miles from Derby that was used by Rolls-Royce as a guesthouse for senior executives. His CR1 engine had been effectively shelved. As Hives had wryly remarked in a letter to

MAP in November 1942, it seemed a magnificent machine but for one flaw – 'we cannot get it to work!'[61]) Assuming Whittle could be induced to join the Derby payroll with a suitably grand title – always the key issue in Roxbee Cox's opinion – Hives probably hoped and believed that a generous investment by his Board in Power Jets might just lead, in time, to a happy convergence.

Perhaps it almost happened. By the middle of April 1943, the groundwork seemed complete. Rolls-Royce had fully assimilated the former Rover operations in Lancashire and had also affirmed a degree of control over the whole jet project that went far beyond Rover's partnering role in the past. Hooker had recommended that Barnoldswick should press ahead with the W.2B/B.23 – which would in due course become the 'RB.23' (RB for Rolls Barnoldswick) and be assigned the name Welland – on which so much effort had already been expended since its initial run as long ago as December 1941. Hives accepted this advice, implicitly setting aside Whittle's insistence that his W.2/500 engine ought to be preferred, and MAP accepted this decision. The first Welland engines would go into line production in September 1943 (and an operating manual for the Welland, produced under MAP's direction in April 1945, would contain two fine illustrations to match the elegance of Rolls-Royce's engineering – *see Fig. 21*). Hives also backed Hooker's desire to devote more work to Rover's 'straight-through' B.26, adapting its best features – and some of the W.2/500's as well – as the basis of another engine, the RB.37 that would later be christened the 'Derwent'. (These two, the Welland and the Derwent, were soon to be famous as the first in a long line of turbojet engines made by Rolls-Royce and named after English rivers rather than birds of prey, as for the piston engines of yore.)

As for the contractual relations between the Derby firm and Power Jets, Hives and Sidgreaves had kept their distance from yet more interminable wrangling between MAP and Whittle's two legal eagles, Pat Johnson and Coll Tinling, over what 'Terms of Reference' should govern relations between the two companies. When their advocacy stretched to asserting parity between Rolls-

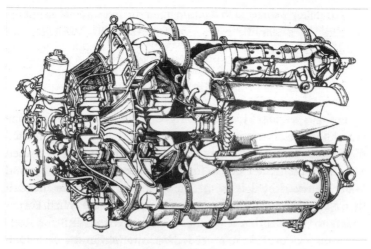

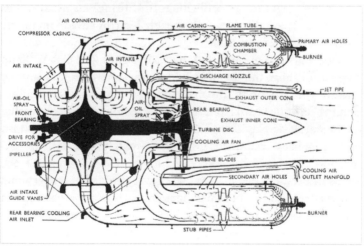

Fig. 21. Rolls-Royce's Welland Mk 1 engine, from
a Ministry manual of April 1945

Royce and Power Jets in almost every way, though, Hives finally
lost patience. In a letter to Linnell, the proverbial fist hit the table
with a bang as he spelt out the realities of the post-Rover regime
in uncompromising fashion:

> Our policy is directed in looking upon the [jet turbine] as just
> another aero engine, and not as a piece of scientific apparatus...
> We do not look upon the turbine engine as a new secret weapon,
> it is just another way of pushing an aeroplane along... [At Rolls-
> Royce] we have created a very enthusiastic team on this job, and
> the progress will be in keeping with our reputation.[62]

On 19 April 1943 Hives and Sidgreaves bearded Whittle in his
lair at Brownsover and told him the time had come to make a
fresh start. They handed him a copy of the letter sent to Linnell
and made clear their desire for a commercial alliance. At first,
Whittle prevaricated as usual. Then, by his own account, he suddenly acknowledged the logic in their proposal. He had always
felt, said Whittle, that it would be improper for him to discuss
a commercial deal 'or so at least I had thought in the past – but
if they were right in fact and this sort of thing was necessary in
order that we could get on with the job, I might have to revise my
attitude in these respects'.[63]

The Rolls-Royce men returned to Nightingale Road, surely
relieved to think the moment had finally arrived for an orderly
takeover of Power Jets. The moment, though, soon passed. That
evening, Whittle heard reports of a momentous occurrence earlier
in the day at de Havilland's aerodrome at Hatfield. A lavish air
display had been put on for Churchill and a retinue of the RAF's
top brass. (Whittle had once again been left off the guest list,
to his understandable dismay.) Halfway through the afternoon,
Gloster's second test pilot Michael Daunt had flown the E.28/39
across the aerodrome at almost 400 mph. It was actually not the
same plane as that flown at Cranwell by Gerry Sayer: a second
prototype had been built by Gloster in the meantime. But this
one, powered by a W.2B engine, had again made a huge impression on all who saw it – and especially the Prime Minister. It was
the first time he had seen a jet aeroplane in the sky. His thunderous
reaction – 'swinging round in order to follow the course of the
E.28/39... so quickly that he very nearly spilt his whisky and soda'
– had caused almost as much of a sensation as the plane itself:
'Mr Churchill was so impressed that he immediately wanted to

know why we had not squadrons of jet fighters'.[64] Churchill's instant response changed the jet's prospects overnight. Plans for the production of the Meteor were immediately stepped up, with orders for a first run of three hundred aircraft. It may also have helped to change Whittle's mind about a merger with Rolls-Royce. If hundreds of jet engines were now going to be in demand, with Churchill's blessing, why should the new factory at Whetstone not be entitled to a sizeable slice of the orders? Hives called him on the telephone next day, 20 April, saying 'they wanted to know how far Power Jets were willing to "let them in", and how much it was going to cost them – particularly the latter'.[65] Whittle brushed off the enquiry, invoking his 'serving-officer' status to avoid the issue yet again.

He turned instead, over the next several days, to assembling the arguments for an alternative future that he had been contemplating for some time. He then pressed his case so hard with Stafford Cripps, and backed it up with such vituperative criticism of Rolls-Royce, that any lingering possibility of a commercial alliance was probably dashed irretrievably. The scheme he proposed to Cripps in a letter of 29 April 1943 called for the state to acquire Power Jets along with all the other operations now involved in the jet-engine project, including the Rolls-Royce facilities in Barnoldswick and Clitheroe:

> As you know, many big commercial concerns are now entering into the gas turbine field, largely as the result of the stimulus provided by my efforts. There are a number of signs that a fierce commercial struggle is likely to develop. In my opinion this should never be allowed to happen... [and] there is a very strong case for complete nationalisation viewed from any political standpoint.[66]

The state had already invested, by his estimate, at least £2 million (£100 million in today's money). Whittle resented the prospect of privately owned firms enriching their shareholders out of a nascent technology to which they – unlike Power Jets' shareholders – had never committed a penny of their own risk capital.

As well as averting this outcome, and pre-empting wasteful competition between the firms, the pooling of all the jet-engine sector's constituent parts would promote, he suggested, a free interchange of technical information far surpassing the efforts of the GTCC and greatly to the benefit of the nation. It would also dispense at a stroke with endless quarrelling over patents and licences in the post-war world. Whittle closed with a plea that his proposal be heeded urgently. He told Cripps that he had done his utmost to prevent Power Jets from becoming involved in any commercial entanglements in order to keep the nationalisation option alive – 'but I may not succeed in doing this much longer the way things are going at present'. He backed up this warning with a swipe at Rolls-Royce that both Cripps and Roxbee Cox found disquieting. The Derby firm seemed likely to 'make an effort to swallow up the organisation which I have done so much to build up… They are an extremely powerful firm and Power Jets has little hope of escape'.

Hives encountered Whittle's change of heart for himself on the last day of April. He went to see him at Brownsover Hall for what proved to a revealing encounter. The meeting had been scheduled ten days earlier, as an opportunity for more discussion of commercial possibilities. Having greeted Hives in the porchway, Whittle ducked out of the meeting and retreated into his study, leaving the most powerful man in the aircraft industry to be hosted by Johnson, Williams and Tinling in the draughtsmen's office. There followed a tense discussion, 'pretty blunt and at times severe in tone'.[67] Pat Johnson had the temerity to ask Hives if he would care to clarify his main concerns, and say whether or not Rolls-Royce was 'interested primarily in ensuring that they did not run up against a monopoly position [owned by Power Jets] which to say the least of it might involve them in great and expensive legal difficulties, post war'. Unsurprisingly, Hives soon tired of this kind of bluster. Rolls-Royce, he informed his hosts, 'intended to be the centre of the whole orbit of jet propulsion, and… intended their activities to become paramount in this sphere'. If Power Jets was willing to enter an agreement with 'a big and powerful brother', that could be arranged. If not, they should be under no illusions about the leadership of the project: 'RR had taken on the job with a great sense of responsibility and... had just got to make a success of it and were going to do so. He stated it was safe to ignore all the other firms because RR were going into this in a big way.'[68]

This powerful statement of intent from Hives, relayed to Whittle in a dense memorandum by Johnson, surely ought to have prompted Whittle to reconsider his stance. He had a perfect pretext for doing so: days later, on 7 May 1943, he took a call from one of Hooker's colleagues, John Herriot, to say the W.2B reworked by Rolls-Royce had excelled itself at the end of its 100-hours test. Herriot had previously worked at Rover – he was seconded to the firm's staff in 1941 having previously been on location at Rover as an official of the Air Ministry's Inspection Department – but he and Whittle had compared notes several times since the start of 1943. They were on good terms together. Whittle was so impressed with the news from Barnoldswick that, notwithstanding the arguments he had just put in writing to Cripps, he immediately penned an effusive letter of congratulations to Herriot and the team he had been leading. (Two years earlier, Rover had rejected a design modification urged on them by Whittle and calling for a five-degree twist to the turbine blades. Much to his satisfaction, Herriot had revived the idea and implemented it – which had undoubtedly contributed to the W.2B's greatly improved performance.) Herriot wrote back in glowing terms, to thank Whittle on behalf of the whole Barnoldswick development team and to stress their respect for what he had bequeathed them: 'the basic design still remains almost 100% in line with your own original ideas, and we feel honoured in having been allowed to play our small part in what we hope has been the first step in putting the jet propulsion engine on the map as a tried and going concern...'[69]

All this mutual admiration might perhaps have been the preface to a promising fresh start for Whittle with Rolls-Royce. But it was not to be. When Stafford Cripps asked him to visit MAP for a talk about the nationalisation proposal that he had put forward in his letter of 29 April, Whittle stuck to his guns – and levelled them at Rolls-Royce, just as before.

He had not yet met Cripps personally, but certainly knew of his formidable reputation. A brilliant barrister and one of the country's most forthright left-wing politicians of the pre-war years – he had been expelled from the Labour Party in 1939 for promoting an alignment with Britain's Communist Party – Cripps had joined Churchill's War Cabinet in 1942, having become a household name: he had served as British Ambassador in Moscow through 1940–42 and was widely credited with helping to cement the West's alliance with Stalin after Hitler's invasion of the Soviet Union in June 1941. Since arriving at MAP, Cripps had been much impressed by its dealings with the aircraft industry. He had quickly seen the Ministry's potential as a future exemplar of central planning. Indeed, he envisaged using MAP's huge investment in the industry's shadow factories as a building block of post-war socialism. So Whittle's nationalisation idea had certainly intrigued him.

At the outset of their meeting on 11 May 1943, Cripps offered some broad observations about the general role of the state that made a strong impression on his visitor. Whittle later confided this to his diary in candid fashion: 'perhaps for the first time I was conscious of the fact that I was in the presence of an intellect very much superior to my own.'[70] Conceivably emboldened by a sense of their shared belief in a socialist future, Whittle saw no reason to hide from Cripps that he was feeling betrayed by events since January. The possibilities inherent in nationalisation then took second billing to an angry indictment of Rolls-Royce's shortcomings. He and his colleagues had long advocated bringing Rolls-Royce into the jet project, Whittle told the Minister, as perhaps the only firm technically 'in the same street' as Power Jets. 'We had however been very disappointed in this respect… They were very arrogant and very powerful and assumed that they could ride roughshod over the Ministry.'[71] No doubt Whittle was under immense strain at this point. And his remarks could, as ever, be attributed to that singular mix of naïveté, directness and single-minded determination that so often resulted in a rather unworldly attitude. Nonetheless, this adoption of an openly adversarial stance towards Hives, in the Minister of Aircraft Production's own office – and just a few days after praising Herriot so generously – suggests that Whittle's mind was by this point in turmoil.

One other factor may have contributed to his mounting distress in May 1943. He had just become aware of vital new intelligence being accumulated about the Germans' progress with jet engines. Late in March 1943 he had been shown a dossier of evidence on the Germans' jet work, compiled by the head of the AI 2(g) section of Aircraft Intelligence, Wing Commander S. D. Felkin. It almost certainly included the highly sensitive 1942 reports on Heinkel's He 280, and perhaps also a more recent report suggesting 'at least one type of jet-propelled fighter might be in limited production by the end of 1943'.[72] What a moment it must have been for Whittle. He had spent years battling virtually alone to build his first jet engine. He had been tormented, almost since the outbreak of the war, by misguided government directives that in his view had delayed the launch of a prototype jet fighter by at least two years. He must have been astonished and appalled to learn that German aircraft firms, working in total isolation from his own project, had advanced so far towards the same end goal. Indeed, if a report shown to him days later in April 1943 was to be given credence, the Germans were well on their way to fulfilling his own youthful vision of stratospheric flight. A recently captured German engineer had told an interrogator that tests were under way on a supersonic plane for the Luftwaffe, capable of flying 1,120 mph at a height of 59,000 feet.[73] By May, MAP was intent on bringing together the half-dozen or so individuals in England with the necessary credentials to monitor this development and to assess what threat, if any, it posed to the Allies. Whittle was one of them.

For the next few months, though, his views would have to be sought largely via written correspondence. Roxbee Cox, not for the first time, had devised a lengthy break for him. It was obvious on many days that he was close to another nervous breakdown. A three-month 'War Course' was just commencing at the RAF Staff College that would run until the second week of August.

It would be no rest camp for Whittle – only the most promising young officers were put up for it – but joining it would offer him the change of scene that he so obviously needed. Cripps heartily endorsed the idea, not least as a way of ensuring that a little more time would be available to weigh the Ministry's best response to Whittle's nationalisation proposal. By a happy chance, the Staff College's Commandant was Air Vice Marshal Roderick Hill, lately transferred from the BAC in Washington. No fellow officer had more admiration for Whittle – Hill's glowing account of the previous summer's US tour had been widely circulated – and it took Roxbee Cox less than an afternoon to clear the necessary arrangements for a latecomer to be added to the class of May 1943.

10

Cornered by Cripps

May 1943 to March 1944

i

The RAF's wartime Staff College occupied a Victorian country mansion at Bulstrode Park, just a mile or so from the town of Gerrards Cross in Buckinghamshire. With its Gothic spires and castellated towers, it was a bigger and grander version of Brownsover Hall – large enough, in fact, to house not only the Staff College but also the main training centre for the Women's Auxiliary Air Force (WAAF). Whittle arrived there on 24 May 1943 accompanied by Mary Phillips, who had been found a suite of rooms in the WAAF quarters. She would help him with his correspondence, and the preparation of some theoretical papers that he was in the midst of drafting. Whittle had promised more than one MAP committee in London that his physical absence for a while would not stop him contributing to their work.

One chairman who particularly welcomed this assurance was Ben Lockspeiser, a stalwart of the RAE who had just succeeded David Pye as MAP's Director of Scientific Research. In response to the astounding report in April of German experiments with a jet plane flying faster than the speed of sound, Lockspeiser had been tasked with forming a 'Supersonic Committee' in Whitehall. Early recruits, in addition to Roxbee Cox and Hayne Constant, included A. A. Griffith and Cambridge's Professor Melvill Jones.

One of the very first places round the table, though, was reserved for Whittle. He had already written a long and deeply thoughtful letter to Roxbee Cox about the possible implications of Wing Commander S. D. Felkin's dossier on the Germans' jet programme.[1] In this letter – dated 7 April, and written before the revelation of a possible supersonic plane – he had concentrated on the intelligence gathered about jet and rocket fuels under development in the Reich: three densely typed pages on compounds and processes attested again to his youthful passion for chemistry. He had also offered, though, a few reflections on high-speed flight, including a judgement that suddenly looked rather prescient: '... it may well be that... the increase [of drag near the speed of sound] is not sufficient to prevent an aeroplane diving through the critical region... and thereafter flying well above the speed of sound'.[2] Eight days before leaving Rugby for his Staff College course, he had confirmed to Lockspeiser's team that he was working on a technical note for them. The effort devoted by the Germans to jet-engine research, as he observed in a letter to the MAP official appointed as secretary to the committee, appeared to have been free of 'the pessimistic outlook' which had dogged Whitehall's general attitude. 'The [German] aeroplane described (the existence of which I do not doubt) is the outcome, and it will be dangerous if we try and delude ourselves into believing that it is not there.'[3] He copied his letter to Roxbee Cox, with a scribbled note in the margin: 'I regard the matter as so important that I want to give as much help as I am able.'

Some were inclined to treat the whole idea of supersonic flight as simply too fantastical to be taken seriously. The President of the National Physics Laboratory, E. F. Relf, spent many hours running his slide rule over aerodynamic equations in the first week of May, only to find they bore out his initial suspicion. As he explained to Lockspeiser: 'I have made an extremely optimistic calculation and come to the broad conclusion that these supersonic speeds are quite out of the question.'[4] Hearing word of the topic later in the month, Henry Tizard was equally sceptical. He wrote to Air Vice Marshal Ralph Sorley – who had just succeeded Jack Linnell as

MAP's Controller of Research and Development – and set down a long list of reasons why no plane could ever fly supersonically. Or, at least, no plane with a pilot hoping to survive the flight: 'owing to the compression effect and frictional drag, the aeroplane may soon get so hot that the pilot's blood will boil and there is no method of cooling it. What is the answer to that one?'

By the time Lockspeiser's committee was ready for its second formal gathering, on 4 June 1943, Whittle had circulated his technical paper. Its theoretical reasoning was unassailable and it swept aside the objections that Relf and others had raised. Whittle presented it in person at the meeting, carrying the whole committee with him and prompting a lengthy discussion that ended on a sombre note:

> It was agreed that it was clear... that the Germans were build-ing jet propelled aircraft, and that possibly some of these were capable of supersonic speeds. We in this country had not studied the problems of aircraft flight at supersonic speeds... and if Germany had, in fact, solved them that country was years ahead of Great Britain or the USA.[5]

This conclusion was to mark the start of a shocked reappraisal across Whitehall over the next few months of the jet engine's importance. And one secret paper after another would acknowledge a desperate truth. With or without supersonic planes, the progress made with the jet concept by German engineers meant Hitler's Luftwaffe might just be about to steal a march on the Allied air forces, with potentially disastrous consequences. The war had taken a more favourable turn since the start of the year – the Germans had suffered a terrible defeat at Stalingrad in January 1943 and Rommel's Afrika Corps had just surrendered in North Africa in May – but losing air supremacy over Europe might postpone any thought of a Second Front in the West for a long time to come.

Whittle's Staff College course followed an exacting timetable, with a rigorous schedule of lectures and frequent excursions that he found 'usually very interesting – to aircraft firms, to the various Command Headquarters, and so on'.[6] He nonetheless found the time to chair various discussions at the college about future gas-turbine projects – one of these looked at 'the requirements for a future long-range bomber for the Far East War' – and he was given special permission to skip some days at college in order to attend important meetings in London. It was all a little reminiscent of his time at Cambridge, when he had combined his undergraduate studies with frequent trips to talk to industrial suppliers round the country (and the outcome, as Roxbee Cox liked to recall in old age, was exactly the same: 'and of course, who came top but Frank Whittle – he had got a brain beyond the normal...').[7]

Whittle appears also to have been included on the distribution list for at least some of the reports about German jet-engine work now trickling steadily out of Felkin's Air Intelligence section. At the third meeting of the Supersonic Committee, held on 6 July 1943, he made a special request. 'Wing Commander Whittle asked whether some recent PRU photographs, apparently of jet-propelled aircraft on German airfields, had been examined. It was agreed that these photographs should be obtained.'[8] Meticulous scrutiny of photographs taken by Spitfire and Mosquito pilots of the PRU had made a significant contribution to Allied intelligence about German jets in 1942. (The de Havilland Mosquito, Freeman's Folly, had been in service with the RAF since November 1941.) Whittle was anxious to see any further photographic evidence that had been collected more recently. While he was waiting for his formal request to be approved, he was able to circumvent the process in a serendipitous fashion. Days after the committee meeting, he discovered to his delight that the War Course timetable provided for a visit to RAF Medmenham, home to the PRU's interpretation section. By the time he walked through the doors of its mock-Tudor mansion perched on a hill high above the Thames on 16 July, we can be sure Whittle's arrival was keenly awaited by the section head, Flying Officer Constance Babington Smith.

Known as 'Babs' to all her colleagues, F/O Babington Smith enjoyed a celebrity status within the WAAF and the intelligence community alike. The granddaughter of a Viceroy of India, the 9th Earl of Elgin, she led her small team with a patrician authority that completely belied her modest rank. Her striking good looks and fondness for strong perfumes no doubt added to a formidable reputation; but this rested first and foremost on her deep knowledge of military aircraft, acquired as an aviation journalist before the war, and her uncanny skill at her job. It entailed extracting highly prized information from photographs of the ground taken from a height of five miles or more. She soon extracted Whittle from the visiting Staff College party, too, and the pair of them spent a memorable few hours poring over prints together. Whittle was fascinated to see how Babington Smith deployed a Leitz magnifying glass – 'the last pre-war German magnifier in London' as she would happily confide to visiting officers – and a clever device called a stereoscope. This 'absurdly uncomplicated little gadget' allowed two prints of the same photograph to be examined through a pair of lenses, one for each eye, so that the brain automatically fused the separate images into one and vested flat photographs with an illusion of depth and perspective.[9]

What especially intrigued Whittle were the pictures Babington Smith was able to show him of German airfields clearly sporting double lines across their grass runways. She felt sure these were scorch marks connected in some way with the existence of German jet aircraft but was puzzled over what was causing them. Whittle had no hesitation guessing the explanation. They were looking at the trails left by aircraft with a jet engine on each wing, but without the tricycle undercarriage that he and Carter had incorporated into the Gloster designs for the E.28/39, lifting its tail plane into the air. It seemed the German jets were 'tail-sitters', having only a conventional wheel under their tailplane. As they accelerated for take-off, the blast from their jet engines was hitting the ground instead of venting backwards horizontally. If this suggested the Germans had fallen short in one crucial respect – and it was an oversight they were soon to correct – the sheer profusion of scorch tracks at half a dozen airfields suggested they were making rapid progress in most other ways. Babington Smith showed Whittle the images she had received in April 1942 of the twin-engined jet planes on the ground at Heinkel's Marienehe airfield, along with other photographs in which she thought she could discern a smaller aeroplane with a single jet engine. By the time he left her for the journey back to Bulstrode Park, Whittle was desperate to discover what further details on the German jets might have been accumulated by the intelligence branch.

He did not have long to wait. Only three days later, on 19 July 1943, the Air Ministry circulated a secret twenty-one-page paper entitled 'Report on German Jet-Propelled Aircraft'.[10] Its contents – which Whittle saw, as a member of Lockspeiser's committee – gathered together summaries of all the intelligence reports dating back to May 1940. Based on PRU work, espionage and the inter- rogation of prisoners of war, these provided grim details on a staggering range of aircraft. In addition to the He 280 ('A few aircraft of this type may be reported in operation within the next few months...') and other two-seater and three-seater monoplanes from Heinkel, the paper described the new jets known to be under development at Messerschmitt, producer of the ubiquitous Me 109 fighter, including the Me 262 and another known within that company as 'Schwalbe' ('Swallow'). (As would only later become clear, these were actually one and the same – and it was the air- craft accounting for the scorch marks pored over by Whittle with Babington Smith.) Other items included a reference to jet engines under development by BMW, and a mention of the supersonic plane with the frightening performance estimates that Whittle had encountered in April. ('Athodyde Propelled Aircraft... It should be able to fly from Berlin to New York in about three hours.')

Even allowing for boastful exaggeration and muddle-headed hearsay, there was easily enough material here to warrant taking a far more urgent approach to Britain's jet-development plans. One of the closing paragraphs in this July 1943 paper referred to a lecture given at Caen in northern France during April by the youngest and most celebrated of the Luftwaffe's commanders, General Major Adolf Galland. According to a prisoner of war who had been in the audience, 'General Galland... told fighter pilots that a Heinkel jet-propelled fighter, manoeuvrable and with a speed well in excess of 500 mph would be in mass production in 1944'. The days of Allied air supremacy, he had reportedly promised them, would soon be over. (Galland had been exhilarated by his first flight in a prototype Messerschmitt 262 early in 1943, exclaiming afterwards – as would become famous after the war – that he had felt 'as though angels were pushing him through the air'.)

According to the official historian of Britain's wartime weaponry, this July paper 'caused some alarm to the Cabinet'.[11] Its impact was soon felt across a wider circle of ministers, alerting them to the likelihood that – as Whittle had been arguing since 1938 – technology existed that could soon allow aerial warfare to make a radical break with its past.[12] But another paper, also dated 19 July 1943 by sheer chance, seems to have made at least as forceful an impression on MAP's Chief Executive, Wilfrid Freeman. It arrived at the Ministry from Derby, as a briefing memo for a forthcoming meeting, under a covering note from the man whose views always mattered so much to Freeman.

The stark message from Hives was twofold. First, since January 1943 Rolls-Royce had come to see the jet project as a matter of the greatest possible urgency. After 'intensive work' on it for six months, 'we are more than ever convinced that we cannot afford to lose a minute in producing satisfactory operational machines. We must anticipate that the enemy at any time might attack us with machines of this type... One can imagine the squeals and commotion which will be raised if the enemy are first in the field with this type of machine.'[13]And second, Rolls-Royce had begun to despair of MAP's handling of the project. Whittle had anguished over this for seven years; but seven months were enough for Hives. He was scornful of the Ministry's performance. Its officials had too often displayed 'lack of interest or faith' in the gas turbine's future. A Rolls-Royce man had just returned from a tour of GE's plant in the US and his report had been sobering: 'it stands out as a certainty that the Americans will also leave us standing.' The Americans had set their best engineers to work on both the engine and the airframe for a jet machine. MAP had to follow suit. 'We do not deserve and we cannot expect to compete with this,' warned Hives, 'unless we give [the Gloster Meteor] some priority.' This required immediate cutbacks on other existing commitments. 'By priority we do not mean just "lip-service". It may mean a sacrifice of 50 Merlins a week, or their equivalent.'

Probably no one else in England at this point, outside Downing Street, could have urged MAP to mandate a lower output of Merlin engines, the lifeblood of the RAF's war machine. Hundreds a week were being shipped out of Rolls-Royce factories in Derby and Crewe, and the demand for them was insatiable. Indeed, the general view was that the latest Merlin (and Griffon) engines – boosted by the introduction of new, higher octane fuels – were so impressive, as George Bulman suggested in a letter to Hives about this time, as to have '[affected] the yardstick against which must be measured the potential value of Jet propelled aircraft from a performance standpoint...'[14] Bulman questioned the wisdom of any recommendations to the Air Staff 'to forego output of reciprocating engine aircraft, to leave more capacity for the Jet types'. Hives thought otherwise, and Freeman was duly astonished. 'At a time when Rolls-Royce are tumbling down [sic] on their programmes,' he replied, with some exaggeration, 'you propose that we should make an additional sacrifice and give up the certainty of Merlins for the uncertainty of the Squirt engines.'[15] Freeman was not a man inclined to use exclamation marks, but his tone here implied two or three might have been appropriate.

Nonetheless, trusting in Hives' judgement, Freeman proposed immediate steps to meet his demands. The outcome was a raft of changes that effectively complemented the switch from Rover to Rolls-Royce made at the start of the year. MAP's supervisory role was to be restructured – in a fashion that acknowledged, in effect, how egregiously the Ministry had misjudged the needs of the jet project since Bulman's first intervention in the early months of 1940. He and Ross would now lose what vestigial influence they had retained over the jet-aircraft initiative since Rover's exit. All responsibility for it would pass to a new 'Special Projects' directorate led by the man who had made such a success of the GTCC as a coordinating body, Dr Harold Roxbee Cox. He was promoted as Director and given his own team of civil servants who would work independently of the Engines directorate. So the jet's progress was at last to be directed by an individual steeped in the mysteries of aerodynamics – the subject of Roxbee Cox's doctorate at Imperial College in the 1920s – and genuinely passionate about the jet engine's future. (After the war was over, he would speak on many platforms as an authority on its origins and development, with an obvious authority second only to Whittle's.) Meanwhile fresh instructions went out to the two companies most directly responsible for the pacing of the jet project. Gloster was directed to slow the production of other aircraft if necessary, in order to focus on the Meteor; and Rolls-Royce itself was asked to plan for jet-engine production at one of its main plants in addition to the modest site at Barnoldswick. Freeman, the champion of both the wooden plane and the plane with no propeller, had acted decisively again – and the prospects for the jet had been transformed.

Just in time, as it transpired, to anticipate Churchill's instant reaction to the July 1943 intelligence paper. It was almost exactly two years since the Prime Minister's 'Action This Day' note to Moore-Brabazon in July 1941, when he had suggested the production of 'say 1,000 Whittles', and three months since he had seen the 'Whittle' in flight at Hatfield aerodrome. In the last few days of the month Churchill insisted on intervening more directly: 'By directive of the Prime Minister... an order for 120 Meteors was given.'[16] By an unhappy coincidence, the second prototype of the E.28/39 that he had watched in March was lost on 30 July, crippled at high altitude by an aileron failure unconnected with the engine. (The test pilot parachuted to safety.) It seems unlikely that Churchill can have been alerted to the accident, but just possibly he did hear of it. On the 31st, he fired off an angry minute to MAP, challenging any lingering pessimists to set aside their doubts about the jet's prospects: 'we cannot afford to be left behind.'[17]

ii

The reorganisation at MAP coincided with Whittle's last few weeks at Staff College. It was not immediately apparent, but his involvement with the continuing evolution of the jet engine was now approaching a pivotal moment. Decisions over his personal situation had hung in the air since the start of the year. In effect, he faced two alternative futures. Writing well after the war, Lance Whyte saw the choice Whittle made between them as the precursor to 'a Greek tragedy in the modern world' that would play out horribly for him over the next eight months.[18] How far he was genuinely free to make a choice of his own may be doubted; but the two ways ahead certainly led in different directions – as Whittle himself documented, in scarcely compatible notes written within the space of just a few days in August 1943.

In promoting him during his Staff College course to the rank of Acting Group Captain, the RAF had made clear that he would not necessarily be returning to Power Jets. MAP's restructuring opened up the possibility that some appropriate new role might be created for him within the Ministry. With Freeman's blessing, Roxbee Cox drove to the Staff College on 17 July to offer him a formal appointment as one of two future Deputy Directors within the new Special Projects directorate. (The other was to be George Watt.) Whittle rejected out of hand the idea of working inside Thames House – Roxbee Cox, he thought, 'seemed rather shaken' – but the notion of leaving Power Jets for some broader role plainly appealed to him and the two men met again six days later in London to talk through some of the practicalities.[19] Over the next three weeks, it seemed to be understood that Whittle would indeed be moving into a MAP-related job. When Roxbee Cox and Watt travelled up to Brownsover Hall on 14 August, for their usual monthly visit to Power Jets, this new job was given 'much discussion'. Whittle had just returned home from his course a few days earlier and had worked it all out in his mind. With his usual attention to detail, he presented Roxbee Cox with a sheet of foolscap paper itemising no less than a dozen specific responsibilities that he envisaged falling to him. It amounted to a full-blown bid to take over the general supervision of 'the design and manufacture of new types of jet propelled aircraft'.[20]

Under his suggested terms of reference – poor Roxbee Cox was this time 'rather startled at the sweeping nature of these' – Whittle proposed that he should run a special projects unit of his own. It would be based at Brownsover with 'a considerable staff to be under the control of FW', comprising draughtsmen, design engineers and experimental engineers. Its purview would cover every aspect of the new aircraft, including airframes and engine production as well as the design and development of new gas turbines. He himself would liaise closely in all matters with Roxbee Cox, without being a 'Deputy Director' but perhaps taking the title of 'Chief Engineer, Special Projects'. He would continue to have ready access to the best of the engineers at Power Jets and his roving brief would also embrace work undertaken for the Supersonic Committee. (He was already thinking about ways of adapting his latest and most powerful engine, the W.2/700, to the demands of a supersonic plane.)

An appointment even approximately along these lines would have meant Whittle leaving behind any responsibility for Power Jets as a business. This would have marked a tacit acceptance of Hooker's advice eight months earlier that he should give up 'trying to compete'. If supported by Hives and Freeman, the outcome might conceivably have been a powerful advisory body to assist MAP and its contractors, led by an individual seen by all as the fount of technical knowledge in the new field of jet propulsion. But it was obviously a plan calling for some turbo-charged optimism. Roxbee Cox, nervous of MAP's reaction, warned that winning over the Ministry might need them to proceed step by step, 'by tactful methods as time went on'. This drew a characteristically feisty response from Whittle: 'I said that I did not like piece-meal methods and would very much prefer to fight for a major change now.'

Yet at precisely this same moment, Whittle was also staking out the rationale for Power Jets to have its role significantly enhanced – in ways that would make no sense at all without his own direct involvement in the business. This was the alternative course before him. Immediately after his return to Rugby, he had been informed by MAP that Stafford Cripps wanted to pay Whetstone a visit. Whittle promptly penned a background briefing for the Minister. After chronicling the company's relocation from Lutterworth since 1942, he pointedly observed that Power Jets was 'in a transition stage from being a small organisation with practically no system to a medium-sized concern'.[21] Key to its future success would be its ability not only to design and develop new engines but also to produce them in modest quantities. Here, once again, was a plea for Power Jets to be allowed to expand its operations in the grey area between development and full line production. For MAP to withhold production contracts from Whetstone, suggested Whittle, would pose a 'fundamental difficulty'. If supplied with the right machine tools, on the other hand, Whetstone could engage in 'batch manufacturing' which would allow its engineering team to identify and resolve any teething troubles in production before handing over the complete package of a new engine to a mainstream manufacturer (with all the skills of, say, Rolls-Royce – though Whittle left this unsaid).

As if to confirm his own personal commitment to an expansion strategy for Power Jets, Whittle followed up this briefing for Cripps by complaining in a note to Roxbee Cox dated 19 August 1943 about the way in which MAP had opted to back an engine from Rolls-Royce (the RB.37) in preference to the next engine under development at Whetstone (the W.2/700). This was Whittle wearing his old hat as the impassioned advocate of Power Jets' interests ('more attention must be paid in the future to the unfortunate effects on the morale of the Power Jets employees…').[22] He even suggested that the company's rivalry with Rolls-Royce put him in mind of its protracted quarrels with Rover in the past. In truth, this memo amply attested to the fact that – as Roxbee Cox had always suspected – Whittle's real sympathies still lay with the company he had refused to abandon in January. If he had been ready in July to contemplate a reassignment by the RAF, Whittle had begun to doubt by the middle of August that he would really be able to walk away from Power Jets. His ties to the team of engineers recruited since 1940 were too strong; his faith in them to help him deliver work of exceptional quality still endured. Herein lay the essence of the tragedy about to unfold. Power Jets had grown too big for Whittle to feel comfortable abandoning it. Yet it was far too small to have any realistic chance, now, of growing into a business fit to compete with Rolls-Royce or any of half a dozen other leading names in the aero-engine business. All of them fiercely commercial rivals.

Whatever the future of his own career, Whittle still clung to his belief in the importance of two structural developments for the future of the jet engine: a wholesale nationalisation of all the key organisations involved with it, and a steady expansion of the operations run by Power Jets at Whetstone. Over the next several weeks, Cripps stymied both developments – and in the process backed Whittle into identifying his personal position more closely than ever with Power Jets. A series of critical decisions by Cripps began with a visit that he made to Whetstone on 21 August 1943. It was not a success. He arrived with his wife on a Saturday afternoon, accompanied by Freeman, Roxbee Cox and half a dozen Ministry officials. The welcoming party assembled by Whittle included Sir Maurice Bonham Carter, representing O. T. Falk and the private shareholders, as well as Williams, Tinling, Johnson and the ever-present George Lees. After a tour of the plant, Cripps gave a short speech extolling the company's achievements. As Whittle had pre-arranged, they then went to see the first, and so far only, completed W.2/700 engine, followed by a running of one of the four fully developed W.2/500 engines. As the home team and the visitors emerged from one of the workshops on their way to the test house, they were confronted by a group of workmen carrying placards calling on Cripps to sack the entire management. The local branch of the Amalgamated Engineering Union had organised the protest to cause the executives maximum embarrassment, and the visitors found themselves surrounded. The AEU's chief shop steward, a man named Hunter, presented Cripps with a list of the management's shortcomings and announced that a union meeting would be convened that evening to discuss the speech that the Minister had given. Only then were the visitors allowed to continue making their way to the test house. After a brief demonstration of the W.2/500, Cripps and his party hastily departed.

Whittle was mortified. Writing to Roxbee Cox a few days later, he blamed the 'very painful' episode on 'a few agitators [who] have played upon some of the poor quality labour we have been getting and have ruined the spirit of the place'.[23] He had penned a fierce speech about 'the wreckers' which he had planned to make on the shop floor two days after the visit. Williams and Tinling had persuaded him to shelve it. 'They felt that the risk was too great and that there might be serious implications if I failed to carry the men with me.' Perhaps Williams and Tinling had a more realistic grasp of the breadth of support for the union. There were signs everywhere that the rapid expansion of the company's workforce, and the difficulty of finding good men locally round Whetstone, had dispelled much of the *esprit de corps* so palpable at Lutterworth. As Whittle explained in a letter to Cripps some time later, 'the employees [earlier in the war] were a small team of enthusiasts. They have since become diluted by a large number of individuals whose interest is limited to their pay packets.'[24] What this implied was an urgent need of more orthodox industrial disciplines. Whetstone seemed woefully short of them. Cripps, who as a young man had briefly been in charge of an armaments factory during the First World War, was quick to grasp this. He wrote a courteous letter of thanks to Tinling for his visit, but sent a more critical note to Whittle: 'I was not happy about the production side and am sending down someone to look into this. I think you need a stronger Works Management than you have got.'[25]

Cripps was just in the throes of weighing up the nationalisation proposal espoused by Whittle – among others – since the spring. A lively debate over the idea had been under way for months within MAP. Whittle had not shown much interest in the political complications, though. A takeover of the entire jet-engine endeavour by the state, he had assured Cripps in June 1943, 'should present no problem'.[26] Taking stock of recent progress and of what he had learned at Whetstone, Cripps was coming to a different conclusion.

After well over two years of disharmony and misunderstandings from late 1940 to the end of 1942, the whole project had moved up a few gears. Gloster had delivered the first batch of F.9/40 Meteor aeroplanes, and at long last flight tests of jet engines were beginning in earnest. De Havilland was flying Frank Halford's Goblin from a base near Newmarket, close to the famous racecourse, which was judged more secure than Cranwell. (Whittle, more anxious than most about German spies, insisted no flights should happen on race days when foreign agents with binoculars might pass as punters.[27]) Rolls-Royce had flown its first RB.23 flight engine in a Meteor at its Hucknall airfield on 12 June 1943 – less than six months since taking over the Barnoldswick plant from Rover's engineers (who in almost three years had produced no flight engine at all). The Hucknall Meteor needed only a little more power, reported its test pilot, 'to make it a very excellent fighter indeed'. Hooker and his colleagues were now intent on a busy test schedule into the autumn, while at the same time continuing the development of their own RB.37 (Derwent) engine. And at Metropolitan-Vickers, the F.2 engine designed with an axial-flow compressor by its Chief Designer, David Smith, assisted by Hayne Constant's team at the RAE, was almost ready for its maiden flight. (It was to happen in the middle of November.) Surveying all this impressive activity, Cripps saw no business rationale whatever for a wholesale nationalisation. Nor did such a course look remotely feasible from a political perspective. Nationalisation, after all, would represent a massive lost opportunity for engine makers as yet confined to the old world of piston-driven power plants, and just waking to the future potential of the jet.

A state purchase of Power Jets alone, on the other hand, looked an entirely different matter. This would require little more than a technical change of ownership, insofar as the company had long been totally dependent on funding by the state. Nationalisation would at last iron out the anomaly, so irritating to many in Whitehall, of direct public funding for a private company. Undoubtedly of far more importance to Cripps, though, was the opportunity of turning Power Jets into a national body supportive of the emerging jet-engine industry. 'Apart from considerations of finance and equity,' as Cynthia Keppel's draft history put it, 'there was an increasing need for a single central research establishment on a strictly non-competitive basis whose services would be available to all firms alike.'[28] This strategic aspect greatly appealed to Cripps, who in due course would turn to creating a state-owned network of research facilities. Perhaps Roxbee Cox had talked to him about Whittle's proposal for a special projects unit based at Brownsover Hall. By one account, Cripps 'sought advice on the best structure and role for a jet engine research centre from Harry Ricardo', who had set up a privately funded research centre for the advancement of piston-engine technology after the First World War.[29] Ricardo's consultancy company was still thriving. Cripps conceived of a similar if rather grander affair for gas-turbine engines. In setting it up at Whetstone, he would also be offering Power Jets a way out of its present difficulties – and averting some political embarrassment over a possible misuse of the substantial state assets at its disposal.

A subsequent enquiry into these difficulties, conducted at Cripps' behest by MAP's Chief Production Adviser, a Mr Eric Mensforth, confirmed that a more robust management structure was urgently needed. With more than nine hundred employees at the latest count, the company's lack of organisational rigour – almost a defining feature of the Cherry Orchard environment at Lutterworth – had begun to lose its charm. The new premises were incomparably larger than the Ladywood Works, covering 80,000 square feet with no less than ten large workshops and an extensive administrative block. Whittle himself had suggested in April that 'a drastic reorganisation of the executive staff' might be needed, but no significant changes had been made.[30] Now the company was looking seriously undermanaged as work pressed ahead on development of the W.2/700. Williams and Tinling remained the joint managing directors, heading Secretarial and Works departments respectively.

'Daddy' Lees had administrative responsibility for all design and development projects. Pat Johnson handled legal and patent issues, while also handling relations with the Gas Turbine Collaboration Committee. None of these individuals had any experience whatever of running a large business, as, of course, Lance Whyte had pointed out to Whittle in July 1941. They were always well-intentioned and utterly devoted to Whittle – but it was not enough. Other senior executives, usually from the motor industry, had put in occasional appearances but most had soon drifted away without making any lasting impression. As one of Whittle's own senior engineers, Reg Voysey, would confess towards the end of the war, the management of Power Jets was simply not up to the job:

> [It] should have been obvious that engineering technicalities were the least of the problems because of the enormous start enjoyed... [but] the firm was never balanced; the manufacturing facilities were grossly inadequate at all stages of the firm's existence. Attempts to correct this consisted of entrusting power to incompetents and rogues, revealing a lack of character-judgment which would have disgraced a shop foreman.[31]

(It is striking that Whittle chose to quote from this document at some length in *Jet*. Although he was 'not in entire agreement' with all its views, he wrote, 'there was not much I would have wished to have toned down'.[32])

Mensforth and one of MAP's regional controllers made at least two visits as part of their investigation. Whittle hosted the first, and devoted some hours to answering questions from the two Ministry men. When they revisited the site on 8 September 1943, though, Whittle was absent. Williams and Johnson took charge, hosting a convivial lunch at which everyone's spirits were lifted by news on the wireless that Italy had just surrendered to the Allies. At the end of the visit, Williams walked out of the factory with Mensforth. What happened next, Williams recorded in a note about the day:

> On his way to his car, Mr Mensforth said that he could not understand why the position of FW had been allowed to go on.

He said that he was very highly strung and should be living a
cloistered life. He asked why he was still in the RAF and I told
him that the Service had been his father and mother for close on
20 years and he felt he owed it a debt.[33]

Almost as revealing as Mensforth's observation is the fact
that Williams, six days later, circulated this note to the rest of the
team at Power Jets, Whittle included.

Whittle heard nothing more from Cripps for several weeks
after the Whetstone visit, nor did he have much contact with
anyone from Rolls-Royce. (Hives was out of the country, spending much of September 1943 on a trip to America.) This might
have been more frustrating had he not been diverted by something infinitely more interesting to him than the politics of
nationalisation: the first stirrings of supersonic flight. When
he learned at a meeting of Lockspeiser's committee that MAP
was preparing to draw up a proposal for a supersonic research
aircraft, Whittle was absolutely delighted. He plunged into making preliminary designs of an aircraft that he thought might be
powered by an upgraded version of his W.2/700 engine. Here
was a challenge that seemed a natural extension of all his work
since 1936. Indeed, it was almost as though someone at MAP
had just read his Cranwell thesis of 1928 and, fifteen years too
late, decided to act on it: in the second week of October 1943,
the Ministry issued an aircraft specification with key targets that
might have struck some inside Thames House as risible, were it
not for the intelligence on the advances being made by German
engineers. The aircraft envisaged in Specification E.24/43 was to
be a monoplane. It had to have a maximum speed of 1,000 mph,
and be capable of cruising at 700 mph at 40,000 feet.[34]

The concept – for an aircraft to be completed within nine
months – was discussed on 9 October 1943 with Phillips and
Powis Aircraft, one of the smallest firms in the industry. Its
Chief Designer was F. G. Miles – the same intrepid Fred Miles
who had lunched at the Savoy with Whittle and Whyte to talk
about building a jet plane, less than twelve months after the

first ignition in 1937. In fact Miles and his brother George had recently taken over Phillips and Powis, which at this point was just changing its name to Miles Aircraft Ltd. The Miles design team wasted no time contacting Whittle to seek his views. By the time they visited Brownsover Hall for a first proper conversation on 17 October, Whittle had almost finished his technical paper setting down his own initial ideas on the layout of a supersonic plane.[35] These were so radical as to dismay the team's Chief Aerodynamicist, Dennis Bancroft ('We were silently horrified...').[36] Whittle had also made a preliminary drawing of the engine he was proposing for the plane, which would be based on the W.2/700 while adding an 'aft fan' as an extension of the turbine blades, designed to boost the thrust. Another feature of this modified W.2/700 would allow fuel to be injected into a flow of air bypassing the core engine. Igniting this flow and mixing it with the exhaust from the aft fan would provide an 'afterburn', or 're-heat', that would add significantly to the engine's power. It was yet another of Whittle's innovations that would one day become a standard feature of modern jet engines – and Fred Miles incorporated it immediately into his proposal for MAP. The contract, for a plane to be christened the 'M.52', would be awarded on 13 December 1943.

Despite this more than welcome distraction, though, Whittle was feeling increasingly unsettled about his future. No formal acknowledgement had been made of Power Jets' role since the July reorganisation within MAP. At the start of October 1943, the Ministry circulated an organisation diagram for the Directorate of Special Projects. It showed both the Royal Aircraft Establishment and the National Physics Laboratory in little boxes of their own, as offshoots of Roxbee Cox's department. The chart made no reference whatever to Whittle, Power Jets or Whetstone. On a visit to Thames House on 8 October 1943, he had a long conversation with Jack Linnell's successor as Controller of Research and Development, Air Vice Marshal Ralph Sorley. He complained to Sorley that his personal position 'was very nebulous... [and] expressed strong dissatisfaction with the organisation for jet propulsion aircraft in general'.[37] He had sent Sorley a private paper in August outlining his ideas about how a nationalised industry might be organised, which the Air Vice Marshal thought was broadly sensible but 'would take time to bring about'. Whittle stopped short of telling the CRD about his meeting with Miles Aircraft. He did mention, though, that he was thinking again about air strategy in the Far East – and the fact that 'if we were to attack the Japanese other than by the slow process of island hopping we needed long range bombers...' (Having once predicted the attack on Pearl Harbor, Whittle was starting to worry obsessively about the course of the Pacific War. US forces had succeeded in driving the Japanese out of several island strongholds since the start of 1943, but had encountered such ferocious resistance in recent months across the Solomon Islands that fighting them all the way back to Tokyo was now a grim prospect.) Then he assured Sorley that his latest calculations at Brownsover Hall suggested that a suitably designed aircraft could indeed fly at 1,000 mph at 40,000 feet. The Air Vice Marshal, noticed Whittle, 'was very considerably shaken by this'. It was a refrain running through many of Whittle's daily notes, these days, that his spoken remarks had left someone or other badly shaken.

Whittle left Thames House that day feeling uneasy. He still had no idea of Cripps' intentions. He had been shown a memorandum from Cripps to the War Cabinet of 29 September, suggesting 'it may well be that, during 1944 and 1945, the enemy will be in a position to put into service, in limited numbers, both fighters and bombers of higher performance than those which we will then have available'.[38] Roxbee Cox told Whittle that Churchill had reacted quite sharply to this, noting the firm evidence of German jets and stressing that everything possible had to be done to speed up Britain's jet project. Cripps had assured the Prime Minister 'everything was being done' but Roxbee Cox privately thought otherwise: 'He... was afraid that one of these days there would be a rumpus because things were not going fast enough and he would get kicked.'[39] Once back at Brownsover, Whittle returned to his supersonic calculations and probably prayed for the rumpus to come soon and decisively enough to push Sorley and Cripps into action.

A fortnight later, he at last received a summons from MAP to meet the Minister in London for a policy discussion. At Thames House on 25 October 1943, Cripps told Whittle of his decision on nationalisation. Or at least, he disclosed one half of it – telling Whittle that he had decided to press ahead with a state takeover of Power Jets. He failed to mention the other half, namely that he had firmly ruled out nationalising the rest of the industry. Whittle reacted enthusiastically to the Power Jets proposal, agreeing with Cripps that tedious matters like the purchase price could be left for another day. There was a clash of views on the composition of a future Board. Most of their conversation, though, dwelt on the implications for the existing company and the changes that might flow from state ownership. Cripps wanted to talk about Williams and Tinling, for instance: they 'would have to go as they were not big enough for the job'. To his credit, Whittle leapt immediately to their defence. It was true, he conceded, that they often made a poor impression on officials. Their courage and per- sistence, though, had been indispensable to Power Jets from the start and 'it would break their hearts if they were thrown out at this stage'. Cripps relented, and the interview seemed to close on an amicable note.

Whittle immediately went to see the Director of Special Projects in his office along the corridor. It was soon apparent to a dismayed Roxbee Cox that Whittle had hopelessly misunderstood Cripps' intentions. Whittle talked of nationalisation as the key that could now unlock a brave new future for the whole jet sector. Why, said Whittle, it might even make sense to let Power Jets take over con- trol of Barnoldswick from Rolls-Royce immediately, even while beginning to plan its own line production of W.2B/RB.23 engines at Whetstone.[40] If Roxbee Cox nodded vaguely through all this in the hope that Whittle might come to a more sober appraisal of his position later, he was to be disappointed. Whittle returned to Rugby that evening. Two days later, a long letter arrived for Cripps from Brownsover Hall.

This extraordinary, not to say poignant, missive dated 26 October 1943 first confirmed that the whole team at Power Jets was agreed in principle on the decision to accept a government offer for the company. Then it set out Whittle's carefully crafted views on how MAP and Power Jets ought to proceed. He laid out his thoughts with a strident clarity implying, in every line of four closely-typed pages, that at last he felt free of all those misconceived MAP constraints of the past ('the Ministry's policy on jet propulsion… was wrong from the beginning'). He addressed Cripps as a confidant and ally, to whom he owed some forthright truths.

The most urgent of these related to the Board for a nationalised Power Jets of the future. Cripps had mooted the idea of appointing prominent individuals from other aero-engineering firms, who would serve the company while retaining their executive positions elsewhere. Whittle was vehemently opposed to this – a measure he thought would virtually amount to handing over the business to the entrenched aircraft industry. He laid bare yet again his abiding distrust of the corporate bosses, born of political conviction but amply nurtured by his resentment at their disdain for the jet over so many years. Far from watching over Power Jets' future interests, 'they might conspire together to "smother the child"'. And this would obviously negate the ambitious nationalisation plans that he and Cripps had discussed together at Thames House – plans that would soon draw in the rest of the industry alongside Power Jets. Cripps deserved some of the blame for this misconstruction of his plans, but Whittle's wildly optimistic expectations were probably also a fair measure of his detachment from reality by now. His usual health problems were becoming acute again, with painful skin ailments betraying his stressed state of mind. Within days he was back in the doctors' hands. He was given a bed at the RAF Hospital in Uxbridge, where Roxbee Cox visited him on 6 November. Whittle pressed the idea that, once discharged, he might be appointed official controller at Whetstone for six months 'to shake the place up a bit', but he made a note of Roxbee Cox's reaction. 'He did not receive this suggestion with enthusiasm.'[41]

The doctors insisted that Whittle needed a proper rest and did their best, with Mary Phillips' help, to cut their patient off from the world for most of the next few weeks. Thinking that he and Cripps were in broad agreement on their objectives, and anyway reluctant to be involved in the legal and commercial terms of any deal, Whittle resigned himself to letting Williams and Tinling handle initial discussions with the Ministry. Meanwhile, he heard nothing from Roxbee Cox, or anyone else, to suggest that he and Cripps were in pursuit of divergent agendas. He was told of several meetings that MAP and Treasury officials attended at Brownsover Hall in November, but nothing further was said about the broader thrust of MAP's policy.

This diplomatic silence kept the peace until Whittle's return home from hospital. Once he was back at his desk, it lasted less than two days. He pressed Roxbee Cox for more details on the Ministry's thinking about next steps – and the strictly limited scope of the Cripps nationalisation plan was almost immediately apparent.

Whittle was distraught. He had trusted Cripps and had inferred from their detailed conversations together that they shared the same agenda. It was now clear to him, with a brutal suddenness, that all his hopes had been misplaced. He was shattered to think he had been naïve in looking forward to the emergence of a state-owned jet-engine industry. (The abrupt end to this dream left him permanently disillusioned with the socialist philosophy that he had seen as a bond between himself and Cripps.) He had resigned himself to the reality that, under any kind of nationalisation scheme, Power Jets was going to lose its independence. The arrangements apparently envisaged by Cripps, though, scuppered any hope of seeing the company evolving as a significant part of a state industry. In particular, it would be turning its back on all thoughts of 'batch manufacturing' and pilot engines. The Minister seemed to confirm as much in a letter to Sir Maurice Bonham Carter late in November, setting out his 'research-centre' rationale: 'we urgently need the plant for general experimental purposes'.[42] The state's takeover of Whetstone, in other words, would mark the end of Power Jets as a unique operation aspiring to develop a new technology through every stage from design to initial production.

It would also involve, as quickly became clear, the acquisition of Power Jets with or without the consent of its founders. Whittle could not believe that Freeman and Sorley were prepared to acquiesce in what seemed to him an obvious travesty. After Roxbee Cox confirmed that they were indeed uncomfortable with Cripps' approach, Whittle pleaded for a concerted stand to be taken on his behalf. On 2 December, Roxbee Cox called him back and reported that Cripps had rejected their protests. Worse, Cripps had insisted that he was only intent, after all, on a policy that Whittle had espoused himself. This disingenuous half-truth was almost too much for Whittle. Deeply upset, he made an unusually emotional appeal to Roxbee Cox for his support. Roxbee Cox was alarmed and suggested he come down to London immediately and put his objections to Cripps in person. Whittle replied that he 'was feeling very, very run down and far from being able to cope with an interview with the Minister'. He rang off, but then called Roxbee Cox again moments later to say 'the whole of the development and efforts of the E.28/39s to date was being belittled...'

> I said the effect of the whole business was to undermine the [socialist] convictions of a lifetime and that I felt so indignant about it that in my present frame of mind I felt like resigning my commission and going overseas... It was intolerable when the Government started behaving like the worst of City sharks.[43]

Whittle knew that he was close to the edge of another breakdown. 'Overseas' could only have meant America. Perhaps he thought another long break in Boston or Los Angeles would let him put the stressful politics of the jet project behind him. If a period of relative anonymity was any part of this fantasy, though, he was about to be abruptly disillusioned. General Hap Arnold and his USAAF staff in Washington had other plans.

iii

Wing Commander Felkin and his colleagues in the AI 2(g) section of Britain's Air Intelligence had acquired a new and highly prized source over the autumn of 1943. Contact had been made between British agents in Germany and an aeronautical engineer 'who for six years ending September 1943 held a high position connected with the RLM in Berlin [i.e. the *Reichsluftfahrtministerium*, Hitler's Air Ministry]'. A secret five-page paper, Report No. 472, compiled by Felkin and circulated in November emphasised that this man was no mere pen-pusher:

> He had daily contact with the leading personalities of both the Luftwaffe and the German Aircraft Industry, and was therefore in a position to be well-informed on current trends of thought and development in the whole field of aeronautical research.[44]

The information he had already provided, apparently in a series of debriefings through October 1943, was of commensurate importance, especially in relation to German engineers' research into jet propulsion and high-speed flight. His disclosures finally swept away any lingering hopes in London that earlier reports of jet planes for the Luftwaffe might have been wildly exaggerated.

At least two gas-turbine engines had in fact been developed, one by a Heinkel subsidiary, Hirth Motoren, and the other by the engine section of the giant Junkers aviation group. The latter, classified as the 'Jumo 004', had an axial-flow compressor and several ingenious design features to cope with cooling problems. Professor Willy Messerschmitt had chosen the Jumo 004 for his Me 262 aircraft. Test flights of the resulting prototypes had so impressed Luftwaffe officers early in the summer ('the aircraft had a flight endurance of one hour, and had touched a speed of 880 kph [547 mph] at optimum height') that the hitherto favoured He 280 had been sidelined. Felkin's informant claimed that he had been personally assured by Willy Messerschmitt that the Me 262 was ready for series production and the RLM had asked him 'how long it would take him to erect factories to produce

1,500 of these aircraft monthly'. That would mean three thousand engines *a month* – ten times the total number of RB.23 Wellands so far ordered from Rolls-Royce by MAP for future production. The only consolation to be drawn from the October debriefings was that a top-level conference, organised by the RLM in June 1943, had apparently ordered a temporary halt to Me 262 production plans, for reasons that were not entirely clear. In every other respect, this latest report on jets in Hitler's Germany could hardly have been more alarming. It could surely not be long before Allied pilots encountered enemy planes flying at hitherto unheard-of speeds.

The AI 2(g)'s usual circulation list included at least one senior officer in US Air Intelligence. So by early December 1943, the implications of Report No. 472 were being weighed at command level on both sides of the Atlantic – and bore directly on a tussle, currently under way, between the British and the Americans over how to handle a first disclosure of the jet's invention to the general public. The Allies were at odds over this, in ways that presaged later and more potent rivalries over the jet engine.

In the wake of Whittle's visit in the summer of 1942, the Americans had duly encountered all the teething troubles to which their British guest had alerted them. His proposed joint venture across the Atlantic, though, had made no headway. By the start of 1943, perhaps taking note of the failed gamble in Britain to rush a jet engine from drawing board to production in 1941–2, Washington had quietly abandoned the idea of a wartime fighter in favour of less urgent plans to encourage commercial production of jet engines in the post-war world. Then the alarming intelligence from Germany about Heinkel's He 280, made available in March 1943, had prompted second thoughts. US engineers had begun visiting England on technical missions and made several excursions from London to Whetstone (where Whittle noted on one occasion how 'the visitors were evidently agreed that it was a great pity that there should not be much closer liaison…').[45] In the space of just six months, a second US aircraft had been commissioned, designed and built for a jet engine – the Lockheed XP-80, later known as the Shooting Star – and by November 1943 it was ready to begin test flights at Muroc Army Air Field with an H.1 Goblin engine shipped from de Havilland. With the test programme for the Bell P-59 ('Airacomet') also expanding steadily at Muroc, a new Fighter Group was set up there devoted to experimental jets.[46]

This posed an obvious problem for the officers on General Arnold's staff in Washington, who had always wrapped the US jet programme in layers of secrecy that bemused British visitors. (Not least the hapless de Havilland engineer who accompanied the H.1 Goblin from England to the West Coast. He ended up in a prison cell in Hollywood for a night: he had no US identity papers and FBI agents checking his story with Lockheed's head office found no one there who knew anything about the XP-80.) The possibility of maverick and ill-informed press coverage about propeller-less planes flying over the Californian desert caused the USAAF so much concern that they decided eventually to pre-empt any leak by unveiling the jet engine to the general public with a formal press release. Word of this reached Wilfrid Freeman at MAP in the middle of November 1943. Freeman took great exception to it, as he explained to his successor at the Air Ministry, Air Vice Marshal Douglas Evill. British engineers had invented radar before the war, Freeman reminded him, only for the Americans to lay claim to it as their own work in ways that had caused much resentment. He feared an encore over the jet engine:

> ... unilateral publicity from [the] USA would undoubtedly give the impression that since the Americans were the first to broadcast the facts, they had been first in the field of development. This, of course, is absolutely untrue, and it would be most unfair to our industry to allow the idea to gain currency.[47]

The British Air Commission in Washington was asked to do everything possible to prevent 'premature publicity', while the Air Ministry pressed Hap Arnold into agreeing that any future public announcement would have to be both prepared and released jointly.

Felkin's intelligence on the advanced state of the Me 262, landing on desks late in November, put this notion to the test. The stark possibility loomed that Allied servicemen in Europe might encounter any day now a jet plane with a swastika on its tail. This might prompt unauthorised press stories far more damaging than any leak based on civilian sightings of a strange plane over the Mojave Desert. Hap Arnold insisted an announcement about the Anglo-American jet programme would have to be made without delay. The Air Ministry accepted this, albeit reluctantly, but stuck to its insistence on a joint approach. Arnold promptly telegraphed over his draft text for the release – and it triggered an entirely predictable contest over the wording. The proposed amendments that flew back and forth across the Atlantic in the days just before and after Christmas 1943 were in effect the opening shots in a delicate battle for ownership of the jet in the public's imagination.

Both governments could see that the alignment of honours for inventing and developing this new technology might have important ramifications. More than pride was at stake. The popular perception of the jet's origins seemed bound to weigh heavily on any post-war legal arguments over claims to the jet's commercial value. It was immediately clear that the Americans were seeking to present the jet engine as a brilliant design coup by the British, the practical application of which had been rather woefully neglected. (This, of course, was not so wide of the mark.) Its future now lay with America's leading aerospace giants, who had already put two jet aircraft into the sky in short order. The RAF men in Washington were desperate to see this version of the story countered from London with amendments presenting the jet engine as, unmistakeably, a triumph of British science and engineering. In their view, there was one obvious way of ensuring this outcome, which could hardly be contested by the Americans: Whittle's personal role in conceiving and creating the first engine had to figure in the text as prominently as possible. Wilfrid Freeman assured the Ministry that he had no objection to acknowledging Whittle's importance in this way and successive drafts from London were tailored accordingly.

Whittle, meanwhile, knew nothing of these exchanges. It was not until 30 December 1943 that he even heard of the plan to break with the long-standing ban on publicity of any kind. Roxbee Cox telephoned him with the news. The decision, he told Whittle, had been taken by Cripps and Sir Charles Portal, the Chief of the Air Staff, in agreement with General Arnold and President Roosevelt. 'My name was to be mentioned,' noted Whittle, adding that Roxbee Cox seemed 'very disturbed about the degree to which the American part was played up...'[48] Visiting Thames House on 3 January to see Cripps on other business, Whittle was asked by Roxbee Cox to approve a biographical note that was to be appended to the Anglo-American statement. This surely ought to have alerted him to what was coming, but Whittle was a complete innocent in such matters and apparently gave the statement no more thought. No one at MAP made any attempt to show him the final text, prior to its release. On the appointed day, Thursday 6 January, Roxbee Cox only talked to him by phone about the idea of his taking a long holiday. The release went out that evening, 'issued today by the War department, Washington' and embargoed for London publication until 11 p.m.[49] At his home in Rugby, Whittle answered a ring on the bell to find a journalist at the front door from the *Daily Herald*. She handed him a copy of the statement, which he read through for the first time – 'I nearly went through the roof' – an hour before hearing it aloud on the BBC's midnight bulletin.[50]

The national papers carried the news next morning without much elaboration. They had been given little time and no technical information on which to build. Jet-propelled fighter aircraft, in the words of the official release, had passed their experimental tests. 'Originally to British design, the improved jet propulsion engines eliminate propellers on the new aircraft.' After 'several hundred [*sic*] successful flights... at high altitudes and extreme speed', plans had been approved for production of 'this new type of aircraft'. The release offered abundant clues, on the other hand, to a human drama in the background that it was thought might appeal to many newspaper editors. Work had begun on the jet engine as long ago as 1933. One man had apparently been behind its success, working out of a 'special factory in England'. The 'greatest credit' for the first flight of the jet was due to him for 'his genius and energy'. A long Editors' Note on Group Captain Whittle retailed all the colourful details of his RAF career, from his days as an apprentice making 'a number of remarkable model aircraft' to his fame for 'one of the most thrilling exhibitions of crazy flying' in 1930 and his roll of honours at Cambridge. A second note was provided, with generous details on the career of Gerry Sayer – but the test pilot was dead, alas, which left Frank Whittle and his family as the sole focus of press enquiries on the Friday. The papers made the most of his story, as the headlines on the Saturday morning suggested:

> Jet Fighters Built in Disused Workshop – Inventor's Wife
>   Kept A Secret 14 Years (*Daily Express*)
>
> Jet-Planes – Men Who Saved Whittle From Despair
>   (*News Chronicle*)
>
> RAF Friends Behind Jet Plane Ace: 40 Minutes Made Air
>   History – and Only 10 Men Saw It Happen (*Daily Mail*)

Through the weekend, the lane leading to Broomfield was clogged with cars. The house was besieged by strangers. Lurid press coverage of the background to the jet engine lasted for days.[51] Whittle was totally unprepared for the furore and badly unnerved. He sent his apologies to the Supersonic Committee for not attending a scheduled meeting on 11 January. Roxbee Cox told the chairman that Whittle had had another breakdown, though this proved to be an exaggeration. He managed to give a short speech that same day to the workforce at Whetstone – he felt acute embarrassment over being given so much credit personally for the jet and grabbed the opportunity to acknowledge, publicly, how much he owed to those around him – and he struggled on for days at Brownsover Hall with a torrent of correspondence. (Characteristically, he thought at first that it was his duty to reply to every letter, however eccentric.) Coming just a few weeks after his

November spell in hospital, though, this fresh crisis undoubtedly threatened to trigger a serious collapse. As he himself admitted to Cripps: 'My health has suffered severely through overwork, frustration, and worry on this project and though I believe the effects to be temporary, there is a possibility that they may be more permanent…'[52]

Whittle looked back on the whole episode as 'a shattering experience'.[53] He himself blamed this largely on the sheer suddenness with which he was forced to exchange years of secret endeavour for an unwelcome celebrity. Perhaps just as telling, though, was the cruel contrast between the adulation being heaped on him in public and the acrimony swirling round him in the background. Behind the scenes, the proposed nationalisation of Power Jets was being adamantly opposed by Whittle and all his closest colleagues.

iv

Though Stafford Cripps took a robust approach to the purchase of Power Jets, it was never his intention to oust Whittle from the project. He and Wilfrid Freeman were agreed early in 1944 that it would be highly desirable to retain Whittle in a leading role at Whetstone. This would encourage the younger engineers around him to stay on, and would boost the calibre of the research centre that Cripps had in mind. So no steps were taken to deprive Whittle of his base at Brownsover Hall, nor were any reductions made to the budget being planned for the Whetstone operation's 1944–5 year. Substantial extra resources were actually promised in some areas, including additional funding for the testing of finished engines, and of course the company's capital structure would now be transformed. Whittle had assumed in November that nationalisation would kill off any chance of being able to manufacture pilot engines. As the takeover negotiations progressed, though, this whole subject went completely unmentioned. (In fact, nationalisation was going to leave Power Jets far more leeway to pursue its ambitions than Whittle thought likely at the time of the takeover.)

Unfortunately, more immediate issues like the price to be paid for Power Jets prompted such rancour over the early months of 1944 that Whittle's own future seemed in doubt. It would look for a while as though his leadership of Power Jets was over.

Reaching a generally acceptable valuation of the company was always going to be a tense affair. The Treasury thought it already belonged to the state, in effect. Dudley Williams thought its shareholders owned the world rights to all future production of the jet engine. The previous June, in early exchanges about the nationalisation idea, Whittle had sent Cripps his own estimate of Power Jets' true value, with a bottom line of £810,000, to include £100,000 for the state's 'moral obligation' to the company.[54] He had suggested that, say, £500,000 might represent a bargain for the Treasury and a price acceptable to the shareholders. This was a negotiation in which MAP held all the cards, however, and Cripps played them ruthlessly. His officials with Treasury advice offered Power Jets' shareholders £100,000. If this was turned down, warned Cripps, the state would simply appropriate all of Power Jets' physical plant – which taxpayers had anyway paid for – and the company would be put into 'cold storage' with paper assets that might eventually be worth nothing at all. After several weeks of tortuous correspondence, the government finally agreed in March 1944 to a price of £135,563. An additional £38,000 was paid to nullify, in effect, any future value claimed for the residual paper assets.[55] The total of £173,563 was certainly a material sum – but a less than extravagant outlay, seen in the context of government spending on the aircraft industry since the start of the pre-war rearmament. (The most authoritative account suggests its expansion 'was achieved by investing more than £350 million in factories and plant for new production between April 1936 and March 1944...'[56])

Leaving aside the clash of views over how much to pay Power Jets' shareholders, three other aspects of this takeover caused Whittle great distress in the immediate aftermath of his traumatic encounter with the press. In the first place, he was tormented by his own financial position. Of the ninety-eight 'A' shares in Power

Jets, he had been assigned fifty-six in 1936 but had agreed (as an officer of the Crown) to hold twenty-four of these on behalf of the Air Ministry's Secretary of State. This left him with thirty-two shares – and in October 1940 he had offered to hand these over to MAP by way of signalling that he personally had no commercial stake in the jet engine: he was motivated solely by the national interest and his sense of duty, as a serving RAF officer. He refused even to transfer his shares to other members of the family, which he thought would be contrary to the spirit of his decision. He resolved over Christmas 1943 to stand by this conspicuously honourable gesture, despite the way he felt he had been ambushed by Cripps over his nationalisation proposal, but it caused him much anguish – not least in persuading Dorothy it was the right thing to do. 'My wife opposed it strongly at first, thinking mainly of the education of the children and being somewhat sceptical about the gratitude of the state,' he told Cripps in January.[57] Over the following weeks, it began to look as though Dorothy had been right.

He was surrendering a stake worth not far short of £50,000 (around £2½ million today).[58] This drew admiring letters from several of his Whitehall correspondents; but when someone suggested a consoling *ex gratia* payment might be appropriate, all sorts of obstacles arose. Whittle remarked to Treasury officials at one meeting that 'when generals and admirals had won important battles the State had made grants of special pensions etc' – but this seemed not to cut much ice.[59] He was warned that a Royal Commission after the First World War had looked into the question of special payments for officers of the Crown who had been engaged 'for the very purpose of research and discovery'. It had been decided that no payments could be made, as a rule. Exemptions might be available, in principle, for cases of 'exceptional brilliance and utility'. In practice, the last war had thrown up not one single case judged to be eligible. Whittle, terrier-like as usual, refused to give up. He had no false modesty about the significance of his achievement. As he explained to the Treasury official in charge of the numbers: 'my aim is to obtain recognition... of the effect [of the jet project] on British prestige, the probable favourable effect on Britain's commercial position generally etc'.[60] Eventually, on 15 March, the Treasury agreed to an *ex gratia* payment of £7,000. (It was subsequently increased to £10,000 – £½ million today – though the cheque did not arrive until a full fourteen months later, in April 1945.)

The award might have been more gratifying to Whittle had the RAF complemented it with some generous adjustments to his rank and pay grade. In the event, the prospects for his career were left more uncertain than ever. This was the second of his grievances. Many of Whittle's civilian contemporaries thought he deserved a special kind of promotion within the service. His engine, after all, was about to entail the creation of an entirely new fighting force for the RAF; and he had been accustomed for four years to dealing regularly with the most important individuals behind the air war – men like Freeman, Tedder and Hives. Instead, the Air Ministry made it clear that if he chose to continue working at Power Jets he might find the door closed to any future promotion at all. It was 'against the policy of the service' for senior officers to be 'overspecialised'. To be eligible for a higher rank than Group Captain, he would have to resume a normal service career by leaving behind his work on the jet project. Freeman, trying to be helpful, suggested he might possibly seek an administrative post in the Technical Branch, so that he could at least apply some of his engineering knowledge.[61] This only perturbed Whittle even more, since he thought the RAF's relative neglect of its Technical Branch spoke volumes about the service's general undervaluation of engineers (too many of the top brass treated them as 'something in the nature of "camp followers"... mainly concerned with maintenance and repair'[62]). There was just one other option open to him: he could resign his commission and become a civilian engineer. Unfortunately, despite joining the service at the age of sixteen, he had not yet completed enough years as a commissioned officer to be eligible for an RAF pension. And now that Power Jets was to be a state-owned company, Whittle was none too sure of his prospects in the commercial world either.

Dudley Williams and Coll Tinling shared his misgivings on this score – which, for them, was a cause of considerable bitterness. Here was the third hugely distressing aspect of the nationalisation episode for Whittle. It soured his relations with the two men who had fired up the jet project in the first place and been by his side for almost nine years. Since the first flight of the E.28/39 in May 1941, they had been looking forward to making their fortunes out of the jet once the war was over. Their belief in Whittle had brought them to the brink of riches neither could have imagined in 1935, sitting in the kitchen at Trumpington with their brilliant young RAF friend. Now the wretched fellow, with his socialism and his endless quarrels with MAP, seemed to have thrown it all away. Nationalisation had never been part of their plans. They (and their wives) hugely resented the fact that Whittle had triggered the whole business with his foolish letter to Cripps of 29 April 1943. The pair had not emerged penniless. Each of them collected almost £33,000 from the Treasury (£1.65 million in today's money). This bonanza, though, hardly compared with the wealth they thought they might have amassed, had Whittle only agreed to quit the RAF before the war. They might now have been looking forward to building a post-war commercial empire – or so Williams supposed – with engine sales all over the world. Of course the man with 'the June temperament' was hopelessly deluded in dreaming of global franchises to be shared with the likes of General Electric, but the grievance he nursed against Cripps was real enough. (Many years later Williams went into politics, hoping for a chance to revenge himself on Cripps in some way. 'Unfortunately he died,' as he confessed to an interviewer, 'and had himself cremated, so I couldn't even piss on his grave.'[63])

The tension between the three of them flared up at the beginning of March 1944 over a relatively trivial issue, which was proxy for the wider breach. Hearing of Whittle's *ex gratia* payment, Tinling suggested in an unguarded moment that he and Williams were entitled to claim a proportion of it under the terms of their original deal struck at Cambridge. Whittle was taken aback. He challenged them to produce a copy of the agreement, thinking it to have been lost long ago. A fraught meeting followed in his Brownsover Hall study. Williams turned up brandishing the document and read out the clause noting their joint entitlement to any awards arising from the jet project. After a moment of silence, he and Tinling evidently realised that Whittle was becoming overwrought. Williams closed the argument with a theatrical flourish: 'RDW threw his copy of the agreement dated 31 May 1935 (which bore my signature) into the fire.'[64]

The nationalisation saga was by this point having a baleful effect on Whittle. He was struggling with the most serious flare-up yet of his troubles with eczema and the recurrent skin infection known as furunculosis that had first been diagnosed in December 1941. The blotched and disfigured skin round his ears and a rash across his forehead were making public occasions even more of an ordeal than they had already become in the wake of the January publicity. ('I was in no mood to be sociable with strangers.'[65]) But some invitations were impossible to decline – and one in particular marked a move up the social ladder that was immensely gratifying for the former Boy Apprentice from Leamington Spa. So on the afternoon of 1 March 1944 Group Captain and Mrs Whittle duly attended a tea party at Buckingham Palace.

Soon after they arrived, and had passed along the reception line to reach the tables laden with cakes and sandwiches and lined by footmen, a Brigadier General sought them out to say that Whittle would be wanted later to talk to the King. In the meantime, the suddenly world-renowned inventor was much in demand among the other guests – they included Arthur Tedder, now immersed with General Eisenhower's staff at their headquarters in St James's Square on the planning for D-Day – and he was summoned over to talk to the two royal princesses, too. They told Whittle they were 'very thrilled by the news' of the jet engine. ('The only outstanding point I remember is that I asked Princess Elizabeth not to ask me to explain how the thing worked.'[66]) When he and Dorothy were finally shepherded over to meet the King, Whittle was impressed to find His Majesty genuinely curious about many aspects of jet propulsion. They talked at some length, and it was apparent that King George had been well briefed – on the details, if not the concept – by Wilfrid Freeman. He wanted to know about the Meteor's fuel consumption, for example, and the advantages of the jet engine's relative simplicity from a manufacturer's perspective. So when he turned to the jet's likely post-war potential, Whittle thought the King ought to hear the truth of it:

> He asked if it would be any use for Civil Aviation, to which I replied that though I was not the one who should be saying so, it was the beginning of a complete revolution in aircraft design. He seemed quite surprised to hear this.[67]

Dorothy probably attracted more public attention that afternoon than she had received over the past several years put together. She had accompanied Whittle on very few important occasions since his graduation ceremony at Cambridge in 1936 and there is no record that she had ever once visited the Ladywood Works, or indeed Brownsover Hall. The King offered her a comforting bromide – 'He turned to my wife and asked if she had helped. She replied that she was afraid she had not and he said, "Of course you have" – but Queen Elizabeth was quite exercised to hear that Dorothy had never yet seen a jet plane.' Whittle said he had tried and failed to fix this several times. Then he asked the Queen if she might be able to arrange it. 'She said instantly that she would see what she could do, and seemed to mean it.' She also showed some concern for Whittle when he apologised for having a croaky voice. He explained that 'something had gone wrong with my voice that day – probably nerves'. The Queen tried to put him at ease ('She then said, "You're not nervous now are you?" I replied that I was not') and she closed their conversation by telling him how much the royal family admired what he had done. 'They all thought it was a most remarkable achievement' – as Whittle proudly recorded later, in a typically detailed note that stretched to thirteen numbered paragraphs.

Before he and Dorothy returned to Rugby that evening, Whittle

called at Thames House to see Wilfrid Freeman again. Though
burdened with the immense pressure of his responsibilities for
MAP's war effort, Freeman always tried to make time for him.
His respect for Whittle's judgement on technical engineering
matters was unbounded. As the wisest and most sensitive of
men, Freeman was also sympathetic to the personal difficulties
that he knew Whittle was facing. He was not surprised to find
Whittle in his office now, anxiously seeking reassurance about
his career. Whittle was struggling to come to terms with the Air
Ministry's insistence in February that his continued focus on jet
engines would render him too 'overspecialised' for promotion.
Freeman gently teased him that he 'could not expect to be an
Air Chief Marshal attached to Power Jets'. Whittle, though,
was there to speak in deadly earnest of a truth that he feared
neither Freeman nor the Air Ministry had yet begun to grasp.
The day was coming soon when he, Whittle, would be one of
very few officers in the RAF fully conversant with the engines
on which the entire service would depend. 'In my opinion, I was
in the act of revolutionizing the technical side and all the other
technical officers were in danger of being then looked upon as
overspecialised.'

There was one other point that Whittle wanted to make that
evening, too. He had heard that his decision to gift almost £50,000
to the state was being misconstrued by some Whitehall officials,
incredulous at his sense of honour:

> I said that I could not afford to have it held that I had foolishly and
> unnecessarily handed over what I need not have done, because it
> was more than possible that my action might be used against me
> as evidence of slight mental instability. He smiled, and putting
> his hand on my shoulder as he left the room remarked that they
> would never do that.[68]

It was a poignant gesture, but Freeman's trust in his Whitehall
peers was not wholly warranted. Whittle's state of mind was a
topic of constant speculation by March 1944, and it seems more
than probable that word of this had reached Brownsover Hall.

Whittle was now extremely frail. By the middle of the month, another period in hospital was starting to look inevitable. It happened that the RAF's principal military hospital, Princess Mary's at RAF Halton in Buckinghamshire, had recently become one of the first in Britain to begin prescribing a new wonder drug. Taken to the US by British scientists in 1941 – another wartime bequest to the Americans of a British breakthrough, not unlike the jet engine – penicillin was being mass-produced by the American pharmaceutical industry. Whittle's doctors suggested that it might be the answer to his skin afflictions. Arrangements were made with RAF Halton – where the fifteen-year-old Frank had failed his medical to join the service in January 1923 – and he was admitted to Princess Mary's Hospital on 20 March 1944. He was to remain in one hospital or another for almost all of the next six months.

11

Messerschmitts and Meteors

March 1944 to May 1948

i

Dear Old Man,

... I hope you are keeping your pecker up and not overworking the old brain. Whatever the Medicos say, they are not just treating a rash but the results of overwork, so for God's sake try and get something out of the enforced rest.

Yours, Coll[1]

The ever-solicitous Coll Tinling need not have worried about the doctors taking Whittle's condition too lightly: from the day he went into Princess Mary's Hospital, Whittle received constant attention from some of the best doctors in the RAF. He was given intensive nursing care for a condition diagnosed as severe eczema with a host of related complications, from otitis and dermatitis to fibrosis and furunculosis. In the affectionate note that he dashed off shortly after Whittle's March admission, though, Tinling was exactly right. It was less the rash than the overwork, and the accompanying stress and frustration, that lay at the heart of Whittle's troubles. After six weeks of treatment – including generous doses of penicillin in creams and sprays – the 'rash' was retreating but Whittle's deeper woes were increasingly apparent.

'He has sustained considerable anxiety over the past few years,' noted a senior consultant early in May 1944, 'and he has many symptoms not connected with his eczema...'. (No reference was made to the patient's long-standing addiction to Benzedrine.) Judged to be less in need of acute care by then, Whittle was transferred by air ambulance to an RAF Officers' Hospital in Blackpool called Cleveley's, where he spent another six weeks. His physical symptoms seemed to be in remission, but he now fell into a severe depression. The staff at Cleveley's struggled with him and Whittle was sent back to Halton on 11 June. The resident psychiatrist offered a bleak opinion:

> ... since March 1944 he has exhibited irritability, tension, insomnia, and during his continuous hospitalisation has been an exacting and difficult patient. Exceptional consideration has not helped. This neurosis has not improved... For several months he has been in disharmony with his circumstances... [and] I think this case should be investigated by the Consultant in Neuropsychiatry. Meanwhile the patient wishes to continue treatment in this hospital. If so [sic], he requires encouragement to dress and obtain fresh air (so far at every opportunity he retires to bed).[2]

An RAF Medical Board ruling a week later tacitly acknowledged the likely source of his problems: Whittle's distressing symptoms in the first months of 1944 had 'coincided with a period of severe mental stress in connection with his research work on gas turbines'.

Whatever the details of the diagnosis, he was in a bad way. His distress over the treatment of Power Jets since the summer of 1943, compounding all his woes over the mishandling of his project through 1940–42, had brought him to another breakdown. His condition caused the doctors at Princess Mary's serious concern over the following weeks: for several days of July he was kept under constant observation, and allowed no visitors. Even Mary Phillips was asked to stay away. She had been given accommodation at the hospital, as at Cleveley's previously – ostensibly so that she could continue to help him with his paperwork, though

it seems plain that her companionship was of rather more importance. Dorothy made occasional visits, but they evidently gave the
patient little comfort. (Bizarrely, Whittle around this time took
to referring to Dorothy in his diary entries as 'the wife' or even
'Mrs Whittle'.) Though he made light of the whole episode in *Jet*,
Whittle did record there that it was late July 1944 before he was
'allowed out occasionally' and not until 29 August was he finally
discharged from Halton. A second Medical Board a fortnight
later decided there was 'no need for further psychiatric overhaul
at present'. Whittle insisted he was feeling fit enough to return to
active duty and assured its members he could 'suit his work to his
physical condition'.

He had recently received at least one cheering piece of news.
Four months earlier, he had written to MAP's Air Vice Marshal
Sorley with an impassioned plea for promotion. (It was not without
some pathos: after all that he had done for the RAF, Whittle was
reduced to explaining that a higher rank would help him mediate
between Power Jets and its suppliers: 'commercial gentlemen…
are apt to think they can wipe their feet on Group Captains'[3]).
Sympathetic to his case, Sorley had run into a flurry of minutes
inside MAP about correct procedure and the impossibility of
changing Whittle's rank.[4] He had eventually decided that Whittle
simply had to be assured of a decent RAF pension, giving him
at least the option of early retirement from the service, so had
insisted on his elevation to Acting Air Commodore at the end
of August. Despite this fillip, though, Whittle returned home to
Rugby feeling very uncertain of his future. Still suffering from a
mild depression, he set about taking stock of the latest momentous developments in the war, and of the implications for the
operations at Whetstone. He had listened obsessively to the BBC's
news bulletins from day to day, so knew the broad thrust of events.
(On the afternoon of D-Day itself, 6 June, he had walked along a
stormy seafront at Blackpool marvelling at the news earlier in the
day of successful landings on the Normandy beachheads despite
high winds all over the weather map.) But he craved more news
of the air war and some detailed briefing, above all, on how far

jet aircraft were yet making an impact – flying for either side. The news on this front came as quite a surprise. Despite all the chilling reports in the second half of 1943 about the imminent deployment of jet planes by the Luftwaffe, none had yet been encountered in the air.

Or at least, none until just a month or so before Whittle began making his enquiries. It turned out that a single German jet had been met in action for the first time on 26 July. One of the RAF's fastest planes, a Mosquito, had been hit with cannon fire from a two-engined jet while on a photo reconnaissance mission over Munich. According to the RAF pilot, who managed to land his damaged plane safely in northern Italy, his attacker had flown at least 100 mph faster than the Mosquito. The incident was mentioned in official papers that were despatched to the chairman of the Supersonic Committee, Ben Lockspeiser, on 4 September 1944 as homework for its next meeting. The papers were shared by him with Whittle, and included Air Ministry Intelligence summaries confirming that the German plane had been a Messerschmitt Me 262. (Only later would it emerge that this had in fact been a prototype aircraft on trials: the Me 262 was yet to come into full production.)

Remarkably, a covering letter with the intelligence summaries sent to Lockspeiser suggested that they were probably not worth circulating more widely and had merely been added 'in case you wish to draw attention to them'.[5] This first reported clash with the Messerschmitt Me 262 was apparently not considered an event of any great moment. Officials within MAP and the Air Ministry had received extensive intelligence briefings since mid-1943 on the jet engines and airframes built by the Germans. War artists had been commissioned to draw impressions of the Luftwaffe's jet planes, which would later prove remarkably accurate (*Figs 22* and *23*). The Luftwaffe's failure yet to deploy them properly, however, had stripped these reports of their earlier menace. Defence sources were happy to release vague details to the press: *The Times* carried a less than alarming first reference to the topic early in August. ('Interesting German aircraft developments are beginning to

Fig. 22. Air Ministry artist's impression of the Luftwaffe's
Arado Ar 234 jet bomber

Fig. 23. Air Ministry artist's impression of the
Messerschmitt Me 262 jet fighter

make their appearance in Germany and France. One is... a fighter driven by rocket-propulsion... It has not yet ventured to attack.'[6]) It seemed fair to suppose that the Germans had run into unexpected difficulties since the summer of 1943 – technical glitches in launching Junkers' Jumo 004 engine into production, perhaps, or problems encountered by the Luftwaffe in flight tests. In fact, this engine had indeed proved to be extremely hard to manufacture, and even harder to fly. The design of its axial compressor, built at the German works equivalent of the RAE, had for some reason departed from the theoretical principles laid down by Griffith in 1926. The result was lethal: any rapid acceleration would induce surging and a total loss of thrust. The protracted trials of the Me 262 had failed to mitigate the Jumo 004's fatal flaw: dozens of young, inexperienced German pilots had been killed trying to cope with it. Arguments between Hitler and his airmen over whether to use the Me 262 as a fighter or a bomber had almost certainly caused additional delays to its launch.

Whatever the true explanation for the late arrival of the Luftwaffe jets, MAP and the RAF had not pursued the launch of the Gloster Meteor with anything like the urgency that seemed to be implied by setting up Roxbee Cox as head of a Special Projects directorate in July 1943. Prototypes of the Meteor went on being tested all through the second half of 1943, with de Havilland's Goblin and Rolls-Royce's Welland engines. The first 'production' version of the Meteor, though, had not flown until January 1944 – and this plane with its Welland engines had been immediately presented to the US government, to honour (at least in spirit) a long-standing promise to the Americans that they would have a jet plane off a British production line by the end of 1943. So it was not until April 1944 that the first Meteors were delivered to the RAF. This pre-dated the introduction of the first Me 262s into active service, but nonetheless marked less than a triumph of timing. Back in the summer of 1941, it had been envisaged that jet fighters would be in service with the RAF by the summer of 1942 at the very latest. By July 1944 only seven had been cleared for deployment, with 616 Squadron stationed in Kent. They were given no combat role in the fighting across Normandy, unleashed a month earlier.

Stanley Hooker and two Rolls-Royce colleagues visited Brownsover Hall early in October 1944, for the first time since Whittle's return from hospital. They shared their assessment as engine designers. 'We were all agreed', as Whittle noted with RAF-style understatement, 'that the British aircraft industry was a bit slow in the uptake about the gas turbine situation.'[7] He heard that Hives had for months been expressing frustration over MAP's half-hearted coordination of the Meteor programme. It was a serious worry for Rolls-Royce, which had equipped not just Barnoldswick but also another factory twice its size at Newcastle-under-Lyme in the West Midlands for the production of jet engines. One year after commencing production of the Welland – more than 150 of them had been built so far – the Derby firm was tooling up to launch the production of its new RB.37 engine, the Derwent (*Fig. 24*). This was the unit that built on the compressor and turbine designs fashioned by Whittle for the Welland, but also incorporated the 'straight-through' combustion chamber adopted by Rover for its B.26. Combining Whittle's aerodynamic components with the greater convenience of the straight-through chamber,

Fig. 24. Rolls-Royce's Derwent engine, run in October 1944

over the reverse-flow original, had turned out to offer the best of both parent engines.

And Rolls-Royce had other calculations to make. Germany's jet-engine rivalry was far from being its sole concern – or indeed its main yardstick of progress on the jet. Hooker had been one of nine engineers – they also included A. A. Griffith – who had spent May 1944 in the United States on a 'Special Projects Mission' led by the RAE's Hayne Constant. He now gave Whittle a copy of the report authored by Constant after their return. It more than endorsed the views aired at Brownsover Hall about MAP's slow progress. In a 'Summary of General Impressions', Constant had sounded a forthright warning about the threat posed by the American aircraft industry's enthusiasm 'in marked contrast to the comparative apathy shown in this country'. With the kind of snooty British disdain that so infuriated many US service chiefs, Constant offered faint praise for American achievements to date ('the offspring of bald-headed enthusiasm rather than scientific calculation'); but he drew attention to an 'American capacity for learning from their mistakes [which] makes it dangerous for us to delay much longer to put [sic] our house in order'. He was especially struck by the immense scale of General Electric's commitment to the jet engine. Constant spelt out the implication for policy-makers at MAP and the Air Ministry, supplying in the process a list of the flaws he discerned in their current approach:

> Unless we can either bring greater resources into the field of gas turbine research and development, or can so organise our existing resources that our effort is not dissipated or frittered away by duplication of effort, by working along unfruitful lines, by lack of vision or by vacillations in policy, this country is likely to be left behind and beaten by the efforts of this single American Company.[8]

Here yet again was the message as so often before: the bungling had to stop. Whatever the risk of being overtaken by the various jet projects supposedly coming to fruition in Hitler's doomed Reich, Constant was clear that the real threat to Britain's post-war leadership of this new sector of aeronautics came from the other side of the Atlantic.

One explanation for the 'comparative apathy' bemoaned in Constant's report was entirely understandable: with no Luftwaffe jets to be countered, jet aircraft had been far from a strategic priority for the RAF in 1944 to date. The jet engine had very high fuel consumption at low altitude. Jet fighters on low-level operations would therefore have limited range and be restricted to defence of the home front. At high altitude, jet-powered interceptors would offer much better range and, of course, superior speeds. Neither of these operational roles, though, had been a priority for the Allied air forces in preparing for the invasion of north-western Europe and the campaigns that were to follow. With air supremacy all but complete in the skies over France, the Allies needed aircraft capable of long endurance at low altitude – fighter bombers that would be able to wreak havoc with air-to-ground attacks on German tanks and French railways. Even supposing the Meteor had been fully available, its jet engines would have enjoyed no advantage in this context over state-of-the-art piston engines like the latest version of the Merlin (the twin-supercharged Merlin 66), Rolls-Royce's Griffon or Napier's Sabre IV. In the event, these engines were powering proven aircraft like the P51 Mustang and the Hawker Typhoon. The Meteor was to be assembled at Gloster Aircraft, but so too was the Typhoon. The construction of Meteor airframes was effectively shelved early in 1944 to free up capacity for making as many Typhoons (and later Tempests) as possible in the months remaining before the launch of Operation Overlord.

A second explanation for the loss of momentum behind the jet, though, was less than strategic. The practical consequences of nationalising Power Jets were proving problematic. In line with Cripps' quest to turn it into a national research establishment, MAP's accountants had transferred all the firm's assets and activities at Whetstone into another entity called Power Jets (Research & Development). Cripps had then ordained a merger between this redefined R&D venture and the operations of the RAE at Farnborough and a second Hampshire base nearby at

Pyestock. He had tried at the start of 1944 to meet Whittle's objections to nationalisation by promising that the resulting combination, while being state-owned, could nonetheless be entirely autonomous and independent of the rest of the aircraft industry. Whittle had wondered at the outset whether it would have any lasting future at all – and Cripps' plans, however well-intentioned, had certainly made a shaky start. The RAE staff under Hayne Constant, reassigned to Power Jets (R&D), found vestiges of the Cherry Orchard culture at the new company completely baffling. They also resented losing the close ties that they had hitherto enjoyed with MAP, and the loss of status that went with a subjugation of their Hampshire activities to the far larger operation at Whetstone. Here was the source of those 'unfruitful lines' and 'vacillations in policy' cited by Constant in his report on the May 1944 mission to the US.

Through the early months of Power Jets (R&D)'s existence, Whittle had still been in hospital. Returning home late in the summer, he was not sure what to make of it. He accepted a provisional title as Technical Adviser in September 1944 but hung back from any meaningful involvement. It was obviously a troubled organisation. He wanted time to decide what role, if any, would be attractive and available to him. By his own account, he came close to severing his links altogether. Only the fear of triggering an exodus from Whetstone of all his old engineering colleagues held him back: 'I did not wish to expose myself to the charge of breaking up the Government company.'[9] Then, week by week, his health steadily improved and he began to re-engage with his old team. They responded enthusiastically to his visits, and were keen to explore with him again the challenge involved in adapting the W.2/700 engine for use in Miles Aircraft's supersonic M.52. He even began work on an entirely new design, to exploit a patent that he had filed in 1936 for a 'turbo-fan' engine: he had in mind a unit with an axial compressor and a huge fan in front of its compressor to draw in air which would by-pass the core engine. It was designated the LR1, standing for Long Range No.1, and he envisaged it going first on a bomber for use in the Pacific war

– and then, once the war was over, on a civilian plane that might cross the Atlantic at 500 mph.

On 11 November 1944 he attended a meeting of the Gas Turbine Collaboration Committee, held at BTH's Rugby plant. Assembled round the table were representatives of the big six engine manufacturers – Rolls-Royce, de Havilland, Metropolitan-Vickers, Bristol Aeroplane, Armstrong Whitworth and D. Napier. Whittle had disparaged their corporate bosses as the wolves at his door early in the war, but he clearly enjoyed being back among his senior engineering peers again – and he received plenty of flattering attention. It was perhaps his first real taste of sincere applause from his peers, which mattered infinitely more to him than all the popular fame that had overwhelmed him at the start of the year. Tedder had remarked to him in February 1940 that the proof of the pudding would be in the eating. Judged by its impact on the Allied war effort, the jet project had obviously fallen short – but the reception given to the Gloster Meteor since the early summer had ruled out any possibility of the jet engine ultimately proving a disappointment. Though given no role in Operation Overlord, the Meteor had shown itself to be a superb aeroplane: within the senior ranks of the RAF just as among the pilots of 616 Squadron, it was already seen by all as the start of a new era. (Word of the Meteor's reputation in the service was spreading fast, too. The newspapers by this time were leaving their readers in no doubt about the impact of the new plane. 'So sensationally successful are Britain's new jet fighters,' as the *News Chronicle* was to declare on 20 November, 'that some of the most famous names in the history of aviation – Spitfire, Hurricane, Tempest – will soon be found only in stories about this war.') Each of the companies at the GTCC meeting made a presentation about their latest progress on the jet projects that they were now pursuing. Even A. A. Griffith had an opportunity to tell the meeting about the latest setback for his CR1 contra-flow engine ('The compressor had undergone more testing and had shown excessive pressure loss in the S-bend simulating the ducting from the low pressure unit…'[10]) When the time came for the Power Jets (R&D) presentation, Hayne Constant handled it, while Whittle took a back seat. But when they all gathered outside the plant for the customary group photographs, it was like a scene from earlier days: a line of men – all dressed in three-piece suits, collar and tie – forming, however unconsciously, a deferential arc around the small capped figure in the RAF uniform at their midst.

Before the meeting ended, Whittle was invited to spend some days at Barnoldswick. Hooker and his team wanted him to help Rolls-Royce prepare for visits to Derby and the Lancashire plant that had been requested by MAP's Sir Wilfrid Freeman and the Chief of the Air Staff, Sir Charles Portal. These were scheduled for the end of November. Whittle was happy to accept, and before setting off for Lancashire he agreed to a meeting with Ernest Hives in Derby. What he heard from Hives made a strong impression on him:

> He said that he was in the process of pointing out to Sir Wilfrid Freeman that we were going to finish this war with an obsolete Air Force unless something was done about it… He asked me to get together with Hooker and others at Barnoldswick with a view to making recommendations as to the types of future power plant which would be required.[11]

The discussions in Barnoldswick over 20–24 November 1944 went well. In fact, they encompassed another exchange of views in the Swan and Royal pub almost as colourful as the famous encounter between Hives and Wilks just before Christmas 1942.

Hooker took Whittle out to lunch with Adrian Lombard, formerly of Rover and the man behind the innovative coupling for the longer turbine shaft that had made the 'straight-through' jet engine into a workable design. With Hives' blessing, Hooker and Lombard confided in Whittle that extraordinary progress had been made since June 1944 on the construction of a huge new jet engine, much larger than the Derwent. Specified as the RB.41 and soon to be named after another British river, the Nene, this unit was going to be capable of delivering a massive 5,000 lbs of thrust. It was a sizeable jump beyond anything contemplated up to this point. Both men were convinced the Nene could be a hugely important engine – which only made it all the more frustrating that MAP had no plans yet for an aircraft capable of accommodating it. The Nene was simply too big for the Meteor. Whittle listened to them anguishing for some moments over this, then asked the two men: 'Why don't you just scale it down?'[12] Slightly nonplussed, they answered a series of questions about the dimensions of the engine. On the back of a paper napkin, Whittle then scribbled down the mathematics to show how virtually the same engine, reduced in scale to fit the dimensions of a Meteor, could produce a thrust of 3,500 lbs. That would compare with 2,000 lbs from the Welland. Hooker and Lombard looked in awe at the numbers. They began work on the smaller Nene days later. It would emerge in 1945 as the 'Derwent V'.

Whittle's insight on this occasion captured the difference between his genius and the brilliance of the best around him. He showed an instant grasp of the mathematical possibilities. Political realities, on the other hand, continued to elude him. Ideally, he might perhaps have seized on this napkin episode as a suitable moment to signal his recognition (at last) that the time had come for Rolls-Royce and others to lead the way. He might have stepped back into an advisory but still influential role, offering Roxbee Cox and MAP some much-needed help with the reshaping of Power Jets (R&D). Instead, he seems to have returned from Clitheroe to Rugby feeling a renewed sense of confidence that the time had come for him to plunge back into development work on his own account. Perhaps, despite all the disappointments of 1944, he could look forward to putting the nationalised Power Jets back at the vanguard of Britain's jet-engine industry?

Attitudes towards the jet engine, after all, were suddenly evolving at a quickened pace that had been conspicuously absent for most of 1944. Hooker confirmed as much at the start of December, in a letter to Whittle giving a lively account of the meetings held with Portal and Freeman. These 'went off very satisfactorily both at Derby and here', Hooker told him.[13] With a sense of urgency that had struck all the Rolls-Royce men, their visitors had pressed them hard over future production plans. Hours of discussion had then been devoted – just as Hives had urged – to the chances of reaching rapid agreement on new jet-engine designs. Portal had at one point suggested going for a jet bomber that could fly at 50–60,000 feet, probably a version of the Avro Lancaster. MAP also wanted to pursue plans for interceptor jet fighters and a high-speed reconnaissance jet to replace the Mosquito. As Hooker wryly noted, this was 'the meat of the discussion for we now get back to Frank Whittle's original specification for a jet-propelled machine'.

It all marked an abrupt change of mood in Whitehall and Whittle felt compelled to act on it. Having battled to prevent the total emasculation of Power Jets on several occasions since 1940, he was not going to let his old Power Jets team be shuffled to the sidelines now, just as the revolution wrought by the jet concept seemed about to come into its own. So it was time, if his health permitted, for him to reassert some leadership over the nationalised organisation at Whetstone. A few days into December he telephoned Roxbee Cox, offering to return to the company 'and take the reins on the engineering side'.[14]

ii

In 1938, Whittle had foreseen a day when a jet fighter might climb from take-off to an altitude of 20,000 feet in less than four minutes, ready to intercept enemy bombers at speeds of around 500 mph. It was clear by November 1944 that this vision had become reality and jet fighters were being deployed in this role with some success – but they were Luftwaffe fighters, pitted against Allied bombers over Germany. Attacks by Messerschmitt Me 262 fighters were still infrequent but had been growing in number and notoriety since early October. Well-informed references to the Me 262 and another German jet, the Me 163, had featured in the British press on several October mornings ('… it is obvious that the Luftwaffe attaches great importance to this new form of propulsion'[15]). So the Luftwaffe's long-rumoured wonder weapon had not proven a mere will o' the wisp after all. It was soon established that the Me 262 had finally gone into full production in October: it had not beaten the Meteor into the sky, but it seemed likely now to appear in far greater numbers. For all those engineers secretly engaged in Britain's jet project since 1940, evidence of the Germans' success was at once galling and horribly compelling. At the GTCC meeting in November, Hayne Constant told its members of a daring commando raid into Germany that had captured a specimen turbine blade used on the Jumo 004 engine. They were hugely intrigued to hear that the Germans had perfected a hollow design, allowing air to circulate inside the blade. The internal air flow offered at least some protection against the intense heat at the turbine. (All modern jet engines employ this concept.) The German engineers had relied on their celebrated pre-war ingenuity to circumvent (in part, at least) the fact that the heat-resistant metals used on Whittle's engines were largely unavailable to the Third Reich in production quantities.

By the middle of December 1944, Constant and his colleagues at Pyestock had been handed a virtually intact Jumo 004 recovered by British ground troops from a Me 262 that had been brought down over Belgium – and the ambition behind the German engine's design, in defiance of severe material shortages and constant Allied bombing raids, left them seriously impressed. With a multi-vaned axial compressor, the Jumo 004 was much more complicated than the units now being manufactured for the Meteor but it was sleeker and seemed more obviously aerodynamic. (With one engine suspended below each wing, the Me 262 had a notably elegant appearance.) The Me 262's combat effectiveness was still being monitored closely by Air Intelligence: pilot reports and analysis of captured data filled many paragraphs of each week's Weekly Intelligence Summary from the Ministry.[16] Those examining the captured engine closely at the RAE were able to confirm that, as long suspected, it had been rushed into active service with some nasty design problems still far from properly resolved. Nonetheless, it had powered the Me 262 into frontline squadrons for the Luftwaffe – the best known of them led by the Luftwaffe's former commander,

General Adolf Galland – and the Power Jets engineers could only wonder at this achievement. Nor was the irony of it lost on them. Many felt bitterly aggrieved over the outcome to this dimension of the Anglo-German 'air race' begun in the 1930s. Reg Voysey probably spoke for many at Whetstone in decrying the way they felt they had been beaten to the finishing tape:

> All around us in this, Allied and other countries, companies are getting down to the practical business of making Jet Propulsion units and turbines. With robust, intelligent attention to pilot production we could have beaten the Me 262 by two years with the W.1A but there was no one to do it and see that there were airframes too.[17]

In Whitehall and the East Midlands alike, it could only be hoped that Hitler's defeat would come soon enough to render such recriminations entirely academic.

American air force generals were less concerned with analysing past delays than with hearing from their RAF counterparts what measures they were intending to take against the German jets. The USAAF's B.17 Flying Fortresses, massed in huge formations on daylight raids over Germany, looked all too vulnerable as targets for the Me 262. When Chief of the Air Staff Sir Charles Portal made a tour of active units stationed in France during November 1944, General Doolittle of the American Eighth Air Force told him how alarmed the bomber crews had been by the new plane. Few B.17s had actually been brought down yet, but the astounding speed of the Messerschmitt jet had already changed combat tactics ('it takes four normal fighters to be sure of destroying a Me 262 if it tries to fight,' Doolittle had explained. 'Of course, if it runs away, they can do nothing…'[18]). Portal's own Air Intelligence section in London had warned him that German jets, if mobilised in sufficient numbers, 'are likely to prove a serious menace both in the tactical and strategical areas'.[19] It was feared that they might even be able to slow down the Allies' land campaign. (As would only become clear much later, in 1943 Hitler had envisaged employing the Me 262 in large numbers as a low-level bomber, capable of devastating any Allied attempt to invade Fortress Europe.) It was thought the Luftwaffe had around a hundred serviceable jets in action by late 1944, but might have 'between three and four hundred first line operational jet fighters and ground attack aircraft by April 1945'. It was no wonder Portal and Freeman had been so keen to visit the Derby and Barnoldswick plants at the end of November, to review Britain's jet-production plans. Days into December, the Air Ministry was being pressed hard by General Hap Arnold from Washington for an assurance that RAF countermeasures were on their way. Where, indeed, was the Gloster Meteor?

The seven Meteors put into active service in July 1944 had won high praise from their RAF crews but they had yet to make any impression on the enemy. The RAF was extremely hesitant about deploying them over the Channel, for fear of losing one in some way that might allow the Germans to salvage an engine. Those flown by 616 Squadron since July had instead reinforced the campaign to intercept V-1 flying bombs. At the outset, Churchill had assumed the speedy Meteor would be at a 'great advantage' in this role and had registered his frustration that a paltry twenty jet aircraft were due for production by the year's end. He had sent Cripps a reminder of his long-standing enthusiasm for the jet on 9 July – 'As you know, I have always taken a great <u>personal</u> interest in this question of jet propulsion ...' – and on hearing of the first encounter with a Me 262 had fired off a second Minute with a dark warning about any failure to stay abreast of the Germans: 'If we are caught behind-hand in jet-propulsion aircraft, it will be a serious reflection on MAP.'[20] This was exactly the situation by November 1944, and the result was a drastic reappraisal of production plans. A much more powerful version of the Meteor, powered by Derwent rather than Welland or Goblin engines, was just going into production. MAP gave directions for the manufacturing capacity to be doubled immediately.

Meanwhile, Portal had changed his mind about using the Meteor overseas. Tactical trials were arranged, pitting Meteors against American Flying Fortresses based in England. The partici- pants were left marvelling at the potential impact of Britain's jet fighter: as an RAF report noted, 'the Meteors could sail in as and when they pleased'.[21] Portal was planning by January 1945 to move 616 Squadron to France 'before the end of this month' – and he favoured 'using our jets with 2nd TAF [Tactical Air Force] as soon as possible' rather than restricting them to interception duties.[22] Portal told Freeman they had no choice but to accept the risk of one of them 'falling into the hands of the Germans'. The new deployment would add again to the urgency of stepping up Meteor production rates. Early in the New Year, Stafford Cripps struck a slightly desperate note in telling the aircraft industry that all jet work was now to have absolute priority: 'we want as many high quality jet aircraft as quickly as possible.'[23] It was tacit recognition that the appearance of the German jets had caused Churchill's Cabinet some embarrassment. Despite all the enthusiasm generated by the May 1941 maiden flight of the E.28/39, the Anglo-American jet project had been overtaken in the skies over Europe by the parallel endeavours of Hitler's aircraft engineers. Towards the end of 1944, a concerted effort was launched by MAP to catch up. Some of the enthusiasm shown for the jet in 1941–2 could be sensed again. In the words of Keppel's draft history, 'the wheel turned full circle, and for the second time the jet propulsion engines and aircraft occupied a predominant position in the plans for the RAF'.[24] The most immediate spur to action was the challenge posed by desperate Luftwaffe commanders.[25] But there was another consideration, too: after Germany's defeat, surely imminent, there would remain the war against Japan.

The sprawling geography of the Pacific theatre put a high premium on carrier-based aircraft able to operate over very long distances. By the end of 1944, MAP was contemplating a range of new jet fighters thought to be candidates for rapid deployment with the Fleet Air Arm, including a jet-propelled version of the Spitfire, already specified as the Supermarine E10/44. The heavy jet bomber flying at very high altitude, as mooted by Portal at Barnoldswick, was conceived as a powerful way of reinforcing the strategic bombing campaign launched over Japan since June 1944 – to rather little effect, so far – by the USAAF's B.29

Superfortresses. Whittle had talked of Pacific air strategies and ocean-hopping jet bombers in 1943, when he began serious work on behalf of Lockspeiser's Supersonic Committee. The notion had at that time struck senior RAF officers – like MAP's Controller of Research and Development, Air Vice Marshal Sorley – as a plaything for slightly eccentric boffins. After a six months' bombardment of south-east England by V-1 flying bombs, the deployment by the Wehrmacht of the V-2 ballistic missile and the Luftwaffe's use of jet-propelled and rocket-propelled aircraft, MAP had been obliged to revise its definition of eccentricity. It had also rediscovered its respect for Whittle himself, an officer known to have had a long-standing interest – since his youthful days as a test pilot, being fired off a ship's deck by catapult – in the strategic use of carrier-borne aircraft.

There was no way that Power Jets (R&D) under Whittle's renewed guidance would be able to augment jet-engine production rates to any significant extent. As the progress already made on the W.2/700 engine showed, however, there was still plenty that the nationalised entity at Whetstone might be able to offer by way of innovative designs. Officials heard from Roxbee Cox, now based at Whetstone himself as chairman of Power Jets (R&D), that Whittle was ready to return to work. On the first day of 1945, Roxbee Cox led a delegation comprising Williams, Tinling and Johnson into Brownsover Hall to propose to Whittle that he should join the company's Board and resume charge of engine development.

To their consternation, Whittle turned them down. Since making his suggestion at the beginning of December 1944 that he should take back control of Whetstone's engineering, he had had second thoughts. As chairman, Roxbee Cox was following the decision taken by Cripps that Power Jets (R&D) had to merge with the RAE. At Whittle's behest, Roxbee Cox had chaired a meeting on 8 December between him and Hayne Constant. The resulting discussion had flushed out immediately the awkward fact that Whittle and Constant harboured clashing views on the proper function of the company: the one envisaged it as a pioneering research *and* engine-development business, the other was already treating it as a quasi-scientific centre for applied research. (Days later, Roxbee Cox had received from Brownsover Hall a typically comprehensive four-pager to explain the difference: 'there is still much confusion of thought due to the different interpretations put on such words as "projects", "research", "development", etc and we were at cross-purposes more than once because of this.'[26]) The delegation on 1 January trooped out of Brownsover Hall without reaching any agreement. Whittle said he was withdrawing his offer to join, in light of what he had learned about the current operation: 'the backcloth would have to be repainted, otherwise the principal actors were likely to be hissed off the stage however well they performed, and I did not want to be one of them.'[27]

Over the next four weeks, Whittle was courted as rarely before. Cripps authorised that all kinds of assurances be offered him, to signal a fresh start for the Whetstone organisation. State-owned or not, it would have complete autonomy and a broad remit to explore the future development of the jet engine. The tiresome squabbles of the past over defining 'development' would be forgotten. Whittle and his men would have carte blanche to design and construct experimental engines. They would be expected to build prototypes, and would have all the resources they needed to push these through 'pilot production'. Here, indeed, was exactly the drastic repainting of the backcloth that Whittle had demanded. On 30 January 1945 MAP formally invited him to join the Power Jets (R&D) Board as Chief Technical Adviser. It was agreed that his continuing health worries made a more directly managerial position impractical. But he would have pride of place on a seven-man Technical Policy Committee, and would effectively have control over all future projects. Setting aside his misgivings, Whittle accepted.

Thus was the stage set for a climactic scene in the drama that his career with the jet-engine had been through most of the war. Alas, it ended all too predictably. Whittle had not spent his long 1944 stay in hospital polishing his interpersonal skills and mastering the arts of compromise. He remained the same fiercely deter-mined perfectionist as ever. He also saw his new appointment as probably the last chance to establish his small team of pioneers irreversibly as the torch-bearer for British aero-engineering in the coming era of the jet that he foresaw. In this respect he needed the demand for jet engines to go on rising quickly – but as the war entered what was surely its final phase, the opposite happened. It became obvious that the Luftwaffe had lost the last shreds of its combat effectiveness over the course of January 1945 – scores of German aircraft had been destroyed on the ground in the closing stages of the Battle of the Bulge – and the alarm in late 1944 over Hitler's jet-aircraft threat turned out, after all, to have been over-played. (Ironically, the flight speeds of the Me 262 proved counter-productive: poor armament meant it could only hit targets at very short range, and its pilots found themselves flying so fast that they usually had only three seconds or so in which to aim at an Allied bomber.) Plans for a deployment of Allied jets in the Far East also dwindled, with the USAAF launching much more effective raids on Japan with its B.27 Superfortresses from February 1945. With these developments it was soon clear that the impetus to expand Whetstone as a production plant was fast slipping away. Tensions over its future rose accordingly.

Whittle plunged into a series of misunderstandings and alter-cations that amounted to an instant reprise of so much that had gone wrong in the past. He began by presenting Roxbee Cox with a breathtaking list of corporate requirements. Whetstone needed another half a million square feet of floor space, 3–4,000 extra operatives and up to 1,800 additional machine tools.[28] To MAP's Technical Director, Sir John Buchanan, Whittle explained why a continuing onus on Power Jets (R&D) to hand over its brightest ideas for development by other engine companies 'was psycho-logically a very bad thing for the engineers concerned' and con-signing them to Rolls-Royce was particularly irksome, since the company towered over its rivals 'and it wasn't healthy that one firm should be so dominant'.[29] He quarrelled with Constant over a variety of engineering issues and with Roxbee Cox over the governance of the Whetstone organisation. By March 1945, there were flashes of the familiar paranoia ('I have the impression that HR-C [Roxbee Cox] has communicated his lack of confidence in me to other members of the Board…') and his hitherto generally amicable relations with Hayne Constant had all but collapsed. It incensed Whittle when Constant was invited to join the Power Jets (R&D) Board, which he thought would only lead to protracted discussion of points that he felt ought to have been settled at his discretion alone ('I complained that my views received too little weight in view of my experience and ability').[30]

Above all, Whittle now ran into a terminal confrontation with his peers in the established aircraft industry. He took at face value the lavish assurances he had been given by Cripps in January. He was confident the Whetstone plant would be allowed to aim for the production rate of thirty engines a year that he thought practical. In the event, it took less than four months for the leaders of Britain's biggest aero-engine companies to smother his plans. They were not prepared to countenance the emergence of Power Jets (R&D) as a competitor to the private sector. Cripps and his officials at MAP were reminded of the post-war history of the Royal Aircraft Factory in 1918–19. It, too, had aspired to a manufacturing role, prompting an acrimonious stand-off with private industry that was only resolved when the Aircraft Factory agreed in 1919 to become the RAE, confining itself to research activities that would be of benefit to the industry as a whole. A similar research-oriented future was now open to Power Jets (R&D), insisted the industrialists, but only if it agreed to give up all thought of actually making engines, even in the very smallest quantities.

Inevitably, Hives was at the forefront of the industry's stand. It may have saddened him to find Rolls-Royce and Whittle cast as adversaries, but he was nonetheless scornful of plans for a Whetstone manufacturing facility which he regarded as moonshine. He actually suspected those around Whittle of being intent on what he called 'a patents racket', using lawyers to stake out a claim to post-war jet-engine revenues all over the world. (If so, as he had warned Roxbee Cox rather ominously in November 1944, 'it would in the end work very much against them'.[31]) Above all, Hives – true to his soubriquet 'the Quiet Tiger' – fought as fiercely as ever for Rolls-Royce's corporate interests. His management of the company had transformed it since 1939 into by far the largest and most powerful of the country's aero-engine firms. (It had employed fewer than 7,000 people when the first Merlin was built; by the end of the war Rolls-Royce had 55,000 employees.) He intended to build on this and knew how he was going to do it. More clearly than any of his peers, he saw that Whittle had been absolutely right to talk from the earliest days of the war about a coming revolution – and now piston engines for military aircraft had indeed had their day. 'When the war is over,' as Stanley Hooker recalled him saying with his customary bluntness, 'you will be able to buy Merlins on any street corner for a bob a dozen. We must press on with these jet engines or we shall have nothing to do.'[32] Given his formidable reputation by April 1945 as one of the foremost architects of the Allies' victory over Germany – 'God knows where the RAF would have been without him', as Freeman had confessed some months earlier[33] – Hives was not a man to be denied in Whitehall.

Nor was he. Teaming up with Frank Halford, Hives managed even before the war was over to coordinate an abrupt cancellation of the expanded role that had been handed to the Whetstone operation in January. Nationalising Power Jets a year earlier, Cripps had set up an advisory panel – the less than jauntily named Gas Turbine Technical Advisory and Coordinating Committee (GTTACC) – that he hoped would smooth the restructured Whetstone company's relations with the rest of the aircraft industry. The GTTACC met for the third time on 18 April 1945 at the headquarters of the Royal Aeronautical Society, an elegant town house just off London's Piccadilly at 4 Hamilton Place. Wartime austerity had scarcely diminished the splendour of the gilded ceilings, the chandeliers and the marble fireplaces that adorned its many rooms. Round its boardroom table on the afternoon of the 18th sat many of the cast that had featured in Whittle's war. Roxbee Cox (rather oddly) chaired the occasion while also leading a delegation from Power Jets (R&D) that included Pat Johnson as its Secretary. MAP was represented by George Bulman and by Ben Lockspeiser, as Director of Scientific Research, and two of its senior

RAF officers. Arrayed opposite them were the envoys of the old Air Ministry Ring: sitting beside Hives and Halford, were senior men from Metropolitan-Vickers, Bristol Aeroplane and Armstrong Siddeley plus Harry Sporborg from BTH. Though he had formal membership of the Committee, Whittle himself was not there – nor, to judge by the official minutes, was he ever mentioned by name. His absence surely helped to expedite what Hives had dictated would be the main business of the day: to impress upon Roxbee Cox that all commercial ties with Whetstone – including the provision of indispensable components and sub-parts – would be severed immediately unless it was reined back and restarted as 'a purely research-minded Power Jets'.

No resistance was offered by the Power Jets delegation. The only note of dissension was voiced by Ben Lockspeiser, but he was given short shrift. ('Mr Lockspeiser asked the industrialists, "Your case is, that if Power Jets make a complete engine, they are in competition?" Major Halford said "yes".') In reaching unanimous agreement, the GTTACC left Cripps and his officials little option but to revise MAP's official stance accordingly. None could have been in doubt about the impact on Whittle. The discussion closed with an oblique reference to the delicate task that Roxbee Cox would face in conveying the Committee's views to the man whose career they were effectively writing off:

> Mr Hives and Major Halford gave the view that unless Power Jets achieve the same position as RAE has achieved in recent years, they will fail; they viewed sympathetically the personnel difficulty which this suggests, for the RAE was not creative, and Major Halford could well imagine that the Chairman of Power Jets had his difficulties, when it was recognised that a large proportion of Power Jets staff had creative minds.[34]

Briefed on the details a few days later, Whittle resigned his GTTACC membership in disgust. He was persuaded, though, not to quit the Power Jets (R&D) Board. Angered by Halford's patronising remarks about the company's 'creative minds', Roxbee Cox decided he would do his utmost to keep those minds working together. They still included, after all, a dozen or so of the best young aero-engineers in the country. He decided they could yet thrive as the core of an independent firm. They would need, though, to go on being inspired by the man who had recruited them all in the first place. Whittle had to concede as much, and he agreed that they should go on with the fight – though in his heart he doubted they could prevail ('The writing on the wall was painfully plain').[35]

iii

'Thrill, Then Tragedy', ran the headline in the *Leicester Evening Mail* on 23 July 1945, 'Vivid Story of Whetstone Jet-Plane Crash'. The employees of Power Jets (R&D) and their families, gathered on a sports field at Whetstone for the company's annual summer gala, had been offered a 'spectacular mystery attraction'. This turned out to be, as all had hoped, an aerobatics display by the company's test pilot in an RAF Meteor III aircraft with Derwent engines. It had ended in tragedy. In full view of the crowd, the plane had made a perpendicular climb to 8,000 feet but had then gone into an inverted dive and plunged headlong into the ground. This was not the first Meteor to crash, nor was it the first Meteor-pilot fatality. But the young man at the controls, Squadron Leader A. O. Moffat, had been an especially popular figure with all Whittle's engineers, having lived for months at the Hind Hotel in Lutterworth to be part of the team. His death was a blow to morale that seemed cruelly timed, given a steady haemorrhaging of confidence at Whetstone since the start of the summer.

The atmosphere had begun to change within days of the war with Germany ending in May. Superficially, the company's routines were unaltered. Plans went ahead for the 'pilot production' of a modest number of W.2/700 engines – in fact no less than forty were built at Whetstone before manufacturing was abandoned – and development work was ostensibly continuing. Williams and Tinling were still busy compiling dense letters of 'clarification' for

Whitehall, hailing the company's post-war business franchise. Pat Johnson was still struggling to assert a coherent strategy over foreign patents, though any legal entitlement seemed increasingly theoretical in the face of practical politics. (The US government's licence to make use of Whittle patents had technically expired with the cessation of hostilities, but the British Air Commission in Washington had readily conceded 'a short-term continuation of the status quo'.[36]) In reality, though, Power Jets (R&D) was being none too subtly refashioned for a different future. Nothing could be done in the workshops at Whetstone without item-by-item clearance from MAP in triplicate, and the paperwork was usually not forthcoming. In line with the stance taken by the GTTACC meeting in April, the Ministry was effectively preparing Whetstone for its new status as a state-owned research centre.

Whittle himself felt increasingly detached from the business – despite the fact that some important work was still continuing on both the LR1 engine and the enhanced W.2/700 lined up to power Miles Aircraft's M.52 supersonic plane. (Lockspeiser's Supersonic Committee would soon be pressing Power Jets (R&D) to work towards 'an engine suitable for an aircraft developed from the Miles E.24/43. Flight at speeds up to say 1.5 x the speed of sound may be envisaged...'[37]) He tried in vain to persuade Cripps to forestall neutering Whetstone as a 'national research establishment', still arguing that an autonomous development company could emerge as a catalyst for Britain's peacetime jet technology. The aero-engine industry, though, remained implacably opposed to the idea. After the election of the Labour government in August 1945, Cripps left MAP for another senior post in Attlee's Cabinet and the Ministry itself was soon being readied for a departmental merger. Whittle found no support from the Attlee government for his vision of a state-owned paragon of aero-engineering. This dispelled what little faith he had left in the socialist ideals of his youth. By the autumn he was finally losing all hope of a future for the team venture he had founded at Lutterworth those five long years ago.

One might have supposed that these were bitter months for Whittle, soured by a sense of personal rejection. In fact he managed a stoic response. Perhaps his long illness in 1944, prompting months of introspection, had left him with a keener appreciation of what he had achieved despite his many disappointments. He could share in the general elation over the war's end and was also buoyed along through the summer and autumn of 1945 by waves of acclaim for the jet engine, a belated celebration that found expression in several ways. Famously, hundreds attended a lecture that he delivered in Westminster on 5 October at the Institute of Mechanical Engineers, tracing the early history of the jet project.[38] (It was such a successful event, and so many people had to be turned away for lack of space, that he was asked to give the First James Clayton Lecture a second time on 11 January 1946 in the larger main hall of the Institute. Once again there was scarcely room enough for the numbers that Whittle's growing reputation attracted.) Notwithstanding all his health problems, he was still only thirty-eight years old and appeared to have lost none of the dynamism he had always brought to public-speaking occasions. At the Institute's request, he set off soon afterwards to give the same talk in its regional branches all over the country.

Nor had he lost his zest for flying. He seized a chance in October 1945 to fly a jet plane for the first time, finding a Meteor I with two W.2/700 engines standing available at the local Bruntingthorpe aerodrome near Whetstone. The experience gave him 'intense satisfaction', as he later recorded. ('The occasions when an engine designer has piloted an aeroplane powered by his own engines must have been very few since the Wright Brothers' first flights in 1903.'[39]) Then, early in November 1945, another opportunity came along. The Air Ministry had authorised an attempt on the World Speed Record with a Mark IV version of the Meteor. A course was laid along the Kent coast at Herne Bay and on this occasion – unlike some in the past – Whittle's name was included on the guest list. After he arrived for the start of the speed trials on 3 November, Whittle discovered that a Meteor III was parked at the nearby Manston aerodrome that was being used for the event. What happened next was afterwards a source of some dispute. Late in the afternoon, an announcement was made on the Tannoy system that all flying was over for the day. As the crowds began to disperse, though, another Meteor suddenly appeared over the sea. It swept from one end of the course to the other at a height of about fifty feet, then climbed, turned and dipped to fly back again. Few watching from the beaches can have guessed the identity of the man at the controls, but they might have appreciated hearing it was Air Commodore Whittle. His senior officers were less impressed. The idea of a Whittle flight had been suggested by the public relations people and had been expressly rejected – as Whittle himself almost certainly knew, when he somehow obtained clearance for take-off at Manston. It probably added nicely to the thrill of the flight that he was once again cocking a snook at those in authority above him: he still had the mischievous instincts that had been such a feature of his youthful flying career. ('I have since been told,' he wrote later to MAP's new head, Air Marshal Sir Alec Coryton, 'that you had refused permission for me to fly the Meteor. If so, I cannot see why...'[40]) On 4 November he signed photographs of the Meteor IV that was waiting, with its Derwent V engines, to make an attempt on the world air-speed record (*Fig. 25*). But he had left Kent for a lecture tour in Wales by the time it flew the Herne Bay course at a record speed of just over 606 mph.[41]

As this suggested, the true scale of the jet project's wartime achievement was being borne out by the way in which the engines derived from the original W.1 and W.2B designs were now undergoing a rapid evolution. Almost as gratifying to Whittle were reports confirming that the Germans' jet engines had never reached a stage of development that would have qualified them for factory production in Britain. Despite these consolations, though, nothing could really atone for the dismal decline of morale at Whetstone over the winter of 1945–6 and portents of the operation's imminent collapse. By January 1946 Whittle was receiving poignant letters of regret from those who had worked with him at Lutterworth, most of them explaining why they would shortly be looking for new posts. Since there was nothing he could say to reassure them, Whittle felt his position was impossible and he resigned from the Power Jets (R&D) Board on 22 January. His decision prompted

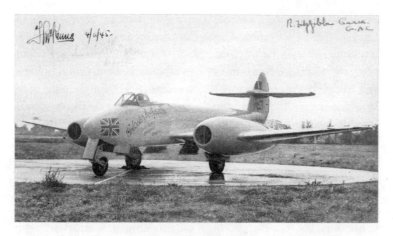

Fig. 25. The Gloster Meteor Mk IV that re-set the world air-speed
record in November 1945

extensive coverage in the press, most of it highly critical of the
government. This caused much embarrassment in Whitehall, and
no little indignation that he should have had the temerity to defy
the government's plan for Whetstone. This troubled Whittle not a
jot. Deploring the state's neglect of the precious asset represented
by his former colleagues, and warning of their departure, his verdict on the structure set up for them by Cripps was pithy enough:
'It is the right crew in the wrong ship.'[42] Fiercely opposed to the
effective disbandment of the engineering operation he had created,
Whittle saw it as more than 'a grave injustice' to the individuals
involved. It was also a betrayal of the national interest, 'in my
opinion... a disaster' depriving the country's aerospace industry
of rare skills that might, by working as one close-knit team, have
made a significant contribution to Britain's post-war fortunes.

As if to confirm his pessimism, the government moved within
weeks of his resignation to cancel a contract awarded in 1944 for
a single LR1 engine – which might yet have been the world's first
turbo-fan, forerunner of an engine type that has since become the
standard power plant for almost all jet airliners in the modern
world. Steps were also taken to kill off the project seen by some

as symbolic of Britain's whole future in aerospace: at a meeting of Lockspeiser's Supersonic Flight Committee on 12 February 1946, it was agreed to call a halt to the M.52 – for which about 90 per cent of all the airframe components had already been manufactured – and to cancel the contract with Power Jets (R&D) for the enhanced W.2/700 engine that had been designed to power it. The rationale for this momentous decision was widely debated at the time and for many years afterwards. Those sceptical of arguments based on the cost of the plane or its projected performance saw other forces at work. The resentment in Whitehall over Whittle's resignation was palpable. Some suspected the M.52 had been cancelled as a way of spiking any further role for him in the aircraft industry. (This was the conclusion of a painstaking post-mortem only finally concluded in 1997 and later quoted in a book authored by a famous test pilot, Eric Brown, who as a young man had been scheduled to fly the M.52.[43]) Whatever the true explanation, the M.52's demise effectively handed the future of supersonic flight over to the American aerospace industry. In the course of the plane's development, in the autumn of 1944, government officials had arranged for representatives of the USAAF and Bell Aircraft to visit the Miles factory. At MAP's explicit request, all data relating to the design and testing of the M.52 were fully disclosed to the Americans. This was supposed to have been the first leg of a reciprocal exercise. Unfortunately, as test pilot Eric Brown would later recall, 'one week after the American visit the MAP told the Miles team that the return visit had been cancelled by the Pentagon for security reasons'.[44] The first supersonic flight was made by USAF pilot Chuck Yeager in October 1947, piloting Bell Aircraft's rocket-powered Bell-X1 – an aircraft sharing several critical design features with the M.52. Whittle had suggested in 1942 that the Americans would inevitably come to dominate the jet-engine business one day – but he had never expected the British government to help things along quite so generously.

He was right in anticipating the departure of his old colleagues: sixteen of those closest to him – including Dan Walker and 'Old Bozzi' Bozzoni, Leslie Cheshire and his deputy R. C. McLeod,

Bob Feilden and Reg Voysey – resigned en bloc in the middle of April 1946. Most of them chose to leave their aero-engineering days behind them, taking their expertise into other sectors of the turbine industry and prompting yet more hand-wringing in the press about the impact of government policy on Britain's leadership of the post-war 'Jet Age'. ('Obviously something has gone seriously wrong,' opined the *Daily Mail*.[45]) The exodus of the 'Jet Men' at least made it easier for the government to build rapidly on their legacy. The Whetstone plant was largely converted to office space, leaving the state-owned research operation based at the RAE's Pyestock premises. It was renamed the 'National Gas Turbine Establishment', reporting to the Ministry of Supply which was MAP's successor, and Roxbee Cox was appointed its first Director. (The NGTE would go on to flourish as a formidable research centre, becoming a bedrock of Britain's aero-engine industry for the next fifty years.) Power Jets (R&D) was reduced to a shell company with a smart office in London – just a few doors down the street from the Royal Aeronautical Society in Hamilton Place – where Pat Johnson sat alone as Managing Director surrounded by his patent files. No further roles were available for Dudley Williams and Coll Tinling. They had devoted themselves to the jet project for ten years. Now their employment prospects looked bleak, and it caused Whittle some anguish that he could do nothing to help them.

As for his own situation – Whittle, too, was effectively jobless in the wake of his January 1946 resignation. Informing him that his Special Posting status had been discontinued, the RAF had no immediate alternative to offer. Nor was he approached by any companies in the private sector, hoping to explore ways of replicating what had been achieved at Power Jets. Here was the denouement of that fateful decision in the summer of 1943, described by Lance Whyte as a Greek tragedy. Whittle had opted to stand by the notion of an autonomous operation at Whetstone rather than accept a redefinition of his role in some way that might have complemented the setting up of MAP's Special Projects directorate under Roxbee Cox. Emerging from the miseries he had endured in

1944 and the vicissitudes of 1945, Whittle now had no obvious place to turn: by the time he resigned from Power Jets, he had managed to alienate the key decision-makers in Whitehall and the business world alike. As a result, post-war Britain apparently had no use for a man generally acknowledged by his peers to have wrought an engineering revolution.

Yet he was still thinking about the future of flying with extra-ordinary insight and imagination. Nowhere was this more striking than in papers he had written in recent months about the coming impact of jet engines on civil aviation. In a memorandum on the vast potential of the LR1 engine, penned three months before the government aborted its development, he had looked forward to seeing a four-engined civil airliner making 'a non-stop flight' from London to New York with a crew of six, cruising at 470 mph at an altitude of 45,000 feet. Many pundits in the aviation world insisted that passenger aircraft of such power would never be needed. They had failed, in Whittle's view, to grasp how profoundly jet airliners would alter the whole experience of flying:

> I am strongly of the opinion that if a passenger had once experi-enced high speed, bumpless flight, at 40,000 ft, with complete absence of vibration and negligible noise, in an aeroplane with no visible moving parts, he would never wish to travel otherwise.[46]

He was by now well aware, though, of being once again a lone voice. He cut short his discussion of high-speed civil aviation in that paper, acknowledging that readers might be puzzled by his steely confidence in its jet-propelled future and there was 'certainly no sign as yet that it is shared outside Power Jets'.

Then, towards the end of March 1946, someone at MAP spotted a gainful way of employing him without having to devise a fresh RAF posting. A well-attended speech by Roxbee Cox in Washington in December 1945 – it was the 9th Wright Brothers Commemorative Lecture at the US Institute of Aeronautical Sciences[47] – had caused quite a stir. Jet-powered flight was suddenly attracting much wider attention in American aviation circles. This was initially gratifying for officials in Whitehall, but many were soon feeling vexed over a string of statements from the other side of the Atlantic suggesting that the jet engine was essentially another fine product of US industrial prowess. Ways had to be found of countering this unfortunate misperception. Whittle had won much acclaim on his 1942 tour of the US, and his reputation as a public speaker and champion of the jet engine had again soared in the wake of his Clayton Lecture round. (He had since then given talks in several European cities including Paris and Brussels.) From MAP, Air Marshal Coryton wrote to him with a novel job offer:

> Recent American publicity about their jet aircraft and engines has reached such vast proportions that we feel the time is opportune to send someone over from this country to lead a campaign [in the US] to emphasise Britain's contribution in the jet development field... and if you feel like doing it, I would like you to lead the jet campaign.[48]

Whittle needed no persuading. He accepted the invitation, and planning for his second tour of the US began a few days later. It would include a heavy schedule of lectures, interspersed with calls at most of the places he had visited on his first trip four years earlier.

If that trip in 1942 had made a strong impression on him, the second confirmed his feelings of a deep affinity with America. The success of the 1946 tour was to turn Whittle from a slightly lost soul with no obvious future in the RAF into a celebrity honoured – even within Britain – for making a unique contribution to the Service and to aeronautics more generally. When he set off across the Atlantic on 17 June, he was still struggling with the RAF over footling rules that forbade him the use of a secretary. When he landed back at Prestwick on 11 September, he was welcomed home on the tarmac of the runway by the Secretary of State for Scotland, a deputation of Scottish MPs and a Scots pipe band. Press reports of his progress over the intervening three months produced this dramatic change of status: it was impossible to ignore the fact that Whittle had been fêted by the Americans everywhere he went – on an epic itinerary. He gave eighteen public lectures, attended twenty engineering symposia, held nine press conferences and made ten extended radio broadcasts in addition to countless interviews.

Helping him to cope with his draining schedule was a twenty-seven-year-old WAAF officer from the Code and Cypher section of the Washington embassy, Staff Officer Jill Shepherd. She was assigned to accompany him everywhere as his personal assistant – and it is clear from Whittle's personal diary that a warm friendship sprang up between them over the summer. He had at first hesitated over her appointment because she could not offer the shorthand skills offered by some available civilian secretaries; but Jill Shepherd was much more worldly, with the social skills of the officer class. She was to prove a perfect tour companion as well as a formidable organiser: Whittle would note 'with JS' against almost all the entries in his diary, covering not only press briefings and formal receptions but also weekend parties, walks beside the ocean and trips to the movies. They enjoyed innumerable dinners à deux in fashionable hotel restaurants over the course of ten weeks. Perhaps there was the hint of a future romance. If so, Whittle took great care to conceal any sign of it in public, wary as ever of suggesting the slightest impropriety, and nothing was to come of it. (They stayed in touch, but only just. 'I have thought out many letters to you in my head when something has brought memories particularly to my mind,' wrote Jill in 1953, by which time she had long been back in England and was married with two children.[49] She left behind a hoard of private papers when she died in 1987 – from which almost all traces of her time with Whittle were conspicuously absent.[50]) Whatever the truth, she was plainly in awe of him and afterwards submitted a glorious if slightly breathless account of their travels, recalling their many extraordinary days together.[51]

Their corporate hosts included GEC and Bell Aircraft, Lockheed and Douglas, Boeing, McDonnell, Martin Aircraft and Westinghouse. Whittle's message for them all was none too subtle. His chief task, as he noted in a subsequent blow-by-blow account of all his meetings, was 'to emphasize (a) that jet propulsion originated in Great Britain and was a prominent feature in reverse lease-lend, and (b) that Britain was still ahead in the field'.[52] However ambivalent some of his audiences may have felt about this perspective, all appeared to respond with an unfeigned enthusiasm that was often wholly spontaneous. When Whittle made an unscheduled appearance at the Cleveland National Air Races in Ohio, one of the US aerospace industry's great annual fixtures, it prompted an announcement over the public-address system: 'My presence resulted in a very generous tribute being paid to the British contribution to jet propulsion by the commentator.' He was ushered into the Event President's Box and was handed the microphone several times to offer his thoughts about the engines on display. It must have made a welcome contrast to the aftermath of his visit to the Herne Bay speed trials, ten months earlier.

'JS' arranged several memorable encounters for him. In New York he dined more than once with Constance Babington Smith, demobbed from her role in Photographic Reconnaissance and now working as a journalist with *Time-Life* magazine. In Dayton, Ohio, he spent an hour talking about aviation with the seventy-five-year-old Orville Wright in his laboratory. In factories, hotel ballrooms and university lecture halls, he spoke to large and animated audiences whose questions often left his timetable in tatters. Whittle's command of his brief was universally admired. Unquestionably, though, the extent of his triumph was also partly a reflection of the extraordinary reputation enjoyed by the RAF in post-war America. Many at the time noted how it seemed to be regarded by Americans as the encapsulation of everything they admired about Britain's wartime fortitude. Air Commodore Whittle and S/O Shepherd, both of them dressed immaculately in uniform at all times, were everywhere hailed as the personification of the Air Force they served (*Plate 14b*).

This happy alignment produced one of the highlights of the trip when the two of them visited the USAAF station at Long Beach, California, on 28 July 1946. Shortly after their arrival, sixteen Lancasters of 35 Squadron Bomber Command landed at the base. The now iconic aircraft were on a goodwill mission across the continent – having flown from Britain via the Azores and Gander – and a huge 'Circus Party' was laid on for all the crews by a millionaire inventor and entrepreneur, Arthur Atwater Kent. Always at Whittle's side clutching her notebook and a Baby Brownie camera, JS noted how both of them were made guests of honour at an extravagant occasion to rival all those trips to the Mocambo nightclub in 1942:

> It certainly was an extraordinary experience to see an old-time circus band and clowns, performing dogs and horses, a camel and an elephant, all in a private garden high up on the Beverly Hills, with a beautiful view of Hollywood and LA stretched out below.[53]

On 1 August the Air Commodore and his WAAF companion boarded a B17 bomber to fly alongside the Lancasters. Whittle noted in his diary: 'JS and self passengers in the B17 which accompanies 35 Sqdn during formation flight over Southlands.'[54]

They enjoyed eight days in Los Angeles with no official engagements. It was too brief a respite, though, from their relentless timetable – and Whittle spent much of it either exploring the mathematics of supersonic aerodynamics or drafting paragraphs for his end-of-tour report. (He was now less resigned than hitherto to the inevitability of American dominance of the jet world. 'There is a large market for British jet engines in the USA if we play our cards right... The more we bring it home to the Americans how much they owe us in this field, the more we are likely to get.') Another four weeks were to be spent criss-crossing the continent. By the time they parted, they had flown about 10,000 miles on commercial flights between twenty cities spread from one coast to the other. Whittle's young companion took a fortnight's leave in Canada – on her own – and returned to Washington 'very proud to have been associated with such a genius'. He flew home utterly exhausted.

Even before his departure from the US, the government in Washington had raised the possibility that he might be invited back again to receive some official acknowledgement of his achievements. Whittle was by now enamoured with all things American, so there was little prospect of him making the sensible decision to avoid further travel for a while. He made the trip back to America by sea, affording him at least some rest, taking six days to cross the Atlantic aboard the *Queen Elizabeth* in November 1946. The indefatigable Jill Shepherd and a fellow WAAF officer joined him for breakfast aboard, two hours after the ship berthed in New York. Thereafter, JS remained at his side for most of the next four weeks, managing his frantic schedule as expertly as she had done in the summer. Whittle gave lectures in Boston and New York, then travelled to Washington to be invested at the Pentagon into the American Legion of Merit, an award made by the US armed forces for distinguished service and a rare distinction for a non-US citizen (*Plate 15b*). He was also awarded the country's top aeronautical engineering accolade, the Daniel Guggenheim Medal, bestowed once a year. This additional honour entailed giving yet more lectures.

By the start of December, the pace of events had all become too much. Jill Shepherd had to return to her normal duties at the embassy and Whittle was soon overwhelmed by all the calls on his time. His health broke down so seriously that a return flight over the Atlantic was suddenly out of the question. The family of Lord Weir had a house in Bermuda, and embassy staff in Washington contacted them to have Whittle invited there for a properly secluded break. He would not return home until March 1947, by which time his productive years as the genius behind the jet were unequivocally over.

iv

The reception accorded Whittle by the Americans caused many of his erstwhile masters in Whitehall some surprise, not to say discomfort. Even leaving aside the whole controversy over MAP's mismanagement of the jet project during the early years of the war, it was hard to ignore the shattering impact of nationalisation on Whittle personally – or the way in which he felt Power Jets had been brought back into the war effort in January 1945, only to be brutally marginalised again three months later. Many in the aero-engineering fraternity thought Whittle's treatment in Britain had done the civil service little credit. Inevitably this view was held most passionately by those who had been his colleagues at Power Jets. The sixteen who resigned in April 1946 orchestrated their group departure as an angry protest against the government's readiness to abandon him. Days earlier, they had gathered for a dinner at the Hind Hotel in Lutterworth to inaugurate a club in Whittle's honour (*Fig. 26*). It was an emotional occasion: Whittle was presented with a miniature impeller made of stainless steel, with a detachable cigarette lighter embedded in the hub. (Whittle was thrilled with it, and is using the lighter in the image on the cover of this book.) Round the base of the impeller were engraved the names of sixty-eight colleagues. They christened themselves 'the Reactionaries' and resolved to meet annually for a dinner to preserve the memory of their work under Whittle's leadership. Many others, too, felt uneasy seeing Whittle cast as the prophet without honour in his own land – including engineering peers quite ready to acknowledge how much they owed to him. As Rolls-Royce's Stanley Hooker confessed to one of the founding Reactionaries, 'To me, whatever shape or form these [jet] engines take, they will always remain Whittle engines.'[55]

Given the enormity of the jet engine's implications for the future, at last obvious to all, it seemed briefly possible by the autumn of 1946 that the RAF might belatedly honour Whittle's unique career by offering him a suitably unprecedented appointment. Roxbee Cox confessed in his old age that he had hoped that Whittle might even have been made an Air Marshal.[56] This would surely have reflected well on the RAF in later years. In the event, no such honour came Whittle's way from the force he had served with such distinction since 1923. Instead his situation attracted attention from a less likely quarter. Treasury officials had been impressed by Whittle's decision in 1944 voluntarily to surrender his sizeable stake in Power Jets to the state. It was they

Fig. 26. An invitation to the first Reactionaries' Dinner,
launched as an annual event

who took the initiative, in October 1946, to arrange a financial
reward for Whittle that might offer him some redress while also
reducing the gap between his US reputation and his standing
in Britain. At their request, the Royal Commission for Awards
to Inventors (RCAI) agreed to act outside its normal brief. This
generally entailed hearing submissions directly from those
who thought they deserved some official reward for a technical
invention utilised by the state. The hopeful applicant would put
his case to the Commission in a courtroom and then be cross-
examined by officials from the Ministry of Supply, not necessarily to his advantage. This approach, all acknowledged at the
outset, would place a strain on Whittle that might be inadvisable.
Instead, plans were made for a senior man from the Ministry –
E. L. Pickles, formerly Head of Contracts – to act as advocate
for his case, on the premise that an award of some size would
definitely be made. The Commission, at the Treasury's request,
would be responsible only for deciding the actual amount. It
was clear by early 1947 that it would need to be a sizeable sum.
In the New Year Honours, Whittle collected only a minor gong

but it carried a striking citation: 'his name will undoubtedly go down in history as one of the great British inventors...'[57] Nothing was yet said to him personally about an RCAI award, however, and the adjudication process inched forward without his knowledge.

Some word of the Treasury's intentions might have been salutary at this point: Whittle was by now seriously ill again. No sooner had he returned to Washington from his month's rest in Bermuda than he retreated to his hotel room and suffered another collapse. The British embassy staff arranged for him to be admitted on 12 January 1947 to the US Naval Hospital at Bethesda, Maryland. Its head of neuropsychiatry advised a course of intensive treatment. This lasted two months and included three sessions of electro-convulsive therapy (ECT), a remedy for depression that was just becoming widely adopted in American hospitals. ('The last of these,' reported a doctor at Guy's Hospital, London, later in the year, '[Whittle] thinks was mismanaged [:] there was a "violent" reaction to it and he experienced confusion and some loss of memory; it was decided to stop the course.'[58]) In addition to the skin ailments that had afflicted him so severely in 1944, Whittle was now suffering from anxiety, insomnia, depression and chronic fatigue. He somehow managed one further short lecture tour, in Canada, in the spring of 1947 but after his return to England succumbed to a sequence of psychiatric crises. He spent almost the entire second half of 1947 in a specialist clinic for nervous disorders at Guy's Hospital. Neither intensive psychotherapy nor several further sessions of ECT in November 1947 produced any lasting recovery. A return home to Rugby that month lasted just two days, ending in a hasty readmission. It must have been a woeful time for poor Dorothy, who had already nursed him through so many bad patches during the war. His medical notes from this period make grim reading: as the doctors regularly acknowledged, his war work had taken a heavy toll on his health in every way. He by this point had little option but to take early retirement. Arthur Tedder, now Chief of the Air Staff, took a hand in this, and met him for 'a friendly talk' which was gratifying to Whittle. He was effectively invalided out of the RAF in April 1948, just short of his forty-first birthday.

Whether Whittle's prolonged absences in any way slowed Whitehall's homework on the mooted financial award is not clear. Whatever the explanation, the Ministry of Supply's preparations dragged on interminably through 1947–8. This snail's pace, though, did have one positive consequence: every passing month appeared to bring further graphic evidence of the revolution that was Whittle's legacy. Hives had been right, of course. As he had predicted, the advent of the jet engine rendered piston engines on fighters and bombers more or less obsolete overnight. Within Britain, the re-equipping of the RAF was proceeding rapidly. By the end of 1947, just over 2,000 jet engines had been delivered to the service, mostly manufactured by either Rolls-Royce or de Havilland.[59] These two companies were also busy selling jet engines overseas. More than 1,400 had been shipped or were awaiting shipment by December 1947. Some were going to countries that had purchased large numbers of Meteors and de Havilland Vampires. (One of the leading customers for the Meteor was Argentina, where the air force was being advised by that erstwhile champion of the Me 262, Luftwaffe General Adolf Galland.) Other engines were being sold as separate units, including – much to the US government's disgust – fifty-five Nenes shipped by Rolls-Royce to the USSR, where Soviet technicians were to prove masters of reverse engineering. (Nene-powered MiG fighters would feature prominently in the Korean War of 1950–53, outpacing all their British and American adversaries.) And in addition to finished engines, Rolls-Royce had a lucrative sideline granting licences to foreign companies keen to make their own versions of its jet engines – especially of the Nene, which represented a quantum jump beyond any previous aero-engine, in terms both of performance and reliability. When the US Navy opted for the Nene to power a new fighter, to be manufactured by Grumman, a licence was granted to one of the leading US engine-makers, Pratt & Whitney, to step up as the supplier. Announcing its plans in May 1947 – as reported in a prominent British aerospace

magazine – P&W paid tribute to Whittle as the jet pioneer 'and
to the fact that the Whittle design... was also the basis for most of
the jet engines now being manufactured in America'.[60]

Mere medals, honours, and media plaudits were apparently
quite insufficient, however, to satisfy Britain's Ministry of Supply
that all requisite boxes had been ticked for any official verdict
linking Air Commodore Whittle directly to the success of the jet
engine. Letters were accordingly sent off to various individuals
who had worked with him, asking in effect for affidavits. Roxbee
Cox began his reply with a mild protest at the absurdity of this –
'It seems to me a little strange that... any appraisal is necessary'
– but he nonetheless provided an elegant encomium to Whittle:

> It is one thing to have an idea. It is another to have the technical
> and executive ability to give it flesh. It is still another to have
> the tenacity of purpose to drive through to success unshaken
> in confidence in the face of discouraging opposition. Whittle,
> whose name in the annals of engineering comes after those of
> [James] Watt, [George] Stephenson and [Charles] Parsons only
> for reasons of chronology or alphabetical order, had these things.
>
> It is, I think, generally admitted that without Whittle's deter-
> mination to turn his idea into reality we should not have begun
> to think about the jet-propelled aeroplane... until the idea had
> been forced upon us by the exploits of the enemy with their jet-
> propelled machines.[61]

Others wrote back equally effectively, if less memorably. By
February 1948 Mr Pickles was ready to begin compiling a lengthy
background paper for the Commission.[62]

His report was submitted on 8 March. Having read it, and
Whittle's James Clayton Lecture, too, the seven members of the
Commission – led by an Appeals Court judge, the Lord Cohen –
invited themselves to Whetstone for a day late in April. A letter
from their secretary about this was the first Whittle heard of
the whole affair. It came as welcome news to him. He had never
denied wanting some kind of financial settlement provided it was
arranged in a dignified manner (or as he had explained to Cripps
in 1943: 'naturally, I want my efforts to receive full recognition,

[but] I would much prefer any reward to be direct from a grateful Nation'⁶³). The Whetstone visit had to be postponed by four weeks, prompting the Commission's members to rescind an invitation to Whittle to attend an informal discussion with them at the RCAI's offices just off the Strand in Somerset House. Whittle was relieved to be spared the private meeting with the Commission and made it known he would not be attending its formal hearing. He was content to remain in Brownsover Hall, to be kept abreast of proceedings by Pickles and the Commission's Secretary. Matters were eventually scheduled to conclude abruptly. A visit to Whetstone on 25 May was to be followed by the hearing next day, at which Pickles would make an oral presentation on the merits of the claim. After being repeatedly assured by the Commission's Secretary that the hearing would be extremely straightforward, Whittle changed his mind and decided to attend in person after all. His only request was that he should be spared any encounter whatever with the press. Lord Justice Cohen gladly agreed to this, and briefed his colleagues that Whittle's presence meant there might be an opportunity to question him after the presentation. ('The Air Commodore is a neurotic type but I have been able to remove many of his apprehensions about these proceedings... [and] have offered him the sanctuary of my room.'⁶⁴)

On the appointed day, Wednesday 26 May 1948, Whittle arrived at Somerset House at ten o'clock, only to find himself immediately confronted by several press photographers. At the hearing itself, an audience of more than sixty people included many reporters. With very little preamble, the hearing was handed over to Pickles – and by all accounts, he spoke with an eloquence that went some way to atone for the long delays through 1947. He even followed his summary of the jet project's achievements with a quotation from Shakespeare to explain Whittle's refusal to lodge a claim on his own behalf. ('We wound our modesty and make foul the clearness of our deservings, when of ourselves we publish them.'). It came from *All's Well That Ends Well* – aptly enough, as matters turned out. After Pickles, the Commissioners heard testimonies from several others including Roxbee Cox. Finally Whittle took the stand himself to answer just three brief questions – 'it would be difficult,' he told the Commission members, 'to over-estimate the engineering training I had received in the RAF, particularly at Cambridge' – and Lord Justice Cohen drew the proceedings to a sudden close. He ushered Whittle straight into the chairman's room, to pre-empt any possibility of his being ambushed by the press. 'All the members of the Commission were there,' noted Whittle later, 'and we had a short general conversation.'[65] Apparently he was given no hint of the size of the award. Roxbee Cox and other officials took him out to lunch at the RAC Club in St James's and then put him on a late afternoon train home.

He took a call at Brownsover Hall the next morning to tell him a letter would be arriving by courier from the Ministry of Supply in the afternoon. This brought him the tidings that he had been awarded £100,000 – approximately equivalent to £5 million in today's money. Whittle was taken aback. He had scarcely had time to digest the news, though, before press photographers and reporters began arriving in the lane up to Broomfield. This prompted a slightly undignified retreat with Dorothy – 'via back door and hole in hedge' – and they hurried up Bilton Road to Mary Phillips' home. Ever dutiful, Mary agreed to spend the evening at Broomfield in their place, fielding press enquiries solely on the strength of a press statement that Whittle had agreed with Roxbee Cox the previous day. She held the fort until well after midnight. Driving over to Brownsover Hall with Whittle in the morning, Mary then had to deal with the waiting press a second time while Whittle hid in the bushes beside the drive until they had all departed.[66]

He confessed to Pickles in a letter of thanks some hours later that it had all been 'a considerable shock, though a pleasant one, both because of the unexpected size of the award and the speed with which it was announced'.[67] The amount was certainly regarded as generous at the time. (It was twice the sum that would be awarded four years later to Sir Robert Watson-Watt, the pioneer of radar.) In retrospect, it seems less so. The final figure appears to have been based almost entirely on a curious analysis prepared for the Commission by the most senior of the RAF's technical officers in 1947, Air Vice Marshal R. O. Jones.[68] In his opinion, 'one could reasonably say that Whittle was, without doubt, responsible for 15 years advance in the art [of jet propulsion]'. This had resulted 'in procuring for Great Britain the monetary advantages gained' over this period, by implication 1932–47. Jones suggested 'we try to assess what those monetary advantages have been' and then credit an appropriate share of the total value to Whittle. A 50 per cent share might be defensible, thought Jones, allowing for other contributions from other parties. ('I think one could fairly say that the Germans should have some credit. In addition, RAE must have some credit, and so must de Havilland and Rolls-Royce. I would not credit the United States with anything.') Allowance also had to be made, though, for the assistance that Whittle had received from government sources and from his Power Jets colleagues. Jones therefore reduced Whittle's rightful 'share' substantially, to just one-sixth.

Estimating the 'monetary advantages' of the 1932–47 period, Jones began with a payment of £200,000 recently made by the US government for all the patents and other technical data on the jet engine that it had received from Britain during the war. British industry, he thought, might have 'profited to not less than that amount, say another £200,000'. Canada and Australia had been passed 'all the information' but he thought they might only have 'earned' £50,000 each. Finally, there had been other miscellaneous sales and licences over the fifteen years that Jones estimated to have been worth £100,000. The resulting total of £600,000 implied an award of £100,000 (one-sixth) for Whittle. He had already received £10,000, which implied a further £90,000 yet to be paid. This, concluded Jones, meant that Whittle could be reimbursed for the equity that he had forfeited during the nationalisation, to which he was certainly entitled 'without question'. Jones was less forthright, though, about the case for an *ex gratia* payment as well. This could be funded by the balance of the £90,000 – 'but I am not suggesting that such an offer should be made to him'.

The Air Vice Marshal readily conceded that his assessment was 'crude in the extreme'. By design, it ignored Britain's future earnings from foreign usage of Whittle's patents – a vexed topic yet to be resolved. (In the event, arbitrary payments were made at intergovernmental level, notably by the Americans. Washington agreed a payment of $4 million over 1949–51 to settle its dues, in effect, for all subsequent US usage of the patents. The sterling value of this, after the pound's 1949 devaluation, was just over £1.4 million – equivalent to around £70 million today, a risible sum by any commercial yardstick.) More anomalous, perhaps, was the failure to heed the jet engine's actual commercial progress to date – despite the fact that some eye-catching military sales figures were being collated by the Ministry of Supply for its 'Request' paper, even as Jones was plucking his feeble numbers out of thin air. By the end of December 1947, the Air Ministry had paid British industry – in effect, Rolls-Royce and de Havilland – an estimated £8.5 million for production engines delivered to the RAF. (Prior development costs of about £12 million had already been reimbursed by the government.) Foreign governments had paid approximately £6 million for engines purchased in 1947 alone (on top of approximately £1 million in 1945–6). Whatever the margin on all these sales, the profits derived from them would have made a nonsense of Jones's estimates. The two leading engine-makers – in exchange for receiving from Whitehall the patents that had been handed down from Whittle to Power Jets and then on via Power Jets (R&D) to the government – had agreed to pay the Treasury an annual sum equivalent to 5 per cent of their overseas sale revenues (and a third of their licencing fees). So more or less at the same time as Whittle's £100,000 award was finally settled, the government was collecting £300,000-worth of commissions from Rolls-Royce and de Havilland based on 1947 sales alone. Presumably Jones was never alerted to these numbers.

It is intriguing to wonder how much more Whittle might have received had his engine shortened the war as he had envisaged in pre-war days. In the event, the Commission's award was effectively a token of thanks not for any military contribution but for the seed that his work had sown of a future British industry, the potential scale of which was now just starting to become apparent. The resulting jet engines – along with those manufactured by rival industries in the US and a host of other countries – were going to change the world in ways that were still unimaginable in 1948, even to Frank Whittle. A financial stake of any real size in that wider transformation would have earned him a fabled fortune indeed.

12

A Vision Fulfilled

Post-1948

i

Passed unfit for further service by an RAF Medical Board in 1948, aged forty-one, Whittle lived for almost another fifty years. Smoking up to sixty cigarettes a day through most of them and moving from Benzedrine to more familiar tipples – a psychiatrist friend described him (rather indulgently) in the 1960s as 'a controlled alcoholic' – he made the most of Air Ministry pension arrangements to keep countless doctors busy tracking a stream of ailments, both physical and psychiatric. They were often totally debilitating, but Whittle somehow surmounted them year after year. His brave resilience entailed an often troubled middle age: some baleful consequences of his wartime ordeal took many years to play themselves out. All was redeemed, though, over the years that followed. Long before he first crossed the Atlantic by Concorde, in 1976, Whittle had the immeasurable satisfaction of seeing his youthful vision of the aeroplane's future fully realised. Far more rapidly and more comprehensively than he had expected, the aeronautical revolution that he had done so much to instigate led to a transformation of the world of aviation – broadly reshaping it along the lines he had envisaged in that Cranwell thesis of 1928. He had foreseen a future of pressurised aeroplanes covering long distances by flying at great speed and at altitudes high enough to be clear of the weather. That defined the nature of modern civil aviation as it began to emerge in the early 1960s – rescuing Whittle from a melancholy decline and lifting him, eventually, to worldwide fame.

As the significance of his pioneering work became more widely appreciated in the immediate post-war years, Britain's engineering fraternity showered him with medals: by 1952 he had a cabinet full of them in which he took great pride. Never a vain man, he nonetheless prized these emblems of a belated recognition. 'I think it probable,' as he confided to the Whitehall author of a note about his career ten years later, 'that my collection of gold medals is unique in the UK and possibly the world.'[1] Less to his liking, the fame he had had to endure in 1944–6 was fanned again, restoring a celebrity that had understandably faded since his return from America. Four weeks after receiving his award at Somerset House, he was granted a knighthood in the June 1948 Birthday Honours List. The BBC featured the turbo-jet as the fifth in a hugely popular series of radio programmes about recent great inventions (*They Found the Secret*) and stories about him appeared regularly in the press.[2] Whittle found himself cast as one of the foremost heroes of the new era in military aviation – the world of fighter jets and rocket planes, public air shows, world speed records and a fascination with the breaking of 'the sound barrier' – that had fired the public's imagination since the end of the war. As in 1946, the British government was anxious to make the most of his status, given the importance of exports to the country's aircraft and aero-engine manufacturers. Whittle's personal story was still a powerful way of advertising Britain's leadership of the Jet Age to the rest of the world. Evidently he felt obliged to go along with some official retelling of the jet engine's origins. He even agreed, rather improbably, to appear as himself in a short propaganda film (*The Wonder Jet*) made by the Central Office of Information in 1949. Its wooden script scarcely referred to his relations with the government in general or MAP in particular. Most of Whittle's troubles, the film suggested, had stemmed from the jet engine's early misdemeanours, with here a leak of burning kerosene and there a crash of rogue blades shattering the turbine.

Whittle thought a fuller account was needed. He worried about versions of the past eventually emerging that would spin a narrative seriously at odds with the truth as he had experienced it. It could accurately be said, after all, that it was only government contracts that had kept his project alive from 1936 to 1940. Accounts of the wartime jet might fairly hail Wilfrid Freeman's interventions for saving it from oblivion in some of the darkest days of the war. They might even acclaim MAP for its prescience in engaging Rolls-Royce, de Havilland and Metrovick in the successful production of the first jet engines. And by 1949 it was clear that Stafford Cripps' merger of Power Jets (R&D) with the RAE had proved successful in the end, with the National Gas Turbine Establishment emerging as an invaluable catalyst for Britain's jet-engine industry. So a sanitised tale of the jet's gestation, merely noting some 'messy' relationships in the early days, might suggest an almost sympathetic stance by government towards his long travails. This interpretation of events would be plausible enough, Whittle feared, to expunge from history what he saw as the gross mismanagement of his epoch-defining invention. The failure to resource his project adequately or to lift it clear of constant and debilitating financial crises in the pre-war years; the repeated attempts by MAP's Engines directorate in the early years of the war to sideline Power Jets or to close it down altogether; the stubborn refusal of the Ministry to heed his counsel, persisting instead with a totally ill-conceived scheme for developing an operational jet engine which effectively delayed its wartime appearance by at least two critical years; and the government's rejection of the post-war future he had envisaged for Power Jets in the vanguard of a world-leading British aerospace industry – all these were features of the story that he was determined should not be forgotten.

He had been impressed, two years earlier, to read the draft official history of the project drawn up between 1945 and 1947 by Cynthia Keppel. Curiously, he had never been approached by her for an interview. Indeed, when sent the text for his comments by the Ministry of Supply in the summer of 1947, Whittle still had no idea of its authorship and assumed a team of collaborators lay behind it. This in no way diminished his regard for 'The Development of Jet Propulsion', which he praised in generous terms: 'The draft narrative is a remarkable piece of work... a very considerable achievement.'[3] (Its only significant flaw, he suggested, was its insufficient emphasis on the technical difficulties caused by Power Jets' lack of funding from 1936 to 1940. 'There is no doubt that the use of unsatisfactory components retarded the technical progress [in those years] very considerably.') In the course of working on the 1949 CIO film, however, he learned that the Cabinet Office had refused the film-makers access to Keppel's work, for fear of fuelling a 'highly coloured film in honour of Air Commodore Whittle'.[4] Evidently promoting him as the hero of the story, once thought such a useful public-relations ploy, was now seen as more problematic for the government. He concluded – presciently enough – that Keppel's work was most unlikely to be published in the foreseeable future. If an accurate account of his story was to gain currency, he would have to write it himself – as no doubt he had long suspected.

Official celebrations of the jet engine's origins included, in 1949, the installation of the first flight engine, the W.1, in South Kensington's Science Museum. The W.1X that had been gifted to GE in 1941 was at the same time presented as an exhibit to the National Air and Space Museum of the Smithsonian Institution in Washington. Whittle attended ceremonies in both places. (In his short speech at the Smithsonian, which touched his American audience, he told them: 'I like to feel that a part of me has a permanent place over here.'[5]) He had hoped to see Sir Henry Tizard at the London event, but Tizard was unable to attend. Writing to him afterwards, Whittle disclosed that he was planning a book. Tizard replied with some tempered encouragement: 'The full history would be of interest but I rather think that some people have taken the precaution of tearing up their remarks in the past.'[6] Tizard can scarcely have imagined how many of 'their remarks' had been written down by Whittle immediately afterwards and squirrelled away in his private papers. And the longer Whittle pored over them, the more resentful he became of past injustices. Above all, he was determined to set down in detail how in his view the possibility of equipping the RAF with jet fighters long before 1944 had been squandered.

Preparing the book must have consumed endless hours. He had begun summarising his handwritten daily diaries even before the end of the war, filling them out with appropriate complementary material. The resulting 'Consolidated Diaries' left him with 786 closely typed foolscap sheets – and they only covered up to April 1942.[7] He could draw on several cabinets full of letters, memoranda, committee minutes and file notes chronicling his life since 1935. Most had been typed and filed by Mary Phillips but she, alas, was no longer by his side. To his great sadness, she had fallen seriously ill in 1948 – shortly before he had finally abandoned Brownsover Hall – and had had to give up work altogether. (Afflicted with some mysterious complaint that the doctors could never fathom – surely not unrelated to the years of intense strain she had shared since 1938 – she was to be virtually bedridden for the next twenty-four years. Power Jets had never been able to fund a pension for her, so Whittle sent her a regular cheque out of his own pocket and paid for special medical attention whenever she needed it.*) He had to juggle with other commitments for a while – he worked as an (unpaid) consultant to the BOAC airline for four years – but by 1952 he was free to concentrate on his memoir with few interruptions. He could complement the written records with his prodigious memory, and he drew liberally on both to depict a drama even more 'highly coloured' than the gentlemen of the Cabinet Office might have feared.

He devoted much of the text to logging the progress of his

---

* He also did his best to comfort her via regular correspondence. His surviving papers contain eighty-eight letters from Mary (CAC/WHTL A.288-300). Before her death in 1972, she went to great trouble to bequeath to the City of Rugby librarian a full set of Whittle's letters to her, but the library later lost all trace of them.

engines from the WU1 to the W.2/700 through their many technical vicissitudes. This left him plenty of scope, though, for some unsparing criticism of those he believed guilty of endangering his project in its early years and then slowing its wartime progress until Rolls-Royce finally took charge. Scathing in his indictment of executives at BTH and Rover, he was excoriating in his criticism of MAP's policy-making, castigating it at several points as little short of a national scandal. The sheer proliferation of detail in his account gave it an immense (and lasting) authority – as its many reviewers universally acknowledged, when it was published as *Jet: The Story of a Pioneer* by Frederick Muller in November 1953.

There was no doubting the popular appeal of the book. It was serialised in the *Sunday Express* and was reprinted almost immediately. (It would sell over 16,000 copies in hardback over the next six years.[8]) Its more perceptive critics were nonetheless at one in discerning, behind the glorious engineering story, a less happy tale. 'A sort of cold justice has been done,' suggested an anonymous review in the *Times Literary Supplement*. 'Full acknowledgement and honour have been given to the inventor and yet the story bears all the marks of personal tragedy.'[9] One of the most respected aviation journalists of his day, E. Colston Shepherd, offered his own take on this in the *Sunday Times*:

> His misfortune was two-fold. He was an officer in the RAF when he became a jet-engine designer and therefore his work was the property of the State; and his engine was so important that it demanded the application of other engineering brains besides Frank Whittle's. He would have been happy to lead them all, but by the time he was ready to do that they had become his competitors… It is the story of frustration for one of the RAF's brightest sons who was both too generous towards his beloved Service and too jealous of his brain-child.[10]

This was a slightly uncharitable view of Whittle's career and took no account of his constant pleas in 1940–41 for a proper executive team to be set up for the jet project, leaving him to serve as Chief Engineer. Given Colston Shepherd's close ties with many in the aviation world, though, the review was probably a fair reflection of a widespread perception that Whittle had been too slow to cooperate with others. It was the price Whittle had paid for objecting to Tizard's non-exclusive approach, and (more importantly) for clinging to an independent strategy for Power Jets in 1943. Colston Shepherd offered another telling comment, too, on how Whittle was now viewed by his peers. He made a point of noting that Whittle had effectively been deprived of any meaningful role in the Jet Age by 1953 ('I am obliged to confess that in Civil Service and industry alike I find little sympathy for the man who started it all'). Oddly, he suggested that *Jet* fell short of explaining why this should be so – though the book's closing chapters on the struggle between Power Jets and the authorities were surely bitter enough to alert even the most casual reader to the grounds for lasting resentment on both sides.

Jet's publication compounded this problem. Many of those targeted by Whittle's judgements were dismayed. Some were embarrassed by his disclosures, as Tizard had foreseen. Others thought he had given far too little attention to the work of the RAE and of fellow engineers like Frank Halford. And there was perhaps another, broader reason why hackles rose in response to the book. Britain's leadership of the Jet Age had been one of the country's great success stories since 1945. It was disconcerting to be told that the Jet Age could and should have been inaugurated years earlier. At a time when the British aircraft industry was riding high, Whittle's unflattering account of the government's handling of the jet engine seemed to some almost unpatriotic. All the more so when, by an unhappy chance, tragedy overtook Britain's Jet Age in the immediate aftermath of the book's publication. The de Havilland Comet, the world's first civil jet airliner, had enjoyed a glamorous debut after its launch in May 1952: the Queen and other members of the royal family had flown on it in June 1953, despite a worrying crash in India a month earlier that had killed all on board. Then in January 1954 a Comet dropped out of the sky for the second time, shortly after taking off from Rome airport. This disaster was followed by another only three months later, also bringing down a flight out of Rome and shattering for ever the Comet's commercial prospects. This setback to Britain's ascendancy in the aerospace industry made *Jet*'s trenchant critique of past policy decisions – and especially its reminder of what had been lost with the resignations of 1946 – an even more uncomfortable read.

It is impossible, anyway, to escape the impression that its author for many years thereafter – until well into the 1960s – was effectively cold-shouldered by most of Britain's aviation establishment. He was never invited to its biennial gathering at Farnborough, launched in 1948. The medals and awards dried up, and *Jet*'s appearance conspicuously triggered no celebrity tours. He was offered no further employment in the aero-engineering industry, nor did the government seek his advice on any matters of consequence. He lost contact with Rolls-Royce after Hives retired in 1955 and would make no further visits to Derby until many years later. When the BBC's Overseas Service in 1959 put out a momentous series of interviews with leading figures in the history of British aviation, Whittle was not among them.[11] For most of the 1950s, working intermittently as an adviser to Shell's research facilities, Whittle lived an increasingly solitary and unhappy life. Having identified so strongly with the RAF since his teens, he felt slightly adrift for years after his early retirement from the service. Personal relationships brought him little consolation. His total immersion in the jet project had made terrible demands on his family for years, and his illnesses after the war had finally proved more than his marriage could bear. He and Dorothy had separated in 1951. (He scarcely mentioned her in his autobiography, in which she was indexed under her maiden name.) He had begun living alone either in London's Dolphin Square or in a farmhouse (Walland Hill) that he acquired on the edge of Dartmoor in the West Country. Though he always attended the Reactionaries' annual lunches if he could, many of his old friendships cooled – he saw little, even, of Coll Tinling, Dudley Williams or Pat Johnson – and he had scant further contact with old RAF colleagues. Adjusting to life with no regular work and no compelling workplace challenge proved no easier as the years went by. He had another nervous breakdown in 1960 which required a long period of convalescence, but he was not a man for whom luxury holidays held any appeal. One forlorn attempt to take a California-style break ended abruptly: he bought a round-the-world cruise in 1963 – but fled from the ship when it reached its first port of call at Naples, as he later explained to yet another Medical Board, 'because he could not stand close contact with his fellow passengers'.[12]

ii

A gradual revival in his fortunes began with the triumph of the jet plane in the American airline industry. The US airlines had neglected the jet's potential for many years after the war, when their marketplace had been swamped with cheap and reliable ex-service carriers, notably the evergreen Douglas DC-4. Jet engines were seen as a purely military technology. The progressive plane makers at Boeing and Douglas had gone on pressing the business case for the civilian jet, but the airline companies had given it no credence. Flying anywhere had therefore remained a privileged affair until the end of the 1950s, almost the exclusive preserve of well-heeled passengers and corporate types. Then Pan American World Airways broke with the past, and gave the plane makers their first orders in 1955. The Boeing 707 and the DC-8 were flying with several airlines by 1960. Initially offered as a luxury service with prices to match, jet travel then became a commodity item with the advent in 1964–5 of the Boeing 727 and the DC-9. What followed was a dramatic 'catching up' with the compelling business model offered by the jet, marking one of the more seismic shifts in the twentieth century wrought by new technology. If you had wanted to cross the Atlantic in 1950, it was cheaper to take a suite on the *Queen Mary* than to buy an airline ticket. By the start of the 1970s, you could buy a transatlantic air ticket – probably on a Boeing 747 jumbo jet – for little more than the price of a night on the tiles at either end. This was the commercial fulfilment of the revolution that Whittle had foreseen – though he was quite as surprised as anyone by the pace at which it unfolded.

From the early 1960s he began attracting a steadily mounting stream of plaudits from across the Atlantic. His postbag brought frequent invitations to attend award ceremonies. The main impetus for this fresh wave of honours – like the Goddard Award (1965), enrolment into the San Diego Hall of Fame (1967) and the Tony Jannus Award (1969, for 'contributions to scheduled commercial aviation') – mostly came not from the engineering profession but from the travel industry and bodies representing the civil airline business. It was their way of celebrating the tumultuous impact, over little more than a single decade, of jet planes on the American way of life. They had transformed not only the routines of passenger travel but the entire logistics, too, of the freight industry. As a consequence of his renewed celebrity in America, Whittle began travelling there more frequently and decided to acquire a small holiday home in the Caribbean, at Montego Bay. He left the practical running of it to his housekeeper and companion in Britain, Margaret Lawrence, who seems to have managed most of his affairs. He also renewed his friendship in America with a woman he had first met when both were patients at the Naval Hospital in Bethesda, Maryland in 1947. A former TWA air hostess, Hazel ('Tommie') Hall was a divorcee now working as a psychiatric nurse in Bethesda. Whittle stayed with her whenever his schedule allowed it on any of his prize-gathering forays, and she regularly stayed as a house guest with him (and Margaret) in Jamaica.

Back in Britain, he found his circumstances ever more dispiriting. He was upset to see a deteriorating financial situation at Rolls-Royce culminate in the company's collapse in 1971. It had embarked on a radical redesign of the jet engine that promised to mark the single most significant advance in a generation. Unfortunately, developing the 'RB211' proved a steep technical challenge and tested the company's cost controls to destruction. Whittle was dismayed by the Derby firm's plight, which seemed to him only too revealing about the status of engineering in contemporary Britain. He had a personal stake in the tragedy, too. While working at Shell in the 1950s he had conceived the design of a jet-powered 'turbo-drill' for the oil industry. The idea had subsequently been backed by Bristol Siddeley Engines, thanks to the support of Stanley Hooker who had left Rolls-Royce many years earlier to become one of the Bristol firm's directors. Sadly for Whittle, Bristol Siddeley had been acquired by Rolls-Royce in 1968. Funding for the turbo-drill had rapidly dwindled, and was swept away altogether by the bankruptcy of 1971. Rolls-Royce's aero-engine business was to be rescued within days via a sale of its assets to a state-owned company, which went on to make a great success of the RB211. Whittle exchanged occasional letters with senior managers of the company over the next few years – mostly in connection with environmental concerns over the supersonic Concorde – but his turbo-drill never surfaced again.

Also troubling him in Britain by the early 1970s was an old friendship that he had rekindled with an oddball psychiatrist based at London's Charing Cross Hospital. Dr John Randall took Whittle on as a patient and began prescribing him anti-depressant drugs, while encouraging him to see alcohol as a useful relaxant. (Whittle did not need much encouragement by this time, and was drinking heavily.) He also persuaded Whittle to assist him through much of 1973–4 with some biblical research for a book he was writing, provisionally entitled *The Mental State of Jesus Christ*. Bizarrely, Whittle plunged into writing a series of papers on theology and ethics, full of cod scholarship and rather crackpot ideas.[13] Only adding to their oddness was the fact that Whittle wrote most of them in a tiny, spidery longhand on corporate stationery headed 'Bristol Siddeley Whittle Tools Limited'. Perhaps he enjoyed reviving memories of being told Bible stories as a child, and the historical origins of the Bible had always been of interest to him. He was also exercised, like Isaac Newton, by the relation-ship between science and Christianity – though Whittle departed from Newton in rejecting any belief whatever in biblical truths. (In a letter to William Hawthorne at Cambridge, he mentioned his renewed readings of the Bible only to pour scorn on it – 'my feeling is that for a load of nonsense it would be hard to beat. It seems quite incredible to me that it should have had such an influence on social history.'[14]) His lack of any Christian faith did not prevent him spending whole days reconstructing John the Baptist's family tree for his friend Randall, or building spreadsheets to enumerate New Testament references to Christ's miracles. It was a strange episode – one has to wonder what kind of drugs he was taking – and it was mercifully brought to a close when he fell out with Randall in 1975. Shaking himself free of the whole business, Whittle decided it was time for a completely fresh start.

Unsurprisingly, he turned to America. He asked Dorothy for a divorce – they had been separated for twenty-four years – and left for a temporary stay with his American friend Tommie Hall. Close to her home in Bethesda, Maryland, was the US Naval Academy in Annapolis. Learning of Whittle's presence in the area, the Academy's faculty heads made contact and early in 1976 they offered him a guest lectureship for their next academic year, 1976–7. After a brief exchange of letters, he accepted. The Concorde began flying between London Heathrow and Washington Dulles Airport in May that year, and the Academy secured him a seat on it for his journey over in September 1976 to begin life as a permanent US resident. By the middle of November, he had married Tommie Hall and abandoned for ever his home in Devon, leaving it with most of its contents to Margaret Lawrence.

Revered at the Naval Academy from the day of his arrival, Whittle turned back to lecturing and serious research on thermodynamics as though his long travails in Britain had been a mere passing interlude. Truly, his new life at the Academy seemed to bring him redemption of a glorious kind. He remained as a fulltime member of staff at its Faculty of Aerospace Engineering until October 1980. With access to all the Academy's laboratories and active support from a team of slightly star-struck postgraduates, he was a man reborn. The moral support he received was probably as important as the practical facilities made available to him. There was no disguising the bafflement felt by his new colleagues over the way his career had been allowed to tail away in Britain, and their perspective on his wartime story was entirely sympathetic. When the Academy's Bulletin on Research Activities announced his elevation as Visiting Research Professor, it recited his many distinctions ('Knight Commander of the British Empire, Commander of the Bath, Fellow of the Royal Society, Air Commodore of the RAF and Honorary Citizen of the State of Oklahoma') and included his authorship of *Jet*, which was described as:

> [the story] of a man of genius and vision faced with formidable engineering problems and the enormous cost of experimental work, and often opposed by those who, through pessimism, apathy, bureaucratic fumbling or short-sightedness, delayed the progress of his work.[15]

(Whittle might almost have penned that himself – and perhaps he did.) By 1980 he was ready to work on a textbook – published as *Gas Turbine Aero-Thermodynamics* – embodying the main conclusions of his work since 1976. Stepping back from his research, he wrote to one of the Academy's senior officers to express his gratitude for the cooperation he had received from all his Faculty colleagues: 'It has been reminiscent of the team spirit which prevailed in the early days of jet engine development.'[16] Now white-haired and mellowed with age, the seventy-three-year-old Whittle was happier than he had been for years. Some of the Reactionaries, visiting from England, encountered the witty, optimistic and purposeful companion they remembered from the earliest days of the war.

He had always been intensely sensitive over his reputation. His later years brought him the satisfaction of seeing two long-standing reputational issues settled in gratifying ways. The first related to the origins of the jet engine, and more specifically the claims of those who persisted in tracing these back to the experimental work at the Heinkel factory before the war. It was a topic that resonated far more in the US than in Britain, for understandable reasons. Many of the young German engineers who had worked on jet and rocket programmes under the Nazis had moved to America in the immediate post-war years. They included men like Helmut Schelp, who had overseen the Third Reich's entire jet programme from Berlin, and Anselm Franz, who had designed the Jumo 004 engine that powered the Me 262. Several remained prominent figures in US aero-engineering over the following decades. (Another highly influential engineer of German extraction, Gerhard Neumann, was the head of General Electric's jet engine division.) Among them lingered a keen awareness of what had been achieved with gas turbines in Hitler's Germany. Constantly reminded of Whittle's achievements in England on the one hand and the wartime feats of General Hap Arnold's American taskforce on the other, the German émigrés were fond of recalling the pre-war achievements of their country's jet programme. So it was gratifying for them to have the man behind Ernst Heinkel's 1939 jet, the He 178, working from 1947 in a prominent research role with the US Air Force. Hans Pabst von Ohain became a director of its Aeronautical Research Laboratories at the Wright-Patterson air base in 1956 and was appointed Chief Scientist there in 1963.

In truth, von Ohain's contribution to the development of the jet engine was nugatory: had the Heinkel unit never flown, it would have made no difference at all to the jet-engine programmes pursued by Junkers and BMW. His design for the He 178 never resulted in a production unit and left no direct legacy of any kind for other aero-engineers (not even as an historical artefact – the 1939 flight engine was destroyed in a British air raid on Berlin in 1943). As one comparative study of the jet engine's evolution in Britain, Germany and the US has it, the Heinkel project produced only 'stunt turbojet engines'.[17] Nonetheless, von Ohain was indubitably the brains behind the first jet engine ever to fly (albeit briefly). This was enough for many of his peers, and especially his fellow German émigrés, to hail him as, at the very least, the 'co-inventor of the jet'. Whittle by contrast had never rated von Ohain's work of any importance. He had made only a single passing reference to it in *Jet*. Dubious of the He 178's merit, and anyway convinced that the German must have had the benefit of seeing his crucial 1930 patent, Whittle had long found the whole business mildly irritating. Too many committee men in the US over the years had written to him as 'the British co-inventor of the jet', usually drawing a polite but firm correction by return of post.

So when invited to meet von Ohain for the first time, in New York in 1966, Whittle had approached the occasion with some misgivings. The BBC arranged their encounter for a film to mark the twenty-fifth anniversary of the E.28/39's first flight – *Jet Propelled*, directed by Ramsey Short.[18] To Whittle's surprise, they took an immediate liking to each other. He visited von Ohain at his home in Dayton, Ohio, nine months later and they talked together for several hours. It was probably helpful that von Ohain had already confirmed during an interview with the BBC, seen by Whittle, that he had indeed had the chance to read the 1930 patent before starting to think about his jet engine – although, much to Whittle's chagrin, this admission was cut from the edited version of the 1966 film. ('I hope that a good deal of the material which was not used is not being destroyed,' Whittle had pleaded in a subsequent letter to Ramsey, 'because in my view it is very valuable for the records, particularly, for example, von Ohain's admission that he had seen my patents before he started work.'[19]) Evidently the true origin of the German jet was not regarded by either man as a serious bone of contention when they met. 'I particularly enjoyed talking with you about your own early work,' wrote Whittle in a letter of thanks.[20] Thereafter they met on many of Whittle's trips to America and became good friends – as, too, did their wives, Tommie and Hanni.

The friendship between two legendary names of the aeronautical world offered those organising trade events an irresistible double bill. Once Whittle had followed von Ohain over the Atlantic and taken up US residency, it was much easier to bring them together for joint appearances and a string of invitations duly followed through the 1980s. Their public conversations were hugely gratifying to Whittle – not least because von Ohain was perfectly happy to confess the 'stunt engine' aspect of his work. The German was essentially a scientist with much less interest in engineering. He readily deferred to Whittle's far greater knowledge of jet propulsion – and was always adept with his flattery, to which Whittle was not immune in his later years. The two men thrilled American audiences with a sense of history merely by turning up on platforms together, and kept them amused with their banter about how and when they had each learned of the other's activities. Since the end of the war, Whittle had generally made light of Nazi Germany's jet programmes. Perhaps just to be consistent, he would now often claim to have known little of them until 1945. This probably helped to perpetuate a myth about the Allies' ignorance of them which had grown up over the years. (It had suited many post-war champions of Britain's Jet Age to say little or nothing of the Luftwaffe's efforts – not least, surely, to avoid awkward questions about how on earth Hitler's engineers had been allowed to get so close to stealing a march on their British counterparts.)

Their reminiscences included some serious reflection, too. Von Ohain was firmly of the view that, in neglecting Whittle's project in the 1930s, the British had lost an opportunity to prevent Hitler's war. As he put it to an audience of engineers at a General Electric corporate event in Cincinnati in February 1985:

> In Germany my idea was tested relatively quickly. In England, Sir Frank's was not. British jet engine development produced [a first] operational aircraft in 1943. One has to wonder what would have happened if – as was possible – this development [had] occurred six or seven years earlier. Would World War II have occurred if the Luftwaffe knew it faced operational British jets instead of Spitfires? I, for one, think not.[21]

More than one serving RAF officer in the Washington embassy was buttonholed by von Ohain at some event in the 1980s and force-fully reminded of Britain's culpability. ('If you people had given Frank the sort of support I got in Germany you could have had a jet fighter in 1936 and we might not have had World War Two', as he insisted to one Air Vice Marshal.[22]) Von Ohain's outspokenness did Whittle's growing reputation in America no harm. On the fiftieth anniversary of the first ignition of the WU1 in April 1987, a party was thrown in his honour at the National Air and Space Museum. Whittle was there in person to hear a stirring message of congratulations read out to the gathering. It came from President Ronald Reagan: 'Sir Frank's invention of the jet engine was a quantum leap forward in aeronautical technology – as significant as the first flight of the Wright brothers in 1903.'

Not for the first time, praise for Whittle in America found an echo in Britain. His achievements had never really been forgotten; but until the late 1970s few opportunities had been taken for almost a quarter of a century to celebrate them (except at Cambridge University, where the Engineering Department led by William Hawthorne, now Master of Churchill College, linked Whittle to three anniversary events over that decade). Indeed, his decision to live in the US attracted occasional criticism in the British tabloids, which were not above suggesting that he had taken his 1948 award and flown the country. Perhaps such jibes helped to prompt more serious media interest in his work. The BBC began planning a film about his life, which was eventually broadcast in May, 1981.[23] His stock in Britain thereafter seemed to rise steadily in the mysterious way that reputations sometimes do – assisted by at least one anniversary party for him organised by a former Power Jets apprentice – and Whittle, who had long yearned for a keener appreciation of his work in Britain, responded to the palpable change as warmly as his poor health allowed. A newly installed management at British Airways adopted him almost as an unofficial ambassador for the airline's expanding ambitions. He was gifted transatlantic flights on several occasions, some of them on Concorde, and this helped to make his UK appearances steadily more frequent. One exchange could often lead to another in serendipitous fashion. When the City of Derby decided to name a major road after him in 1984, Rolls-Royce endorsed the idea. Soon afterwards, Whittle was invited to visit its Derby plant as a guest of honour. Whittle wrote back to the company without hesitation to say how much he 'would be delighted to renew the always happy association between myself and Rolls-Royce'.[24] English friends who visited him at home in Maryland found memorabilia from his wartime past, hitherto stored away, had been taken out and hung back on the wall as in days gone by at Broomfield.

If his move to America in 1976 had caused any resentment in Britain, it seemed long forgotten by the middle of the 1980s. In 1986 he received another invitation to Buckingham Palace, this time to have tea with the Queen and to receive the insignia marking his appointment to that most exclusive of honours, the Order of Merit. A few days later he was invited to 10 Downing Street. True to form, he made a detailed record of his forty-five-minute conversation with the Prime Minister. They spent much of the time discussing the recent Challenger space-shuttle disaster. Margaret Thatcher asked her guest what he thought had gone wrong, which perhaps elicited a more detailed response than she had expected ('Referring to the just published report I said that... important points had been overlooked... [such as] the basic stupidity of using O rings of only 0.28' sect. dia. on a cylinder of about 12' diameter. I explained why this was a serious mistake.'[25]) Afterwards Thatcher issued a generous note to the press, congratulating Whittle on his elevation to the OM and drawing a moral for the times. His career, she noted, had been 'an object lesson on the creativity and inspiration of British engineering at its best'.[26]

He never opted to live in England again, although in truth he missed it terribly. He greatly enjoyed a return visit in 1987 to attend a celebratory dinner marking both his eightieth birthday and the WU1's fiftieth. Rolls-Royce alumni also hosted two memorable dinners for him at the company's Duffield Bank guest house outside Derby.[27] Thereafter the frequency of his trips back to England dwindled away. He went on gracing the odd event nearer home. He and von Ohain were hosted by the First Flight Society at Kitty Hawk, North Carolina, in 1991, for example, to remember the E.28/39's maiden flight at a suitably evocative location. That same year, the two men were jointly awarded the Charles Stark Draper Prize, the ultimate accolade in the American engineering world. Whittle was now generally happier at home, though, immersing himself in books on a wide range of intellectual passions – he loved history, archaeology and geology in particular – with undimmed curiosity.

Reaching his advanced age was little short of a medical phenomenon, given his long history of illness and disability, but the cigarettes caught up with him in the end. In 1996 he was diagnosed with terminal lung cancer. That July, as his strength began to fail, he received a letter from William Hawthorne confirming that his private papers had been safely deposited, as Hawthorne had requested, at the Churchill Archives Centre in Cambridge. They would be preserved, wrote Hawthorne, as 'an authentic account of the major revolution in aircraft development since the first flight'.[28] Whittle had rounded off his epic documenting of his jet-engine years in style. He spent his last weeks at home with his wife Tommie in one of the four apartments they owned at his lakeside residence in Columbia, Maryland. His younger son Ian joined them there – having just arranged the funeral in England for Dorothy who by chance had died earlier in July. Towards the end, the British embassy sent down one of its RAF officers as a mark of respect. Group Captain Iveson arrived at the bedside in his RAF uniform, a nice touch that brought a smile to Whittle's face. He died the next day, on the evening of 8 August 1996, aged eighty-nine.

He was cremated in Maryland, but his ashes went on two journeys before interment and both showed an attention to detail that Whittle would have applauded. In its fleet of airliners christened with individual names, British Airways had a Boeing 777 that was called the Sir Frank Whittle. Alerted to his death by the embassy in Washington, the company made this aeroplane available to carry his ashes back to England. It seemed briefly that they might be interred in the Royal Air Force Chapel of Westminster Abbey. This proved not to be possible – though a memorial stone would later be placed there – but a lavish memorial service followed at the Abbey in November. The main eulogy was delivered by the head of the Air Force. The RAF then came up with an alternative resting place for the ashes. It required a lengthy delay, but took good advantage of the 1998 Air Show at Farnborough. The show's arrangements involved having two antique aircraft on stand-by at Bournemouth airport on the south coast – a Gloster Meteor and a de Havilland Vampire. The RAF negotiated to borrow them both for a day. So it came about that Whittle's remains made their last journey by jet, in a Gloster Meteor piloted by a retired Air Marshal who flew them, with a second jet as an escort co-piloted by his son Ian, to RAF Cranwell in Lincolnshire, to be interred in the grounds of the college where his service life had begun all those years ago – as Whittle, F., Boy 364365.

The Whittle Engine's Family Tree

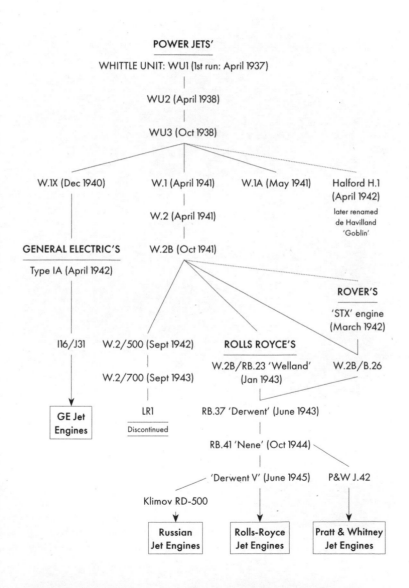

List of Characters

Beaverbrook, Lord (Max) (b. 1879). Installed by Churchill as head of new Ministry of Aircraft Production (MAP) in May 1940 to bulldoze aside all obstacles to industry's support for the RAF. Disrupted so many existing development plans that chaos ensued and jet project was briefly imperilled. Later gave it his support but to little effect. Left MAP in May 1941.

Bramson, Morgens (Bram) (b. 1895). Consultant engineer whose independent report on FW's jet-engine proposal in October 1935 urged O. T. Falk & Partners to invest in it.

Bulman, George (b. 1892). Civil servant who oversaw much of Whitehall's relationship with the aero-engine industry from 1919 until his departure from MAP in February 1944. As head of Engine Development until October 1938 and subsequently head of both the Development and Production arms of MAP's Engines directorate, he exercised unusual influence for a middle-ranking official and had powerful hold over policy towards jet engine until Wilfrid Freeman distanced him from it in January 1943. Became *bête noire* of Power Jets team.

Carter, George (b. 1889). Chief Designer at Gloster Aircraft from 1937. Responded quickly to Whittle's approach in 1939 and thereafter led team responsible for E.28/39 (Pioneer) and F.9/40 (Meteor). Worked with FW to launch E.28/39 in May 1941 and later backed idea of adopting it as an operational fighter.

Cheshire, Leslie (b. 1905?). Turbine engineer at BTH who worked with FW from earliest days of jet project and was eventually seconded to Power Jets. One of FW's most important assistants throughout the war, who remained a close friend in later years.

Collingham, R. H. (Bob) (b. 1888). Deputy Chief Turbine Engineer at BTH in Rugby until 1938, when he succeeded Samuelson as Chief. Frequently at loggerheads with FW. Retired 1948.

Constant, Hayne (b. 1904). Academic and RAE engineer, ran supercharger section at Farnborough from 1936. Initially championed axial compressor, but later argued for FW to be given urgent support with centrifugal compressor. Headed RAE's Engines directorate from 1941, transferring to Power Jets (R&D) in 1944 as head of the two organisations' combined Engineering Division. Later director of National Gas Turbine Establishment, and eventually Chief Scientist (RAF) at Ministry of Defence.

Cripps, Stafford (b. 1889). Labour member of Churchill's War Cabinet, appointed Minister of MAP in November 1942. With strong socialist background, appeared to FW to be an ally in push for nationalisation of whole jet project. Opted instead for a state buyout of Power Jets alone, in March 1944. Sympathetic to FW's subsequent plans but unable to overrule industry objections in April 1945 to continuing role for company as independent manufacturer.

Farren, William (b. 1892). Close colleague of Melvill Jones at Cambridge until joining Air Ministry in 1937. Leading figure in wartime aeronautical research, first at MAP then at Farnborough where he was key to expansion of RAE to prepare for jet-engine revolution.

Fedden, Roy (b. 1885). Designer of the Jupiter engine and greatly respected Chief Engineer at Bristol Aeroplane from 1920 to 1942. Ignored letter from FW re jet idea in February 1931 and remained sceptical of the jet well into the war.

Freeman, Wilfrid (b. 1888). Senior RAF officer put in charge of Research and Development at Air Ministry in 1936. Led successful rearmament of RAF thereafter. Served uneasily under Beaverbrook at MAP until November 1940 when he was made Vice-Chief of the Air Staff. Left RAF to return to MAP as its civilian Chief Executive in October 1942, remaining there until almost end of the war. Always sympathetic towards FW, but used strong rapport with Ernest Hives to urge ahead Rolls-Royce's leadership of jet project.

Griffith, A. A. (b. 1893). Renowned government scientist who pioneered theoretical work on the gas turbine. Modelled a first axial compressor while head of the Air Ministry's science laboratory in late 1920s, envisaging gas turbine with propeller. Failed to respond when alerted by the young FW to possibilities of jet propulsion. Inexplicably set aside turbine research while running Engine Research at RAE in 1931–6. Later joined Rolls-Royce where he pursued work on contra-flow jet engine ('CR1'), eventually abandoned.

Halford, Frank (b. 1894). Distinguished aero-engine designer given introduction to FW by Tizard in December 1940. After initial misunderstanding, received help from FW in his work on a variant of the design pursued at Power Jets. Sponsored by de Havilland and built H.1 ('Goblin') engine which powered first Meteor. Forthright opponent of commercial future for Whetstone plant.

Hives, Ernest (b. 1886). General Manager of Rolls-Royce from 1936. Dominant figure behind his firm's rise to pre-eminence in aero-engine business and close confidant of Wilfrid Freeman. Early convert to future potential of jet engine after first flight in May 1941. Pushed through Rolls-Royce's takeover of Rover's role in jet project at end of 1942 and cemented its leadership of jet-engine sector by 1945. Led industry's opposition to Stafford Cripps' proposal that Power Jets survive under Whittle's lead as independent producer of prototype engines after the war.

Hooker, Stanley (b. 1907). Head of supercharger section at Rolls-Royce from 1938. Great admirer of FW, and keen to foster ties with Power Jets from mid-1941. Sent by Hives to run jet-engine facilities in Lancashire, taken over from Rover in January 1943. Played key role in developing Rolls-Royce's first jet engines.

Johnson, W. E. P. (Pat) (b. 1903). Distinguished pilot and Chartered Patent Agent in City. Met FW while an instructor at Central Flying School in 1929, and helped him to file initial patent for jet engine. Retired from RAF in 1932 but returned as instructor in 1938. Joined Power Jets in 1940 as one of FW's core team – but never did manage to fly jet plane.

Jones, Bennett Melvill (b. 1887). Cambridge professor of aeronautical engineering (appointed in 1919) who encouraged FW to persevere with ideas for jet engine even while studying for Tripos exams. Subsequently acted as adviser to Power Jets and mediated between FW and Whitehall.

Keirn, Donald J. (b. 1905). Engineering officer in the USAAF, sent to England by General 'Hap' Arnold in August 1941 to assess the state of the jet project. Charged with escorting the W.1X over the Atlantic the following month. Accompanied FW on US tour of summer, 1942 and appointed member of GTCC in September 1942.

Lees, George ('Daddy') (b. 1897). Officer in RAF Education Branch who taught FW at Cranwell and at Henlow. Joined Power Jets in 1940 on 'Special Duties' and became FW's personal assistant.

Lindemann, Frederick (b. 1886). Close friend and scientific adviser to Churchill, given peerage as Lord Cherwell in July 1941. Alerted Churchill to jet engine and urged support for Gloster Meteor. Acrimonious relationship with Tizard helped to undermine latter's role in Whitehall.

Linnell, F. J. (Jack) (b. 1892). Senior RAF officer appointed Controller of Research and Development at MAP in June 1941. Sided with officials in support of Rover but changed his mind by late 1942, recommending switch to Rolls-Royce. Re-posted abroad in April 1943.

Lockspeiser, Ben (b. 1891). Career scientist at RAE who succeeded Pye as Director of Scientific Research in 1943. Recruited FW to Whitehall's Supersonic Committee, set up in 1943, which gave FW access to secret reports on progress of German jet engines.

Moore-Brabazon, John (b. 1884). Famed as a pre-1914 pioneer aviator. Succeeded Beaverbrook as political head of MAP in May 1941. Largely ineffectual in role and survived less than ten months. Sacked by Churchill. Later chaired the Brabazon Committee, laying plans for the post-war development of Britain's civil aviation.

Phillips, Mary (b. 1911). Hired by FW as secretary at end of 1938. Shared FW's office/study at Brownsover Hall from August 1940. Took rooms at Staff College in 1943 and at hospitals in 1944–5 to keep his paperwork going and provide valuable companionship for FW. Supported by FW financially after the war, when her health collapsed and left her bedridden until her death in 1972.

Pye, David (b. 1886). Aeronautical scientist and authority on piston engines. Director of Scientific Research at Air Ministry from 1937 to 1943. Initially sceptical of jet project, but hugely impressed by WU3 engine on visit to Lutterworth in June 1939. Instrumental in award of government contracts to Power Jets in first three months of the war.

Reactionaries. Name adopted by those alumni of Power Jets who honoured its memory with annual reunion lunches from 1946. Included most of FW's handpicked engineering colleagues such as Geoffrey Bone, Bruno Bozzoni, Leslie Cheshire, Bob Feilden,

William Hawthorne, Mac Ogston, Reuel van Millingen, Reg Voysey and Dan Walker.

Roxbee Cox, Harold (b. 1902). Former RAE scientist brought into Whitehall in July 1940 as Deputy Director of Scientific Research. Backed FW and Power Jets from start, often intervening to counter MAP's support for Rover. Given effective control over jet-engine plans as Director of Special Projects in July 1943. Appointed head of nationalised Power Jets (Research & Development) by Cripps in April 1944. Remained as chairman of National Gas Turbine Establishment. Ennobled as Lord Kings Norton in 1965.

Samuelson, Fred (b. 1878). Chief Turbine Engineer at BTH in Rugby, who rejected FW's first approach in 1930 but agreed to contract in 1936. Retired in 1938.

Shepherd, Jill (b. 1919). WAAF Staff officer in British embassy in Washington who spent ten weeks as FW's personal assistant on his official tour of USA in summer of 1946. (Married as Jill Grey.)

Sidgreaves, Arthur (b. 1882). Managing Director of Rolls-Royce from 1929 to 1945. Was behind appointment of Hives as General Manager, and backed him over jet engine.

Sporborg, Henry (Harry) (b. 1877). Chief Engineer and Board Director of BTH. Unimpressed with FW's early efforts, which he insisted in 1937 be relocated from Rugby to Lutterworth. Remained sceptical of jet's future and early in 1941 pulled BTH back from originally intended production role.

Tedder, Arthur (b. 1890). Air Vice Marshal of RAF with responsibility for research at Air Ministry in 1939–40, later transferring to MAP in similar role. With no scientific or engineering background, struggled to reconcile conflicting views of officials over policy towards FW. Outspoken critic of Beaverbrook at MAP. Potentially a valuable ally for FW, but re-posted abroad in

November 1940. Later had distinguished wartime career, serving as Eisenhower's Deputy Supreme Commander. Assisted FW in retiring from RAF in 1948.

Tinling, Collingwood (Coll) (b. 1900). Business partner of Dudley Williams and fellow director of Power Jets. Assumed chairmanship after departure of Lance Whyte in 1941. Assiduous advocate of company's legal and commercial rights. Remained on Board after nationalisation but resigned in 1946 after departure of FW's 'Jet Men'.

Tizard, Henry (b. 1885). Scientist, academic and government adviser on defence matters. By 1940 had been leading member of Aeronautical Research Committee for twenty years and had played key role in construction of Britain's radar network. After leading scientific mission to USA, was asked to succeed Freeman at MAP late in 1940 and tried to steer jet project forward, with only mixed success. Often struggled with personality clashes and lacked authority to counter Bulman. FW thought him insufficiently supportive in battles with Rover through 1941–2.

Tobin, Denis (b. 1912?). Official at MAP appointed as Technical Representative to Power Jets. Was FW's day-to-day contact at Ministry, then at Directorate of Special Projects.

Von Ohain, Hans Pabst (b. 1911). German physicist and designer of jet engine sponsored by Ernst Heinkel, which flew in August 1939. Emigrated in 1947 to USA, subsequently taking various senior posts with USAF. Met FW in New York in 1966 and joined him at many US aerospace events over next thirty years to reminisce in public about origins of jet engine.

Watt, George (b. 1908). New Zealander and qualified engineer who had joined RAF in 1933. Arrived at MAP as Wing Commander in 1942 to become Roxbee Cox's deputy in Special Projects.

Whittle, Dorothy (*née* Lee) (b. 1904). Married FW in 1930 having met him in his last year as an apprentice at Cranwell. Devoted herself to FW, the family home and their two sons, David (b. 1931) and Ian (b. 1934), but had virtually no involvement with FW's work. They separated in 1951 and divorced in 1976. She died a few weeks before him in July 1996.

Whittle's engine (b. 1937). Christened Whittle Unit (WU), it passed through several design permutations – WU1, WU2 and WU3 – and then two flight versions, W.1 and W.1A, with non-flight version, W.1X, going to General Electric in the US. A major revision, W.2, was quickly superseded by W.2B, subsequently adopted and modified by Rolls-Royce as the RB.23 ('Welland'). Two later designs were the W.2/500, which Rolls-Royce drew upon for its RB.37 ('Derwent'), and the W.2/700 which FW intended to adapt for the proposed supersonic M.52 until this plane was cancelled by the Attlee Government in February 1946.

Whyte, Lance (b. 1896). Cambridge physicist and writer, turned investment banker with O. T. Falk & Partners. Instigated launch of Power Jets in 1936, taking chairmanship. Antagonised many of company's Whitehall contacts with his personal manner. Dismissed by FW from executive role in 1941 after disagreement over ambitious growth plans for Ladywood Works.

Wilks, Spencer (b. 1891). Prominent figure in Midland car industry and Managing Director of Rover Company. Took on shadow-factory contracts for aero-engines and built plant in Lancashire for manufacturing to FW's designs. Quarrelled frequently with FW and lost patience with jet project by autumn 1942. Struck deal with Hives to hand over Rover's role and assets to Rolls-Royce.

Wilks, Maurice (b. 1904). Brother of Spencer and renowned engineer in car industry. Led Rover's engine team in Lancashire, coordinating work with subcontractor Joseph Lucas Ltd.

Williams, Rolf Dudley (Willie) (b. 1908). Ebullient ex-RAF friend who in May 1935 helped to persuade FW to resume work on jet-engine project. Director of Power Jets and one of three main private shareholders. A constant presence at Power Jets during 1937–46 and strong proponent of expansion at Whetstone. Left Board with Tinling after FW's resignation. Later became Tory MP.

Note on Primary Sources

This book has drawn on primary material from three main sources, starting with Frank Whittle's own private papers which are held in the Churchill Archives Centre at Churchill College, Cambridge. The collection (CAC/WHTL) runs to ninety-seven boxes, as befits the life of a man who for many years kept a written account of his every conversation. He himself distilled much of this material into his memoir, *Jet: The Story of a Pioneer*. He was able to embroider its text with further reminiscences when he assisted John Golley and Bill Gunston in the writing of *Whittle, The True Story*, published in 1987 (and republished with a different title in 1996) which was initially envisaged as an authorised biography but ended up as a modestly expanded version of *Jet*.

The second principal source was The National Archives (TNA) in Kew, where one series of the Air Ministry's papers, TNA/AIR 62 comprising 150 subcategories, is solely devoted to Whittle and the development of the jet engine. Additional material came mostly from TNA/AIR 40 (papers and reports relating to Air Intelligence in the Second World War), TNA/AVIA 8 (Air Ministry papers on inventions and Research & Development) and TNA/AVIA 10 & 15 (papers relating to the wartime work of the Ministry of Aircraft Production).

The third source was the collection of papers held by the Rolls-Royce Heritage Trust (RRHT) in Derby. In addition to the papers of Ernest Hives, this collection includes records from many different sources selected and copied by the late Ken Fulton. The surviving Ken Fulton archive (KFA) fills fifteen boxes and was catalogued by Alec Collins in 2013–15.

Other primary sources included:

The Tizard Papers at the Imperial War Museum;

The Kings Norton Papers at Cranfield University;

The Whittle Papers at Peterhouse College, Cambridge;

Miscellaneous Whittle Papers at the Dana Research Centre of London's Science Museum;

Miscellaneous Whittle Papers at the RAF Museum, Hendon.

Notes

Chapter 1: False Starts

1   A. A. Griffith, 'An Aerodynamic Theory of Turbine Design', Royal Aircraft Establishment (RAE) Report No. H-1111, July 1926, Ken Fulton Archive (KFA) Box 10.

2   'The Present Position of the Internal Combustion Turbine as a Power Plant for Aircraft' by A. A. Griffith, AML Report No. 1050A (paragraphs 3 and 4), November 1929, KFA Box 15.

3   W. L. Tweedie to FW, 5 December 1929, Avia 8/394, KFA Box 1. It is quoted in Glyn Jones, *The Jet Pioneers, The Birth of Jet-Powered Flight*, Methuen, 1989, p. 25, but misdated there to September 1929.

4   Hayne Constant to M. M. Postan, 7 December 1961, TNA/CAB 102/213, KFA Box 11.

5   Frank Whittle, *Jet, The Story of a Pioneer*, Frederick Muller, 1953, p. 14.

6   John Golley, *Whittle, The True Story*, Airlife Publishing, 1987, pp. 4–6.

7   Obituary by John Golley, *Independent*, 10 August 1996.

8   Whittle, *Jet*, p. 15.

9   Golley, *Whittle, The True Story*, p. 9.

10 T. E. Lawrence, *The Mint*, Penguin Books, 1978, p. 156.

11 Ibid., p. 219.

12 FW, English Literature Note Book 1926–28, CAC/WHTL A.42.

13 FW Diary, 12 January 1948, CAC/WHTL A.185.

14 The original Letters to Barbara are held in the RAF Museum, Hendon. Copies are in KFA, Box 15.

15 Golley, *Whittle, The True Story*, p. 8.

16 Ibid., p. 10.

17 Whittle, *Jet*, p. 17.

18 Filmed interview in 1986 with Glyn Jones and Nicholas Jones, subsequently incorporated into their jointly produced BBC Horizon documentary *Genius of the Jet*, broadcast on 20 March 1997.

19   Quoted in Russell Miller, *Boom, The Life of Viscount Trenchard*, Weidenfeld & Nicolson, 2016, p. 249.
20   Andrew Boyle, *Trenchard*, Collins, 1962, p. 363.
21   FW to Barbara, 19 July 1926, KFA Box 15.
22   *Flight*, 5 August 1926, p. 482.

Chapter 2: From Thesis to Turbo-Jet

1   FW to Barbara, 19 July 1926, KFA Box 15.
2   Andrew Boyle, *Trenchard*, Collins, 1962, p. 363.
3   Frank Whittle, *Jet, The Story of a Pioneer*, Frederick Muller, 1953, p. 19.
4   Patrick Bishop, *Air Force Blue: The RAF in World War Two – Spearhead
of Victory*, William Collins, 2017, p. 37.
5   Quoted in Glyn Jones, *The Jet Pioneers, The Birth of Jet Powered Flight*,
Methuen, 1989, p. 22.
6   FW to Barbara, 10 November 1926, KFA Box 15.
7   CAC/WHTL A.169–270.
8   'Memorandum on Aero Engine Design and Development', 1944, TNA/
CAB 102/50, KFA Box 11, para 59.
9   Book II Chemistry Thesis, 1927, uncatalogued papers held by Ian Whittle.
10   Science Museum archives, MS/0556.
11   A. A. Griffith, 'An Aerodynamic Theory of Turbine Design', Royal Aircraft Establishment (RAE) Report No. H-1111, July 1926, Ken Fulton
Archive (KFA) Box 10.
12   John Grierson, *Jet Flight*, London, 1946, p. ix.
13   Engine Sub-Committee's 48th Report to the Aeronautical Research Committee, October 1928, DSIR 23/10421, KFA Box 6A.
14   David Mondey, *The Schneider Trophy*, Robert Hale, 1975, p. 238.
15   Whittle, *Jet*, p. 24.
16   'An Encounter Between the Jet Engine Inventors, 3–4 May 1978, at
Wright-Patterson Air Force Base, Ohio'. The event was taped and a
transcript was published by Air Force Systems Command Publications
in 1986. It can be found at CAC/WHTL A.75. The quoted passage is
extracted from p. 75.
17   See www-g.eng.cam.ac.uk/125/achievements/whittle/Chronology.htm
18   Minutes of the Aeronautical Research Committee, 1926–8, para 888,
DSIR 22/5, KFA Box 6A.
19   See minutes of the Engine Sub-Committee's Internal Combustion Turbine Panel (H.E.1) meetings of 4, 11 and 20 February and 18 March 1930,
DSIR 22/68, KFA Box 6A.

20 Report of Panel H.E.1 to the Engine Sub-Committee, April 1930, DSIR 23/2964, KFA Box 6A.

21 Under-Secretary for Air to the British Interplanetary Society, 1934, quoted in Roy Hattersley, *Borrowed Time, The Story of Britain Between the Wars*, Little, Brown, 2007, p. 260.

22 Roland Cooper manuscript, CAC/WHTL A.34–37.

23 Whittle, *Jet*, p. 30.

24 John Golley, *Whittle, The True Story*, Airlife Publishing, 1987, p. 48.

25 The application date was 16 October 1930. It was approved as UK Patent No. 347766 ('Improvements relating to centrifugal compressors and pumps') on 7 May 1931.

26 A copy can be found at CAC/WHTL C.1.

27 A digest of the paper by Alec Collins can be found in *Archive*, the privately published bulletin of the Rolls-Royce Heritage Trust (Derby & Hucknall branch). See 'How Whittle Invented the Jet Engine' in No. 90, Vol. 30, Issue 2, August 2012, pp. 11–19.

28 Whittle, *Jet*, p. 40.

29 Bill Gunston, *Fedden – The Life of Sir Roy Fedden*, Rolls-Royce Heritage Trust Historical Series No. 26, 1988, pp. 254–6.

30 F. M. Green, Chief Engineer, to FW, 6 March 1931, CAC/WHTL B.1.

31 Dr Hatfield of Atlas Steels to FW, 18 November 1941, Consolidated Diaries p. 651, CAC/WHTL B.131.

32 Golley, *Whittle, The True Story*, p. 52.

33 Whittle, *Jet*, p. 39.

34 'The Turbo-Compressor and the Supercharging of Aero Engines', *Journal of the Royal Aeronautical Society*, No. 251, Vol. 35, November 1931, pp. 1047–1074.

35 Stanley Hooker, *Not Much of an Engineer, An Autobiography*, Airlife Publishing, 2002, p. 65.

36 Reavell & Co. to FW, 26 November 1931, CAC/WHTL B.2.

Chapter 3: The Cooperation Squadron

1 John Golley, *Whittle, The True Story*, Airlife Publishing, 1987, pp. 57–8.

2 Patent Office to FW, 22 November 1933, Ian Whittle papers.

3 Frank Whittle, *Jet, The Story of a Pioneer*, Frederick Muller, 1958, p. 44.

4 Golley, *Whittle, The True Story*, p. 64.

5 Whittle, *Jet*, p. 46.

6 Interview with Reg Voysey, quoted in Golley, *Whittle, The True Story*, p. 129.

7   Rolf Dudley Williams to FW, 15 May 1935, CAC/WHTL B.4.

8   The applications went in on 16 and 18 May 1935. They were both accepted on 16 November 1936 as UK Patent Number 456976 ('Improvements relating to centrifugal compressors') and UK Patent Number 456980 ('Improvements relating to propulsion of aircraft'), respectively.

9   M. L. Branson, 'This Must Be Done!', 12 November 1968, *Engineering Case Library ECL 172B*, ed. Prof. G. Kardos, Stanford University 1971, available at CAC/WHTL A.75.

10   FW memo to M. L. Bramson, 23 August 1935, CAC/WHTL B.4.

11   Obituary in *British Journal for the Philosophy of Science*, Vol. 24, Issue 1, 1 March 1973, pp. 91–2.

12   L. L. Whyte, *Focus and Diversions*, Cresset Press, 1963, pp. 102–3.

13   L. L. Whyte, 'Whittle and the Jet Adventure', *Harper's Magazine*, June 1954. Reprinted in *Focus and Diversions*, Chapter X, pp. 136–50.

14   M. L. Bramson, 'Report on the Whittle System of Aircraft Propulsion (Theoretical Stage) – October 1935', *Journal of the Royal Aeronautical Society*, Vol. 74, pp. 128–33, February 1970.

15   FW to Williams and Tinling, 1 November 1935, CAC/WHTL B.5.

16   Held today at the Lutterworth Museum.

17   Roy Lubbock to the Air Ministry, 27 December 1935, CAC/WHTL B.5.

18   R.D.E.1 (W. L. Tweedie) to Director of Contracts, 3 October 1935, TNA/AVIA 8/415, KFA Box 1.

19   Memorandum from George Bulman to David Pye, 8 January 1936, TNA/AVIA 8/413, KFA Box 1.

20   'The Four-Party Agreement', 27 January 1936, CAC/WHTL B.7.

21   Andrew Nahum, *Frank Whittle, The Invention of the Jet*, Icon Books, 2017, p. 34.

22   *Harper's Magazine*, June 1954.

23   'The Whittle Gas Turbine Used in Jet Propulsion: Pioneer Development Work as carried out by The British Thomson-Houston Co Ltd', privately printed by BTH, undated (1946?), Science Museum collection, Item 2006-164. For some reason, all its illustrations have been redacted.

24   Golley, *Whittle, The True Story*, p. 149.

25   31 March 1936, Consolidated Diaries p. 14, CAC/WHTL A.246.

26   FW, 'The Early History of the Whittle Jet Propulsion Gas Turbine', First James Clayton Lecture, Institute of Mechanical Engineers, June 1946.

27   *Flight*, 12 March 1936, p. 276.

28   Golley, *Whittle, The True Story*, p. 76.

29   Air Ministry to the Chief Instructor of the CUAS, 11 March 1936, Ian Whittle papers.

Chapter 4: 'Making the Thing Work'

1   John Golley, *Whittle, The True Story*, Airlife Publishing, 1987, p. 149.
2   J.A.W. to AMRD Wilfrid Freeman, 20 July 1936, TNA/AVIA 8/413, KFA Box 1.
3   The annual diaries for most years until 1991 (some quite sparse) are archived at CAC/WHTL A.171 to A.245. An abridged version of the 1935–42 years ('Consolidated Diaries') is available as a paginated typescript at CAC/WHTL A.246 to A.265 and B.128 to B.136.
4   D.R. Pye to FW, 4 December 1935, CAC/WHTL B.5.
5   See Frank Armstrong, 'Farnborough and the Beginnings of Gas Turbine Propulsion', *Journal of Aeronautical History*, Paper 2020/02, published online by the Royal Aeronautical Society, April 2020.
6   Consolidated Diaries, p. 19, CAC/WHTL A.246.
7   Tizard to Whyte, 5 October 1936, Consolidated Diaries, p. 24, CAC/WHTL A.246.
8   Ronald W. Clark, *Tizard*, Methuen, 1965, p. 96.
9   A.A. Griffith, 'Report on the Whittle jet propulsion system', RAE Report No. 3545, February 1937, CAC/WHTL B.11.
10 Clark, *Tizard*, p. 97.
11 Frank Whittle, *Jet: The Story of a Pioneer*, Frederick Muller, 1958, p. 56.
12 G.B.R. Feilden and Sir William Hawthorne, 'Sir Frank Whittle', *Biographical Memoirs of the Royal Society*, 1998, p. 439.
13 FW diary 12 April 1937, CAC/WHTL A.172.
14 See, for example, James Dyson's praise for Whittle at https://www.youtube.com/watch?v=_JBePAEHIeA
15 Whittle, *Jet*, p. 61.
16 Golley, *Whittle, The True Story*, p. 90.
17 Whittle, *Jet*, p. 63.
18 Consolidated Diaries, p. 43, CAC/WHTL A.248.
19 Ernst Heinkel, ed. Jürgen Thorwald, *He 1000*, Hutchinson, 1956, p. 240.
20 Quoted in Andrew Nahum, *Frank Whittle, The Invention of the Jet*, Icon Books, 2017, p. 39. The Harvard historian was Robert Schlaifer, co-author with S.D. Heron of *The Development of Aircraft Engines and Fuels*, Harvard Business School, 1950.
21 FW diary 27 May 1937, CAC/WHTL A.172.
22 FW diary 2 June 1937, CAC/WHTL A.172.
23 Consolidated Diaries, p. 39, CAC/WHTL A.247.
24 Tizard to Whyte, 22 June 1937, Consolidated Diaries, p. 41, CAC/WHTL A.247.

25   Golley, *Whittle, The True Story*, p. 94.
26   FW diary 8 July 1938, CAC/WHTL A.173.
27   Nahum, *Frank Whittle*, p. 39.
28   FW diary 29 June 1938, CAC/WHTL A.173.
29   Glyn Jones, *The Jet Pioneers, The Birth of Jet-Powered Flight*, Methuen, 1989, p. 64.
30   FW diary 3 March 1938, CAC/WHTL A.173.
31   Golley, *Whittle, The True Story*, p. 176.
32   George Bulman, *An Account of Partnership – Industry, Government and the Aero-Engine*, ed. M. C. Neale, Rolls-Royce Heritage Trust Historical Series No. 31, 2002, p. 228.
33   Ibid., p. 250.
34   Ibid., p. 230.
35   Ibid., p. 171.
36   Ibid., p. 26.
37   TNA/AIR 6/58, SSPM No. 188, quoted in Anthony Furse, *Wilfrid Freeman, the Genius Behind Allied Survival and Air Supremacy, 1939 to 1945*, Staplehurst, Spellmount, 1999, p. 94.
38   'The Whittle Gas Turbine Used in Jet Propulsion: Pioneer Development Work as carried out by The British Thomson-Houston Co Ltd', privately printed by BTH Co., undated (1946?), 122 pp., Science Museum, Collection Item 2006-164, p. 3.
39   Golley, *Whittle, The True Story*, p. 134.
40   FW, 1938 Diary, CAC/WHTL A.173.
41   FW, 'The Early History of the Whittle Jet Propulsion Gas Turbine', First James Clayton Lecture, Institute of Mechanical Engineers, June 1945.
42   FW diary 11 May 1938, CAC/WHTL A.173.
43   FW, 'Memorandum on Conversation at the BTH', 13 December 1938, CAC/WHTL B.20.
44   FW diary 13 January 1938, CAC/WHTL A.173.
45   Bulman, *An Account of Partnership*, p. 253.
46   H. Constant memorandum, 23 August 1937, CAC/WHTL B.13.
47   FW diary 30 March 1938, CAC/WHTL A.173.
48   FW, 'Memorandum on the Jet-Propelled Interceptor Fighter', 25 October 1938, CAC/WHTL B.169.
49   Consolidated Diaries, p. 104, CAC/WHTL A.249.
50   Author's interview with Ian Whittle, 18 April 2017.
51   Consolidated Diaries, p. 108, CAC/WHTL A.249.
52   'History of the E.28', TNA/AIR 62/606.

53 FW, 'Memorandum on Visit to Gloster Works', 29 April 1939, CAC/WHTL B.23.

54 Consolidated Diaries, p. 112, CAC/WHTL A.249.

55 FW diary 18 August 1937, CAC/WHTL A.172.

56 Golley, *Whittle, The True Story*, p. 122.

57 A translation of the articles by M. Flint can be found in CAC/WHTL B.6.

58 Whittle, *Jet*, p. 84.

59 Consolidated Diaries, p. 116, CAC/WHTL A.250.

60 FW, 'Memorandum on Visit of Pye and Whyte, 30 June 1939', CAC/WHTL B.25.

61 Whittle, *Jet*, p. 89.

62 Arthur Wagner to FW, 13 January 1987, Ian Whittle papers.

63 Consolidated Diaries, p. 117, CAC/WHTL A.250.

64 FW, 'Preliminary Specification for Aircraft for Flight Tests of Unit', and 'General Specification of Unit for Flight', both dated 7 July 1939, CAC/WHTL B.25.

65 'Air Scientific Intelligence Monthly Summaries Nos 3 and 4', June–July 1940, para 14, TNA/AVIA 15/445.

66 FW to Hayne Constant, 1 September 1939, KFA Box 10.

Chapter 5: The Jet and the Dragonfly

1 Consolidated Diaries, p. 128, CAC/WHTL A.250.

2 George Carter to FW, 6 September 1939, CAC/WHTL B.26.

3 Carter to FW, 14 September 1939, CAC/WHTL B.26.

4 FW, 'Memorandum on Visit to Gloster Aircraft Co, 15 September 1939', CAC/WHTL B.26.

5 Lance Whyte, 'Memorandum on Mr Sopwith's Visit to Lutterworth, 20 September 1939', CAC/WHTL B.27.

6 FW, 'Power Jets' Relations with the BTH', 25 March 1940, CAC/WHTL B.37.

7 'A Personal Memoir' by W. E. P. Johnson, Documents.1942, Box 92/2/1, Imperial War Museum.

8 John Golley, *Whittle, The True Story*, Airlife Publishing, 1987, pp. 129–30.

9 Memoir by Edwin Lawrence Meeson, 'The Reactionaries, 1946–2001', ed. Robert Dale, privately printed by Cullum Detuners, 2nd edn, 2001, p. 231.

10 Golley, *Whittle, The True Story*, p. 123.

11 Lance Whyte, 'Memorandum on Visit by H. Constant to Lutterworth, 4 October 1939', CAC/WHTL B.28.

12 Minutes of Farnborough Group Discussion, 13 October 1939, CAC/

WHTL B.29 and Minutes of Pioneer Conference at Harrogate, 29 November 1939, CAC/WHTL B.32.

13 L.L. Whyte to Group Captain R.H. Liptrot, 8 December 1939, TNA/ AVIA 15/211, quoted in 'Fire in the Belly' by Nick Stroud, *The Aviation Historian*, Issue No. 20.

14 Consolidated Diaries, p. 158, CAC/WHTL A.251.

15 FW, 'Memorandum on Visit of S/L Reynolds to Lutterworth, 26 September 1939', CAC/WHTL B.27.

16 Lance Whyte, 'Memorandum on Visit by Sir Henry Tizard to Lutterworth, 24 January 1940', CAC/WHTL B.33.

17 Roderic Owen, *Tedder*, Collins, 1952, p. 120.

18 FW, 'Memorandum on Visit of Air Vice Marshal Tedder and S/L Ridley, 29 January 1940', CAC/WHTL B.33.

19 Lord Tedder, *With Prejudice, The War Memoirs of Marshal of the Royal Air Force Lord Tedder G.C.B.*, Cassell, 1966, p. 11. (Most of Tedder's account of his first sighting of the engine, it has to be said, was a figment of his imagination.)

20 Arthur Tedder to FW, 2 February 1940, CAC/WHTL B.33.

21 Consolidated Diaries, 7 July 1941, p. 591, CAC/WHTL B.128.

22 Bulman, *An Account of Partnership – Industry, Government and the Aero-Engine*, ed. M.C. Neale, Rolls-Royce Heritage Trust Historical Series No. 31, 2002, p. 81 and p. 319.

23 Consolidated Diaries, pp. 150–51, CAC/WHTL A.251.

24 FW, 'Memo on Visit to Air Vice Marshal Tedder (Harrogate), 6 February 1940', CAC/WHTL B.34.

25 FW to W.S. Farren, 16 February 1940, CAC/WHTL B.34.

26 Frank Whittle, *Jet, The Story of a Pioneer*, Frederick Muller, 1958, p. 103.

27 Arthur Tedder to FW, 19 February 1940, CAC/WHTL B.34.

28 FW, Memo on Conference at the Air Ministry, 26 March 1940', CAC/ WHTL B.37.

29 Whittle, *Jet*, p. 104.

30 Tedder, 'Whittle Engine – Policy', TNA/AVIA 15/421.

31 FW, 'Immediate Plan for Manufacture of Development Engines', 25 March 1940, CAC/WHTL B.35.

32 TNA/AVIA 15/421.

33 George Bulman, *An Account of Partnership*, p. 316.

34 Consolidated Diaries, p. 195, CAC/WHTL A.252.

35 FW, 'Memo on Visit to the Air Ministry, 10 May 1940', CAC/WHTL B.39.

36 Consolidated Diaries, p. 207, CAC/WHTL A.253.

37 Sir John Slessor, BBC broadcast, *Tribute to Freeman*, 15 September 1953,

quoted in Anthony Furse, *Wilfrid Freeman, the Genius Behind Allied Survival and Air Supremacy, 1939 to 1945*, Staplehurst, Spellmount, 1999, p. 117.

38 Whittle, *Jet*, p. 110.

39 Golley, *Whittle, The True Story*, p. 144.

Chapter 6: Conference at Farnborough

1 George Bulman, *An Account of Partnership – Industry, Government and the Aero-Engine*, ed. M. C. Neale, Rolls-Royce Heritage Trust Historical Series No.31, 2002, p. 269.

2 Tedder to FW, 20 May 1940, CAC/WHTL B.40.

3 FW to Tizard, 2 June 1940, CAC/WHTL B.40.

4 Transcript of telephone conversation, 18 April 1940, TNA/AVIA 15/421.

5 Anthony Furse, *Wilfrid Freeman, the Genius Behind Allied Survival and Air Supremacy, 1939 to 1945*, Staplehurst, Spellmount, 1999, p. 139.

6 Frank Whittle, *Jet, The Story of a Pioneer*, Frederick Muller, 1958, p. 131.

7 Consolidated Diaries, p. 229, CAC/WHTL A.253.

8 FW, 'Memo on interview with Lord Beaverbrook, 9 July 1940', CAC/WHTL B.41.

9 'Air Scientific Intelligence Monthly Summaries No. 2', May 1940, para 6, TNA/AVIA 15/445.

10 Secret Report No. 2168, from Air Intelligence 2(g), 28 April 1943, TNA/AIR 40/168.

11 It can be seen at https://www.youtube.com/watch?v=zdb3oLLq8L8

12 'Air Scientific Intelligence Monthly Summaries Nos 3–4, July 1940, para 14, TNA/AVIA 15/445.

13 Consolidated Diaries, p. 259, CAC/WHTL A.255.

14 See Glyn Jones, *The Jet Pioneers, The Birth of Jet-Powered Flight*, Methuen, 1989, Chapter 7 passim.

15 FW, 'Memo on Telephone Conversation with Mr Tobin, 10 July 1940', CAC/WHTL B.41.

16 Consolidated Diaries, p. 241, CAC/WHTL A.254.

17 Cynthia Keppel, 'The Development of Jet Propulsion and Gas Turbine Engines in the United Kingdom', TNA/AIR 62/2, p. 260.

18 'Schedule of Power Jets employees', 2 December 1940, CAC/WHTL B.48.

19 G. B. R. Feilden, 'Memoirs of Sir Frank Whittle', *RAF Henlow Magazine*, March 1962, CAC/WHTL F.21.

20 Consolidated Diaries, p. 65, CAC/WHTL A.247.

21 Lubbock to FW, 15 January 1940, TNA/AIR 62/21. I am indebted to Chris Weir for his assistance with this story.

22   Whittle, *Jet*, p. 135.
23   Consolidated Diaries, p. 250, CAC/WHTL A.254.
24   Tedder to L. L. Whyte, 21 August 1940, CAC/WHTL B.43.
25   FW, 'Visit of Air Vice-Marshal Tedder, 23 August 1940', CAC/WHTL B.43.
26   Consolidated Diaries, p. 267, CAC/WHTL A.255.
27   Whittle, *Jet*, p. 116.
28   Consolidated Diaries, p. 267, CAC/WHTL A.255.
29   John Golley, *Whittle, The True Story*, Airlife Publishing, 1987, p. 149.
30   Ibid., p. 150.
31   FW memo, 'Visit to Air Vice-Marshal Tedder, 6 September 1940', CAC/ WHTL B.44.
32   A. P. Young: MSS.242/SW/25, KFA, Box 15.
33   FW, 'Notes for Professor Lindemann', 2 October 1940, CAC/WHTL B.45.
34   FW, 'Talk with Mr Tobin (London)', 2 October 1940', CAC/WHTL B.45.
35   FW, 'Visit to Prof. Lindemann (London), 2 October 1940', CAC/WHTL B.45.
36   FW to Lindemann, 4 October 1940, CAC./WHTL B.53
37   FW, 'Phone Call to Sqn Ldr. Ridley, 4 October 1940', CAC/WHTL B.45.
38   FW to Tedder, 4 October 1940, CAC/WHTL B.46.
39   FW, 'Phone talk with Mr Tuck, 7 October 1940', CAC/WHTL B.46.
40   FW to Tedder, 10 October 1940, CAC/WHTL B.46.
41   FW to Lindemann, 10 October 1940, CAC/WHTL B.46.
42   Ibid.
43   FW, 'Conference at RAE Farnborough, 11 October 1940', CAC/WHTL B.47.
44   Keppel, TNA/AIR 62/2, pp. 239–41.
45   Ibid., pp. 237–8.
46   FW, 'Visit of Air Chief Marshal Sir Wilfrid Freeman, 18 October 1940', CAC/WHTL B.47.
47   Lord Tedder, *With Prejudice, The War Memoirs*, Cassell, 1966, pp. 15–16.
48   Keppel, TNA/AIR 62/2, para 69.
49   The exchange is quoted in Furse, *Wilfrid Freeman*, p. 137.

Chapter 7: 'Say, 1,000 WHITTLES'

1   Frank Whittle, *Jet, The Story of a Pioneer*, Frederick Muller, 1958, p. 132.
2   FW, 'Phone call with Mr Tobin, 28 November 1940', CAC/WHTL B.48.
3   FW, 'Visit of Sir Henry Tizard and AVM Tedder, 9 November 1940', CAC/WHTL B.47.
4   Tizard, 'Whittle Scheme', 12 November 1940, Tizard Papers, File 262.

5   Tizard to FW, 6 December 1940, CAC/WHTL B.48.
6   FW, 'Visit of Major Halford & de Havilland colleagues to Lutterwoth, 30 December 1940', CAC/WHTL B.49.
7   FW, 'Memo on the Roundtable Conference at BTH in Rugby, 2 January 1941', CAC/WHTL B.50.
8   Cynthia Keppel, 'The Development of Jet Propulsion and Gas Turbine Engines in the United Kingdom', TNA/AIR 62/2, p. 239.
9   Treasury to A. F. Forbes, 29 January 1941, TNA/AVIA 15/2619.
10   Diary for 3 January 1941, Tizard Papers, File 18.
11   Consolidated Diaries, p. 394, CAC/WHTL A.260.
12   Stanley Hooker, *Not Much of an Engineer*, Airlife Publishing, 2002, pp. 63–6.
13   FW, 'Visit of Roxbee Cox, Major Bulman and Mr Tobin, 28 January 1941', CAC/WHTL B.52.
14   Tizard to Minister, 11 January 1941, Tizard Papers, File 262.
15   George Bulman, *An Account of Partnership – Industry, Government and the Aero-Engine*, ed. M. C. Neale, Rolls-Royce Heritage Trust Historical Series No. 31, 2002, pp. 318–19. His text incorrectly dates the meeting September 1940.
16   Ibid., p. 315.
17   Ibid., p. 281.
18   Tizard to FW, 5 March 1941, CAC/WHTL B.54.
19   FW to Henry Tizard, 17 December 1940, CAC/WHTL B.49.
20   FW, 'Note on visit to Lutterworth of Dr Foster, [?] February 1941', CAC/WHTL B.53.
21   FW, 'Visit of Major Bulman, Dr Roxbee Cox and Mr Tobin to Brownsover, 14 February 1941', CAC/WHTL B.53.
22   Bulman, *An Account of Partnership*, pp. 60–62.
23   Ibid., p. 317.
24   FW, 'Note on Telephone Conversation with Tobin, 22 February 1941', CAC/WHTL B.53.
25   FW, 'Phone Mr Tobin, 3 March 1941', CAC/WHTL B.54.
26   'D.E.D.P. Notes of Meeting at the Rover Co Ltd, Chesford Grange, Kenilworth, March 5th 1941 on Rover Whittle Supercharger Production', CAC/WHTL B.54.
27   FW, 'Meeting at Chesford Grange, 5 March 1941', CAC/WHTL B.54.
28   FW to Tizard, 8 March 1941, CAC/WHTL B.55.
29   FW, 'Note on Meeting at Brownsover, 19 March 1941', CAC/WHTL B.55.
30   G. B. R. Feilden, 'Memoirs of Sir Frank Whittle', *RAF Henlow Magazine*, March 1962, CAC/WHTL F.21.

31   FW, 'Visit to Vauxhall, 26 November 1940', CAC/WHTL B.48.
32   FW, 'Notes on visit to Rover Co, Chesford Grange, on Wednesday, 5 February 1941', CAC/WHTL B.52.
33   FW, 'Meeting at MAP London, 25 March 1941', CAC/WHTL B.56.
34   Tizard memorandum to Minister, 'Whittle Engine', 14 February 1941, Tizard Papers, File 262.
35   Carter to FW, 30 March 1941, CAC/WHTL B.56.
36   Whittle, *Jet*, p. 148.
37   John Golley, *Whittle, The True Story*, Airlife Publishing, 1987, p. 227.
38   Consolidated Diaries, pp. 519–20, CAC/WHTL A.264.
39   John Grierson, *Jet Flight*, London, 1946, pp. 34–5.
40   Robert Dale (ed.), *The Reactionaries*, privately printed by Cullum Detuners, 2001, p. 48.
41   Eric Brown, *Wings on my Sleeve*, Weidenfeld & Nicolson, 2006, pp. 11–12.
42   Whittle, *Jet*, p. 152.
43   The footage is included in a DVD, *Whittle – The Jet Pioneer*, first produced by Quanta Films for The History Channel in 2005 and re-released with additional material in November 2019.
44   Ronald W. Clark, *Tizard*, Methuen, 1965, p. 301.
45   Diary note, 17 May 1941, Tizard Papers, File 18.
46   Minute from Sir Henry Tizard to the Director of Technical Development, 20 May 1941, quoted in Cynthia Keppel, 'The Development of Jet Propulsion and Gas Turbine Engines in the United Kingdom', TNA/AIR 62/2, para 91, p. 244.
47   FW Note, 'Demonstration Flight of the E.28/39, 21 May 1941', CAC/WHTL B.59.
48   Clark, *Tizard*, p. 303.
49   FW, 'Note on Meeting Held in Sir Henry Tizard's Rooms', 22 May 1941, CAC/WHTL B.59.
50   Consolidated Diaries, p. 559, CAC/WHTL A.265.
51   Keppel, 'The Development of Jet Propulsion', p. 254.
52   Tizard, 'Whittle Engine', Note to Minister, 12 June 1941, KFA Box 15.
53   Elizabeth Freeman to Hives, [?] March 1945, Freeman Files, Rolls-Royce Heritage Trust.
54   Hives to Freeman, 24 June 1941, quoted in Anthony Furse, *Wilfrid Freeman, the Genius Behind Allied Survival and Air Supremacy, 1939 to 1945*, Staplehurst, Spellmount, 1999, p. 172.
55   Diary note, 10 June 1941, Tizard Papers, File 18.
56   FW Note, 'Talk in Tizard's office at MAP, 16 June 1941', CAC/WHTL B.62.
57   FW, 'Meeting at Rolls-Royce Ltd, Derby 17 June 1941', CAC/WHTL B.62.

58   Whittle, *Jet*, p. 179.
59   I am indebted to the late Alec Collins for this story, told to him directly by Geoff Wilde.
60   FW, 'Diary of transactions with Rolls-Royce', TNA/AIR 62/608.
61   Hooker, *Not Much of an Engineer*, pp. 66–7. Hooker wrongly ascribes the comments to a conversation in 1940.
62   John Golley, *Whittle, The True Story*, Airlife Publishing, 1987, pp. 178–9.
63   FW to Rolls-Royce, for the attention of S. Hooker, 22 June 1941, CAC/WHTL B.63.
64   Bulman, *An Account of Partnership*, p. 316.
65   I am indebted to the late Alec Collins for this account of the W.1A engine.
66   Quoted in Clark, *Tizard*, p. 303.
67   Filmed interview with Glyn Jones and Nicholas Jones, 1986.
68   Whittle, *Jet*, p. 227.
69   'Notes of a Meeting held in the room of the Minister on 18 July 1941, to discuss the Prime Minister's Minute regarding the Whittle Aircraft', KFA Box 15.
70   Churchill to Moore-Brabazon, 30 July 1941, quoted in Peter Pugh, *The Magic of a Name, The Rolls-Royce Story*, Part Two: *The Power Behind the Jets*, Icon Books, 2001, p. 11.
71   Hayne Constant, 'Memo on I.C. turbine development', July 1941, KFA Box 15.

Chapter 8: The Cherry Orchard

1   Tizard to FW, 19 June 1940, CAC/WHTL B.41.
2   Report No. 159 of the National Advisory Committee for Aeronautics, 1923, quoted in Dan Whitney, 'America's First Jet Engine', *Journal of the American Aviation Historical Society*, Summer 2000.
3   Report of the US National Academy of Sciences, 10 June 1940, quoted in Glyn Jones, *The Jet Pioneers, The Birth of Jet-Powered Flight*, Methuen, 1989, p. 176.
4   Anderson to FW, 1 July 1940, CAC/WHTL B.41.
5   Quoted in David Zimmerman, *Top Secret Exchange, The Tizard Mission and the Scientific War*, McGill-Queen's University Press, 1996, p. 96.
6   Air Ministry minute from Director of Contracts, 'Whittle Patents', 7 September 1940, TNA/AVIA 15/655.
7   Zimmerman, *Top Secret Exchange*, p. 94.
8   Letter from Miss Geary, 28 December 1954, Tizard Papers, File 708, Box 531, Imperial War Museum.

9   Papers re Technical Mission to America, Tizard Papers, File 706, Box 531, Imperial War Museum.

10   'British Technical Mission – Information Given to US Authorities' by A. E. Woodward Nutt, Secretary to the Mission, 28 October 1940, Tizard Papers, File 706, Box 531, Imperial War Museum.

11   Roxbee Cox to Director of Contracts, 8 March 1941, TNA/AVIA 15/655 and KFA Box 3A.

12   See Edward W. Constant II, *The Origins of the Turbojet Revolution*, Johns Hopkins University Press, 1980, pp. 220–21.

13   Quoted in Glyn Jones, *The Jet Pioneers, The Birth of Jet-Powered Flight*, Methuen, 1989, p. 184.

14   Beaverbrook memorandum, 11 April 1941, quoted in Daniel Ford, 'Gentlemen, I Give You The Whittle Engine', *Air & Space* magazine, October/November 1992.

15   Harold H. Arnold, *Global Mission*, Hutchinson, 1951, p. 150.

16   Interview quoted in Daniel Ford, 'Gentlemen, I Give You The Whittle Engine', *Air & Space* magazine, October/November 1992, pp. 88–98. My summary draws heavily on this excellent account.

17   FW, 'Talks with Tizard, 17–18 May 1941', CAC/WHTL B.59.

18   'Monograph on American Liaison' by Sqd Ldr Adderley, September 1945, TNA/AVIA 46/234, p. 2.

19   Frank Whittle, *Jet, The Story of a Pioneer*, Frederick Muller, 1958, p. 93.

20   Ibid., p. 218.

21   'Monograph on American Liaison' by Sqd Ldr Adderley, September 1945, TNA/AVIA 46/234, p. 2.

22   Jones, *The Jet Pioneers*, p. 186.

23   Minutes of MAP meeting, 9 September 1941, TNA/AIR 62/1009.

24   Lyon to Arnold, 20 September 1941, quoted in Hermione Giffard, *Making Jet Engines in World War II, Britain, Germany, and the United States*, University of Chicago Press, 2016, p. 139.

25   Official note of meeting at MAP, 14 July 1941, CAC/WHTL B.65.

26   Whittle, *Jet*, p. 167.

27   Ibid., p. 168.

28   L. L. Whyte, *Focus and Diversions*, Cresset Press, 1963, p. 147.

29   FW to Whyte, 2 July 1941, CAC/WHTL B.64.

30   Whyte to Roxbee Cox, 13 July 1941, CAC/WHTL B.65.

31   FW, 'Visit of Mr A. H. Hall, 22 July 1941', CAC/WHTL B.66.

32   Stanley Hooker, *Not Much of an Engineer*, Airlife Publishing, 2002, p. 66.

33   FW, Consolidated Diaries, 21 October 1941, p. 638, CAC/WHTL B.130.

34   Roxbee Cox to FW, 17 November 1953, CAC/WHTL C.57.

35 Extracted from BBC transcript for 'Jets', 9 August 1976, CAC/WHTL D.38.

36 FW, 'Paper for the GTCC on Collaborating Firms', 23 January 1942, TNA/AIR 62/1006.

37 FW, 'Paper for GTCC on Surging', 21 November 1941, TNA/AIR 62/999.

38 Keppel, 'The Development of Jet Propulsion', p. 289.

39 Air Marshal Sholto Douglas to Air Vice Marshal Sorley, 27 August 1941, TNA/AIR 20/1778.

40 George Bulman, *An Account of Partnership – Industry, Government and the Aero-Engine*, ed. M. C. Neale, Rolls-Royce Heritage Trust Historical Series No.31, 2002, p. 328.

41 Linnell to S. B. Wilks, 8 October 1941, TNA/AVIA 15/421.

42 David S. Brooks, *Vikings at Waterloo – the wartime work on the Whittle jet engine by the Rover Company*, Rolls-Royce Heritage Trust Historical Series No. 22, 1997, p. 15.

43 Whittle, *Jet*, p. 160.

44 Moore-Brabazon to FW, 24 September 1941, CAC/WHTL B.70.

45 FW to Hives, 20 November 1941, CAC/WHTL B.73.

46 FW, 'Comments on Cynthia Keppel's The Development of Jet Propulsion', p. 4, TNA/AIR 62/2.

47 Note from Technical Department, copied to Linnell, 12 December 941, TNA/AVIA 15/1923, File 28A.

48 Whittle, *Jet*, p. 184.

49 Ibid.

50 FW Medical Records 1939–81, CAC/WHTL A.468.

51 Ibid.

52 Andrew Nahum, *Frank Whittle, The Invention of the Jet*, Icon Books, 2017, pp. 85–6.

53 W. E. P. Johnson, 'Memo on Meeting at Joseph Lucas, 23 December 1941', CAC/WHTL B.74.

54 W. E. P. Johnson, 'Visit to MAP, 30 December 1941', CAC/WHTL B.74.

55 Whittle, *Jet*, p. 185.

56 'Memorandum of Visit by Air Marshal F. J. Linnell on the 13th January 1942', CAC/WHTL B.76.

57 W. E. P. Johnson, 'Memorandum for MAP, 12 January 1942', CAC/WHTL B.76.

58 'Report by Mr Cheshire on visit of Rolls-Royce Representatives on Friday, 9th January 1942', CAC/WHTL B.75.

59 Hives to FW, 12 January 1942, CAC/WHTL B.75. It is quoted, along with FW's reply, in Whittle, *Jet*, p. 191.

60   FW to Hives, 14 January 1942, CAC/WHTL B.76.

61   George Lees, 'Visit of Rolls-Royce Officials: 14.1.42', CAC/WHTL B.75.

62   'Diffusers used on W.2B Type units', January 1942, TNA/AIR 62. The best account of the problem over surging and its resolution is a post-war paper by Leslie Cheshire, *Proceedings of the Institute of Mechanical Engineers* 1945, Vol. 153, pp. 434–6.

63   FW to Linnell, 20 January 1942, Consolidated Diaries, p. 685, CAC/WHTL B.132.

64   G. Lees to M. Wilks, 28 January 1942, Consolidated Diaries, p. 703, CAC/WHTL B.133.

65   W. E. P. Johnson, 'Memo on Visit to Rolls-Royce, Derby, on 21 January 1942', CAC/WHTL B.75.

66   FW, 'Visit to MAP (London)', 24 January 1942, CAC/WHTL B.78.

67   FW to Linnell, 27 January 1942, CAC/WHTL B.78.

68   FW, 'Visit of Mr Hives and Mr Sidgreaves (RR), 30 January 1942', CAC/WHTL B.75.

69   FW, 'Talk with Mr Hives (RR) at Derby, 31 January 1942', CAC/WHTL B.75.

70   'August 1941: No.10. Secret. Design Proposal, "Gloster" Jet propelled Bomber Aircraft', CAC/WHTL B.67.

71   FW, 'Diary of Transactions with Rolls-Royce', undated, TNA/AIR 62/608.

72   Whittle, *Jet*, p. 194.

73   FW, 'Memo on phone call with A. A. Ross, 28 January 1942', CAC/WHTL B.78.

74   J. H. Larrard, 'Gloster F9/40, Review of Production Position as at 15 January 1942', TNA/AVIA 15/1923.

75   Quoted in Peter Pugh, *The Magic of a Name*, Part Two: *The Power Behind the Jets*, Icon Books. 2001, p. 8.

76   Peter Pugh, *The Magic of a Name*, Part One: *The Rolls-Royce Story: The First 40 Years*, Icon Books, 2000, p. 283.

77   Brooks, *Vikings at Waterloo – the wartime work on the Whittle jet engine by the Rover Company*, p. 56.

78   'MAP Notes of Discussion held on 11 February 1942 at Bankfield Works', with accompanying Memo by W. E. P. Johnson, CAC/WHTL B.79.

79   FW, 'Note of phone call with W/Cdr Watt', 3 April 1942, CAC/WHTL B.82.

80   FW to Linnell, 17 May 1942, CAC/WHTL B.88. See also Whittle, *Jet*, pp. 199–215.

81   W. E. P. Johnson, 'Memo on Conversations at Gloster Co on 10/11 March, 12 March 1942', CAC/WHTL B.80.

82   Quoted in the Consolidated Diaries, p. 781, CAC/WHTL B.136.

83   'Conference on scheduling', 8 April 1942, CAC/WHTL B.83.

84   W. E. P. Johnson, 'Visit of Lord Cherwell on 25 May 1942', CAC/WHTL B.90.

85   FW to Linnell, 12 April 1942, CAC/WHTL B.83.

86   R. D. Williams, 'Memo on Visit to Roxbee Cox, 15 May 1942', CAC/WHTL B.88.

Chapter 9: Reckoning with Rolls-Royce

1   D. N. Walker to FW, 21 October 1941, TNA/AIR 62/1009.

2   CAC/WHTL E.1.

3   Frank Whittle, *Jet, The Story of a Pioneer*, Frederick Muller, 1958, pp. 219–20.

4   Ibid., p. 225.

5   FW to George Lees, 7 July 1942, TNA/AIR 62/1010.

6   FW to Roxbee Cox, 7 July 1942, TNA/AIR 62/1010.

7   They are now to be found in TNA/AIR 62/1010. Quotations about his visits are taken from here.

8   Whittle, *Jet*, pp. 223–4.

9   FW to Air Marshal Roderick Hill, 8 August 1942, TNA/AIR 62/1010.

10   Ibid.

11   D. N. Walker to FW, 21 October 1941, TNA/AIR 62/1009.

12   FW to Air Marshal Roderick Hill, 8 August 1942, TNA/AIR 62/1010.

13   Ibid.

14   Roderick Hill to Linnell, 16 August 1942, TNA/AIR 62/1010.

15   FW, 'Visit to MAP, 19 August 1942', CAC/WHTL B.92.

16   See internal MAP memorandum, quoted Glyn Jones, *The Jet Pioneers, The Birth of Jet-Powered Flight*, Methuen, 1989, pp. 136–7.

17   Linnell to S. B. Wilks, 5 August 1942, TNA/AVIA 15/421.

18   'D.E.D. Note of Meeting with… Power Jets Ltd', 20 July 1942, TNA/AVIA 15/421.

19   Bulman to Williams, 31 July 1942, TNA/AVIA 15/421.

20   FW to Linnell, 17 May 1942, CAC/WHTL B.88.

21   Whittle, *Jet*, pp. 226.

22   Stanley Hooker, *Not Much of an Engineer*, Airlife Publishing, 2002, p. 70.

23   FW to W. H. Hatfield of Atlas & Norfolk Works, 2 October 1942, CAC/WHTL B.94.

24   David Price, *The Crew, The Story of a Lancaster Bomber Crew*, Head of Zeus, 2020, p. 139.

25   FW, 'Diary of Transactions with Rolls-Royce', TNA/AIR 62/608.

26   Note by J. G. Larrard, 'Gloster F.9/40 and Meteor', 31 October 1942, TNA/ AVIA 15/1746.

27   'Minutes of meeting held in CRD's office on 2 November 1942 to consider the future of the W.2B design and the possibility of abandoning the design', TNA/AVIA 15/1708.

28   Tizard to Linnell, 13 November 1942, TNA/AVIA 15/1708.

29   WEPJ Note, 'Rolls-Royce Visit to Whetstone, 23 October 1942', CAC/ WHTL B.95.

30   Hives to Roxbee Cox, 17 November 1942, Hives Papers, Gas Turbine Engines – General, RRHT.

31   Tobin Note, 'Points discussed with Dr Roxbee Cox, 16 November 1942', CAC/WHTL B.95.

32   Tinling to Hives, 16 November 1942, Hives Papers, Gas Turbine Engines – General, RRHT.

33   WEPJ Note, 'Visit to Gloster, 26 August 1942', CAC/WHTL B.93.

34   Anthony Furse, *Wilfrid Freeman, The genius behind Allied survival and air supremacy 1939 to 1945*, Staplehurst, Spellmount, 1999, p. 251.

35   Wilfrid Freeman, Draft Air Ministry paper, 8 May 1942, TNA/AIR 20/ 3072.

36   Minutes of GTCC meeting, 2 May 1942, Science Museum MS 0507.

37   AI 2(g) Report No. 2026, 'New Types of German Aircraft', 5 February 1942, TNA/AIR 40/2164.

38   Constance Babington Smith, *Evidence in Camera, The Story of Photographic Intelligence in World War II*, Chatto & Windus, 1958, p. 238.

39   AI 2(g) Report No. 2073, 'German Fighter Development', 2 July 1942, TNA/AIR 40/2164.

40   Item 4 of Notes on Discussions at 5th Meeting of GTCC, Metropolitan-Vickers, 18 July 1942, Science Museum archives, MS 0507.

41   Intelligence Reports of May and November 1942, summarised in Report No. 3004, 'Report on German Jet-Propelled Aircraft', 19 July 1943, paragraphs 1.15 and 2.15, TNA/AIR 20/2690.

42   A/M Linnell, Note to Chief Executive, 29 November 1942, TNA/AVIA 15/1708.

43   FW, 'Diary of Transactions with Rolls-Royce', TNA/AIR 62/608.

44   Linnell to Hives, 4 December 1942, TNA/AVIA 15/1708.

45   FW note, 'Phone call: Mr Hives', 10 December 1942, CAC/WHTL B.95.

46   Whittle, *Jet*, pp. 237–40.

47   FW note, 'Phone call: Dr Roxbee Cox', 19 December 1942, CAC/WHTL B.96.

48 FW note, 'Phone call from Mr Hives', 21 December 1942, CAC/WHTL B.96.

49 Hooker, *Not Much of an Engineer*, pp. 73–4.

50 Roxbee Cox to his mother, 20 December 1942, CRANLA/LKN, Kings Norton Papers, Box 21.

51 'Rolls-Royce – Rover Organisation', MAP note on discussion at Power Jets, 5 January 1943, TNA/AVIA 15/1806.

52 Hooker, *Not Much of an Engineer*, p. 75.

53 FW Memo, 'Visit of Mr B. J. Tams, 9 February 1943', CAC/WHTL B.98.

54 FW, Consolidated Diaries, 11 July 1941, CAC/WHTL B.128.

55 E. S. Moult to FW, 5 January 1943, CAC/WHTL B.97.

56 G. Lees note, 'Phone call with Tobin and Watt', 31 December 1942, CAC/WHTL B.96.

57 Michael Daunt to FW, 28 February 1943, CAC/WHTL B.98.

58 George Watt to WEPJ, 2 March 1943, CAC/WHTL B.99.

59 FW Note, 'Talk with Dr Roxbee Cox at MAP, 17 March 1943', CAC/WHTL B.99.

60 Interviewed by Ken Fulton, 26 March 1996, CRANLA/LKN, Kings Norton Papers 2000.311.

61 Hives to MAP, 17 November 1942, Hives Papers Cabinet 11, Rolls-Royce Heritage Trust.

62 Hives to Linnell, 27 March 1943, CAC/WHTL B.99.

63 FW memo, 'Meetings at Rolls-Royce, Derby – 19 April 1943', CAC/WHTL B.100.

64 John Grierson, *Jet Flight*, London, 1946, p. 63.

65 FW, 'Phone call with Hives', 20 April 1943, CAC/WHTL B.100.

66 FW to Stafford Cripps, 29 April 1943, CAC/WHTL B.101. See also Whittle, *Jet*, pp. 262–3.

67 WEPJ note, 'Conversation with Mr Hives', 30 April 1943, CAC/WHTL B.101.

68 Ibid.

69 Whittle, *Jet*, pp. 243–5.

70 FW memo, 'Interview with Sir Stafford Cripps, 11 May 1943', CAC/WHTL B.102.

71 Ibid.

72 Report No.2154 'German Single-Seat Fighter Development', 29 March 1943, TNA/AIR 40/2165.

73 'Notes on MAP meeting held 4 May 1943 to discuss AI (K) Report 184A', TNA/AVIA 15/1908.

Chapter 10: Cornered by Cripps

1   FW to Roxbee Cox, 7 April 1943, CAC/WHTL B.100.
2   Ibid.
3   FW to H. M. Garner, 16 May 1943, TNA/AVIA 15/1908.
4   E. F. Relf to B. Lockspeiser, 6 May 1943, TNA/AVIA 15/1908.
5   Minutes of the 2nd meeting of the Supersonic Committee, 4 June 1943, TNA/AVIA 15/1908.
6   Frank Whittle, *Jet, The Story of a Pioneer*, Frederick Muller, 1958, p. 255.
7   Interviewed by Ken Fulton, 26 March 1996, CRANLA/LKN, Kings Norton Papers 2000.311.
8   Minutes of the 3rd meeting of the Supersonic Committee, quoted in Eric Brown in association with Dennis Bancroft, *Miles M.52, Gateway to Supersonic Flight*, Staplehurst, Spellmount, 2012, p. 176.
9   Constance Babington Smith, *Evidence in Camera, The Story of Photographic Intelligence in World War II*, Chatto & Windus, 1958, pp. 84 and 240.
10 Report No. 3004, Department of Information (O), Air Ministry, 19 July 1943, TNA/AIR 20/2690.
11 M. M. Postan et al., *Design and Development of Weapons, Studies in Government and Industrial Organisation*, HMSO, 1964, p. 221.
12 F. H. Hinsley et al., *British Intelligence and the Second World War, Its Influence on Strategy and Operations*, Vol. 3, Part I, HMSO, 1979, pp. 334–6.
13 Hives to Freeman, 19 July 1943, Freeman files, Hives Papers Cabinet 11, Rolls-Royce Heritage Trust.
14 Bulman to Hives, 28 July 1943, Bulman files, Hives Papers Cabinet 13, Rolls-Royce Heritage Trust.
15 Freeman to Hives, 21 July 1943, Freeman files, Hives Papers Cabinet 11, Rolls-Royce Heritage Trust.
16 Postan et al., *Design and Development of Weapons*, p. 224.
17 Sir Winston Churchill, *The Second World War*, Vol. V, Houghton Mifflin, 1952, p. 579.
18 L. L. Whyte, 'Whittle and the Jet Adventure', *Harper's Magazine*, June 1954. Reprinted in *Focus and Diversions*, Chapter X, pp. 136–50.
19 FW notes, 'Visit of R-Cox to RAF Staff College, 17 July 1943' and 'Talk with R-Cox at MAP, 23 July 1943', CAC/WHTL B.104.
20 FW Memo, 'Visit of Roxbee Cox and Watt on 14 August 1943', CAC/WHTL B.104.
21 FW memo, "Power Jets Limited", prepared for Minister's Visit to Whetstone, August 1943', CAC/WHTL B.104.

22   FW to Roxbee Cox, 19 August 1943, CAC/WHTL B.105.

23   FW to Roxbee Cox, 25 August 1943, CAC/WHTL B.105.

24   FW to Cripps, 11 January 1944, CAC/WHTL B.110.

25   Stafford Cripps to FW, 24 August 1943, CAC/WHTL B.105.

26   FW to Cripps, 16 June 1943, CAC/WHTL B.103.

27   Glyn Jones, *The Jet Pioneers, The Birth of Jet-Powered Flight*, Methuen, 1989, p. 204.

28   Cynthia Keppel, 'The Development of Jet Propulsion and Gas Turbine Engines in the United Kingdom', TNA/AIR 62/2, para 196, p. 335.

29   Andrew Nahum, *Frank Whittle, The Invention of the Jet*, Icon Books, 2017, p. 108.

30   FW to RDW, JCBT, WEPJ and GL, 22 April 1943, CAC/WHTL B.100.

31   R. G. Voysey undated private paper [December 1944?], CAC/WHTL B.117.

32   Whittle, *Jet*, p. 303.

33   RDW, 'Memo of W. D. Roberts' Visit on 8 September 1943', CAC/WHTL B.106.

34   Brown and Bancroft, *Miles M.52*, p. 21.

35   'Preliminary note on Miles-Power Jets very high-speed aircraft by Group Captain Frank Whittle, 23 October 1943', printed as Appendix 1 in Brown and Bancroft, *Miles M.52*, pp. 151–5.

36   Brown and Bancroft, *Miles M.52*, p. 33.

37   FW note, 'Talk with CRD at MAP, 8 October 1943', CAC/WHTL B.107.

38   'Memorandum by MAP Minister to War Cabinet Defence Committee (Operations), 28 September 1943', TNA/AIR 20/2690.

39   FW, 'Talk with Dr Roxbee Cox at MAP, 8 October 1943', CAC/WHTL B.107.

40   FW note, 'Talk with Roxbee Cox at MAP, 25 October 1943', CAC/WHTL B.107.

41   FW memo, 'Visit of Roxbee Cox, 6 November 1943', CAC/WHTL B.107.

42   Cripps to Bonham Carter, 26 November 1943, quoted in Nahum, *Frank Whittle*, p. 109.

43   FW note, 'Phone Call from Roxbee Cox, 2 December 1943', CAC/WHTL B.108.

44   S. D. Felkin, A.D.I.(K) Report No. 472/1943, 19 November 1943, TNA/AVIA 15/1908. Also in KFA Box 3B.

45   WEPJ, 'Visit of Aircraft & Turbine Specialists, 29 September 1943', TNA/AIR 62/1011.

46   Sterling Michael Pavelec, *The Jet Race and the Second World War*, Naval Institute Press, 2007, pp. 130–41.

47   Freeman to Evill, 22 November 1943, TNA/AIR 2/7070. See also Hermione Giffard, *Making Jet Engines in World War II: Britain, Germany and the United States*, University of Chicago Press, 2016, pp. 201–4.

48   FW note, 'Phone call with Roxbee Cox, 30 December 1943', CAC/WHTL B.108.

49   It is reproduced as Appendix B in Giffard, *Making Jet Engines in World War II*, pp. 243–7.

50   'G/Capt. F. Whittle's Talk to the Works on Tuesday 11 January 1944', verbatim record, TNA/AIR 62/1023.

51   Copious cuttings can be found at CAC/WHTL B.110.

52   FW to Cripps, 11 January 1944, CAC/WHTL B.110.

53   Whittle, *Jet*, pp. 259–61.

54   FW, 'The Assets of Power Jets' and letter to Cripps, 16 June 1943, CAC/WHTL B.103.

55   Circular to Power Jets shareholders, 31 March 1944, CAC/WHTL B.113.

56   Sebastian Ritchie, *Industry and Air Power: The Expansion of British Aircraft Production, 1935–41*, Routledge 1997, p. 256.

57   FW to Cripps, 11 January 1944, CAC/WHTL B.110.

58   Sam Brown to FW, 4 March 1944, CAC/WHTL B.112.

59   FW, 'Talk with Sir Harold Scott and Sam Brown', 15 February 1944, CAC/WHTL B.111.

60   FW to Sam Brown, 9 March 1944, CAC/WHTL B.113.

61   FW, 'Talk with Sir Wilfrid Freeman at MAP', 1 March 1944, CAC/WHTL B.112.

62   FW to Air Marshal Sorley, 26 April 1944, CAC/WHTL B.115.

63   Quoted in Nahum, *Frank Whittle*, p. 113.

64   FW, 'Talk with RDW and JCBT on 3 March 1944', CAC/WHTL B.112.

65   Whittle, *Jet*, p. 261.

66   FW note, 'Party at Buckingham Palace, 1 March 1944', CAC/WHTL B.112.

67   Ibid.

68   FW note, 'Talk with Sir Wilfrid Freeman at MAP, 1 March 1944', CAC/WHTL B.112.

Chapter 11: Messerschmitts and Meteors

1   Tinling to FW, 25 March 1944, CAC/WHTL B.114.

2   FW Medical Records 1939–81, CAC/WHTL A.468.

3   FW to R. S. Sorley, 26 April 1944, CAC/WHTL B.115.

4   Minutes relating to FW promotion, 26 June to 8 August 1944, TNA/AVIA 15/2093.

5   C. B. Baker to Deputy Director of Scientific Research (Ben Lockspeiser), 4 September 1944, TNA/AVIA 15/1908.

6   *The Times*, 3 August 1944.

7   FW note, 5 October 1944, TNA/AIR 62/588.

8   Hayne Constant, 'Report on the Special Projects Mission to U.S.A. – May 1944', p. 3, TNA/AVIA 10/101.

9   Frank Whittle, *Jet, The Story of a Pioneer*, Frederick Muller, 1958, p. 280.

10   'GTCC: Notes on discussion at the 15th meeting on 11 November 1944', Science Museum archive, MS 0507.

11   FW note, 'Four day Visit to RR, Barnoldswick, 20–24 November 1944', CAC/WHTL B.116.

12   I owe this account, celebrated within Rolls-Royce but largely ignored in histories of the jet, to the late Alec Collins.

13   Hooker to FW, 1 December 1944, CAC/WHTL B.116.

14   FW note, 'Talk with Roxbee Cox, RDW, JCBT and WEPJ, 1 January 1945', CAC/WHTL B.118.

15   *The Times*, 2 October 1944. Further details appeared in the paper on 5 October and 18 October.

16   TNA/AIR 22/78. Also available in KFA Box 7.

17   R. G. Voysey undated private paper [December 1944?], CAC/WHTL B.117.

18   Portal to Secretary of State Sir Archibald Sinclair, undated, TNA/AIR 20/2690.

19   Deputy Chief of the Air Staff to Secretary of State, 22 November 1944, TNA/AIR 20/2690.

20   Churchill to Minister of Aircraft Production, 9 July 1944, TNA/AVIA 9/43, and 30 July 1944, TNA/AVIA 15/2101.

21   Whittle, *Jet*, p. 279.

22   Portal to Freeman, 10 January 1945, TNA/AIR 20/2690.

23   Quoted in Keppel, 'The Development of Jet Propulsion', para 187, p. 325.

24   Ibid., pp. 325–6.

25   Combat film footage of the Me 262 and the Me 163, taken by aircrews of the US Eighth Air Force in the late autumn of 1944, can be seen online at www.youtube.com/watch?v=lQkYn_hOyIo

26   FW to Roxbee Cox, 8 December 1944, CAC/WHTL B.117.

27   FW note, 'Talk with Roxbee Cox, RDW, JCBT and WEPJ, 1 January 1945', CAC/WHTL B.118.

28   FW to Roxbee Cox, 20 February 1945, CAC/WHTL B.118.

29   FW, 'Memo on Talk with Sir John Buchanan at MAP, 21 February 1945', CAC/WHTL B.118.

30   FW, 'On Power Jets', policy paper, 1 March 1945, CAC/WHTL B.119.

31   Hives to Roxbee Cox, 1 November 1944, Hives Papers Cabinet 11, GT Engines, Rolls-Royce Heritage Trust.

32   Stanley Hooker, *Not Much of an Engineer*, Airlife Publishing 2002, p. 94.

33   Quoted in Peter Pugh, *The Magic of a Name, The Rolls-Royce Story*, Part One: *The First 40 Years*, Icon Books, 2000, p. 220.

34   Minutes of the 3rd Meeting of the Gas Turbine Technical Advisory & Coordinating Committee, 18 April 1945, CAC/WHTL B.120.

35   Whittle, *Jet*, p. 283.

36   Minutes of 23rd Power Jets (R&D) Board Meeting, 24 August 1945, CAC/WHTL B.123.

37   Eric Brown in association with Dennis Bancroft, *Miles M.52, Gateway to Supersonic Flight*, Staplehurst, Spellmount, 2012, p. 201.

38   TNA/AIR 62/4.

39   Whittle, *Jet*, p. 287.

40   FW to W. A. Coryton, 9 November 1945, CAC/WHTL B.123.

41   A British Pathé newsreel of the record flight can be seen at www.youtube.com/watch?v=6kzX2OzlYLk.

42   FW to Roxbee Cox, 22 January 1946, CAC/WHTL B.124.

43   Brown and Bancroft, *Miles M.52*, pp. 102–7.

44   Ibid., p. 62.

45   *Daily Mail*, 15 April 1946.

46   FW, 'A general note on the Power Jets (R&D) LR.1 project', 27 November 1945, TNA/AIR 62/750.

47   Subsequently published in the *Journal of the Aeronautical Sciences*, Vol. 13, No. 2, pp. 53–87, February 1946.

48   Sir Alec Coryton to FW, 27 March 1946, CAC/WHTL G.77.

49   Jill Grey (*née* Shepherd) to FW, 16 November 1953, CAC/WHTL C.57.

50   The Jill Grey Collection is held at the British Schools Museum in Hitchin, Hertfordshire.

51   Staff Officer J. E. Shepherd, 'Report on Tour of the USA as Personal Assistant to A/Cmdr Frank Whittle CBE', CAC/WHTL E.4.

52   FW, 'Trip to the USA, 17 June to 10 September 1946', CAC/WHTL E.2.

53   Shepherd, 'Report on Tour of the USA', CAC/WHTL E.4.

54   FW Diary, 1 August 1946, CAC/WHTL A.182.

55   Stanley Hooker to R. B. McLeod, 29 April 1946, CAC/WHTL B.126.

56   Interviewed by Ken Fulton, 26 March 1996, CRANLA/LKN, Kings Norton Papers 2000.311.

57   Cited in January 1947 appointment as Companion of the Order of the Bath.

58 Medical notes from York Clinic of Guy's Hospital, September 1947, CAC/WHTL A.468.

59 This total, and all other figures relating to the background to the Royal Commission's 1948 award, are taken from papers to be found in KFA, Box 12. These comprise a selection from TNA/AVIA 53/47 and 53/261.

60 *The Aeroplane*, 16 May 1947.

61 Roxbee Cox to P. H. Goffey, 2 October 1947, TNA/AVIA 53/47. Also quoted in Whittle, *Jet*, p. 307.

62 'Request by Ministry of Supply to the Royal Commission on Awards to Inventors on the Question of an Award to Air Commodore Whittle', undated, TNA/AVIA 53/47.

63 FW to Stafford Cripps, 16 June 1943, CAC/WHTL B.103.

64 Correspondence relating to the Award, Part II, KFA Box 12.

65 FW Diary, 26 May 1948, CAC/WHTL A.185.

66 FW Diary, 27–28 May 1948, CAC/WHTL A.185.

67 FW to E. L. Pickles, 28 May 1948, Correspondence relating to the Award, Part I, KFA Box 12.

68 R. O. Jones, Memo to Ministry of Supply, 17 February 1947, reproduced as Appendix VI to 'Request by Ministry of Supply to the Royal Commission on Awards to Inventors', TNA/AVIA 53/47.

Chapter 12: A Vision Fulfilled

1 FW to Central Office of Information, 1 March 1962, CAC/WHTL A.38.

2 The BBC script can be found at CAC/WHTL D.25.

3 FW, 'Comments on Jet Engine Narrative', submitted to Ministry of Supply on 13 August 1947, TNA/AIR 62/2.

4 Quoted in Hermione Giffard, *Making Jet Engines in World War II, Britain, Germany, and the United States*, University of Chicago Press, 2016, p. 215.

5 Address to Smithsonian, from 'Trip to the US and Bahamas, 3 November to 3 December 1949', CAC/WHTL E.8.

6 Tizard to FW, 9 November 1949, uncatalogued papers held by Ian Whittle.

7 CAC/WHTL, A.245–65 and B.128–36.

8 FW to Robert Meyer of the US National Air and Space Museum, 25 September 1972, CAC/WHTL C.60.

9 *Times Literary Supplement*, 18 December 1953.

10 *Sunday Times*, 13 December 1953.

11 The BBC's six-episode series of 1959 can be heard via the National Aerospace Library Sound Archive.

12   FW Medical Records 1939–81, 31 October 1963, CAC/WHTL A.468.

13   More than a dozen of these papers can be found in CAC/WHTL A.16-23.

14   FW to W.R. Hawthorne, 24 April 1973, CAC/WHTL G.12.

15   May 1978 Bulletin on Research Activities, US Naval Academy.

16   FW to Commander Hewett, 16 January 1980, CAC/WHTL G.40A.

17   Giffard, *Making Jet Engines in World War II*, p. 195.

18   A copy of the film is available at the Imperial War Museum, catalogue No. MGH 210.

19   FW to Ramsey Short, April (?) 1966, CAC/WHTL D.41.

20   FW to von Ohain, 7 October 1966, CAC/WHTL E.22.

21   Transcript of speech by Hans von Ohain at General Electric Corporation's Evendale Engineers' Day in Cincinnati, 18 February 1985, CAC/WHTL E.50.

22   Cited in discussion following paper by Ian Whittle, published in *RAF Historical Society Journal 39*, 2007, p. 16.

23   *Frank Whittle: Jet Pioneer*, produced and directed by Brian Johnson, with a commentary by Raymond Baxter.

24   FW to Rolls-Royce (John Wragg), 3 February 1985, CAC/WHTL E.52.

25   FW, 'Interview with the Prime Minister on Friday 13 June 1986, 11.30–12.15 pm', uncatalogued papers held by Ian Whittle.

26   Statement from Downing Street by Margaret Thatcher, July 1986, uncatalogued papers held by Ian Whittle.

27   Author's interview with Dave Piggott.

28   Hawthorne to FW, 5 July 1996, uncatalogued papers held by Ian Whittle.

Image Sources and Credits

The following images were sourced from the Rolls-Royce Heritage Trust and are owned by, and reproduced by kind permission of, Rolls-Royce who reserve all rights in the material: **Plates 2a** and **13**; and **Figure 17**.

The following are the copyright of Ian Whittle and are reproduced with his kind permission: **Plates 1b, 1c, 2b, 3, 7a, 8a, 8b, 10a, 10b, 11a, 11b** and **12a**; and **Figure 3**.

The following were sourced from, and are reproduced by courtesy of, Warwickshire County Council, Rugby Library No. 48: **Plates 6, 7b, 9b, 12b, 14a, 15a** and **15b**. (The original copyrights, now lapsed, belonged to F. Lumbers of Leicester and *Illustrated* magazine, or were Crown copyright.)

The following were sourced from Lutterworth & District Museum: **Cover image** (original by F. Lumbers), **Plate 1a** (photographer unknown); and **Figures 6, 9, 10, 11, 21a** and **21b** (the originals of which were the property of British Thomson-Houston or Crown copyright).

The following were sourced from the Mary Evans Picture Library: **Plates 5a** (© Illustrated London News Ltd/Mary Evans Picture), **5b** (© John Frost Newspapers/Mary Evans Picture Library) and **9a** (© *The Royal Aeronautical Society Journal*).

The following were sourced from, and are reproduced courtesy of, the Churchill Archives Centre at Churchill, College, Cambridge: **Plate 16a** (CAC/WHTL F.66); and **Figures 1** (CAC/WHTL B.169), **15** (CAC/WHTL B.53), **18** (CAC/WHTL B.87), **19**

(CAC/WHTL E.1), 20 (CAC/WHTL B.167), 24 (CAC/WHTL D.23) and 26 (CAC/WHTL F.19).

The following were sourced from the Lord Kings Norton archive and are reproduced courtesy of Cranfield University: **Figures 12** and **25**.

Plate 4 was sourced from the Dana Research Centre and Library (Collection Item 2006-164) and is reproduced courtesy of the Science Museum.

Plate 14b was sourced from the papers of Mrs Jill Grey and is reproduced by kind permission of the Hitchin British Schools Trust.

Plate 16b was kindly provided by Mrs Jean Collins.

The following images in the public domain were sourced from The National Archives: **Figures 2** (TNA/AIR 62/1011), **5** (TNA/AIR 62/14), **7** (TNA/AIR 62/871), **8** (TNA/AIR 62/1), **13** (TNA/AIR 62/23), **16** (TNA/AIR 62/61), **22** and **23** (both TNA/AIR 40/256); **front endpapers and back endpapers** (both TNA/AIR 62/873).

).

Bibliography

Articles

Armstrong, Frank, 'Farnborough and the Beginnings of Gas Turbine Propulsion', *Journal of Aeronautical History*, Paper 2020/02, published online by the Royal Aeronautical Society, April 2020.

Collins, Alec, 'How Whittle Invented the Jet Engine', *Archive*, bulletin of the Rolls-Royce Heritage Trust, No. 90, Vol. 30, Issue 2, August 2012.

Collins, Alec, 'The 75th Anniversary of the First Flight of Whittle W.1', *Journal of the Rolls-Royce Heritage Trust*, December 2016.

Feilden, G. B. R., 'The contributions of Power Jets Ltd to jet propulsion', *Journal of the Royal Aeronautical Society*, Vol. 97, No. 962, February 1993.

Feilden, G. B. R. and Hawthorne, William, 'Sir Frank Whittle, O.M., K.B.E.', *Biographical Memoirs of the Royal Society*, 1998.

Ford, Daniel, 'Gentlemen, I Give You The Whittle Engine', *Air & Space* magazine, October/November 1992.

Golley, John, 'Working with a Genius', *Aeroplane Monthly*, September and October 1998.

Jones, Glyn, 'The Jet Engine – anniversary of a missed opportunity', *New Scientist*, 27 November 1980.

McDonnell, Patrick, 'Beaten to the Barrier', *Aeroplane Monthly*, January 1998.

Roxbee Cox, Harold, 'British Aircraft Gas Turbines', *Journal of the Aeronautical Sciences*, Vol. 13, No. 2, February 1946.

Whitney, Dan, 'America's First Jet Engine', *Journal of the American Aviation Historical Society*, Summer 2000.

Whittle, Frank, 'The Turbo-Compressor and the Supercharging of Aero Engines', *Journal of the Royal Aeronautical Society*, Vol. 35, No. 251, November 1931.

Whittle, Frank, 'The Early History of the Whittle Jet Propulsion Gas Turbine', First James Clayton Lecture, *Proceedings of the Institute of Mechanical Engineers*, June 1945.

Books

Arnold, H. H., *Global Mission*, Hutchinson, 1951.

Babington Smith, Constance, *Evidence in Camera, The Story of Photographic Intelligence in World War II*, Chatto & Windus, 1958.

Barnett, Correlli, *The Audit of War, The Illusion & Reality of Britain as a Great Nation*, Macmillan, 1986.

Bishop, Patrick, *Air Force Blue: The RAF in World War Two – Spearhead of Victory*, William Collins, 2017.

Boyle, Andrew, *Trenchard*, Collins, 1962.

Brooks, David S., *Vikings at Waterloo – the wartime work on the Whittle jet engine by the Rover Company*, Rolls-Royce Heritage Trust Historical Series No. 22, 1997.

Brown, Eric, *Wings on my Sleeve*, Weidenfeld & Nicolson, 2006.

Brown, Eric, in association with Dennis Bancroft, *Miles M.52, Gateway to Supersonic Flight*, Staplehurst, Spellmount, 2012.

Bulman, George, *An Account of Partnership – Industry, Government and the Aero-Engine*, ed. M. C. Neale, Rolls-Royce Heritage Trust Historical Series No.31, 2002.

Cairncross, Alec, *Planning in Wartime: Aircraft Production in Britain, Germany and the USA*, Palgrave Macmillan, 1991.

Clark, Ronald W., *Tizard*, Methuen, 1965.

Close, Frank, *Trinity, The Treachery and Pursuit of the Most Dangerous Spy in History*, Penguin Allen Lane, 2019.

Constant II, Edward W., *The Origins of the Turbojet Revolution*, Johns Hopkins University Press, 1980.

Dawson, Virginia P., *Engines and Innovation, Lewis Laboratory and American Propulsion Technology*, University Press of the Pacific, 2005.

Edgerton, David, *Britain's War Machine*, Allen Lane, 2011.

Edgerton, David, *England and the Aeroplane: Militarism, Modernity and Machines*, Penguin Books, 2013.

Furse, Anthony, *Wilfrid Freeman, the Genius Behind Allied Survival and Air Supremacy, 1939 to 1945*, Staplehurst, Spellmount, 1999.

Giffard, Hermione, *Making Jet Engines in World War II, Britain, Germany, and the United States*, University of Chicago Press, 2016.

Glancy, Jonathan, *Spitfire, The Biography*, Atlantic Books, 2006.

Golley, John with Gunston, Bill, *Whittle, The True Story*, Airlife Publishing, 1987.

Grierson, John, *Jet Flight*, Sampson Low, Marston, 1946.

Gunston, Bill, *Fedden – The Life of Sir Roy Fedden*, Rolls-Royce Heritage Trust Historical Series No. 26, 1988.

Hamilton-Paterson, James, *Empire of the Clouds, When Britain's Aircraft Ruled the World*, Faber and Faber, 2010.

Harvey-Bailey, Alec, *The Merlin in Perspective – the combat years*, Rolls-Royce Heritage Trust Historical Series No. 2, 1983.

Harvey-Bailey, Alec, *Rolls-Royce – Hives, The Quiet Tiger*, Rolls-Royce Heritage Trust Historical Series No. 7, 1985.

Hattersley, Roy, *Borrowed Time, The Story of Britain Between the Wars*, Little, Brown, 2007, 1985.

Heinkel, Ernst, ed. Jürgen Thorwald, *He 1000*, Hutchinson, 1956.

Hinsley, F. H., *British Intelligence and the Second World War, Its Influence on Strategy and Operations*, Vol. 3, Part I, HMSO, 1979.

Hooker, Stanley, *Not Much of an Engineer, An Autobiography*, Airlife Publishing, 2002.

Howard, Bill, *The Jet Engine Story: A Review*, Farnborough Air Sciences Trust (FAST), Monograph No. 004, January 2019.

Jones, Glyn, *The Jet Pioneers, The Birth of Jet-Powered Flight*, Methuen, 1989.

Kay, Anthony L., *Turbojet, History and Development 1930–1960*, Vol. 1, *Great Britain and Germany*, Crowood Press, 2007.

Lawrence, T. E., *The Mint*, Penguin Books, 1978.

McKinstry, Leo, *Spitfire, Portrait of a Legend*, John Murray, 2007.

McKinstry, Leo, *Hurricane, Victor of the Battle of Britain*, John Murray, 2010.

Miller, Russell, *Boom, The Life of Viscount Trenchard*, Weidenfeld & Nicolson, 2016.

Mondey, David, *The Schneider Trophy*, Robert Hale, 1975.

Nahum, Andrew, *Frank Whittle, The Invention of the Jet*, Icon Books, 2017.

Overy, Richard, *The Bombing War, Europe 1939–1945*, Allen Lane, 2013.

Owen, Roderic, *Tedder*, Collins 1952.

Pavelec, Sterling Michael, *The Jet Race and the Second World War*, Naval Institute Press, 2007.

Postan, M. M., Hay, David and Scott, J. D., *Design and Development of Weapons, Studies in Government and Industrial Organisation*, HMSO, 1964.

Price, David, *The Crew, The Story of a Lancaster Bomber Crew*, Head of Zeus, 2020.

Pugh, Peter, *The Magic of a Name, The Rolls-Royce Story*, 3 vols, Icon Books, 2000–2002.

Ritchie, Sebastian, *Industry and Air Power: The Expansion of British Aircraft Production, 1935–41*, Routledge, 1997.

Schlaifer, Robert and Heron, S. D., *Development of Aircraft Engines: Two Studies of Relations between Government and Business*, Harvard University, 1950.

Shute, Nevil, *No Highway*, William Heinemann, 1948.

Taylor, Douglas R., *Boxkite to Jet – the remarkable career of Frank B. Halford*, Rolls-Royce Heritage Trust Historical Series No. 28, 1999.

Tedder, Arthur, *With Prejudice, The War Memoirs of Marshal of the Royal Air Force Lord Tedder G.C.B.*, Cassell, 1966.

Tobin, James, *First to Fly, The Unlikely Triumph of Wilbur and Orville Wright*, John Murray, 2003.

Vann, Frank, *Willy Messerschmitt*, Patrick Stephens, 1993.

Wark, Wesley K., *The Ultimate Enemy: British Intelligence and Nazi Germany, 1933–39*, I. B. Tauris, 1985.

Whyte, L. L., *Focus and Diversions*, Cresset Press, 1963.

Whittle, Frank, *Jet: The Story of a Pioneer*, Frederick Muller, 1953.

Wilson, Gordon A. A., *The Merlin – The Engine that Won the Second World War*, Amberley Publishing, 2018.

Winchester, Simon, *Exactly – How Precision Engineers Created the Modern World*, William Collins, 2018.

Zimmerman, David, *Top Secret Exchange, The Tizard Mission and the Scientific War*, McGill-Queen's University Press, 1996.

Index